The Iroquois Struggle for Survival

An Iroquois Book

The Iroquois Struggle for Survival ✧✧✧✧✧✧✧✧✧✧✧✧✧✧✧✧✧✧✧✧✧

World War II to Red Power

Laurence M. Hauptman

SYRACUSE UNIVERSITY PRESS

The paper used in this publication meets the minimum requirements of American
National Standard for Information Sciences—Permanence of Paper for Printed Library
Materials, ANSI Z39.48-1984. ∞™

Library of Congress Cataloging-in-Publication Data

Hauptman, Laurence M.
    The Iroquois struggle for survival.

    (An Iroquois book)
    Bibliography: p.
    Includes index.
    1. Iroquois Indians—Government relations.
2. Indians of North America—Government relations—
1934–   . 3. Iroquois Indians—History. 4. Indians
of North America—History—20th century. I. Title.
II. Series.
E99.I7H34   1986   973'.0497   85-22306
ISBN 0-8156-2349-6 (alk. paper)
ISBN 0-8156-2350-X (pbk.: alk. paper)

For Beth and Eric

Laurence M. Hauptman is Professor of History at the State University of New York College at New Paltz. He is the author of *The Iroquois and the New Deal* (Syracuse University Press) and co-editor of *Neighbors and Intruders: An Ethnohistorical Exploration of the Indians of Hudson's River.* Professor Hauptman holds a Ph.D. in American History from New York University.

Contents

Preface

> It is imperative that Indian history move immediately into this
> century, whether or not historians consider the twentieth century
> to be history.
>
> Vine Deloria, Jr.[1]

The Iroquois are among the most studied and written about Indians
of North America. Despite their importance and the sizeable body
of anthropological and literary works devoted to these Indians, most
historians of Indian-white relations have virtually ignored the writing of the past two hundred years of Iroquois history.[2] Surprisingly,
the last book-length historical survey of these Indians was published
in 1905. Out of sheer necessity, scholars are forced to rely on the recently published Volume 15 of the Smithsonian *Handbook of North
American Indians* that, although excellent, is synoptic in nature and
largely incomplete in dealing with the more contemporary history
of the late nineteenth and twentieth centuries.[3] Thus, in sharp contrast to scholars' continuing fascination with the Iroquois in the period of the beaver wars, forest diplomacy, and imperial struggles for
domination of North America, recent Iroquois history is largely un-
written.

While completing an earlier monograph on the twentieth-century
Iroquois, I began to realize why historians have failed to see the importance of writing twentieth-century Iroquois history. The essential
research methodologies require historians to go well beyond sifting
through old documents in Washington or in Albany, and are more
costly in time and financial commitment. The historian must make
face-to-face contact with living people, an alien thought to most colleagues in the discipline who specialize in forensic history.

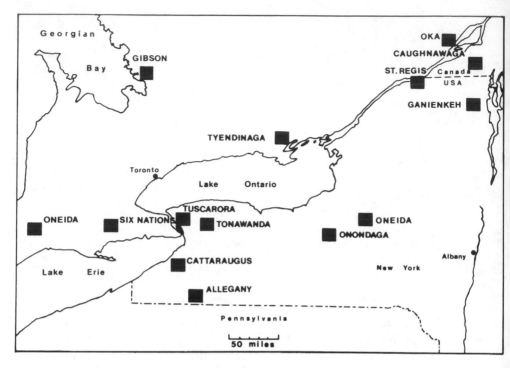

Eastern Iroquois Settlements. Map by Jo Mano.

The Iroquois in New York, Oklahoma, Wisconsin, and Canada have been viewed as being distinct from each other in their culture, history, and institutions ever since the late eighteenth and first half of the nineteenth centuries. Indeed, they are six separate nations historically—Mohawk, Oneida, Onondaga, Cayuga, Tuscarora, and Seneca —and occupy fifteen separate settlements today. Each of these Indian nations has beliefs in its individual tribal sovereignty and many, though not all, have a collective belief in a body called a league. At the present, two Iroquois leagues continue to function, one centered at Onondaga near Syracuse, New York, and the other at the Six Nations Reserve near Brantford, Ontario. Despite this second supralevel affirmation of Iroquois sovereignty, governmental officials in Washington, D.C., and Ottawa historically have recognized Iroquois sovereignty only in the existence of individual tribal or band governments,

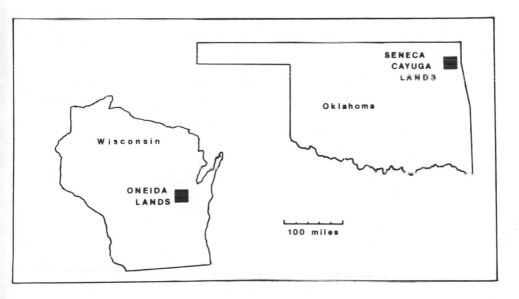

Western Iroquois Settlements. Map by Jo Mano.

in certain tribal judicial authorities, such as the Peacemakers' Court of the Seneca Nation, and in the acceptance of some features of Indian customary law. The continuous rejection by the United States and Canada of this idea of collective Six Nations Confederacy sovereignty has frequently motivated many of these Iroquois League supporters to protest against policy makers and their policies.

The Iroquois, one of the largest groups of Native Americans in North America, have many common threads tying their individual communities, reservations, and reserves together: ceremonials, conservatism, kinship, land claims assertions, language, reaffirmations of historic federal-Iroquois treaty relationships, religion and religious revitalization movements, and views of Washington and Indian Service officialdom. Significantly, each community was never isolated entirely from another despite separation by sizeable distances. Although severe divisions plague Iroquoia today, the movement of ideas back and forth reinforced their common historic memory bank to make them Iroquois in outlook and identity.

From 1940 onward, the Iroquois in each of their communities

faced major crises that threatened their land base and undermined the cultural underpinnings of their existence. Out of these battles came a renewed sense of Iroquois nationalism, one that was clearly recognized by Edmund Wilson in his work, *Apologies to the Iroquois*, in 1959. Wilson maintained that this nationalistic trend was caused by "the gluttonous inroads on the tribal property by state and federal projects."[4] Earlier, Wilson had written to Van Wyck Brooks, explaining how he accidentally discovered "an Iroquois national movement — not unlike Scottish nationalism and Zionism — with a revival of the old religion and claims for territory of their own."[5] Wilson fell rather accidentally onto the subject of renewed Iroquois nationalism, and made many mistakes in his portrait of the Iroquois' struggle for survival. He focused on what to him appeared to be the exotic nature of Iroquois. Nor did Wilson fully understand that this growing sense of Iroquois nationalism had a wrenching and virulent side to it, namely the increased internal disputes within each of the communities and between communities about leadership and strategies to follow in dealing with the outside world. Paradoxically, Iroquois nationalism which reemerged in the postwar world also gave rise to a divided polity.

The Iroquois Struggle for Survival carries the history of the Six Nations to the present, and details both the historical origins of this renewed sense of Iroquois nationalism, much more complex than Wilson imagined, and its long-range consequences. This work has much in common with *The Iroquois and the New Deal*. The Iroquois in New York, Oklahoma, Wisconsin, and Canada are treated together; nevertheless, the present study does not give equal treatment to all the Iroquois people. The Six Nations' contemporary historical experience in Canada is treated briefly in chapters on World War II, the Saint Lawrence Seaway, and Red Power, and is itself deserving of a book-length study. Furthermore, because the largest number of Iroquois reside in New York, and the East is the historic center as well as home to the mother culture of Iroquois existence, the Oklahoma Seneca-Cayugas and the Wisconsin Oneidas receive somewhat less attention. As in *The Iroquois and the New Deal*, I chose to base my conclusions both on my analysis of documents in government and private archives and on interviews and fieldwork in every Iroquois community in the United States and several in Canada.[6]

I have purposefully chosen to end my analysis with the takeover at Wounded Knee in the winter-spring of 1973 and with the United States Supreme Court's rendering of the Oneida decision in January 1974. Iroquois politics since that time has become difficult, if not impossible, to analyze because of its increased fragmentation and

because of the emotional level created by both of these events. My
major goal is to focus on the emergence of the contemporary Iroquois,
not a full discourse on Iroquois Red Power, which itself is worthy of
separate scholarly attention.

My obligations to people who aided in my research are many.
I should especially like to thank the numerous Iroquois people who
aided in my research. The following were especially helpful in under-
standing the modern Iroquois: Chief James Allen, Ruth Baird, Ernest
Benedict, Salli Benedict, Roy Black, Julius Cook, Ruby Diebold, John
Fadden, Ray Fadden, Gloria Tarbell Fogden, the late Norbert Hill, Sr.,
Roberta Jamieson, Jeanne Marie Jemison, Winifred Kettle, Gordie Mc-
Lester, Kay Olan, Keith Reitz, and Pauline Seneca. I should also like
to thank Professor Barbara Graymont of Nyack College and Doctor
Jack Campisi of Red Hook, New York, who have taught me the value
of undertaking fieldwork to gain a clearer understanding of the Iro-
quois and who have encouraged my research from its inception. They
have also provided me with an important critical reading of an earlier
draft of this manuscript. Doctor William N. Fenton, Distinguished
Professor Emeritus of Anthropology at the State University of New
York, Albany, and Professor William T. Hagan, Distinguished Professor of History at the State University of New York, Fredonia, were
also helpful in their critique of some chapters of this manuscript.
Many fine archivists and librarians throughout the United States and
Canada, too numerous to thank personally in print, were essential
to my research. Grants from the Research Foundation of the State University of New York and the American Philosophical Society provided
in part some of the funding to hasten completion of the study.

My greatest debt goes to my "tribe," to my wife Ruth and my two
children, Beth and Eric, whose tolerance of my incessant traveling and
commitment to this project was an act of patience, devotion, and true
love.

New Paltz, New York   Laurence M. Hauptman
Spring 1984

1

One War Ends,
Another Begins

The goal of our whole program [of federal Indian education] should be . . . to develop better Indian Americans rather than to perpetuate and develop better American Indians. . . . The present Indian education program tends to operate too much in the direction of perpetuating the Indian as a special-status individual rather than preparing him for independent citizenship.

United States House of Representatives,
Report No. 2091 (1945)

World War II had a significant impact on contemporary Iroquois history. Although some of the changes affecting the Iroquois had their roots in the New Deal era and earlier, mobilization, participation in a war overseas, and events at the home front from 1941 to 1945 shaped American Indian existence for decades to come. Ironically, at a time when large numbers of Indians were serving in the armed forces, the United States government was beginning plans for the withdrawal of federal services and the postwar end of federal-Indian treaty relationships. During the war, Indian policy makers, reversing their earlier positions, tried to ride out the storm of cost-conscious politicians in Congress seeking to cut the federal budget. They also attempted to counter the numerous Indian and non-Indian criticisms of the Bureau of Indian Affairs that labeled the agency "paternalistic," mismanaged," and even "communistic" in its approaches to native peoples and their problems.[1] In the process, these policy makers were forced to make compromises that seriously undermined their significant New Deal accomplishments of the 1930s, including the elimination of virtually all federal programs designed to permit Indians the opportunity to preserve and retain many forms of their cultural expression.

1

The substantial participation by Indians in the war effort also contributed to a warped perception of native peoples. Americans perceived tribesmen just like other "citizens" and in the context of mainstream American values. In part because of their limited awareness of the special historic, legal, and political status of Indians, many Americans began to support the Indians' amalgamation into American society. Why should Indians, the argument went, who fought so bravely and side by side with the white man against Hitler and Tojo, now return to the terrible poverty of segregated reservations? By the end of the war, new calls from conservatives and liberals alike urged that the Indians be set free from the imprisonment of reservations, which were falsely equated with Nazi concentration camps. The Indians had to be liberated from tyranny and over-regulation by the Bureau of Indian Affairs. The Indians, whether they liked it or not, had to be removed from the debilitating effects of the Indian reservation system.[2] From this logic, it is clear that new catchwords would appear in congressional and policy-maker parlance: emancipation, federal withdrawal, relocation, and termination.

Despite these renewed attempts to assimilate them, the Iroquois —Mohawks, Oneidas, Onondagas, Cayugas, Tuscaroras, and Senecas —resisted each and every governmental effort to accomplish this objective. However divided by geography, historical experiences, political structures, or religion, the Iroquois consistently reaffirmed their distinct and special status as set forth in federal treaties: Fort Stanwix (1784), Jay (1794), and Canandaigua (1794). Even today, the Iroquois— Christian or Longhouse, individual nation or Confederacy—largely define their status and sovereignty based upon agreements made immediately after the American Revolution.[3] From 1940 onward, these Indians took on diverse opponents—federal and state Indian policy makers, Canadian customs officers, the New York State Power Authority, the New York State departments of Education and Transportation, the United States Selective Service System, and the Army Corps of Engineers—in defense of their sovereignty. Yet, the threats to the Iroquois were not only by those agencies seeking Indian lands or by congressional or legislative attacks on the Indians' separate cultural, political, and religious existence. The largely insulated and isolated setting of American Indians was rapidly being transformed by the communications revolution, by the changes from a barter to a cash economy, by rapid urbanization, and by a world at war. From 1941 to 1945, the war itself tested the Iroquois' physical, cultural, and political resilience and prepared them for their postwar struggle to survive.

Numerous Iroquois men and women, between 1800 and 1900

in number, served in the United States and Canadian armed forces during World War II. At Allegany, eighty-two out of approximately 800 reservation residents were in the armed services in 1943; 102 young men and women out of a total community population of 625 people at Tonawanda were in the military in 1944.[4] Iroquois participation was highlighted in an article written by Secretary of the Interior Harold Ickes in 1944 in a widely circulated magazine. Ickes focused on the Iroquois commitment to fight the Axis and to counter Nazi atrocities. The secretary described the family of Mrs. Jerry Crow, "a widow woman of the Seneca-Cayuga nation," who "gave her five sons to the armed forces."[5] It is important to note that several Iroquois were captured by the enemy and spent considerable time as prisoners of war during World War II. Moreover, nine Mohawks from the Saint Regis (Akwesasne) Reservation were killed in action during the war, an unusually high percentage of casualties for a small community.[6]

In Canada, Iroquois Indians were already serving in the armed forces long before the Japanese attack on Pearl Harbor. At the Six Nations Reserve, 225 Iroquois enlisted in the war effort.[7] These Indians, seeing themselves as historical allies of Great Britain since the colonial era, viewed England's plight as their own. The *Pine Tree Chief*, the Iroquois newspaper at this reserve, spoke of Nazi atrocities, British heroism, and the Iroquois obligation to fulfill their commitment of alliance to England: "One by one defenceless nations have fallen helpless victims to the monster's greed. England alone dared to stand against thundering roars and the fiery breath of the dragon of Naziism."[8]

This same newspaper had its own war correspondent, Private Max King of the Canadian Army, a non-Iroquois Mississauga (New Credit) Indian, who reported back about the Indians' reactions to basic training and the war overseas. Besides lauding the work of the Young Men's Christian Association and Salvation Army mobile canteens, King praised the local English people for making the Iroquois and Mississauga soldiers feel at home, allowing the troops to spend leave time at their homes. Perhaps recalling the prejudice toward the Indian in Ontario, he continued: "They [the local British] are really swell, working-class people and in their distress they show a spirit which we never find in Canada." This affinity for the people and the grueling training undergone in preparation for battle led King to confidently assert: "Let it be said that we are ready."[9] Exactly nine months later, Max King, his brother Elliott and two Iroquois Indians from Ohsweken were killed in action at the Canadian military disaster at Dieppe.[10]

The war also affected the Iroquois in ways unrelated to the actual combat. Reservation populations were seriously depleted because many Indians moved to towns and cities to work in defense plants. Out-migrations of Iroquois to Buffalo, Chicago, Detroit, Milwaukee, New York City, Oklahoma City, Rochester, Syracuse, and Tulsa had actually increased just prior to Pearl Harbor since New Deal programs centering on community building, artistic and language enrichment, conservation, and overall work relief had been winding down in scale since late 1939. The national focus had changed from butter to guns, especially after the fall of France in June 1940, and increased mobilization offered job opportunities that did not exist during the Great Depression.[11]

Rochester was a case in point. Iroquois of diverse backgrounds had been making the city their home since World War I. Encouraged by employment opportunities and the presence of the prominent attorney George Decker, who had defended their legal interests and pursued their land claims, many Iroquois had migrated there in the 1920s. The city had also become an Indian cultural center attracting Mohawks, Oneidas, and Senecas partly as a result of Arthur C. Parker's efforts in building the Rochester Museum and Science Center into a major force in Indian and non-Indian life in western New York in the late 1920s and 1930s. Indians took pride and participated in Parker's educational outreach services that took the form of historic pageants and commemorations. The local Neighborhood Indian Society founded by Parker and Arleigh Hill, a Seneca from the Six Nations Reserve in Canada and a confidante of Parker, became a major social force in promoting Iroquois nationalism by frequently sponsoring events and celebrating Indian Day in Ellison Park. Equally important, the success of the Iroquois professional lacrosse teams in the city in the 1930s, in which Hill, Francis Kettle, and Harry Smith (later known as Jay Silverheels—Tonto in his acting career in Hollywood) served as a magnet attracting Iroquois from Canada and other parts of the United States.[12]

By World War II, Rochester, despite its fifth rank in size of urban Indian populations in New York State,[13] was a major center of eastern Iroquois existence. Many members of the local Neighborhood Indian Society worked in war industries, polishing binoculars and searchlights at Bausch and Lomb, the manufacturer of key optical equipment for national defense. In local newspapers, the Iroquois were featured as patriotic Americans rising to "meet the country's need." Iroquois Indians worked in plant security at Bausch and Lomb, operated the heavy equipment at the Rochester productions division of General Motors, and held jobs at Kodak. Yet the war also helped to undermine Indian life substantially in the city. The war produced a temporary breakdown of community cohesiveness. According to one newspaper account: "The war has scattered the local Indian population. Meetings of the Neighborhood Indian Society, held regularly until two years ago, were abandoned because of irregular working hours and lack of time. National Indian Day, an annual event at Ellison Park, is another war casualty."[14]

Iroquois participation in the war effort was reflected in other areas of employment. Senecas and Tuscaroras worked at constructing warplanes at Curtis-Wright in Buffalo. Aluminum plants, such as Alcoa, located along the Saint Lawrence River, near the Saint Regis (Akwesasne) Reservation sought ever more Indian workers to fill the labor shortage caused by World War II enlistments. Mining companies such as National Gypsum, a focus of tribal contempt but operating under and adjacent to the Tonawanda Reservation near Akron, New York, hired more Senecas in their extraction operations. Consequently, because of out-migration to the cities and increased employment adjacent to some reservations, the New York State Board of Social Work insisted in its annual report that the coming of war had virtually eliminated reservation unemployment in the state.[15]

Despite the economic turnaround, the Iroquois faced major crises on the home front during World War II, each of which had a sizeable impact on postwar Iroquoia. Despite Indian willingness to participate actively in the war effort, the Iroquois in New York were uniformly against the application to them of the 1940 Selective Service Act. For the first time in the United States, the federal government conscripted Indians against their will into the armed forces. During World War I, the United States classified Indians as noncitizens and did not subject them to conscription; however, in 1924, the Congress passed the Indian Citizenship Act. The Iroquois, following their own views of sovereignty, insisted that the Selective Service Act and the earlier Indian Citizenship Act did not apply to them since they had never accepted the 1924 law and considered themselves foreign nationals, not United States citizens. Both laws, they maintained, had been promulgated unilaterally by Congress and without their consent; thus, the Iroquois rejected the doctrine of plenary power or federal supremacy over Indians and Indian affairs.[16] The prominent Tuscarora, Chief Clinton Rickard, explained: "We were not United States citizens, no matter what the government said. We were Six Nations citizens."[17] Rickard's organization, the Indian Defense League of America, counseled Indians to register for the draft, but only as "alien non-residents." They protested at the main post office in Buffalo with placards reading: "We did not fingerprint the Pilgrims when they arrived in our Native America."[18] Although not against participation in war on moral or patriotic grounds, the Iroquois clung to traditional beliefs about their sovereignty. Consequently, many were arrested and some were prosecuted as draft evaders, even after the United States gave them warnings.

Subsequently, to test their status, they brought a case, *Ex Parte Green*, to federal court. The United States Court of Appeals for the Second Circuit rejected Iroquois contentions and upheld the Selective Service Act's application to these Indians.[19] In two later draft cases, *United States v. Claus* (1944) and *Albany v. United States* (1945), involving Mohawk Indians from the Six Nations and Caughnawaga reserves, the federal courts went even further, holding that the Selective Service Act was applicable to Indian non-citizen aliens from Canada residing in the United States. The courts rejected arguments by the Mohawks that, since Canada did not conscript Indians during World War II, the United States had no right to draft Canadian Indians. The courts dismissed the Mohawks' contentions that the Jay Treaty, granting the right of free passage back and forth across the international boundary, exempted them from being drafted into military service in the United States.[20] In spite of the Iroquois failure to gain recognition from the federal courts on the issue of conscription, these legal appeals reinforced the separate Indian beliefs about their sovereignty and nationhood at a time when the dominant white society was beginning to talk about absorbing the Indian into the mainstream.

In response to the continued jailing of young Indians under the act, Iroquois leaders urged their tribesmen to enlist before being faced with the issue of conscription.[21] In addition, in order to counter the unfavorable effects of media coverage of Iroquois draft resistance, which was misunderstood by the American public at large, a group of six well-known Iroquois, without formal approval of most of the Six Nations, "declared war" against the Axis on the Capitol steps in Washington, D.C., on June 11, 1942: "Now, therefore, we do resolve that it is the sentiment of this council that the Six Nations of Indians declare that a state of war exists between our Confederacy of Six Nations on the one part and Germany, Italy, Japan and their allies against whom the United States has declared war, on the other part."[22]

After adding that a formal resolution declaring war would be considered by a special conference of the Six Nations within a month, the "declaration of war" added that the "atrocities of the axis nations is violently repulsive to all sense of righteousness of our people, and that this merciless slaughter of mankind upon the part of these ene-

Chief Jesse Lyons and one faction of the Iroquois declaring war against the Axis at the Capitol, Washington, D.C., June 1942. Also shown are Vice President Henry Wallace, Senator James Mead, Congressman James J. Wadsworth, and Assistant Commissioner of Indian Affairs William Zimmerman, Jr. Photograph courtesy of the National Archives.

mies of free peoples can be no longer tolerated."[23] In response to the Iroquois statement and commitment that they would present a formal resolution to the full Six Nations' leadership on July 18, 1942, President Franklin Roosevelt sent each of the individuals a letter of appreciation, stating: "It is good to know that you feel so strongly concerning the atrocities of the Axis Nations and that you are so eager to see the more completely recognized inalienable rights to freedom of life and the pursuit of happiness."[24]

This carefully orchestrated event, which never received endorsement by the full Six Nations' leadership in council at Onondaga, was intended to stem the tide of draft arrests. The attorney for the Iroquois in the Green case concluded that this action would lead to "wholesale" enlistments of Indians which "should be beneficial to the interests of the country."[25] The United States government, at the same time, saw it as a useful way to generate war propaganda against Germany and reinforce the worthiness and even greatness of America's crusade.[26] For at least two months prior to the Iroquois declaration of war, the Department of the Interior had planned the event, had alerted the media, had prepared an itinerary and a visit to the White House for the six delegates—Jesse Lyons (Onondaga), William Rockwell and Hilton Nicholas (Oneida), Louis David and Peter Oake (Mohawk), and Uly Pierce (Cayuga)—and had arranged for hotel and travel expenses. Wilfred Hoffman, along with Assistant Commissioner of Indian Affairs William Zimmerman, Jr., and Senator James Mead of New York, had worked out all the details relating to the Capitol Hill show. The Department of the Interior had arranged for Vice President Henry Wallace's presence at the event. They also booked the Iroquois for June fourteenth on the half-hour Columbia Broadcasting System radio show "We, the People at War," where the Indians would reread their declaration, and alerted the major newspapers, the Associated Press, and other media "bigwigs" to that fact.[27]

The message was clear, as reflected in Commissioner John Collier's press release preceding the events:

> The New York Indians, in making a separate declaration of war against the Axis powers do not question the sovereignty of the United States Government but they are simply giving full expression, in their democratic traditions, to a supreme cause which has upset the internal affairs of the various members of the historic Confederacy. Like millions of families throughout the United States, the New York Indians have sent their sons into the armed forces and their daughters into war jobs off the reservation.

To Collier, the Iroquois' "taking the warpath against Hitler and his Axis pals" was a clear signal that the 400,000 American Indians did not take cognizance of German propaganda about violations of minority rights in the United States.[28]

The repeated attention throughout World War II to the so-called Iroquois declaration of war against the Axis underscores its importance to the American propaganda effort.[29] The event, widely covered by newspapers, was a foil to the extensive reporting of Iroquois draft resistance which continued right through the war. Now the Iroquois were stereotyped as heroic warriors ready to go on the warpath in defense of their Uncle Sam. Newspapers carried first-page news stories about Iroquois participants in the event, especially their dinner in the Senate restaurant with Vice President Wallace and Senator Mead. Prominently placed photographs of Chief Lyons and Vice-President Wallace carried the caption: "Big Chief Sees Assistant White Father." One newspaper presented the Indians as having been wronged by the United States in the past but willing, in the words of Chief Lyons, to "forget the past. Look to the future and win this war. Our people are one with you in this."[30] The Indian had become, in order to save humanity, the "Kemosabe's" trusted friend in a twentieth-century Hollywood western.

Senator Mead, in helping to organize the Iroquois "declaration of war," had also announced before the event that one of his aims was for the announcement to be widely broadcast through the Americas since the declaration was "expected to carry weight with Indians in South and Central America" and encourage them to resist the Axis. Moreover, Mead had hoped to encourage more publicity by having the chiefs appear in full regalia—Plains, not Iroquois, garb. Perhaps as a concession to Iroquois beliefs that they are sovereign and independent nations, he had arranged for the presence of State Department officials as well as representatives of foreign nations.[31] Despite its general interpretation as a dramatic act of sovereignty on the part of the "Grand Council of the Iroquois" or a renewal of the Six Nations declaration of war against Germany in 1917, both of which it was not, the entire episode was a direct result of the draft crisis of 1940 to 1942 and the American government's propaganda drive to sell the war effort to Indian and non-Indian alike. Just like every "red-blooded American," the message went, the Iroquois support Uncle Sam against Hitler, "the man-who-smells-his-mustache."[32]

This tendency to treat Iroquois and other Indians in the context of mainstream America was to contribute to the second home front crisis facing the Iroquois in World War II. Since American Indians were now viewed as being just like other Americans, New Deal programs and government agencies that encouraged Indian control and political separation were viewed askance. The target for the renewed criticism of Indian administration was Commissioner John Collier and the Indian New Deal. The exaggerated sell of Collier's program had never matched the reality of its accomplishments, although it was a better era than that preceding or following it.[33] Despite gains in certain areas, Indians continued to be the nation's poorest group. To complicate matters further, Congress had shifted funds and slashed the Bureau of Indian Affairs budget to unmanageably low levels. In addition, during World War II, the bureau's offices had been shifted to Chicago. Many of the BIA's most skilled employees had left the agency, joining the armed forces, or had transferred to agencies involved in the war effort. Because of the war, BIA-administered facilities were in disrepair, including Indian hospitals, schools, and reservation roads. A severe shortage of physicians also plagued the Indian Service throughout the war.[34]

As a whole, the New Deal reform—tribal reorganization, land acquisition, and federal credit programs—had had limited success. The New Dealers were never able to solve the complicated problem of heirship lands; 45,000 Indians in 1944 were heirs to six million acres of largely unproductive holdings. Many Indian allottees who inherited these lands had refused to give them up or sell them to tribal ownership under the Indian Reorganization Act.[35] The Indian New Deal among the Iroquois had led to an increased tribal land base and stronger tribal structures in both Oklahoma and Wisconsin, and to cultural resurgences in New York and in Wisconsin. Nevertheless, the Iroquois in New York remembered and strongly resented Collier's efforts at selling the Indian Reorganization Act in 1935. Iroquois land claims advocates also believed that the commissioner had co-opted their legitimate movement for tribal justice and redemption. Moreover, Iroquois communities in the East and West continued to view the bureau with suspicion if not outright resentment.[36]

Under intense congressional fire, Commissioner Collier in 1943 and 1944 admitted that the Indian New Deal had not accomplished many of his objectives.[37] The controversial and much-maligned commissioner had come under renewed attack, especially from conservative congressmen. On June 11, 1943, the Senate Committee on Indian Affairs issued *Report No. 310* which ostensibly summarized the findings of the committee's lengthy hearings—*Survey of Conditions of the Indians of the United States*—begun in 1928. In effect, however, *Report No. 310*, and a subsequent supplemental report issued by the committee, was an indictment of the Indian New Deal. The report called for the dismemberment and ultimate liquidation of the BIA, concluding with thirty-three recommendations, each calling for the elimination of certain bureau service functions.[38] In 1943, the House of Representatives adopted a resolution sponsored by Karl Mundt of South Dakota, calling for a separate investigation of Indian affairs. The Mundt Report that followed this investigation insisted that the goal of policy was to encourage the Indian "to take his place in the white man's community on the white man's level and with the white man's opportunity and security status." The report was also highly critical of the bureau for failing to provide adequate economic and educational opportunities and for not encouraging the removal of restrictive regulations on Indians. The report, in direct challenge to Commissioner Collier, suggested that Indians be allowed to withdraw from the Indian Reorganization Act through an electoral process.[39]

Collier soon realized that Congress would not allocate to the bureau all the moneys needed for Indian services in economic development, education, and health. In bureaucratic self-defense, the commissioner, in February 1944, recommended to Congress that the Indian Service be "relieved of federal supervision" over certain tribesmen and concentrate its responsibilites on fewer tribes. Collier, in testimony in 1944, classified Indians into three categories according to their "level of acculturation": (1) 93,000 Indians; (2) 124,000 semiacculturated Indians; and (3) 150,000 acculturated Indians. Those so-called acculturated Indians in the third category were to be "released" from bureau supervision entirely. Among the tribes listed by Collier as acculturated peoples "capable" of operating without the bureau were "New York Indians," namely the Six Nations, and the Wisconsin Indians at the Tomah Agency that included the Oneidas.[40] Culturally myopic and oriented to the Southwest in his judgments of "Indianness," Collier in his political compromise with Congress had given liberal credibility to the postwar movement for withdrawal of federal services from Iroquoia. At the same hearing, he urged the creation of an Indian claims commission "toward the final solution and terminating of the Indian problem."[41] The New Deal had gone stale. A new age of termination which stressed assimilation into mainstream America was now underway.

Collier was not the only policy maker in Indian affairs making compromises with past positions. Willard Beatty, the noted progressive educator and director of Indian education, also shifted in his policy directives. During his most innovative years as director, from 1936 to the outbreak of World War II, he established more day schools, in place of boarding schools, on reservations; began in-service summer teaching programs to inculcate Bureau of Indian Affairs teachers with a common progressive educational approach; held curriculum planning conferences on reservations for teachers and administrators; decentralized educational administration by setting up regional staffs in order to attempt to satisfy individualized Indian and tribal needs; and launched *Indian Education,* a newsletter.

Working closely with anthropologists, educators, and linguists,

Beatty encouraged the development of a new curriculum, some of it bilingual, for Indian schools. Special pamphlets on tribal cultures, the Indian Life series, were written by BIA personnel, translated and illustrated by Indians, and employed to meet the special needs of students. Beatty's attempt at bilingualism proved ahead of its time, largely because there were too few teachers capable of instructing in Indian languages.

World War II and its aftermath virtually wiped out Beatty's prewar innovations. In the cost-conscious era bilingual experiments ended; boarding schools were resurrected; in-service training disappeared; and cultural relativism and cross-cultural educational ideas were abandoned, replaced by a philosophy of assimilating Indians into the mainstream of white culture. Faced with new political and economic realities, Beatty increasingly emphasized that Indian schools should be vehicles for cultural change and integration into off-reservation life.[42]

In 1945 and 1946, Beatty, upon the urging of the New York State Education and Social Services departments, made two reports on Indian schools in New York that shaped educational policies for the next quarter century. Philip Cowen, of the research division of the New York State Department of Education, had made an extensive study in 1940 which had praised New Deal efforts at encouraging Indian arts and cultural expressions. Through a variety of programs, educators had "shown a desire to respect the rights of individuals and to be guided by the decisions of Indian groups." This report stressed improved English instruction, emphasized the Indian's racial heritage, urged the training and hiring of more Indian teachers, and encouraged administrators to work with Indian elders, committees, and organizations to help in the direct preparation of Indian curricula. Cowen's report praised but did not advocate the continued movement to off-reservation day schools, a movement begun with the closing of two schools on Tonawanda Reservation in 1930 and 1931. The report lauded the work of the Thomas Indian School, the eighty-five-year-old boarding school for orphan or dependent Indians located on the Cattaraugus Reservation, and urged the enlargement of its facilities.[43]

Beatty's reports in 1946 dealt with the same subjects; however, his conclusions were nearly diametrically opposed to those of Cowen. Beatty, along with his staff and representatives of the New York State Education and Social Welfare departments, made on-site inspections in May 1945 of all of the Indian schools on the reservations in New York. His report, *New York State Indian Schools*, condemned state Indian educational policy, calling it a "disgrace." New York at the time led "the nation in its per capita expenditures for education"; however, state officials had failed to take advantage of federal hot lunch programs, housed Indians in totally archaic school facilities, and provided inadequate teaching supplies and books. Seeing the situation as an emergency, Beatty urged New York to follow new federal educational policies by encouraging "Indian children to attend public schools with non-Indian children as early as possible." Unlike the Cowen report, Beatty's report insisted that the schools had "some obligation to contribute to adult assimilation of non-Indian culture patterns" and that Indian and non-Indian schools be integrated as quickly as possible, except where extensive distances made travel for the early grades (kindergarten through the third grade) impractical.[44]

In his second analysis, *An Informal Report on the Thomas Indian School,* Beatty strongly objected to the prison-like institutional setting of the school. Although he recognized that the general classroom instruction was "probably slightly better" than the surrounding white schools, he insisted that "the advantage which would accrue to these Indian children by going to school side-by-side with whites would outweigh most of the advantages" of maintaining the school. Beatty urged that all students above the fourth grade be transferred out under contractual agreements to the Gowanda schools which, at the time and apparently unbeknownst to Beatty, were viewed by the Indians as hostile environments for their school children.[45]

Beatty's two reports were symbolic of the change in Indian policies. No longer were bilingual, bicultural expressions valued and the right to be Indian paramount. Four and a half years of war and budgetary restrictions on domestic spending had shifted priorities once again to assimilating Indians. Ten years after Beatty's reports, Governor Averell Harriman closed the Thomas Indian School during its centennial year. In his announcement, Harriman maintained that the closing was "the culmination of a program of integration through which Indian children are now being reared and educated in the community like all other children by sending them to regular public schools and placing them in family boarding homes and child-care institutions."[46] Harriman had rejected a movement by prominent Indians and educators alike to convert the massive school complex into a model vocational high school and/or Indian junior college in the manner of Haskell in Lawrence, Kansas. Ironically, a school founded in the mid-1850s to further assimilationist educational goals had by the mid-twentieth century emerged as a symbol to many Iroquois of community control of education and Indian resistance to assimilation. Although there were those who remembered the repressive nature of the Thomas Indian School earlier in the century and objected to its continuance, and others who were seriously concerned about what they considered the substandard academic quality of the institution, many Iroquois were extremely bitter about the failure to convert the school and its total abandonment by the New York State Department of Social Services.[47] Budgetary constrictions, assimilationist goals, the United States Supreme Court decision *Brown v. The Board of Education of Topeka, Kansas* (1954), and the continued movement of consolidation and centralization of rural district schools led to the closing of all but three of New York's Indian schools by 1965.[48]

World War II had ended the New Deal for Indians. Experimentation and community building by administrators in the Indian world had now given way to budget-cutting, conformity, and mainstreaming. Fighting off the new congressional threats to cultural separatism and federal-Indian treaty relationships soon became the first order of business for those servicemen and women who returned to the reservations after the defeat of Japan.

Despite the early draft protest, the Iroquois were extremely proud of their participation and accomplishments in World War II. They paid tribute to those who returned and those who fell in battle with special ceremonies at the end of the war on nearly every reservation. The first all-Indian American Legion post was founded in 1946 on the Cattaraugus Reservation. Other veterans' associations were founded on New York reservations and at Oneida, Wisconsin. Almost immediately, a new leadership class, centering around the social events of the Veterans of Foreign Wars and the American Legion, challenged the older tribal leaders who had been educated at the Hampton and Carlisle institutes.[49] By recounting their heroism along distant overseas warpaths, these Indians, as in former days, slowly attained political power and tribal offices.

One war had ended while a longer war, more directly threatening to Iroquois existence, had just begun. It was to last uninterrupted for the next twenty years. In order to maintain their cherished beliefs in their separate nationhood, these Indians began building trenches to stop an old enemy, one who was soon knocking at the legislative doors at Albany and Washington.

2

Forness

> All leases made with the Seneca Nation as lessor, which are de-
> linquent in rental payments this 4th day of March, 1939, . . . are
> hereby cancelled as of this date.
>
> Seneca Nation of Indians
> Council Resolution

In January 1942, the United States Circuit Court of Appeals for the Second Circuit of New York handed down *United States v. Forness, et al.*, one of the most momentous decisions affecting Iroquois peoples in their history. The case involved a five-year legal brouhaha between the Seneca Nation and delinquent non-Indian leaseholders on Indian lands in the City of Salamanca, which, strange as it may seem, is entirely on the Allegany Reservation of the Seneca Nation. The federal court ruled against Fred and Jessie Forness, the operators of a large garage in the city, who, along with over 800 non-Indian leaseholders at Salamanca, were delinquent in their payments to the Seneca Nation. The United States Department of Justice brought the test case on behalf of the Senecas to determine if the Indians had the right to cancel Forness's and other federally authorized leases because of non-payment. The Fornesses had not paid rent on property in the central business district for eleven years, and were a total of forty-four dollars in arrears on a ridiculously undervalued lease of four dollars per year. The Circuit Court of Appeals also questioned a New York State law that provided for the acceptance of a tender of payment of rent in arrears, even within six months after execution of judgment. This provision in state law had allowed the Fornesses to pay after the cancellation of their lease. The lower federal district court had previously refused to apply the state law but had rendered judgment for Forness anyway on the common law ground that his tender of payment prevented forfeiture of his lease.[1]

Finding against the Fornesses, the higher court also restricted the application of the state law, insisting that the lessees were "customarily lax about paying their rent"; that all-too-frequently in the past they had been in default; and that the Senecas had attempted to cancel leases in the past. In one earlier instance, the Department of the Interior had blocked the Indians because of restrictions regarding the use of tribal funds in hiring an attorney. In the court's view, the "present action by the [Seneca] Nation, then, represents the culmination of a long struggle by the Indians to enforce their economic rights."[2] The Senecas, according to the opinion written by Justice Jerome Frank, had made a timely effort as best they could under the circumstances. According to this noted New Dealer, legal scholar, and jurist:

> Circumstances like these cannot be excused by the lame apology that others were doing likewise, and that the Senecas were known to be long-suffering. Even if such an excuse were not tantamount to an astonishing claim of a vested right in wrongdoing, preventing any correction of an evil condition, it would still fall short of proving laches on the part of the Indians. It would be both impractical and unfair to require the Indians to bring suit each year for the paltry sum owed on this plot, a suit costing more than the amount which it would yield, and it would be equally impractical and unfair to hold that they must expend part of the rent for badgering defendants and their neighbors into prompt payment. To hold that the Senecas cannot cancel this lease because they have treated defendants and others generously in the past would, in these circumstances, be a miscarriage of justice.[3]

The attorneys for the Fornesses and the lessees of Salamanca argued that the Senecas had no right to cancel the leases since they were procedurally barred by the New York Civil Practice Act. Yet, Frank maintained in overturning an earlier federal district court decision, the congressional intent in confirming the Salamanca leases in 1892 had to be determined first. After all, Frank added: "We cannot believe that Congress intended that, in our times, the rights of American Indians as landlords should be determined by the early 17th century views of Coke—an antique dealer in obsolescent medieval ideas—commenting enthusiastically on the 15th century writings of Littleton, a medieval lawyer."[4] Certainly, in 1892 when the Salamanca leases were confirmed, Congress still had a trust responsibility to Indians as guardians to protect them from exploitation. Thus, since Congress had not permitted application of the New York Civil Practice Act, it did not apply to the circumstances of the case. After all, "state law cannot be invoked to limit the rights in lands granted by the United States to the Indians, because . . . state law does not apply to the Indians except so far as the United States has given its consent."[5]

The origins of this case go far back into Iroquois and New York history and throw light on the entire relationship of the Indians with the people of the southwestern part of the state. From the last half of the nineteenth century until World War I, the Seneca Nation fought off efforts by New Yorkers to gain title to Indian lands. The targets of these attempts were the two largest Iroquois reservations in the state: Allegany with its more than 30,000 acres and Cattaraugus with its more than 21,000 acres. This movement, like the movement for termination after World War II, became tied to efforts at assimilating Indians into the mainstream of American society.

In the mid-nineteenth century, the Senecas began leasing rights-of-way through portions of their reservations to several railroads, including in particular the Erie Railroad and its component spur lines. White farmers or those in service occupations for the railroads and their employees, began to occupy tracts of land within the Allegany Reservation. They subsequently leased these reservation lands at low rentals from the Seneca tribal council or from Senecas who claimed individual possessory rights to such lands in conformity with ancient usages and customs. Because some of these leases were of highly dubious legality, and in view of the significant economic investment of whites on the reservation, Congress officially confirmed the leases in 1875. This date marked the beginning of the major thrust for allotment of Seneca lands by these same lessees and their representatives. By 1875, some of the non-Indians had already made sizeable profits by subleasing Indian land; 420 leasing arrangements had been made and the total white investment on the Allegany Reservation had reached 1,359,775 dollars. Consequently, several non-Indian communities, including the City of Salamanca, were founded within the Allegany Reservation. Approximately one-third of this reservation was leased to non-Indians. By 1900, Salamanca's white residents outnumbered the Indian population on Allegany by five to one.[6]

To make matters more complicated and the pressures for allotment even more acute, an oil and natural gas rush took place in and around the Seneca lands. In the 1890s, a non-Indian venture—the Seneca Oil Company—leased parcels of the Allegany Reservation, obtaining a ninety-nine-year lease at one-eighth royalty to the Indians. The company proceeded to develop these lands and struck oil in 1897. By 1899, 75,695 barrels were being produced. On January 1, 1900, the Seneca Oil Company sold its leases to the South Penn Oil Company, a subsidiary of Standard Oil, for two million dollars transferring forty wells with a production of 200 barrels a day. With "oil fever" in southwestern New York, pressure for allotment of Indian lands reached its zenith in this period, led by its sponsor, Congressman Edward B. Vreeland, a partner in the Seneca Oil Company.[7]

Although the long history of the Ogden Land Company's claim to Seneca lands is beyond the scope of this book, the company's relationship to these lands needs some elaboration because of its significance to the period under discussion. To this day, the Ogden Land Company still owns what has been legally interpreted as a first right to purchase the Allegany and Cattaraugus reservations if the Indians ever decide to sell their lands. According to Gerald Gunther of the Stanford University School of Law, the "Ogden claim has been a pervasive source of difficulty in the handling of New York Indian matters."[8] This assertion is an understatement of one of the most perplexing problems involving aboriginal land tenure in the United States.

On September 12, 1810, David A. Ogden of New York City purchased for himself and his associates the Holland Land Company's interests in Seneca lands in New York. The Ogden Land Company, not a corporation but comprising the heirs of Ogden and his partners, contributed to Seneca suspicions of the motives of white people. Tempered only by the activities of well-meaning Quaker missionaries, the Ogden Land Company continually interfered in Seneca politics throughout the first half of the nineteenth century. As land speculators, the company sought to remove the Indians from New York State in order to profit from the sale of their lands. It pursued this objective through bribery, whiskey, the threat of force, and deliberate misrepresentation of facts. The company was instrumental in one of the most flagrant land swindles in New York history, the Treaty of Buffalo Creek of 1838, in which a majority of the Iroquois chiefs in New York were prevailed upon to sell the remainder of their reservations in the state to the company. Only after considerable agitation by many of the Indians and their white friends were the Senecas able to sign the Second Treaty of Buffalo Creek, the so-called compromise treaty, which returned to the Indians in 1842 the Allegany and Cattaraugus reservations. These events and their impact caused the political upheaval of 1848 which led to the formation of the Seneca Nation of Indians.[9]

Bitter memories of the machinations of the Ogdens and other

land speculators lingered in Iroquois country throughout the nineteenth century. Nevertheless, and ironically, the Ogden Land Company's preemptive claim helped to cloud the issue of allotment and let the Senecas keep their land. The question arose how Congress or New York State could partition Seneca land and allow for its sale to whites other than the Ogden Land Company. Both Washington and Albany, pressured by the white lessees and their political representatives, grappled with the issue of buying the company's preemptive right during the second half of the nineteenth century and well into the twentieth. Congressmen and assemblymen repeatedly introduced legislation to extinguish the claim. Despite the government's recognition of the legality of the claim, the Indians questioned whether the Ogden Land Company had any rights to their land at all. Significantly, at the same time, the Senecas resisted government efforts to extinguish the claim because they believed extinguishment would be the first step in separating them from their land. Meanwhile, the Ogden Land Company held out for more settlement money, demanding more than Congress believed they deserved. Thus, this impasse helped the Senecas hold onto their land base, resist the threat of allotment, and survive as a people.[10]

The movement for allotment of Seneca lands did not arise suddenly with the bills Vreeland introduced in the House of Representatives early in the twentieth century. From 1875 onward, bills and riders dealing with this question were submitted almost every other year in Congress and in the New York State Legislature. In Congress, New York representatives drafted legislation to allot Seneca lands outright or attached amendments to Indian appropriation bills calling for the United States government to extinguish the preemptive claim of the Ogden Land Company. In the New York State Legislature similar attempts were undertaken. These early attempts eventually resolved the jurisdictional question in favor of Congress, and, at the same time, recognized the official standing of the Ogden Land Company. They also showed that there was little support both in and out of Congress for paying out large sums of public moneys to extinguish the company's claim. At the turn of the century, Vreeland discovered a magic formula for convincing a large number of his budget-minded colleagues of the advantages of this action. His plan was to have the Seneca Nation itself pay off the Ogden Land Company with part of the two million dollars it had obtained in a court decision adjudicating its claims in Kansas. The two reservations would then be divided among individual Indians under an allotment formula that would facilitate land transfer and sales to non-Indians.[11]

Vreeland, Republican congressman from Cattaraugus County and president of the Salamanca National Bank, was the chief architect and promoter of allotment of Seneca lands and led the fight in Congress. Vreeland was aided by the favorable climate for allotment in the country, which had produced the Dawes Act in 1887, as well as by previous attempts at securing allotment of Seneca lands. Through effective public relations work and political finesse, he sponsored two bills—H.R. 12270 and H.R. 7262—and managed them successfully through the House of Representatives, but they were to be defeated in the Senate. Despite Vreeland's failure to secure passage, interest in allotment of Seneca Nation lands continued through World War I.

The longevity and strength of Vreeland's movement to allot Indian lands was, in part, a result of support by influential reform groups, such as the Indian Rights Association and the annual Lake Mohonk Conferences of Friends of the Indian. They viewed allotment as part of their four-point plan of forced assimilation—Christian proselytizing; compulsory education in white American ways and values; the breakup of tribal lands and allotment to individual Indians to instill personal initiative, supposedly required by the free enterprise system; and finally, in return for accepting land-in-severalty, the reward of United States citizenship.[12] Vreeland was armed by several studies made by committees of the New York State Legislature, most importantly one headed by James S. Whipple, a Salamanca attorney and friend of Vreeland. In a report of 1888–89, the Whipple Committee urged the United States government to extinguish the Ogden claim in order to solve the so-called "Indian problem" and begin a "radical uprooting of the whole tribal system, giving to each individual absolute ownership of his share of the land in fee."[13] In this report, which has bred resentment toward the New York State government down to the present day, Iroquois family life, land claims, lifestyle, and religious practices and traditions were held in contempt to emphasize the "need for the changes in landed patterns and tribal governments."[14]

In the tight-knit power structure of Salamanca politics, which changed little through World War II and after, the motive for the movement to pass the Vreeland bills was clear. Whipple's son was married to Vreeland's daughter and the congressman's brother served as special counsel for the New York State Legislature's Whipple Committee investigation. The co-editor of the local newspaper, the *Cattaraugus Republican*, now the *Salamanca Republican-Press*, A. W. Ferrin, was also the Indian agent for the New York Agency and in favor of the legislation.[15] In 1902, the day his first allotment bill passed the House, Vreeland openly expressed his objective: "I represent 8,000 people who live upon these reservations; who hold ninety-nine year leases from these Indians, and want to get a title to their lands."[16]

Although the movement for allotment of Seneca lands had died out by the 1920s, a bitter legacy remained. Because of the resentment caused by the Vreeland bills, the Senecas associated efforts, whether noble or base in motive, such as the Indian Citizenship Act of 1924 and the Indian Reorganization Act of 1934, as renewed attempts to get at their land base.[17] The civic-minded white leaders of Salamanca, led by the same families as in the 1890s, such as the Vreelands and Whipples, never completely lost hope of securing title. After a while, many just stopped paying their rents to the Seneca Nation. They took these payments for granted as "inconsequential" obligations, in part because they were infinitessimal and in part because they assumed the Indians were powerless to force them to pay. By 1939, over twenty-five percent of the leases within the Allegany Reservation were in default. Moreover, over 200 had been delinquent for more than seven years.[18]

Tied to the movement to forcibly assimilate Indians into the mainstream by allotting tribal lands was a movement to shift the Iroquois from federal to state jurisdiction. For years, the United States government and New York State frequently clashed over who had paramount jurisdiction over the Iroquois. Although the federal government provided little monetary aid to the Iroquois until the New Deal, the New York Agency of the BIA paid and distributed annuities under federal-Iroquois treaties, collected rentals on leases, provided educational loans and scholarship programs beyond state schools, administered special federal work relief programs such as the New Deal's Indian Civilian Conservation Corps, and made special investigations and prepared annual reports to Washington. New York State, through the Department of Social Services in Buffalo, administered the Thomas Indian School, almost all social welfare and work relief programs, as well as payment of state annuity moneys to the Mohawks, Onondagas, and the scattered Cayugas. The New York State Department of Health was in charge of administering to the health needs of reservation Indians. In the educational realm, the chief of the Special Schools Bureau of the State Education Department administered district schools on the reservations and worked with public schools which some Indians attended in towns adjacent to the reservations; beyond high school, the state provided aid for students attending state normal schools and colleges. The State Department of Highways financed the construction and maintenance of highways on the reservations. With the expansion of federal government services to the Iroquois in the 1930s and the change from a federal operating budget of the New York Agency of a few thousand dollars, the ambiguities between state and federal jurisdiction became more accentuated.[19]

Despite the opinion of legal scholars, including the late Felix Cohen, the foremost authority on Indian law and a solicitor for the Department of the Interior in the 1930s and 1940s, that federal-Iroquois treaties of the 1780s and 1790s "had the effect of placing the tribes and their reservations beyond the operation and effect of general state laws," New York continued to exercise *de facto* concurrent jurisdiction over Indian affairs from the 1790s onward.[20] The state entered into treaties with the Iroquois without prior federal approval or supervision, passed legislation regulating tribal affairs, chartered tribal governments, "sanctioned" the actions of certain tribal councils, and expended money to provide social services, health care, and highway maintenance on reservations.[21]

New York State legislators and representatives in Congress, inspired largely by assimilationist goals, myopic philanthropy, a need for legal order, or less-than-noble motives of land and resource acquisition, sought increasing control over Indian affairs in the last quarter of the nineteenth century until the mid-twentieth century. At the time of the Whipple Committee and again in 1906, 1915, 1930, and 1940, legislators attempted to effect this change. The Iroquois waged a major battle, especially in 1930, to fight off state jurisdiction. Even though the jurisdiction bill of 1930, one introduced by influential conservative Republican Congressman Bertram Snell of Potsdam, had provided for a formal recognition of property rights guaranteed by treaties, the Six Nations, suspicious of non-Indian motives, feared it as a "contravention of treaty rights" and an effort that would subject them to the uncontrollable whims of state politics.[22] According to Chief Clinton Rickard:

> In 1930 a serious threat faced our Six Nations people in the form of the Snell Bill in Congress, which would give control of our Six Nations to New York State. We Indians have always feared being under the thumb of the state rather than continuing our relationship with the federal government because it is a well-known fact that *those white people who live closest to Indians are always the most prejudiced against them and the most desirous of obtaining their lands.* We have always had a better chance of obtaining justice from Washington than from the state or local government. Also, in turning us over to the state, the federal government would be downgrading our significance as a people and ignoring the fact that our treaties are with the United States. [Emphasis added.][23]

Jurisdiction and leasing seemed to be separate issues and were viewed by policy makers as unrelated; nevertheless, the Indians never viewed them as entirely distinct largely because in the past those New Yorkers who pushed for jurisdictional changes were so often the same attorneys or legislators who represented non-Indians in their legal struggle against the Iroquois. It is important in this regard that the Snell Bill of 1930 had been drafted by Henry Manley, the assistant attorney general of New York State. Later, in the early 1940s, Manley was one of the attorneys for the Fornesses and other Salamanca lessees in their legal appeals to stop the Senecas from initiating eviction proceedings. In the 1950s, Manley worked on behalf of the New York State Power Authority in its successful fight to condemn Tuscarora lands for a reservoir. Moreover, Daniel Reed, a congressman from Dunkirk, New York, and a protégé of Bertram Snell and his brand of upstate conservative Republicanism, was the main voice in protecting the interests of his southwestern New York constituents in their legal tiffs with the Seneca Nation; as a highly influential member of the House of Representatives Ways and Means Committee, Reed was the legislative "point man" in getting his conservative Republican colleague Hugh Butler of Nebraska to introduce legislation leading to New York State jurisdiction in Indian criminal and civil matters in 1948 and 1950.[24]

The background to Judge Jerome Frank's ruling in the Forness case, which raised anew the question of jurisdiction, must be examined in order to understand the emotional backlash on the part of the white lessees and their legislative representatives. After years of seeking redress, the Seneca Nation in the 1930s found a favorable ear at the public lands division of the United States Department of Justice. Aubrey Lawrence and, more significantly, Charles Cleaves Daniels, the brother of the powerful southern Democrat and Roosevelt supporter, Josephus Daniels, took up the Seneca cause. During the New Deal, C. C. Daniels was a special assistant to Attorney General Nicholas Biddle and specialized in Indian legal matters. Although viewed by his noted kin as the black sheep of the family for his legal and propaganda work for Henry Ford's anti-Semitic crusades of the 1920s, Daniels' fame rested largely on his work on behalf of Indians.[25] Daniels "put the fear of the law into the hearts of many Pale Faces. It was a time when a resourceful minority seemed to look upon exploitation of the Indians as a lucrative pastime."[26]

Daniels' interest in the protection of Indian civil liberties stemmed from three sources. As a young attorney, he had migrated to the Cherokee strip in Oklahoma Territory in the 1890s. There he had witnessed the terrible injustices done the Indians during the hal cyon days that followed the land rushes in the late 1880s and the work of the Dawes Commission in the 1890s. During Woodrow Wilson's presidency, Daniels had been appointed special assistant to the United States attorney general. Soon he was assigned to investigate and prosecute a number of cases in which the Chippewa Indians had been defrauded of timber land and large sums of money.[27]

Importantly, in the early 1930s, Daniels met Lulu Stillman, a non-Indian activist who served as a legal advisor and confidante to Indian traditionalists at the Saint Regis (Akwesasne) and Tuscarora reservations. Stillman had served as clerk-stenographer and researcher for the New York State legislative committee investigating the so-called Indian problem from 1919 to 1922, better known as the Everett Commission. The report of Chairman Edward Everett of Potsdam, New York, though never published, had concluded that the Iroquois were fraudulently dispossessed of over six million acres of land in New York.[28] Although Daniels was never involved in the Iroquois claims movement, he was influenced by both Stillman and Everett's report. In a memorandum to the attorney general in 1934, Daniels wrote, however "much the conclusions of the Chairman [Everett] may be questioned, there can be little doubt that he was honest and sincere in his effort to get at the very bottom of the New York Indian situation." In this memorandum, Daniels thanked Stillman for helping him obtain a rare copy of the Everett Report, gave a brief history of the jurisdictional question affecting the Iroquois, insisted that the Indians were almost entirely suspicious of and opposed to state supervision over tribal matters, and enclosed Everett's findings for the attorney general's perusal.[29] From his years in Oklahoma Territory, his earlier prosecution of Chippewa land fraud cases, and his research into the history of land claims and jurisdictional confusion affecting the Six Nations, Daniels was eminently qualified to take on the lessees in and around Salamanca.

After a visit to Salamanca preceded by contact with the BIA central office in Washington in late 1934, Daniels prepared a memorandum which suggested it would be proper procedure for the council of the Seneca Nation to cancel the leases. Daniels' preliminary investigation suggested that all leases in Salamanca be investigated to determine whether they warranted cancellation; that legal action be taken to repossess lots and collect back rent where the facts warranted it; that after cancellation, new leases more favorable to the Indians be written; and that all tenants, whether in default or not, be encouraged to accept new, more equitable leases that would benefit the Seneca Nation and the growth of the locality.[30]

The seriousness of Daniels' preliminary investigation as well as the Department of Justice's commitment to prosecute delinquent lessees was taken lightly by New York Indian agent W. K. Harrison in 1935: "It is doubtful if the United States Attorney or the Federal Court will take cognizance of those cases owing to the small amount involved."[31] Harrison, who had served as Indian agent at Salamanca for nearly three decades, had survived by not rocking the boat of Indian and white politics. The Justice and Interior departments collaboration with the Seneca Nation on the Forness case came only after Harrison's retirement in 1938 and his replacement by Charles H. Berry, the upgrading of the agency to the status of a superintendency, and the shifting of the office to Buffalo, away from the Republican politics and political influences of Salamanca.[32] Although the motivation for the Department of Justice's sudden move on behalf of the Indians is not altogether clear, it was not initiated simply because of C. C. Daniels' moral concern with helping the Senecas. It was not beyond the realm of the Roosevelt administration to punish Congressman Reed and his largely Republican constituency for their opposition to Social Security and other New Deal programs.

By March 1935, Commissioner Collier requested that Harrison cooperate with Daniels by holding discussions with the Senecas concerning the attorney's recommendations. Nevertheless, the push for tribal reorganization under the Indian Reorganization Act, the resulting Indian opposition to it, and its bitter legacy in New York delayed further consideration of Daniels' suggestions about the leasing questions until the late 1930s.[33] On March 4, 1939, at a regular session of the tribal council, the Seneca Nation finally decided to take Daniels' advice and cancel all delinquent leases.[34] Two months later, the Lease Committee of the Seneca Nation, composed of Cornelius Seneca, Wilford Crouse, Theodore Gordon, Jr., Cephas Watt, Adlai Williams, and Ulysses Printup, held a meeting at the Dudley Hotel in Salamanca attended by Daniels and Aubrey Lawrence. The Seneca Nation Lease Committee authorized the two Department of Justice attorneys to proceed with the "test cases of certain leases cancelled by the Council . . . for the purpose of establishing through proper legal procedure the fact that the Council of the Seneca Nation has legal authority to cancel any and all delinquent leases on the basis of delinquency."[35] Despite the cancellation of the leases, the Seneca Nation left open the Indian willingness to negotiate new leases at two and a half percent of the appraised value of land and insisted that the cancellations were done only when the defaulting lessees refused to enter into negotiations, and that the intention of the Indian action has never been "to work any hardship upon the defaulting lessees or any third persons." Under the Seneca Nation formula, the Forness's four-dollar-per-year rental of choice commercial property would have been raised to 230 dollars per year. Since these ninety-nine-year leases had no accelerator clauses and had been negotiated at bargain-basement rates, the Indians saw the Forness case as an open door to rectify the abuses of the past.[36]

Although three test cases were originally contemplated by Daniels and Lawrence, only two proceeded to court with Forness, the most undervalued lease in default, being the center piece of Department of Justice and Seneca concern.[37] The Department of Justice won firm support from a powerful ally, Secretary of the Interior Harold L. Ickes, who saw the issue as righting a terrible past wrong done to the Indians. Nominal rentals of one dollar a year and insignificant rentals in the heart of the business district led Ickes to conclude that the "question should be settled in favor of the protection of the Indians' interests and rights in this matter," not simply the acceptance of past rents due with interest. He recommended that the test cases be prosecuted to a final legal conclusion since it would lead other delinquent lessees to negotiate with the Indians for new, more equitable leases.[38]

The Seneca lease case, however, did not proceed without serious roadblocks. In response to Seneca actions, the leaseholders deposited their rent money, 8,000–9,000 dollars, in the Salamanca banks since the Senecas, after lease cancellations, had refused to accept money from delinquent lessees. The delay in securing judgment from the federal courts caused extreme hardship to the Senecas since the nation depended on this lease money to operate. Other problems included the lack of a smooth working relationship between the attorneys of the nation and the Department of Justice. In addition, Daniels and Seneca officials had to contend with large gaps in the documenting of the case since twenty-five years of tribal records and minutes had been "misplaced," in part because of a series of corrupt Indian leaders and councils in the early 1900s.[39]

While preparing the Department of Justice's case, Daniels discovered that the Senecas had repeatedly sought to deal with the delinquent leases. In 1911, a full-scale investigation of this situation was undertaken by the Department of the Interior. Each year, the Indian agent of the New York Agency prepared a list of delinquent lease holders. In 1931 and 1932, an audit of the books of the Seneca Nation revealed the seriousness of the problem. Moreover, on several separate occasions prior to the cancellation of the leases, the *Salamanca*

Republican-Press had quoted the mayor of the city as urging the prompt payment of rentals.[40]

The Forness case finally reached the United States District Court in 1941. The decision of the lower court rendered by Judge John Knight found against the Senecas, but focused largely on the role of Superintendent Berry, rather than on whether the Senecas had the right to cancel delinquent leases. Berry had sent notices on Department of the Interior stationery to various lessees notifying them that rent was due on February 19, 1939, and that an interest payment would be charged on rents not paid by the twentieth of April. Knight insisted that Berry was not simply an agent of the United States government but also "clearly the agent of the Indians." The judge maintained that the Seneca Nation had implicitly ratified the acts of the agent since this procedure of notice and extension had been undertaken for many years. Moreover, since the tender of payment occurred before the twentieth of April, the "right to re-enter" a lease under common law protected Forness from ejectment. Despite his emphasis on Berry's role, Judge Knight rejected applying the laws of the state to the Seneca Nation since it "occupies the position of a quasi independent Nation." He raised the issue of state jurisdiction indirectly in his decision, insisting "the Indians are not subject to state laws and the process of its courts."[41] Nevertheless, the Senecas had no satisfactory redress and had the added burden of operating without the Salamanca lease money which was now tied up by the court proceedings.

The Department of Justice refused to concede and appealed the decision. By November 1941, Daniels was cooperating with the personnel in the Department of the Interior in preparing supplementary memoranda of law and hinting that he was prepared to take the case to the United States Supreme Court. Daniels, frustrated by the setback at the lower court, accused the United States Attorney's office in Buffalo of not working hard enough on the case and suggested that Judge Knight had made a poor decision and exhibited prejudice in the case.[42] Finally, on January 20, 1942, the Federal Circuit Court of Appeals for the Second Circuit reversed and remanded Judge Knight's earlier decision.[43]

Even after the United States Supreme Court refused to grant a *certiorari* hearing to Forness's attorneys, the Salamancans persisted in their efforts at resisting the implications of the Federal Circuit Court of Appeals' decision, namely to negotiate new leases at higher rates with the Seneca Nation.[44] Daniels, in retaliation, advised the Justice and Interior departments and the Seneca Nation to "give 'em both barrels" since only then would the lawyers and lessees in Salamanca believe that the "government is dead in earnest to secure the protection of its wards without further delay." He added that the "persons whose leases have been cancelled will fall over each other to secure new leases when they realize the danger of delay—paying heavy costs, attorneys fees and possible loss of their lots."[45] The Senecas then began eviction proceedings with the support of the Justice and Interior departments against the hold-out delinquent leaseholders who refused to negotiate and sign new leases.[46] The City of Salamanca, at the recommendation of their new attorney, Henry Manley, then sought injunctions to stop these evictions. These efforts were denied by judges in both federal and state courts. It is clear from the delay tactics employed by Manley that he sought to put economic pressure on the Indians since they were wanting 13,000 dollars in rent moneys tied up by the legal dispute.[47]

The Salamancan-Seneca lease war ended in 1944. By that time, most Salamancans had reluctantly accepted new leases. These new leases had been drafted and researched by Superintendent Berry and three BIA personnel specially assigned to check hundreds of land descriptions contained in available maps and county records to insure their correctness. Out of 839 leases, 627 were renegotiated upward. Twenty of the remaining 181 leases were in the process of renegotiation while the remainder were held "by persons whose whereabouts were unknown" or parties uninterested in retaining possession. As a result, the United States Attorney's office in Buffalo called a halt to these proceedings in April.[48]

The consequences of Seneca and Justice and Interior department actions had by that time resulted in an anti-Indian backlash of immense proportions. As early as August 1942, Daniels had seen the potential of a political backlash to the Indian victory in the Forness decision. Looking into his crystal ball, the North Carolinian reflected that the lessees and their supporters hoped "within three years" to elect a Congress "not in sympathy with the policy of protecting the Indians" as "the present administration has shown." In Daniels' opinion, "they may after numerous failures to do so, have Congress pass an act turning over to the 'tender mercies' of the State the Indians." He concluded: "The sort of treatment that they would get can be understood when it is remembered that the State becomes a party against the Government in practically every case brought to protect the 'wards of the nation' from graft and exploitation."[49]

Daniels' prediction was almost entirely accurate. The winds of anti-Indian feeling that arose anew as a result of the Forness decision swept out of Salamanca and the southwestern part of New York to

Albany and then to Washington. Instead of Daniels' estimate of a three-year process, Congress passed the so-called jurisdiction bills six to eight years later in 1948 and 1950, inspired by the political influence of the New York congressional delegation and its major Senate ally, Hugh Butler of Nebraska.

3

Backlash

You must listen to the thunder for even now the sky is black all around us and we must decide what we shall do.

Ernest Benedict (Mohawk)
KA-WEH-RAS (Mohawk newsletter)
1947

On July 20, 1942, Assistant Commissioner of Indian Affairs William Zimmerman, Jr. answered an inquiry put to him by Superintendent Berry concerning questions of jurisdiction of New York State courts over the affairs of the Tuscarora Indians. Zimmerman insisted that the jurisdictional question "is one of long standing about which much has been written and doubtless more will follow" and will remain that way until the "issue is crystallized or put at rest by Congressional enactment" some time in the future. Suggesting that the issue in the particular Tuscarora case was a moot point, he concluded that the BIA was concerned with more important issues, although he offered a personal observation that the Indians were not wholly immune from the operations of all state laws. His warning to his superintendent to drop all consideration of the issue was explicit: "We close with the observation that, at times, it is wise to let sleeping dogs lie."[1]

The sleeping dogs were already howling by the time of Zimmerman's warning. The Forness case had opened Pandora's box whether or not the assistant commissioner wanted to ignore it. The Forness case had thrown into question the general belief among New York officials that laws passed in Albany took precedence where federal laws left off. The implications of the case were important because the decision implied that the Iroquois were beyond the reach of state

civil and criminal courts and statutes. Consequently, the Iroquois were
subject only to the federal Ten Major Crimes Act of 1887. Confusion
was everywhere. Could an Indian be arrested by state police for reck-
less endangerment while driving his car on a state-maintained highway that traversed a reservation? Did state social services statutes apply to problems affecting Indian families on the reservation?[2]

Although there were many legitimate questions about the legal
complications that had arisen because of the decision, the Indians
were unfairly pictured as threats to whites, especially in Massena,
Salamanca, and other communities in proximity to large Indian populations. The fear that the Indians were beyond the pale of law enforcement was further intensified since only two Iroquois nations in New
York had their own courts of civil jurisdiction, and there was no en-
forceable codified Indian law for the punishment of criminal offenses
except what was contained in the 1887 federal statute. These concerns
combined with the bitterness expressed by many Salamancans and
their representatives in Albany and Washington about the Seneca Nation's cancellation of leases. On the other side, the Iroquois distrust
of the state caused by its past Indian policies, its lack of protection
of Indian civil and treaty rights, and its overall insensitivity to the
needs and aspirations of Indian people produced a near-universal Iroquois belief that the storm clouds were signaling a new Indian war.[3]

The backlash started on November 8, 1942, after the Salamancan leaseholders had exhausted all legal and legislative hope of redress-
ing or delaying the application of the Seneca eviction proceedings.
After allocating 10,000 dollars for Indian social assistance in the
county, the Cattaraugus County Board of Supervisors, egged on by the
prominent Salamanca attorney, Charles E. Congdon, and A. Page Bedell, county supervisor from Salamanca's second ward, recommended
cutting off additional county and state funds to the Indians on the
grounds that the Forness case had ruled against the application of state
laws to the Indians. Although New York State never went along with
the county's decision, Congdon insisted that the resolution "offers a
chance to save money for Cattaraugus County, and also to start a movement that may save a lot of money to the state."[4]

In its coverage of this and subsequent events, the *Salamanca
Republican-Press*, which throughout the controversy took the side of
the lessees, recounted how much the state, county, and municipality
had done for the Indians, how much taxpayer money had been expended on the Senecas in the form of educational and medical services, and how the non-Indians had transformed "only a frontier town
on land then chiefly a swamp" into a city of 10,000 hardworking Amer-

ican citizens. The newspaper attacked the federal government for supporting this action, even for helping to cancel leases of servicemen overseas fighting the "Nazis and Japs." In the newspaper's account, the enemies were Commissioner Collier and Superintendent Berry, who had sided with that "Southern devil" C. C. Daniels who came to Salamanca to "get even with the Northerners."[5]

The BIA, as well as the Indians themselves, became the most convenient targets. Whenever the agency was cut during the war, the newspaper gloated. In one editorial, the *Salamanca Republican-Press* focused on the retrenchment of federal personnel, especially those in Interior. The article, "They Never Will Be Missed," concluded that the BIA's budget of 30 million dollars a year cost the public about 500 dollars per family per year and that additional cuts in personnel and overhead should be made. The newspaper sarcastically wrote that the news of staff cutbacks did not include information to determine if "the corps of young attorneys who spent so much time going through records in Salamanca and Little Valley in search of material that could be used as ammunition in the war being waged on Salamanca leaseholders by the Indian Office and the Department of Justice" had been dismissed. The article wryly commented that it "would be just too bad if any of them had to don a uniform and help fight the Nazis and Japanese."[6] Hence, it was no coincidence that the movement for jurisdictional transfer to the state also included the push to close the New York Indian Superintendency.

After continued attacks on the Senecas as unpatriotic Americans for their cancellation of leases of Salamancans who were in the armed forces, one Indian replied that if he refused to pay the rent on his apartment in Buffalo, even on one that he personally had improved with "new paint or fresh wallpaper, he would still be evicted. Because the Indian does not maintain a police force to forcibly demand their $1 rent at the end of the year, the leaseholders have assumed that 'try-and-get-it' attitude." After all, the Indian maintained: "Our boys from the reservation are fighting and dying on the African front" against Hitler. "They are fighting in the Pacific for Uncle Sam and for what he stands"; he added sarcastically, "even for such as those who live in Salamanca."[7]

The Senecas attempted to counter the actions of the Salamancans. On the twenty-sixth of November, President Cornelius Seneca insisted that "if it is illegal for the state to spend money on our reservations, it is also illegal for the state to collect taxes from railroad property and utilities located on the reservations." According to Seneca, outsiders failed to realize that the state has collected millions of dollars in taxes on railroad and utilities assessments on reservations. The Seneca president blamed the action of the County Board of Supervisors on the part of a "few disgruntled Salamanca people. They are angry because we Indians finally have demanded our just rights, and are trying to break the control of a certain element in Salamanca over tribal affairs."[8] Despite Seneca's counterattack, the fear within the nation persisted. One Seneca mother, fearing that her sister's three children would be denied school transportation because of the Salamancan bitterness toward the Indians, wrote to Eleanor Roosevelt, long considered a friend of the Iroquois, to get assurances that this would not happen. Mrs. Roosevelt forwarded the letter to the BIA. An assistant to Commissioner John Collier assured her that the Senecas were protected by Article XIV of the Constitution of the United States against "unreasonable discrimination." If the local authorities chose to discriminate against the Senecas, court action could be taken. He added that the federal government "might be able to exert considerable persuasive force upon the local authorities inasmuch as Federal funds are contributed to the State for relief purposes and might be withdrawn if the State refused aid to all of its citizens without discrimination."[9]

Alarmed by the implications of the Forness decision, especially in challenging concurrent jurisdiction of the state and federal governments in Indian matters, the New York State Legislature, under pressure from southwestern interests in the state, created the Joint Legislative Committee on Indian Affairs on March 8, 1943, to deal with the "more or less continuous state of confusion" about state authority over Indian reservations."[10] The joint legislative committee's intentions were made clear by its make-up and by the way it operated in its first year. Like the earlier Whipple Committee of 1888–89, the 1943 committee was dominated by New Yorkers from the southwestern corner of the state. Although the committee's membership consisted of nine legislators, including ones from Brooklyn, Manhattan, Binghamton, and Rochester, its chairman, William H. Mackenzie, its vice chairman, George H. Pierce, and its most important voice and chief counsel, Leighton Wade, were from southwestern New York. Wade was from Olean, as was State Senator Pierce, while Assemblyman Mackenzie represented Allegheny County. A fourth committee member, Leo P. Noonan, represented Cattaraugus County. The committee quickly scheduled nine hearings throughout the state in 1943, with the first in the series to be held at Salamanca in August of that year.

Indian suspicion about the motives behind the hearings were

evident from the beginning. Cornelius Seneca later testified in 1948 that Indians questioned the committee's objective even before the opening of the hearings in 1943: "Why did they come to Salamanca? Why didn't they start in some other part of the State?"[11] The hearings began on the fourth of August. The committee first heard testimony from Thomas Wilson, mayor of Salamanca; Thomas H. Dowd, formerly a state Supreme Court justice and local attorney for the Home Owners Loan Corporation who had been involved in the original movement for congressional confirmation of leases in 1892; and George H. Ansley, attorney for the City of Salamanca. Numerous Salamancans, including James Whipple and Hudson Ainsley, whose ancestors were involved in the New York State legislative committee of 1888–89 and the original ninety-nine-year leases, represented the lessees' position and testified at the hearings. The Department of the Interior was represented by John Reeves, BIA attorney and specialist on New York Indian legal matters. Only Wilford Crouse, the newly elected president of the Seneca Nation, was allowed to present the Indian side of the leasing question. According to Reeves, the committee's procedures were highly irregular. Besides loading the witnesses in favor of the Salamancans' position, witnesses were not even sworn in before testifying. Moreover, testimony was abruptly suspended at noon on the fifth of August when Chairman Mackenzie announced that the committee was scheduled to visit the Thomas Indian School that afternoon. According to Reeves's report to the Department of the Interior, only after Cornelius Seneca, then the treasurer of the Seneca Nation and known for his gentlemanly qualities and moderate politics, protested and demanded an opportunity to be heard, claiming he had prepared an extended statement, did the state committee finally agree to return to Salamanca to hear additional Indian testimony.[12]

The Seneca tribal treasurer received his opportunity to counter the efforts of the lessees when the Joint Legislative Committee on Indian Affairs returned to Salamanca on the seventh of September. Seneca enunciated the Iroquois' general feeling that they were opposed to state supervision and changes in the federal-Indian relationship since "our treaty and dealings were originally with the federal government"; that the state's historic coercive policies in the past had only contributed to this attitude; and that Indian suspicions about the state had increased since outstanding Indian land claims had never been settled by Albany. He then criticized the committee for earlier denying Indians the right to testify against what Salamancans had presented about the Indians: "Now, I feel that we have been misrepresented to some of the people of the City of Salamanca by some of the publicity given we Indian people, the council body, and also the Indian Leasing Committee, of which I happen to be a member." He accused the state, and by implication the joint legislative committee, of favoring the Salamancans. Seneca added that the Indians, contrary to the testimony and news stories slanted against the Indian position, did not intend to "dispossess people in Salamanca, run business out of the City of Salamanca, in plain words, tear down the City of Salamanca." He added: "All we are asking for was just rent, not excessive rental." In an effort to counter what he saw as the inevitable path to legislative action unfavorable to the Indians, Seneca attempted to win favor with the committee by suggesting that the Seneca Nation had begun judicial reforms, had approached the federal government for the creation of a tribal police system, and had warned its tribal members that "if we Indians don't behave ourselves, some outside agency will come in and make us behave."[13] Seneca, a wise, politically shrewd, self-educated ironworker, looking back into tribal history to the time of the Seneca political revolution of 1848, understood full well that a new era of outside political interference in Indian affairs was brewing and that the Indians had to walk a tight rope to prevent disaster.[14]

As early as December 1943, Wade and the joint legislative committee had drafted in rough form two bills dealing with the state assumption of criminal and civil jurisdiction over the Iroquois. Committee members met on several occasions with Reeves, Berry, and Assistant Commissioner Zimmerman. BIA personnel, at one meeting in New York City in December 1944, emphatically insisted that if civil jurisdiction were awarded to New York, Indian reservation lands, estate matters, and annuities be exempted from the reach of state courts. There was little agreement, especially on the question of civil jurisdiction. Zimmerman wrote Mackenzie that there was "considerable difference of opinion as to the extent of the jurisdiction over Indians which the United States should cede to the State of New York, and there is even more difference as to the method or exact language by which this cession would be made."[15]

On another front, Judge Thomas H. Dowd was attempting to win favor in Democratic political circles, lobbying with highly placed Department of Justice personnel. He insisted that those lessees like himself who were not officially in default in payment of rentals to the Seneca Nation should not be treated like those who were delinquent and that the "old rate of rental shall continue without change" to lessees in this category. The elderly attorney, in a manner of Salamancans from a past era, revealed his motive: "If accepted by you [assistant attorney general] and the Department, and the Indians, it gives a *permanency of title* [emphasis added] to the property owners here in Salamanca, and without that permanency of title, property values in Salamanca will almost disappear." Although Dowd had alluded to leases, his use of the words "permanency of title" is especially revealing given the past history of the Seneca leases. Long after the era of allotment had drawn to a close, the ghosts of the heirs of the Seneca Oil Company and Congressman Vreeland were still around and occupying the city hall and business district of Salamanca.[16]

Other Salamancans echoed Dowd's concerns and carried the judge's points even further. A leaseholder, in a letter-to-the-editor in the *Salamanca Republican-Press*, maintained on September 11, 1943, that "what we want and what I am optimistic enough to believe we will actually have, is not a lease of the land but a deed of it." He added that federal government plans for the Kinzua Dam on the Allegany River was bound to make the Salamanca-Seneca Nation controversy passé. Hence, the Indians better settle now with the Salamancans before the federal government through condemnation proceedings takes the land anyway. Despite the Ogden claim and obvious Indian opposition to his suggestion, he proposed the simple purchase of Seneca land by the federal government and its resale to the leaseholders of Salamanca.[17]

After its closing hearing in October 1943, the joint legislative committee issued a report in February 1944 that focused almost entirely on the Salamanca lease controversy and the questions of jurisdiction. The report recounted the history of the leases and emphasized the lack of state jurisdiction over reservation Indians as a result of the Forness decision, which it characterized as a "reproach" both to the state and the nation. It recommended that Congress take appropriate legislative action and that the Indian tribes, the BIA, and New York State officials hold a conference to deal with the dispute. The report suggested that there were two alternatives: an increased recognition of state jurisdiction or an increased awareness that the federal government assume the state's annual burden of 400,000 dollars by taking over education, health, highway, and social services to reservation Indians.[18] The language of the report was loaded in favor of transfer of jurisdiction. The report failed to mention that highways and bridges maintained on reservations were used by all the state's peoples or that "they were not built or maintained for the especial use of the Indians."[19] Another section of the report was entitled the "Ogden Land Company Title." The report concluded about the Ogden's preemptive claim: "The existence of this claim is a *continuing obstacle to purchase* [emphasis added] by the City of Salamanca of the 3,570 acres of Reservation land occupied by the municipality."[20] The old Iroquois fear, that "reform" meant new threats to their dwindling land base and that state efforts to solve the "Indian problem" by jurisdictional transfer were actually less-than-nobly motivated, seemed to be confirmed in the Indians' minds.

As a result of Commissioner Collier's policy statement in 1944 that the Indians in New York were ripe for withdrawal of federal services, the Department of the Interior became increasingly receptive to overtures for jurisdictional changes made by the joint legislative committee. Unable to function as an agency because of cutbacks, the BIA had to concede. In the same year, Wade's committee had already drafted two transfer bills.[21] Nevertheless, by January 1945 the Department of the Interior was still unwilling to concede totally to New York State demands about full transfer. Abe Fortas, Acting Secretary of the Interior, wrote Wade stipulating three criteria for transfer of jurisdiction. The future justice of the United States Supreme Court required that the transfer "must be qualified so as to preserve the capacity of the Federal Government to take appropriate action for the protection of restricted Indian property and for the discharge of all treaty obligations." Fortas also required that the appropriate administrative agencies such as the Department of the Interior or the courts define the "necessary exceptions to a general transfer of jurisdiction." Before agreeing to any transfer, the Department of the Interior had to have more assurances that "the Indians had no objection to it or that their objections were not justified."[22] Within three and a half years, the Department of the Interior was to reverse this last stipulation about Indian consent and favor the passage of a transfer bill that was opposed by ninety-nine percent of all Indians in the state of New York.

On January 4, 1945, the joint legislative committee held a conference in Albany to discuss transfer. Members of the committee were joined by representatives from the Onondaga, Saint Regis (Akwesasne) Mohawk, Seneca, and Tuscarora Nations. Other invited participants included Felix Cohen and J. C. McCaskill, both representing the Department of the Interior. The meeting was also attended by Lulu Stillman. Stillman was neither invited nor welcomed since her strident position on the sanctity of federal-Iroquois treaties and her suspicion of state motives about the impending legislation were already well known from her past activism. Stillman's position was that treaties had to be carried out first before the Iroquois should accept any new legislation from Washington. Only one of nine Indians, Moses White, a Mohawk from the Saint Regis (Akwesasne) reservation, voiced support for an extension of state jurisdiction. His testimony was challenged by his brother Alec. The historic, often tragic, divisions among the Mohawks, that exist right down to the present day, were revealed in this confrontation between the White brothers. While Moses defended the state-recognized elected system and the need for jurisdictional changes, Alec opposed both. Despite the fact that Moses White represented a minority position among the Mohawks and that even many who supported the elected system opposed jurisdictional transfer, his testimony in 1945 was used to rationalize New York State's assumption of paramount jurisdiction in Iroquois matters. At this same meeting, Cornelius Seneca, attempting to delay the momentum building for the transfer of jurisdiction to the state, urged the tabling of the efforts for transfer because many Iroquois were away from the reservations because of the war. McCaskill, reporting to Zimmerman on the meeting, wrote that "the objection of the Indians to State jurisdiction is a deep-seated and emotional objection; the stated objections are pure rationalizations" including fears of land loss, taxation, destruction of local government, and "inability to get fair treatment in the State courts because of racial discrimination on the part of non-Indians living in the vicinity of the reservation."[23]

The January meeting had revealed an open wound that was to plague Iroquois efforts at stopping the determined joint legislative committee effort to transfer jurisdiction. Bitter political struggles, especially at the Saint Regis (Akwesasne) Mohawk and Tonawanda Reservations, between elected and life chiefs frequently erupted into personal vendettas, threats of violence, and frequent appeals to Washington and Albany officials to intercede. At Saint Regis (Akwesasne), the officially recognized Mohawk government was a council of three tribal members incorporated in the nineteenth century under New York State law. A rival body, supported by Stillman, functioned as a traditionalist alternative claiming that the Mohawks were a sovereign foreign nation, not subject to any federal or state laws and only responsible to themselves. In part because of these assertions of Iroquois independence from Washington and Albany, the Department of the Interior and the joint legislative committee recognized only the three-chiefs system and frequently alluded to the life chiefs as a "rump organization."[24]

Two political organizations existed at Tonawanda. A council of chiefs, but modified once again by state Indian law to the extent of electing officers each year, operated on the reservation. A rival council composed of Longhouse people, followers of the Old Way of Handsome Lake, an Iroquois religion, frequently fought with the council of chiefs claiming not to recognize the state Indian law but only federal law. On each reservation in the mid- and late 1940s, the rival council had the larger number of followers but were out of power since their supporters often boycotted the polls, refusing to partici- pate in elections under laws passed by state authorities.[25] The bitter- ness of the conflicts spilled over into every hearing of the period and helped rationalize the state's position about bringing a new system of law and order to the reservations. Wade's arguments for state juris- diction were bolstered by frequent Indian complaints about their own kin, about the unfairness of tribal inheritance customs, about the cor- ruption and authoritarian behavior of tribal councils, and the lack of judicial institutions to protect their rights. Although few Indians at a major Senate hearing of 1948 supported transfer, Wade perceptively gave the impression to Interior and Congressional leaders that more Indians supported the bills and that the state was actually providing a service to the Indians even if many of them did not realize it them- selves.[26]

On March 15, 1945, the Joint Legislative Committee on Indian Affairs issued its report on jurisdiction. The report included two draft bills, which recommended congressional approval of transferring crimi- nal and civil jurisdiction to New York State, and offered to cooper- ate with Congress in securing these laws. The report concluded that committee members seriously doubted that an "overwhelming ma- jority" of the Indians on the reservations would ever unite in favor of these bills and stated that "the moving force to accomplish these reforms must come from without." The only Iroquois government to endorse the proposed bills were the elected chiefs under state charter at Tonawanda. In a vaguely worded statement, the report claimed that letters "were received from other individual Indians, residents of res- ervations in various parts of the State, expressing complete approval of the proposed legislation." The report, after recounting the January fourth conference at Albany with various Indian groups, discounted Indian opposition as based merely on "pride in the Indian tradition and a resentment against outside interference" and "deep-rooted sus- picion of the white man" based justifiably on "the exploitation of In- dian property rights during an earlier but unforgotten era."[27]

The report quite accurately pointed out Indian inconsistencies. It chastised Indians for wanting it both ways. Most Indians in New York accepted state services, while, at the same time, denying state jurisdiction and claiming independent Indian nationhood. While op- posing state authority, nevertheless, they "welcome the benefits of the educational, social welfare and varied other services being rendered by the State." Notwithstanding this valid point, the report, by emphasizing that the proposed bills were reforms, by no longer even mentioning the Salamanca leases, by ignoring the seriousness of current race tensions between white and Indian, and by highlighting the present state services to reservations, was intended to sell the idea of transferring jurisdiction. The committee soon forwarded its report to Congress.[28]

Despite continued vocal opposition to the legislation, the joint legislative committee won the active support of Congressman Reed, the future head of the House Ways and Means Committee. Wade and Reed worked in tandem to win supporters for the legislative action in Washington. Reed assured Mackenzie and other committee members in early 1946 that he would work on Zimmerman to win BIA support. Yet the agency, under new commissioner William Brophy's leadership, continued, to Reed's and Wade's regret, to insist that transferring jurisdiction be conditioned on a favorable vote by the Indians in a referendum.[29]

Reed was raised just off the Seneca's Cattaraugus Reservation at Silver Creek, New York; he was a conservative congressman, largely committed to nineteenth-century agrarian values, believing that the federal government had grown too big and that the states should take over more of the responsibilities that Washington had assumed. His upstate brand of conservative Republicanism identified with presidential hopeful Robert Taft of Ohio and advocated a return to "rugged individualism" to overthrow the Democrat "heresy," the New Deal.[30] Despite Reed's efforts on behalf of the joint legislative committee and the continued lobbying by Wade of congressional leaders, as late as June 1947, the congressman regretfully reported to Wade that there "is not the slightest chance of such a bill receiving a favorable report from the Office of Indian Affairs, and furthermore, as the legislative program now stands it would be impossible to get any legislation of this character through Congress at this time." Reed interjected a political comment, that only when the Republicans controlled the White House, could they hope to straighten out "this Indian difficulty in New York."[31]

Reed's pessimistic forecast proved incorrect largely because he badly misread the mood of Congress in the postwar era. Congressmen continued to look for ways to cut back on federal Indian programs. They saw the BIA as overly bureaucratic, terribly ineffective, and damaging to Indian self-esteem and economic development, as well as blocking the Indians' path to assimilation into mainstream America. To Congress, as well as to many Indians of the time, the BIA was a self-perpetuating agency that did not service Indian nations or individual needs well enough to warrant its continuance. More-over, at a time when the Truman administration was beginning to champion civil rights, the Indians' separate status was seen as an anomaly. The bureau, in every hearing on Capitol Hill, was rebuked by liberals and conservatives for fostering guardianship, paternalism, and segregation, especially since the Indians had played an important role in the nation's defense during World War II. To congressmen of different political persuasions, the Indians had to be "emancipated" from bureau control for their own good.[32]

Just as Collier had to abandon his New Deal positions under the threats of congressional budgetary cuts, postwar bureau officials had to signal retreat also. After the death of Superintendent Berry in 1946, Commissioner Brophy clearly sounded the bugle for federal with-drawal. In September 1946, Brophy wrote: "I feel that we should set a time limit within which we should liquidate that agency."[33] Less than two months later, Brophy appointed William B. Benge, an attor-ney, as superintendent. Benge announced on his arrival in New York that his major goal was "to clarify the legal and jurisdictional status" of the Indians of New York since it was more complex and "unlike any other in the country."[34]

When Brophy contracted tuberculosis in 1946, Assistant Com-missioner Zimmerman assumed the supervisory role over the bureau. On February 8, 1947, under severe congressional pressure to cut the bureau's budget by "emancipating" some Indian groups, Zimmerman, in hearings before the Senate Post Office and Civil Service Commit-tee, proceeded to divide the Indians into three categories, much as Collier had done three years earlier. The first group of ten tribes in-cluded all Six Nations in New York, who Zimmerman believed could be "released" immediately from federal supervision. The second group of twenty tribes included the Oneidas of Wisconsin and the Seneca-Cayugas of Oklahoma who, according to the acting commissioner, could be "released" in ten years. A third group was composed of thirty-five other tribes who could be "freed" from control some time in the future. Zimmerman defined four criteria for BIA withdrawal: degree of acculturation; economic resources and condition of the tribe; will-ingness of the tribe to be relieved of federal supervision; and state willingness to take over federal responsibilities.[35]

The Zimmerman plan placed the Iroquois of New York in the same category as the Klamaths and Menominees, two Indian tribes who were terminated in the 1950s. Since New York officials for years had urged federal withdrawal and were willing to assume jurisdiction over Indian tribes, the acting commissioner had given impetus to a movement that was well developed and well organized. All it needed was a competent leader with the political clout to push it through Congress even without securing what Collier, Brophy, and Zimmerman had previously insisted upon, namely Iroquois approval. Like a giant thunderstorm out of the Great Plains came a son of the pioneers to lead the fight to "emancipate" the Iroquois.

4

Termination

The Iroquois in New York

... the laws enacted by Congress [in 1948 and 1950] established
a pattern for Federal legislation.

New York State Joint
Legislative Committee on
Indian Affairs,
Report, 1962

Although policy makers used varied terms to describe postwar Indian policy, including "emancipation," "federal withdrawal," or "readjustment," the most frequently employed, and perhaps the most descrip-
tive word to characterize the shift, was "termination." In actuality,
termination was both a philosophy and specific legislation applied
to Indians. As a philosophy, the movement encouraged assimilation
of Indians as individuals into the mainstream of American society
and advocated the end of the federal government's responsibility for
Indian affairs. To accomplish these objectives, termination legislation
fell into four general categories: (1) the end of federal treaty relationships and trust responsibilities to certain specified Indian nations;
(2) the repeal of federal laws that set Indians apart from other American citizens; (3) the removal of restrictions of federal guardianship and
supervision over certain individual Indians; and (4) the transfer of services provided by the BIA to other federal, state, or local governmental agencies or to Indian nations themselves.

Among other things, these "termination laws" of the Truman and
Eisenhower administrations ended federally recognized status for 109
Indian groups, totaling 13,263 individuals owning 1,365,801 acres of
land; removed restrictions on Indian trust lands to allow for easier
leasing and sale; shifted Indian health responsibilities from the BIA

45

to the Department of Health, Education, and Welfare; and established relocation programs to encourage Indian out-migrations from reservations to urban areas. Even the creation of the Indian Claims Commission in 1946 became tied in with congressional efforts at "getting the United States out of the Indian business."[1] In legislative efforts affecting New York, Congress in effect partially terminated the Iroquois between 1947 and 1954 by transferring civil and criminal jurisdiction to the state and forcing the BIA to close its New York Superintendency. Congress also rearranged the procedures by which the Salamanca lessees made payment on their rentals to the Seneca Nation; however, congressional proponents of complete termination attempted unsuccessfully to abrogate the federal-Iroquois treaty relationship by trying to commute the Canandaigua Treaty of 1794.

Since Indian affairs and policies were a backwater area to most congressmen in the postwar period, a few single-minded conservative individuals, operating through the subcommittees of the Senate and House Interior and Insular Affairs committees and the Senate Public Lands Committee, emerged to mold Indian policy in the late 1940s. Congressional liberals, although often in conflict on other matters, were increasingly swayed by their conservative colleagues about the malfeasance of the Indian office and the need to provide civil liberties to another oppressed minority group. Moreover, in the postwar years, both Democrat and Republican congressmen sought to promote parks, dams, and other development projects that on occasion impinged upon Indian tribal rights and land holdings. The policies they formulated from 1943 onward, with the reluctant, tacit, or open support of Department of the Interior, led to so-called termination legislation.

The most important voice in Congress advocating federal withdrawal from Iroquois affairs during the Truman and first Eisenhower administrations was that of Nebraska Senator Hugh Butler, chairman of the Senate Public Lands Committee. In 1947 alone, Butler introduced bills attempting to end the federal trust responsibility to the Hoopa, Mission, and Sacramento tribes in California, the Flatheads of Montana, the Menominees of Wisconsin, the Osages of Oklahoma, the Potawatomis of Kansas, the Turtle Mountain Chippewas of North Dakota, and the Iroquois in New York State.[2]

Butler's background reveals insights into his motivation on Indian legislation. Born on the Iowa frontier in 1878, he moved with his family by covered wagon to a homestead in Nebraska six years later. Extremely proud of his pioneer heritage, Butler, by attaining public office in 1940, was emulating his great uncle William Butler's

Senator Hugh A. Butler of Nebraska, 1941. Photograph courtesy of Nebraska State Historical Society.

path to success. William, the former state treasurer of Illinois in frontier days, had befriended and housed a young, promising Springfield attorney named Abraham Lincoln. His great uncle's early association with Lincoln became part of Butler family folklore. After his graduation from Doane College in 1896, Hugh Butler worked for the Burlington Railroad, became a grain company manager, and eventually made a large fortune as head of the Butler-Welsh Company, one of the largest concerns on the Omaha Grain Exchange. Butler was elected to the United States Senate on a strong anti-New Deal platform in 1940 by cultivating his image as a self-made man, his pioneer background, his concern for farmers, and his philanthropic activities on behalf of Doane College. In the Senate, Butler championed governmental budgetary restraints and Taft Republicanism throughout his fourteen years. Cast in the same mold as Congressman Daniel Reed of New York, Butler reflected the conservative's hostility toward big government and manifested distaste for much of the social experiments of the 1930s. It was in this context that he opposed treating Indians as separate nations within the nation. Frequently using Lincolnesque metaphor, Butler insisted that Indians be emancipated from BIA restraints, that the chains enslaving them to the federal bureaucracy be broken, and that they be allowed and encouraged to be just like other Americans.[3]

On July 21, 1947, Butler introduced three bills into Congress directly dealing with the Iroquois in New York State. Bill S. 1683 aimed "to confer jurisdiction on the courts of the State of New York with respect to offenses committed on Indian reservations within such state." A companion bill, S. 1687, dealt with New York State jurisdiction in "civil actions between Indians or to which Indians are parties." The third bill, S. 1686, attempted to "provide for the settlement of certain obligations of the United States to the Indians of New York" with a single lump-sum payment to the Indians in lieu of the treaty cloth annuity provided under the Treaty of Canandaigua.[4] The Butler bills became the congressional model for later legislation in the era of termination. Public Law 280, passed in 1953, transferring federal jurisdiction in Indian matters to five states, was largely a direct outgrowth of what Congress enacted with respect to the Iroquois in 1948 and 1950.[5]

The Iroquois were well aware of this legislative trend during the fight over the bills. After returning from a Capitol Hill hearing in 1948, the prominent Mohawk Ernest Benedict put the Iroquois struggle into a larger context: "I am inclined to accept the statement made by one of the Senators [Arthur Watkins] that they themselves did not think of these bills as a way of placing the Iroquois at the mercy of New York State, but merely as part of a nation-wide drive to place Indians more nearly in the status of the rest of the people, and thus eliminate the need for the Indian Office."[6] As newspapers announced congressional intentions to "free Indians" from government supervision, the Iroquois became even more assertive in their calls for tribal sovereignty and the retention of "time-honored" treaty rights. When Senator Butler introduced S. 1686 which dealt with commuting the Canandaigua Treaty of 1794, an inviolate document for the majority of the Iroquois, at the same time that he pushed for the transfer of jurisdiction, the Indians identified the bills as a packaged attempt to force them to end their tribal existence.

Importantly, Iroquois associated legislative bills dealing with Indians in other states in the context of the Iroquois struggle. They quickly perceived that certain congressional leaders, particularly Butler, Arthur Watkins, and Wesley D'Ewart, were enemies of Indian peoples.[7] Benedict, seeing the events as a pattern, wrote about congressional motivations behind the so-called emancipation bills:

> Masquerading under the high-sounding cover of "setting the Indians Free" are a series of Bills which strike at the very roots of Indian economy, and if passed would reduce whole Indian populations to poverty and dependence. These bills, which might, to an unsuspecting friend of Indians, sound like pro-Indian legislation because of the holy guise of "emancipation" wrapped about them, are actually being pushed by the big business interests who want to get hold of Indian property. These interests are many and greedy; the big cattlemen of the Plains who want Indian grazing lands; the liquor industry that wants a free hand to debauch and exploit Indians; the mining interests; the timber barons; the fishing industry. It is significant that the proposed legislation affects mainly those tribes still having valuable assets left to their ownership. There seems to be no particular haste to "free" those tribes whose lands are worthless and who own no valuable property.[8]

Benedict informed his readers that Senator Watkins, the chairman of the Indian Subcommittee of the Senate Committee on Interior and Insular Affairs, had remarked that the federal government was getting tired of acting as guardian to the Indian peoples and intended to drop some of its obligations. The young Mohawk journalist queried: "What about solemn treaty commitments? Can an honorable Nation, just because it is tired, shrug off its responsibilities regardless of the wishes

Ernest Benedict with Lulu Stillman at Indian Defense League
parade commemorating the Jay Treaty, Niagara Falls, mid-1940s.
Reproduced by Ron Kohl. Photograph courtesy of Akwesasne
Museum.

and condition of the ward?" Angrily, he wrote: "Perhaps Indians are
tired too! Tired of poverty and ignorance and disease. They are weary
of neglect and broken promises and fruitless hoping."[9]

Butler, in presenting his Iroquois bills, entitled his Lincolnesque
speech, "It is Time to Give Serious Consideration to Setting American Indians Free."[10] Yet, he and Watkins at the time were not in any
way sympathetic to the Indians. They could never fully comprehend
the symbols that meant so much to Iroquois identity. Putting a monetary value on the Treaty of 1794 to him meant commuting a "little
sentimental token," as he put it in 1948, no more. Unable or unwill-

ing to see that an annual distribution of treaty cloth by the federal government reaffirmed in the Iroquois mind their sense of sovereignty, he and Watkins insulted Iroquois leaders by minimizing the importance of the yearly treaty renewal by putting a lump-sum monetary value on it and by suggesting the procedure was an anachronism.[11] Angrily, Alice Lee Jemison, the well-known Seneca political activist from Cattaraugus Reservation, retorted in response to Butler's questioning: "We have kept our shares of the treaties, and we are here to ask that you keep yours. The little amount of calico [treaty cloth] for which the money is appropriated each year by this Congress doesn't amount to very much per person, but it is the significance of that calico which means something to all of us."[12]

Similar sentiments were expressed by Indians from all over Iroquoia. Watkins, in a similar vein as Butler's, asked Andrew Beechtree, representing the Oneida Tribe of Wisconsin who had come to the support of his kin in New York, why his tribesmen were willing to get a fifty-two-cent annuity per year from the federal government instead of a lump-sum large settlement. Beechtree insisted that it was because of Indian pride. Beechtree had previously answered him sarcastically: "Yet, you would lose the identity of this Indian because someone seems to think that the Federal outlay of approximately $5,000 a year in the execution of this treaty is endangering the economic structure of this great Nation."[13]

The extent of Indian opposition to the proposed bills was made clear months before the Capitol Hill hearings in March 1948. William Benge, the new superintendent of the New York Superintendency, who was strongly disliked by the Iroquois, reported in late 1947 that "nearly all of them [Iroquois] with whom I have talked have expressed opposition to the enactment of such laws." The Indians attributed the legislation to "part of a scheme ultimately to make it possible for the state to subject their lands to taxation and destroy their existence as Indians." Benge added that there was a general Indian belief that "racial prejudice against Indians would prevent their obtaining justice at the hands of the state courts." While disparaging tribal criticisms of the bills, Benge observed that Indians insist they can run their own affairs without interference from state or even federal officials, while at the same time appealing to outside authorities to help them secure justice and protection from the acts of tribal courts or councils.[14]

(Benge's latter point about Iroquois inconsistencies was especially true during the decade of the 1940s. Because of intense factionalism and party conflict,) Iroquois from five of the seven reservation communities in New York made appeals to Washington for federal inter-

vention to overturn disputed elections, challenge the existing legitimacy of the tribal structure, or attack laws, regulations, and actions
of tribal councils. The historic divisions and rivalries of elected and
traditional councils at Saint Regis (Akwesasne) and Tonawanda erupted
periodically and petitions from one side or the other were sent to the
president or urgent calls issued for an emergency meeting with the
"Great White Father."[15] These frequent Indian appeals for legal intervention reinforced the position of Wade and Butler that state jurisdiction was needed to provide the aggrieved Indians with an outside
forum.

   The nature of the existing tribal court system added important
support needed for the passage of jurisdictional transfer. Only at Allegany, Cattaraugus, and Tonawanda reservations was there a clearly
defined judiciary, the Peacemakers' Courts. A separate surrogate's court
also operated on the reservations of the Seneca Nation. The Saint Regis
(Akwesasne) Reservation, beset by the existence of two rival Mohawk
councils, had a council of elected chiefs with the power to settle narrow disputes under the laws of New York State. The Onondaga and
Tuscarora reservations were governed by councils of life chiefs or Longhouse governments who kept little or no records of legal decisions,
and, in the words of Undersecretary Oscar Chapman, there was no
"clear idea of the nature or extent of the council's powers." Thus, Chapman and others rationalized forced transfer of jurisdiction as a necessary reform since the Indians were allegedly unwilling to remedy
these problems themselves.[16]

   In fairness to Wade and Butler, some Iroquois had little recourse
available to them against the arbitrariness of tribal councils. The
Cayugas, who had been landless in New York since the late eighteenth
century and who lived on the Seneca Nation's Cattaraugus Reservation, frequently made appeals about the denial of their rights. In Seneca customary law, Cayugas held only life leases on the reservation
and were subject to expulsion from their homesteads. Although the
Senecas had generously allowed the Cayugas to settle among them
for over 160 years, the Seneca tribal council at times lacked sensitivity in dealing with these landless Iroquois. In one case, that of Elsie
Hill, a Cayuga woman, the Seneca tribal council, after a decision from
the Peacemakers' Court, issued orders to eight men to forcibly evict
her and her two children from her home, after the death of her father,
a Seneca. Since her mother was Cayuga, the largely matrilineal Iroquois in New York by custom viewed her as Cayuga, thus having no
tribal property rights on the Cattaraugus Reservation. Cayuga Chief
Elon Eels, in response to the Hill eviction and the manner in which

it was carried out, wrote a protest to President Truman about the unfairness and authoritarianism of the Seneca tribal council. Similarly, during the hearings on the Butler bills in March 1948, Lenore George, who had attended Carlisle Institute and Cornell University and was a representative of the Cayugas of the Cattaraugus Reservation, poignantly described her tribe as a law-abiding, stateless people entirely at the mercies of the Senecas. Although never endorsing the bills, George asked Congress to help provide some remedies for the Cayugas to appeal beyond the actions of the Seneca judiciary system and tribal council. By asking for panaceas from Washington, the Iroquois were opening the door for "federal snake oil," a cure that, on occasions, was worse than the disease.[17]

A major conference discussing the three proposed bills was held in Buffalo early in December 1947, which nearly one hundred members of the Iroquois nations attended, representing different political and religious points of view. Superintendent Benge heard Iroquois, except Nick Bailey of Tonawanda, rant and rave against the bills. Most agreed that they would rather suffer through chaotic conditions than accept state jurisdiction since all New York agencies and courts, they insisted, were prejudiced against the Indian. Above all, they expressed the fear that the legislation would sever treaty relations between the United States and the Iroquois and ultimately "deprive the Indians of their lands through taxation and destroy their existence as Indians."[18] As a result of this constant concern, the Butler legislation was amended to include statements guaranteeing hunting and fishing rights under treaties, an important point to the Iroquois who had been deprived of these rights since 1927.[19] Because of Iroquois protests, the civil jurisdiction bill, which finally passed in 1950, eventually went further than the criminal jurisdiction bill, by providing for the recognition of existing annuities, pending land claims, and customary law, as well as hunting and fishing rights; it also explicitly stated that it did not authorize or imply the alienation of Indian lands or state taxation.[20]

By early 1948, the Iroquois perceptions of the three bills had led them to lobby against the proposed legislation. One young Mohawk high steel worker, Julius Cook, wrote to Eleanor Roosevelt in an attempt to win support from America's most prominent liberal who had aided the Iroquois in the 1930s.[21] Others, such as Elmer Thompson, wrote to Department of Justice officials and the Commissioner of Indian Affairs objecting to the Butler bills. Thompson, having served on the Seneca council for nearly forty years, argued that reservation legal conditions were "not as deplorable as some agitators" have pictured. While certain reforms were necessary, Thompson attacked the Butler bills as "drastic measures," that were largely the inspiration of George Pierce of Olean and "another Indian-hater, Senator Hugh Butler of Nebraska."[22]

Even before the Senate hearings on the Butler bills, the Department of the Interior had shifted its position on the proposed legislation. Undersecretary Oscar Chapman clearly broke with Commissioner Zimmerman in a letter sent to Senator Butler on March 1, 1948: "Although the Indians of the Six Nations place a high sentimental value on the fulfillment of their treaties with the United States and have firmly rejected proposals to commute the payments, I have no objection to the enactment of S. 1686." Chapman, later appointed Secretary of the Interior, justified his policy shift by stating that conditions "have changed vastly in the 153 years since the signing of this treaty, and aside from its significance as a symbol of good will, the annual appropriation of $4,500 contributes little to the welfare of the Indians of the Six Nations." Moreover, for Chapman, the issuance of an annuity check of fifty-two cents to the Wisconsin Oneidas and the distribution of but a few yards of treaty cloth per person to the Iroquois in New York appeared to be outdated practices and a monumental waste of time.[23]

The Senate hearings began on March 9, 1948, and continued for three days. Out of more than thirty witnesses of Iroquois heritage, only four openly supported all or parts of the bills: Nick Bailey (Nicodemus Billy) and Mrs. Hanover Spring of the Tonawanda Reservation; Louis R. Bruce, Jr., a Mohawk-Oglala Sioux; and Moses White, a Saint Regis (Akwesasne) Mohawk. Chief Bailey spoke for the only Iroquois council that had supported the move. Once again, bitter tribal politics came to the fore. Bailey insisted that clarifying the jurisdictional confusion would aid in his efforts to abolish the rival council, a government by chiefs, and foster the substitution of a "new, simple, and modern all-elective form of government in the pattern of the town law." Bailey added that if Congress did not pass S. 1683 and S. 1687, the two transfer bills, during this period of distress and internal disorder, "we have nowhere to turn to for relief. Congress has no remedy for our situation, and the Indian Office over the years has never seen fit to intrude into the relationship of New York State with the Tonawanda people." By passing the jurisdiction bills, local peace officers and justices would have the "green light to retake the reservation within their fold."[24] Later, after the hearings, Bailey suggested to Senator Watkins that he was in favor of the "cloth bill," commuting the treaty to a lump-sum payment to the Iroquois, if it could be used in the creation of an educational scholarship program for Indians.[25]

Both Moses White and Mrs. Hanover Spring stressed the competent job New York State was doing with regard to education, welfare, medical care, and road improvement, as well as overall Indian needs. White criticized Stillman and the life chiefs' traditional council, emphatically endorsed the bills, insisted that there were no impediments to maintaining Indian land title in the bills, and minimized Mohawk land claims. He asserted: "Our Indian courts conducted by our chiefs are both incompetent and inadequate; that is in settling land disputes and personal property and probating of wills." Spring strongly supported the civil jurisdiction bill since in tribal courts "prejudice influences decisions in a community as small as our reservation." Spring, herself a state employee in her position as director of the Tonawanda Indian Community House, added that she also supported the criminal jurisdiction bill since it would save considerable time in the event a peace officer was needed to quiet a disturbance on the reservation. She suggested that an Indian be appointed as a deputy with a salary and "with the authority of the State behind him." Spring, however, held back any endorsement of S. 1686, maintaining that the commutation bill was a "violation of existing treaty rights unless the Indians themselves wish such a change."[26]

The testimony of Louis R. Bruce, Jr. reflected another side of the split within the Iroquois polity. Bruce, the former head of the National Youth Administration's Indian program in New York State in the 1930s and Commissioner of Indian Affairs from 1969 through 1972, had become by the Truman era a force in national Indian politics. He served as an official advisor to President Truman, becoming involved in helping the Navajo Indians in the late 1940s. In 1949, he became executive director of the National Congress of American Indians. Bruce also served as an unofficial advisor to Governor Thomas Dewey of New York on general Indian affairs. Moreover, for years, he had been strongly involved in civil rights matters as a friend of Eleanor Roosevelt, even before the issue came to the fore during the Truman administration. Bruce's family background also shaped his response at the 1948 hearings. For years, his father, a Mohawk Indian and Methodist missionary at Onondaga and Saint Regis (Akwesasne), had pushed for full Indian political participation in American society as citizens of the United States. Although both father and son were extremely proud of their Iroquois heritage and Louis R. Bruce, Jr. worked in New Deal programs to preserve Indian culture—art, dance, music, oral traditions —they were both products and captives of earlier missionary and reformist thinking about "Indian progress." It is important to note that Louis R. Bruce, Sr., and his good friend, the nationally known and influential reformer and Seneca anthropologist Arthur C. Parker, sent letters in support of the three Butler bills that were placed into the record at the 1948 hearing.

Louis R. Bruce, Jr. endorsed the jurisdiction bills, S. 1683 and S. 1687, as ways to protect reservation communities, but questioned the rightness of commuting the Canandaigua Treaty. Aware of his father's and Parker's support, he made an Eleanor Roosevelt-like address about civil rights, and indirectly attacked the commutation bill by insisting that the treaty relationship between the United States and the New York Indians be continued. Although not an uncompromising Iroquois nationalist as were other critics of the Butler bills, Bruce reflected the overwhelming view held by the Six Nations that Indian peoples, despite opinions held by some Department of the Interior personnel, were capable of administering their own affairs.[27] Nevertheless, the testimony of Bailey, Bruce, Spring, and White was used by the supporters of the Butler bills to rationalize the need for legislative action. Despite the limited Indian support, some newspapers of the time gave the impression that the Iroquois were split down the middle over the need for the bills.[28]

Legislative proponents of the bills attempted to use various tactics to win support for passage. Senator Butler questioned Acting Commissioner Zimmerman about his previous testimony in 1947 categorizing Indian readiness for release from federal supervision. Butler emphasized, during the cross-examination, that the commissioner had suggested a year previously that the New York Indians and nine other Indian nations were in the first group of tribes immediately ready for federal withdrawal.[29] Throughout the hearings, Wade, Butler, and Congressman Reed stressed the monetary savings to the federal government of closing the New York Superintendency and ending the federal-Indian relationship, and praised New York for its past commitment to helping its Indian peoples. Reed also claimed it was necessary "to protect the law-abiding Indians on their reservations, as well as the white people who travel the roads on the Indian reservations or have occasion to do business there."[30] Wade, using scare tactics, added that we "don't want to have a legal 'no-man's land' or six of them throughout the State, and that is the primary objective as I see it." The argument went that since most Indians were employed off the reservation at places like Buffalo, Massena, Niagara Falls, Rochester, and Syracuse, extensive contact with non-Indians also necessitated the assurance of law and order.[31]

Despite Indian assurances to the contrary, this latter argument was most effective. Tuscarora chiefs Elton Greene and Harry Patterson boldly stated that Tuscaroras were capable of providing law on the reservation and suspected that after jurisdiction was legislated, "we do not know what is going to come afterward."[32] Seneca delegates, Calvin John, Wynn Printup, George Heron and Dean Williams, insisted that their nation had their own system of courts — surrogate and peacemakers' courts — and that jurisdictional transfer might lead to prejudicial decisions against Indians and the neglect of Indian custom. Some Senecas such as Cornelius Seneca maintained that his nation was capable of developing more courts and law enforcement procedures if allowed and given the time to do so.[33] This point was challenged by Interior and Justice departments personnel as well as by proponents of the bills. Wade minimized Indian abilities claiming that such an undertaking would overshadow the "accomplishments of Napoleon, Lycurgas, and Justinian."[34] A letter from George Grobe, United States attorney in the Buffalo office, added weight against this argument by insisting that since the federal government was unwilling to spend moneys for improvement of much-needed law enforcement and legal reforms, he supported jurisdictional transfer to New York State.[35]

From the testimony at the hearings and from the lobbying that followed, it is clear that the Indians perceived the Butler bills as largely growing out of a backlash from the Forness decision. The appearance of attorney Henry Manley at the hearings and his advocacy of the bills before the Senate subcommittee only confirmed this belief.[36] Reva Cooper Barse, an outspoken Seneca woman, explained it in the following manner: "The whole business of Butler Bills has been a disgraceful procedure, as they are definitely SPITE BILLS in retaliation for the collection of back leases in the city of Salamanca in 1939."[37]

The Indians were most adamant in attempting to hold onto the status quo with respect to civil and treaty matters. The Indians feared that the state would intrude in areas of customary law — rights to tribal membership, to inherit property, to hold political office, to maintain ceremonies. Even more significantly, the Iroquois feared that S. 1686 would abolish them as a federally recognized entity and lead to their extinction as a people. In this context, it is little wonder that the Iroquois from as far away as Ontario and Wisconsin came to testify about the importance of the Treaty of 1794.[38]

Sovereignty-minded Iroquois brought out their fears that the bill was the first stage of a larger legislative effort to destroy them as a people. Benedict insisted he was a citizen of the Six Nations, not a "New York Indian." He added that Congress had no "right to regulate the internal affairs" of his people since the Six Nations have their own constitution and laws by which to abide.[39] This position was reinforced by statements made by Lulu Stillman, the non-Indian advisor to Iroquois traditionalists.[40] The Iroquois Confederacy *Tadodaho* or spiritual leader, George Thomas, insisted that the Butler bills were "forced legislation" and consequently unacceptable to the Six Nations. He asserted that if new legislation was required, both parties—the Iroquois and the federal government—must concur. Thomas, an Onondaga, maintained that the Iroquois were unwilling to accept any new legislation since there had been no settlement of outstanding Iroquois land claims. He added that if the Six Nations accepted these bills, they would be working backwards and would not "be able to progress toward the things that we want."[41] Thomas then recounted the history of the report of the Everett Commission of 1919 to 1922 in order to emphasize that an Iroquois claims settlement had been too long in coming. In a similar manner, Oneida chief William Rockwell, who had testified before the Everett Commission, and Cecilia (Delia) Cornelius Waterman expressed the view that their nation had been waiting for 154 years for Congress to carry out its promises of federal trust responsibility to the Indians by settling land claims.[42]

Trying to stem the tide against the Butler bills, Tillie John of the Allegany Reservation wrote to Congressman Reed in June 1948, attempting to convince him to oppose the legislation by invoking a combination of Christianity, traditional wisdom, and historical analogy. She maintained that if the Iroquois accepted the Butler bills they would be no better off than Esau who sold his birthright "for a mess of pottage." Claiming that her people were sovereign nations, John insisted that the state could not assume jurisdiction anymore than it could over England, France, and Spain. Interestingly, she compared the Iroquois plight in 1948 to that of China in the nineteenth century: "We have only to behold the sad and bitter experience of China with her unequal treaties, foreign priveleges [sic], and foreign jurisdiction over civil and criminal cases on Chinese territory."[43]

Despite the overwhelming Indian oposition to the Butler bills and the Iroquois desire to be left alone, the House and Senate passed the criminal jurisdiction bill S. 1683 in late June. It was signed into law by President Truman on July 1, 1948. Because of the stronger Indian opposition to the transfer of civil jurisdiction and the commutation of the Treaty of 1794, and the legal complexities of implementing S. 1686 and S. 1687, these two bills never reached a floor vote.[44] Providing law and order and protection to and from Indians appeared to be a more pressing need as a result of largely non-Indian testimony. Hence, New York attained paramount jurisdiction in criminal matters affecting Indians, an objective the state had been seeking since the report of the Whipple Commission of 1888–89.

Within twenty-six months, Congress had ironed out all the complexities over transferring civil jurisdiction. Part of the delay was a result of Iroquois efforts themselves to lobby against the legislation. They effectively used the media to counter arguments made by Butler, Reed, and Wade.[45] Led by Tuscarora Chief Clinton Rickard, they took their case to the sidewalks outside the United Nations building in New York City as well as to the banks of the Potomac, demanding that New York "cease its aggressions" against the reservations and respect federal-Iroquois treaties.[46] The Tonawanda Seneca Chiefs' Council sent an elaborate legal brief to President Truman condemning New York for not settling Indian land claims, while, at the same time, interfering in Indian lives. They claimed that the state discriminated against Indians; did little for Indian educational and medical needs or for reservation road improvements; treated Indians as merely charity cases; and collaborated with vested interests, especially public utilities involved in power development and private corporations involved in mineral extraction, to keep the Indians divided and economically deprived.[47]

The Iroquois were aided by long-time friends in their battle against the remaining two Butler bills. Two ministers to the Iroquois—Emery Kocsis, a Baptist minister and chaplain of the Indian Defense League of America; and Glenn Coykendall from Angola, New York and Episcopal minister to the Senecas on the Cattaraugus Reservation—organized a letter-writing campaign to national leaders as well as to newspapers in the state.[48] Coykendall, writing jointly with LeRoy Snow, a councillor of the Seneca Nation, pointed out the long history of the Seneca Peacemakers' Courts. Both clergymen insisted that the Iroquois, in general, considered New York the enemy of Indian peoples because of the state's broken promises in the past. They argued that before "state courts seek to pass judgment upon Indians they should be empowered to pass judgment upon their own officials who have robbed and defrauded the Indian." According to them, the state had not finished making payment to the Cayuga Nation in an international tribunal decision made in the 1920s nor had done anything to redress other existing Indian claims. They expressed a commonly held belief of the Senecas that the entire push for civil jurisdiction was based on state attempts to have legal authority and jurisdiction over the Seneca leases.[49] Once again, the Salamanca leases and the leaseholder and state reaction to the Forness decision was tied in with jurisdictional transfer in the minds of the Indians.

The fears of both the Iroquois and their supporters intensified when the Butler bill commuting the Treaty of 1794 passed the full

Senate in 1949. Although the Senate-approved version never became law, the possibility of its future passage sent shock waves from Massena, New York all the way west to Green Bay, Wisconsin. When the Department of the Interior closed the New York Superintendency in Buffalo in 1949 and ended its subsidy of a medical clinic on Cattaraugus Reservation, the Iroquois in New York saw themselves as potentially being the first Indian group subject to full congressional termination.[50] One Tuscarora chief reiterated Iroquois concerns about civil jurisdictional transfer and new congressional legislation over tribal objections, insisting, before the House Subcommittee on Indian Affairs, that the Iroquois "want you to leave us alone and let us live peaceably."[51] Lulu Stillman, attempting to use analogies from the current tensions of the Cold War, once again filed her petitions with national leaders on behalf of the Six Nations Confederacy. She insisted, "You cannot condemn Russia if you insist upon forcing legislation over the protests of these Indians."[52] Maxwell Garrow, clerk of the Mohawks, in a letter to Senator Herbert H. Lehman, similarly referred to the coercive nature of the legislation, maintaining, "think how you would react to an alien such as Russia taking away, in the same manner, any of your rights as an American."[53] Jesse J. Cornplanter, the noted Seneca author, artist, raconteur, and "show Indian," attempted to use his political influence by appealing to Senator Lehman, whom Cornplanter had adopted into the Senecas during the time of Lehman's governorship in the late 1930s. Worried more about the Butler commutation bill, Cornplanter saw the larger meaning of the Iroquois struggle, namely, that the legislation "would terminate our connection with the Federal Government."[54]

Proponents of the two bills were aided by intense lobbying by four political leaders from southwestern New York. Burdette Whipple, direct descendant of the chairman of the historic Whipple Commission of 1888–89, and Judge Thomas H. Dowd, now well over ninety, attempted to win bipartisan support for the civil jurisdiction bill, reintroduced by Butler and by Senator Irving Ives of New York and renumbered S. 192. Claiming vast experience and expertise in Indian affairs, they challenged Indian custom, especially Iroquois laws of tribal descent and inheritance, and accentuated a hardship case involving an Indian husband who abandoned his responsibility to a dying wife.[55] Wade, in pushing for civil jurisdiction, somewhat bent the truth when he wrote Butler urging the senator to continue his efforts on behalf of the legislation seeking jurisdictional transfer of civil matters: "I have the word of various Indians who opposed the bills at the hearing in Washington last March that they believe the change has worked to the advantage of Indians generally."[56]

Congressman Reed was extremely important in the final passage of the civil jurisdiction bill. Although referred to as the Butler-Ives Bill, Reed's work in Congress was second only to that of the Nebraska senator himself. Viewing himself as extremely knowledgeable about Iroquois matters because he had lived near these Indians for more than half a century, Reed, in a letter to a congressional colleague, dismissed the Indian criticism of the bill as merely the work of a few "unscrupulous agitators." He attacked Senator Joseph O'Mahoney of Wyoming for stalling legislative efforts in an area thousands of miles away from his own constituency. He reiterated his belief that New York had done more for Indians than any other state in the union and should be awarded jurisdiction. Playing politics, the congressman from Dunkirk, New York viewed the legislation as his bill for his constituents and held that it should not be stopped by protests "lodged with some Member or Members far removed from the scene of the action."[57] Once again, both Reed and Butler worked in tandem with Wade and the New York State Joint Legislative Committee on Indian Affairs which continued to lobby on behalf of the legislation.[58]

The legislative showdown on the civil jurisdiction bills came in the summer of 1950. Reed, in congressional debate, once again observed how, over a thirty-nine year period from 1911 to 1950, New York State generously provided 415,384.15 dollars *per annum* for Indian welfare; in contrast, the United States only provided an annual average of 8,700 dollars. Incredibly stretching the truth, Reed insisted that the Indians wanted civil jurisdictional transfer.[59] Reed's arguments were dismissed by Congressman Eugene O'Sullivan, a Democrat from Nebraska. O'Sullivan, the leader of the opposition in congressional debate, recounted the whole sorry episode of the Seneca leases and the backlash that followed the Forness decision. He viewed the bill as originating out of base motives: "Everything indicates that we are now on the 1-inch line and greed and injustice is going over the goal quite soon for a touchdown, if the people's great safety man, President Truman, does not stop the ignoble ball carrier with a smacking veto, which I hope he does." Questioning Reed's statement about the size of Indian support for the bills, O'Sullivan added, "Today our boys are fighting for the right of self-determination in Korea. Why not self-determination for the Seneca Indians?"[60]

On the fourteenth of August, O'Sullivan offered an amendment to the Butler-Ives Bill which called for a majority vote in favor of the bill in plebiscites conducted in Iroquois communities before the legislation would go into effect; his amendment was quickly defeated. Nevertheless, two amendments introduced by Toby Morris, Democrat of Oklahoma, were accepted by voice vote.[61] These amendments attempted to safeguard future Iroquois tribal claims and to preserve customs that the Indians wished preserved. As a result, both the House and Senate voted overwhelmingly for the bill. On the first of September, the joint conference committee further amended the bill by permitting courts to recognize and give effect to tribal laws and customs "which may be proved to the satisfaction of the courts."[62] Importantly, the burden of proof was on the tribes to record within a year any customs that they wished retained, the record to be forwarded to the Secretary of the Interior. Indian resentment about the bill, which was signed into law on the thirteenth of September by President Truman, was total and not one of the tribes complied with this provision about filing.[63]

To add insult to the indignities already faced by the Iroquois, Congress, the following year, at the urging of Butler, Reed, and Wade, passed the Seneca Rental Bill. Because the New York Superintendency was now closed, leaseholders under the provisions of the act paid their rental moneys directly to the City of Salamanca; the city would then forward the money to the Seneca Nation. Although this facilitated payment and replaced the role of collection undertaken in the past by the Indian agent, the legislation created the false impression that the city had paramount authority over "its residents" and that the Indians were simply ordinary landowners, not quasi-sovereign Indian nations.

The Seneca Rental Bill, the closing of the New York Superintendency, and the transfer of jurisdiction in civil and criminal matters to the state did not end Senator Butler's efforts to fully sever the federal-Iroquois treaty relationship. Until his death in 1954, Senator Butler continued to push to commute the Canandaigua Treaty into one final cash payment to the Iroquois in New York. Butler's effort was aided by the introduction and passage of House Concurrent Resolution 108 in August 1953, which specifically targeted these tribesmen:

> That it is declared to be the sense of Congress that at the earliest possible time, all of the Indian tribes and individual members thereof located within the States of California, Florida, New York, and Texas, and all of the following named Indian tribes and individual members thereof, should be freed from Federal supervision and control and from all disabilities and limitations specifically applicable to Indians.[64]

Early in February 1954, Butler introduced two bills which called for the final discharge of the federal government's responsiblity to two of the Iroquois nations under the Treaty of Canandaigua. Since the Six Nations had been in effect partially terminated by the closing of the New York Superintendency and the transfer of civil and criminal jurisdiction to the state, Butler now hoped to end the federal-Iroquois relationship entirely.[65] Ironically, Senator Butler's bills had been fueled by Iroquois criticisms of the Department of the Interior and particularly of the BIA. For decades, prominent Iroquois leaders had urged the total abolition of the BIA. Since the 1930s, Iroquois political activists such as Alice Lee Jemison had called for the end of the bureau's authoritarian supervision, mismanagement of Indian affairs, and excessive paternalism.[66] Although Jemison's arguments were used by congressional critics of the bureau and proponents of termination in the early 1950s, she and other activists among the Iroquois saw the dangers of the proposed legislation of the Truman-Eisenhower administrations. In her newsletter published in February 1954, Jemison predicted with startling accuracy the dangers facing the Indians. She insisted that the "present proposals will accomplish only one thing with any certainty—the termination of Federal expenditures for the benefit of the Indians, and will leave the Indians suspended in a twilight zone of political nonentity, partly tribal, partly State. And twenty years from now another Congress will be considering measures to correct the mistakes of this experiment."[67] It is noteworthy that Congress in 1973, nearly twenty years after the passage of the first termination bill, restored the Menominee Tribe of Wisconsin to federal recognition.

One of Butler's bills, S. 2866, attempted to "provide for the distribution of funds belonging to the Seneca Nation and Tonawanda Band of Senecas," while the other, S. 2867, provided "for the capitalization of a treaty annuity paid to the Six Nations of Indians." The second bill, like Butler's bills of the late 1940s, was an attempt to commute to a capitalized sum an annuity payment under the Canandaigua Treaty of 1794. Unwilling to accept the symbolic importance of the annual cloth distribution to the Iroquois and their beliefs in sovereignty, Butler in 1954 made Jemison's Seneca peoples a "standing offer" to accept a lump-sum monetary settlement. Secretary of the Interior Douglas McKay, who favored the bill, held two meetings with Iroquois representatives who strongly protested Butler's actions "because they fear this action would end all obligations of the United States to the New York Indians under this treaty." Although there was still talk of terminating New York tribesmen right through the Kinzua Dam crisis into the 1960s, the movement to end the 4,500-dollar annuity for distribution of cloth and to provide for a final settlement with the two Seneca bands lost its leader as a result of Senator Butler's sudden death on July 1, 1954.[68]

The three Butler bills left a bitter legacy among the Iroquois in New York. The most longlasting result was increased Indian suspicion of the state and its officials. Leighton Wade's continued presence as counsel to the joint legislative committee until the early 1960s reminded Iroquois leaders, making their annual obligatory visits to Albany, of their first postwar struggle and loss of their separate political-legal existence. Yet, the worst was still ahead for these Indians as well as for their kin in Wisconsin and Oklahoma.

5

Termination

The Wisconsin Oneidas and
the Oklahoma Seneca-Cayugas

Now the United States Government has offered the Oneida Indians a cash settlement (the sum of $60,000) claiming it cost the
government too much money to write out the checks. . . . We the
Oneida Indians of Wisconsin have rejected this offer. . . . Thus, if
we were to consider giving up our priceless heritage for a few pieces
of silver, we would be untrue and unfaithful to the causes our ancestors had given their lives for, so that Freedom may be born and
live. Therefore, we are unable to entertain any thoughts of a cash
settlement for our treaty rights of 1794.

Oneida Fact Finding Board
Resolution
Milwaukee, Wisconsin
1952

The Indians in New York were not the only Iroquoian nations whose
existence was threatened in the late 1940s and 1950s. The Oneida
Tribe of Wisconsin and the Seneca-Cayuga Tribe of Oklahoma came
close to being fully terminated in the postwar years. Both nations
had small land bases and had developed new governmental political
structures under the Indian New Deal in the 1930s. Both had similar concerns and were plagued by similar problems, including tribal
land claims, economic and cultural survival, and rampant tribal factionalism.[1]

As the only two Iroquois communities affected by federal allotment policies from the Dawes Act of 1887 onward, the Oneida and
Seneca-Cayuga land bases were largely checkerboard parcels of land
owned by individuals, not the tribes themselves. At the death of the
allottee, these lands were further divided or fractionated into smaller

parcels. Over time these so-called heirship lands came to be jointly owned by more than one Indian who had inherited equal portions of the original allotment under provisions of the Dawes Act. By the 1950s, in some instances, hundreds of Indians held an interest in the same original allotment. Bureau of Indian Affairs regulations, which Indians criticized as excessive, required the consent of a majority of owners before heirship lands could be partitioned and sold. The land often sat idle or was leased because in many cases heirs could not be found. Congressional bills of the 1950s tried to deal with this heirship mess, which still affects American Indians, by removing many of the regulations on these lands; however, these bills provided little or no protection against alienation of lands from Indian hands.[2]

From the late 1940s onward, the Oneida Tribe of Wisconsin, which had incorporated under the Indian Reorganization Act in 1935, fought against jurisdictional transfer, commutation of the Canandaigua Treaty, and total federal withdrawal of services. They also had to contend with a new commissioner of Indian affairs, Dillon S. Myer, appointed to office by President Truman in 1950. Myer, a career administrator who had served in numerous posts in the Department of Agriculture, headed the War Relocation Authority from 1942 to 1944, and had been a commissioner of the Federal Housing Authority since 1946. Strange as it may seem today, his wartime experience with another minority group, the Japanese Americans, led Secretary of the Interior Oscar Chapman to recommend him to President Truman to be commissioner of Indian affairs. As head of the War Relocation Authority, he supervised the tragic removal and detention of tens of thousands of Japanese Americans, who were held at special camps, some of which were located on Indian reservations. In suggesting that Truman appoint Myer, Chapman discussed his qualifications for the job: "He did an outstanding job in the maintenance and relocation of the Japanese evacuated from the Pacific Coast region, which program was fraught with many troublesome aspects, including the maintenance of good public relations during the emotionalism of war." Chapman added: "I feel that this total experience well fits him for the position of Commissioner of Indian Affairs."[3]

Almost immediately upon assuming office, Myer focused his agency's attention on the step-by-step transfer of bureau functions. Building on early Department of the Interior plans for federal withdrawal, Myer was also aided by the postwar climate of the country. The Cold War with the Soviet Union and the early days of the Korean War had produced an extreme sense of American nationalism and less tolerance of differences both outside and inside American society. Increasingly, many Americans saw Indian reservations, not as native people's homelands, but as strange anomalies irrelevant to modern times. Moreover, the increased awareness of civil rights and growing repudiation of segregation during the Truman administration helped reinforce the overly optimistic belief that reservation life segregated Indian peoples from the benefits of joining the mainstream of American life.[4]

Myer's policies were also aided by other factors. Commissioners Collier and Zimmerman had previously indicated the readiness of certain tribes for federal withdrawal. In addition, Commissioner Myer had at his disposal massive surveys that reinforced his position. The Special Presidential Commission on the Organization of the Executive Branch of the Government, better known as the Hoover Commission, filed a task-force report on Indian affairs in 1949, that, among other suggestions, advocated the transfer of federal programs to the states; urged policies which would encourage and assist Indians to leave the reservation and enter the mainstream of American life; and called for the "ending of tax exemption and of privileged status for Indian owned land and the payment of the taxes at the same rates as for other property in the area."[5] Myer's predecessor as commissioner, John Nichols, a former member of this task force, had announced in early 1949 that "the time should soon arrive when Indian peoples would be dealt with as other Americans and that all special designations and treaty restrictions would be set aside."[6] Myer had also contracted with Princeton University in 1950 to furnish an independent and detailed analysis of bureau functions in order to help determine a national Indian program. The report of this academic group concluded that Indians should be given services that were ordinarily provided for other citizens by other state, local, or federal agencies. It recommended that the bureau assist the "Indians in the process of assimilation into society as co-equals of other citizens—a process which should result in the eventual termination of Bureau activities."[7]

Even Oliver LaFarge and his pro-Indian New Deal American Association on Indian Affairs had moved to a more outwardly assimilationist position. The noted reformer began to see as "inescapable fact" that the nation's mood was leading to the conclusion that Indians be integrated into the mainstream of American society, that the "basic over-all theory or policy is that Indians must become absorbed into the general population." LaFarge added: "Our problem is so to guide and protect the process of amalgamation that it will be carried through with benefit to both groups, with justice, and with humanity." Significantly, LaFarge maintained that his organization favored first the "withdrawal of federal control over Indians in California, New York, and Oregon."[8]

The Myer program of termination was aided substantially by a new BIA rapprochement with Congress. The bureau, even at a loss of its supervisory role in its dealings with certain tribes and the transfer of all health care administration from its control, cooperated with Congress at every turn. Secretary Chapman had certain initial qualms about House Joint Resolution 490 introduced by Congresswoman Reva Bosone of Utah in 1950, that required the BIA to designate tribes for termination and produce a workable federal withdrawal program in two stages by January 1952. Yet, it and subsequent congressional bills were in the end enthusiastically endorsed by the secretary as well as the commissioner, with Myer and his successors giving the tribes the false impression that termination was inevitable for all Indians.[9] In 1952, Congressional Resolution 698 required that the bureau name "tribes, bands, or groups of Indians now qualified for full management of their own affairs" and to recommend "legislation for removal of legal disability of Indians by reason of guardianship by the federal government."[10] The BIA's lengthy response, which appeared in House Report 2503, answered the congressional request by naming the Oneidas of Wisconsin as being ripe and the Seneca-Cayugas of Oklahoma as being conditionally ready for termination.[11]

The cooperation between congressional leaders and Department of the Interior personnel continued even after Myer left office in 1953. Glenn Emmons, the new commissioner, an opponent of the New Deal and an ally of pro-terminationist New Mexico Senator Clinton Anderson, agreed with much of Myer's thinking. During his early tenure at the BIA, Emmons joined with congressmen who sought to dismantle the bureaucracy of Indian affairs, discourage Indian dependence, and promote Indian "progress" by assimilating Indians into mainstream white society. He believed, as did Myer before him, that Congress should speed up removing the excessive restrictions on Indian trust lands, which even many Indians viewed as overly paternalistic.[12]

On August 15, 1953, Congress passed Public Law 280. With a few exceptions, the act transferred criminal and civil jurisdiction over Indian affairs to the states of California, Minnesota, Nebraska, Oregon, and Wisconsin, in the same manner as the Butler bills of 1948 and 1950:

> As a practical matter, the enforcement of law and order among the Indians in the Indian country has been left largely to the Indian groups themselves. In many States, tribes are not adequately

organized to perform that function; consequently, there has been created a hiatus in law-enforcement authority that could best be remedied by conferring criminal jurisdiction on States indicating an ability and willingness to accept such responsibility. Similarly, the Indians of several States have reached a stage of acculturation and development that makes desirable extension of State civil jurisdiction to the Indian country within their borders.[13]

The Oneida Tribe of Wisconsin was one of the Indian nations directly affected by this legislation.

Besides jurisdictional transfer, the BIA had developed by September 1952 an Oneida "withdrawal programming report." The Great Lakes Area Field Office, which prepared the report, concluded that the Oneida "tribe is ready for complete withdrawal of Bureau responsibility for services and termination of trusteeship responsibilities." The report insisted that the BIA was furnishing "very little service" to these Indians and that numerous Oneidas "have demonstrated ability to get along in the competitive world." The report, however, warned that there were two drawbacks to complete termination: (1) the need for legislation to "assist in clearing the land status," or more specifically the heirship problem; and (2) "treaty obligations involving annuity payment."[14]

One month later, BIA officials began to sell their withdrawal program to the Oneidas. In response, the Oneida Tribal Executive Council, headed by Dennison Hill, Irene Moore, Charles A. Hill, and Mamie Smith, expressed dissatisfaction with the continued workability of the political structure created under the Indian Reorganization Act to solve the Oneidas' many problems. The Tribal Executive Council maintained that the Indians' major needs were housing as well as economic and educational programs, not new termination legislation. They also expressed their dissatisfaction with the shifting nature of BIA policies from year to year and questioned whether tribal consent was not necessary before federal withdrawal could take effect.[15]

Throughout 1953, the bureau intensified its campaign to convince both Indian and Wisconsin politicians of the value of Oneida termination. Don C. Foster, the BIA area director, E. J. Riley, the administrative officer of the BIA's Great Lakes Consolidated Agency, Commissioner Myer, and Acting Commissioner W. Barton Greenwood worked out a deal to offer the Oneidas a $60,000 lump sum payment to commute the Canandaigua Treaty.[16] Myer, writing to Wisconsin Senator Joseph McCarthy, counteracted unfavorable publicity about the bureau and its policies toward the Oneidas. He told McCarthy that he and the Oneida Tribal Executive Council were jointly negotiating for the "complete independence of the Oneida Tribe of any need for the special services and the supervision of the Bureau."[17] On the fifteenth of May, bureau officials replied to a questionnaire prepared by the House Committee on Interior and Insular Affairs. The BIA's summary statement reiterated that the Oneidas were "ready for complete withdrawal of Bureau responsibility for services and for termination of trusteeship responsibilities," and once again raised the problems of unclear land status and treaty obligations involving annuity payment. Yet, the BIA's answers to the questionnaire gave the impression that complete Oneida termination was inevitable.[18]

In December 1953, Riley held a major meeting with Oneida tribal leaders at the parish hall of the Episcopal Church of the Holy Apostles at Oneida, Wisconsin. At the meeting, he presented a proposed congressional bill "to settle once and for all, the problem of perpetual annuities," which, according to Riley, were "costing his office $2,200 a year to pay the Oneidas their $1,800 yearly annuity." Riley insisted that the proposal was "not one dreamed up by the Bureau of Indian Affairs," but placed the blame on Congress which was seeking a solution to what it called the "Indian Problem." After maintaining that the bill did not abrogate the Canandaigua Treaty, the BIA official further pointed out to the Indians that "many Indian tribes had shown a desire to withdraw from the protective custody of the Federal government," and cited the cases of the recent move in that direction by tribes in California and Oregon. Despite his insistence that the legislation under consideration did not pertain to federal withdrawal, Riley, under intense questioning by tribal leaders, admitted to the assembled Indians that there was "no use kidding ourselves, that the Bureau of Indian Affairs is going to continue." Significantly, during this questioning, Riley discussed the proposed Menominee termination bill as further proof of congressional intentions. The Oneidas, led by Oscar Archiquette's strong opposition, answered Congress by voting fifty-three to zero at the meeting to reject a final cash settlement of annuities under the Treaty of Canandaigua.[19]

Despite this rejection, talk of fully terminating the Oneida Tribe of Wisconsin continued until as late as 1957. This movement was fueled by efforts at terminating the Oneida's Wisconsin Indian neighbors, the Menominees. On January 4, 1954, Assistant Secretary of the Interior Orme Lewis wrote to Vice President Richard Nixon listing all the tribes that the Department of the Interior considered capable of termination. Two weeks later, bills calling for the termination of the Alabama-Coushattas, the Klamaths, the Menominees, and other tribes were introduced into Congress. Following Lewis's memorandum nearly to the letter, these bills, which became law, called for the end of the federal-Indian relationship and federal services for these tribes.[20]

The Oneidas, despite their unanimous opposition to termination at the December 1953 meeting, were soon weakened by severe political divisions that erupted in the early 1950s. Although the vast majority of Oneidas continued to oppose commutation of the Canandaigua Treaty, the issue of termination became intertwined with the vitriolic family feuds that made up the volatile political world of Oneida. Throughout the early part of the decade, the Tribal Executive Council (Tribal Business Committee) at Oneida, headed by Julius Danforth and later by Dennison Hill, Irene Moore, and Mamie Smith, faced major political battles with a group of powerful Oneidas living in Milwaukee. These urban Oneidas, who sought the city for employment opportunities, were led by Oscar Archiquette and Morris Wheelock, who were, ironically, the founders of the original Tribal Business Committee elected system at Oneida under the Indian Reorganization Act of the 1930s.[21]

This Milwaukee group saw the political advantage of leading the fight against termination and hoped to come to power again at Oneida. This same group, which had opted for economic development and tribal political reorganization in the 1930s at the expense of pursuing tribal land claims, by the 1950s had done a complete about-face. Now they were among the leaders of the Oneida land claims movement and were passionately urging the preservation of the Canandaigua Treaty. This long-established Milwaukee community had never lost contact with kin in the Green Bay area. Moreover, they had established an Oneida "fact-finding committee" to investigate the actions of their political opponents at Oneida in the 1950s. Although charged by the Tribal Executive Council as the "fraud-finding committee," the Milwaukee Oneidas played a key role in the Oneida fight against termination during the Eisenhower administration.[22]

Archiquette was an eloquent speaker of the Oneida language and a political leader of these Indians for nearly forty years until his death in 1971. He was well known in both Indian and non-Indian circles. Through his contacts with anthropologists, art critics, conference directors, hobbyists, legislators, linguists, museum administrators, and the general public in Wisconsin, he was afforded entré to audiences beyond the reach of his political opponents at Oneida. As a famous Midwestern personality and a kind of Indian ambassador to the outside world, he could operate effectively in a world apart

Oneida Indian "Fact-Finding" meeting at Milwaukee home of Cornelius Baird to discuss economic problems, federal efforts to commute annuity payment, and internal tribal politics, 1957. Left to
right: William Wheelock, Morris Wheelock, Cornelius Baird
(back), Oscar Archiquette, Ruth Baird, and John Danforth. Photograph courtesy of the Milwaukee Public Museum.

from that of Oneida. Although he returned to political power at Oneida
in the 1960s, he exerted his most effective leadership throughout his
career from behind the scenes.[23] A frequent correspondent to the commissioner of the BIA, Archiquette would file Oneida objections to
policies and policy makers. Although largely self-taught, he would not
hesitate in doing battle with Commissioner Emmons in arenas far
distant from Green Bay.[24]

    October 18–20, 1956, an Oneida delegation composed of Julius
Danforth, Cecil Skenandore, and Irene Moore, took part in a BIA meet-

ing for Wisconsin and Iowa Indians held in Des Moines. One of the major subjects on the agenda was "readjustment and withdrawal of Bureau of Indian Affairs services." Once again, Department of the Interior officials, including Commissioner Emmons, insisted that termination was inevitable, while the Oneidas lobbied for increased appropriations for economic development and educational and health services. The Oneidas also pushed for a convalescent home, the retention of their OCC building "if Oneidas are disbanded," aid "for drainage on IRA (New Deal Land)," and the creation of a seventeen-acre Oneida Memorial Park. The long shadow of House Concurrent Resolution 108 was everywhere at the meeting and raised in discussions. The Oneida delegates, in desperate economic straits and hard pressed by the excessive restrictions on their trust lands which made tribal and economic improvement nearly impossible, left the meeting with the feeling that termination was a *fait accompli*. However, the three delegates, upon return to their Oneida community, reflecting on the conference at Des Moines, and seeing the overwhelming tribal opposition to federal government withdrawal policies, rejected termination.[25]

Independently of Moore, Danforth, and Skenandore, the Milwaukee Oneidas also developed a strategy to counter efforts at termination. They would find out the itineraries of key BIA personnel and then follow them to meetings, including the Des Moines meeting, where the Oneidas would ask embarrassing questions, disrupt the gatherings altogether, or just keep tabs on the progress of termination legislation. In late 1956, they claimed that the bureau had prepared another full-scale withdrawal plan for the Oneidas, that Riley had approached some individual Oneidas about its acceptance, and that a congressional bill was being drafted. When Archiquette exposed these findings at a tribal meeting at Oneida, the Oneidas once again unanimously rejected congressional termination.[26]

Although Archiquette's and the Milwaukee dissidents' roles were significant in the period, the United States Congress did not decide not to terminate the Oneidas simply because of their activities. Unlike their Wisconsin neighbors the Menominees, who owned over 200,000 acres, the Oneidas tribally held only 2,209 acres. The Oneidas owned no timber land, and had a major heirship land problem. These Indians at this time had not even a long-shot chance for economic self-sufficiency. Their poor economic condition, which had led more than half of the 3,500 Oneidas to migrate from the environs of Great Bay, stood in sharp contrast to the Menominees. Oneida poverty in the 1950s undoubtedly made the Wisconsin congressional delegation think twice about carrying out termination for fear that the state would assume an increased financial burden.[27]

During the Eisenhower administration, the Seneca-Cayuga Tribe of Oklahoma also came close to congressional termination. The Seneca-Cayugas were incorporated in 1937 as a consolidated tribe under provisions of the Oklahoma Indian Welfare Act. Members of each of two smaller Iroquois tribes in Oklahoma, the Senecas and the Cayugas, saw strength in numbers by merging together under one tribal business committee to take advantage of loan and land acquisition policies of the Indian New Deal. Although the two nations were now united under one council, cultural, land claims, and political differences continued to separate the two groups long after the merger. It was these differences that came to the fore in the early 1950s, precisely at the time the Seneca-Cayugas were threatened by termination, leading almost to their destruction.[28]

Oklahoma Indians for years had petitioned Congress for the removal of federal trust restrictions on their lands. Vocally chiding the BIA for its excessive paternalism and its historic mismanagement of Indian lands and resources, Indians from the state, more amalgamated into the body politic than most, had urged their congressmen to lift some of the restrictions. The American Indian Federation, a largely Oklahoma-based national organization that lobbied until the mid 1940s, had urged final settlement of outstanding Indian claims and "emancipation" of Indians from bureau wardship since 1934. Congressman O. K. Chandler, a Cherokee Indian attorney from northeast Oklahoma and a leading lobbyist for the federation, continued to urge, after World War II, that the BIA be abolished since it was too expensive and extraneous to Indian life because Indians no longer needed a federal guardian. Although Oklahoma's Indians frequently rejected the American Indian Federation's assimilationist orientation, they, nevertheless, could agree with its criticisms of the bureau and administrative paternalism.[29]

In 1952, the BIA prepared withdrawal reports for all of the eight tribes of the Old Quapaw or Miami Agency in northeastern Oklahoma: Eastern Shawnees, Miamis, Modocs, Ottawas, Peorias, Quapaws, Seneca-Cayugas, and Wyandottes. In the end, the Modocs, who were included in the Klamath termination bill, Ottawas, Peorias, and Wyandottes were either fully or partially terminated. Hence, fifty percent of the Seneca-Cayugas' neighboring tribes in Ottawa and Delaware Counties, Oklahoma were affected by congressional termination legislation. Yet the 965 Seneca-Cayugas barely escaped the "withdrawal program" which the bureau and congress had been pushing. By the time of their withdrawal report in 1952, the tribe had 1,052 acres of tribal lands and 6,387 acres of restricted trust allotments. As in the case of the Oneidas, the Seneca-Cayugas lived in a checkerboard-style community—a result of tremendous land loss under allotment legislation. A poor community, they had little commercial timber and few cattle. By 1952, the bureau had little supervisory or financial responsibilities over tribal welfare except in the administration of the Seneca Indian Boarding School in Wyandotte, Oklahoma, that had at the time a small percentage of Seneca-Cayuga children.[30]

The 1952 withdrawal report for the Seneca-Cayugas, in contrast to those for the other tribes in northeast Oklahoma with the possible exception of the Quapaws, was cautious in its conclusions. It insisted that the tribe not be terminated until its claims, which had been filed in 1951 before the Indian Claims Commission, had been adjudicated. This withdrawal report came at the time the Seneca-Cayugas were increasingly divided in tribal affairs.[31]

In the 1950s, bitter political squabbles, partially motivated by past internal rivalries of Cayugas and Senecas, erupted between a tribal faction led by Chief David Charloe, head of the elected council recognized by the federal government, and a rival group calling itself the Western Band of Cayugas, who were not recognized by the Department of the Interior. Although Seneca-Cayugas were a consolidated tribe incorporated under the Oklahoma Indian Welfare Act, some Cayuga members resented sharing their New York annuity and their future claims award with non-Cayuga members of the tribe. Grover Splitlog, who referred to himself as chief of the Western Band of Cayugas, objected to Charloe's methods and the policies of the Seneca-Cayuga Tribal Business Committee. They petitioned the Interior and Justice departments as well as Oklahoma congressmen to help them turn out the Tribal Business Committee and Chief Charloe, claiming overall tribal governmental misconduct and dictatorial methods of rule. They accused Charloe's council of being responsible for financial and voting irregularities, the lack of a tribal grievance committee, the failure to update tribal rolls, and the loss of tribal minutes and other records. Both Charloe's and Splitlog's factions went so far as to ask BIA officials to step in and take charge of tribal affairs in order to settle internal political disputes. Consequently, these Indians' open invitation for federal officials to intervene in tribal affairs gave impetus to government efforts to terminate the tribe. By March 1956, factionalism and the recriminations that resulted even led some members to suggest the total dissolution of the existing tribal organization.[32]

These dissident Indians increasingly won support from the BIA's

Quapaw Area Field Office and the Muskogee Area Office. Consequently, the BIA conducted two major audits of tribal affairs that found discrepancies. The BIA, under E. E. Lamb of the Quapaw Area Field Office, conducted a special investigation of tribal affairs, after a disputed election held at the tribal ceremonial grounds in 1955. When Charloe was reelected chief by the slimmest of margins, thirty-seven to thirty-five, Splitlog and his group accused the newly elected chief of allowing under-aged tribal members to vote. After a series of appeals by both factions to the bureau and individual congressmen, Charloe was forced to resign as chief on April 6, 1957. He was replaced by a compromise interim candidate, Hayden Spicer, an original member of the tribal business committee of the 1930s. These serious internal squabbles from 1951 to 1957 made the Seneca-Cayugas ripe for termination. It is also clear that the Department of the Interior, especially Lamb and Paul Fickinger of the Muskogee Area Office, tried to sell the idea of termination to the tribes in northeast Oklahoma. As E. J. Riley had done in Wisconsin, Lamb and Fickinger presented termination as inevitable since federal withdrawal was mandated by Congress. They did not attempt to explain properly the implications of the bills or the overall impact of termination on the tribes unless pressured by Indians at tribal meetings.[33]

During the winter and spring of 1954, BIA personnel held staff meetings concerning a termination bill affecting the eight tribes of the Quapaw jurisdiction and the preparation of final tribal rolls as required under House Concurrent Resolution 108. As a result of these conferences, Homer Jenkins, a BIA program officer, was sent to the Quapaw Area Field and Muskogee Area Offices to prepare a major report on termination. Jenkins was ordered to consult with the tribal business committees of the eight tribes that would be affected by new legislation.[34] On the twenty-fourth of September, Jenkins met with Seneca-Cayuga leaders. He reviewed Interior's departmental policies, congressional intention in House Concurrent Resolution 108, six bills already enacted by Congress "terminating or readjusting tribal-Governmental relationships in other jurisdictions," as well as specific withdrawal legislation for the tribe, and general tribal problems.[35] Termination was presented by Jenkins as practically a *fait accompli* which would be mandated by Congress with or without tribal approval. The Seneca-Cayuga leaders in attendance, Charloe, Ruby Charloe Diebold, Lillian Johnson Emarthla, and Amanda Bearskin Harjo (Greenback), had no other recourse except to play for time and win small concessions wherever possible.

The Indians, as was true of other Iroquois communities threatencd in the 1950s, expressed concern for their treaties and especially for the disposition of their annuity received from New York State, which they feared would be affected by termination. Employing a strategy of delay, the Indians proposed that termination be completed over a three-year period. Fearing new and excessive burdens of taxation, they requested that lands of original Indian allottees "be exempt from taxation during the lifetime of said Indian allottee or until the said allottee ceases to be the owner of the land." They insisted that any new legislation provide for the continued tribal ownership of the twenty-acre stomp grounds near Grove since the land was of religious significance "as the churches are to the white people."[36] Perhaps thinking of the days of the allotment frauds after the Dawes Act, the Seneca-Cayugas insisted that once tribal lands were sold off, individual tribal members be given preference in purchasing them back. The Indians also demanded that there be statements in any proposed legislation guaranteeing them water rights in the future and that their Indian Claims Commission case would not be affected by termination. Although apparently willing to accept a lump-sum settlement of their annuity, they nevertheless expressed their discontent about the lengthy process and time consumed in the adjudication of their claims.[37]

In August 1956, the Ottawas, Peorias, and Wyandottes were terminated in one congressional act. The Ottawas, through the single-handed and arbitrary manner of their chief, had agreed to the move. The Peorias, a consolidated tribe numbering only 440 members, had accepted the legislation because they had virtually been terminated anyway since 1915 when all restrictions on selling their lands were removed. The Wyandottes, with only ten percent of their membership of 984 in Oklahoma, had been induced to accept the legislation by promises of special programs of education for tribal members; these Indians were also given assurances that their two-acre cemetery in downtown Kansas City would be recognized as tribal property, and that when the land was sold off, their ancestors' bones would be removed with dignity and reburied on land in northeast Oklahoma.[38] One historian has perceptively observed that these tribes had been targeted because of their "lack of large populations, funds, legal expertise, and absence of support from powerful friends, especially in Congress."[39]

The Seneca-Cayugas would have been included in the Ottawa-Peoria-Wyandotte termination bill of 1956 except for three major factors. First, their termination was delayed because the Seneca-Cayugas had significantly more trust lands, and hence more confusion about heirship lands, than other Indians in northeast Oklahoma. As late as

December 1957, the BIA had no precise statistics about Seneca-Cayuga properties. The tribal affairs officer at Miami, disturbed by this fact, wrote the Muskogee Area Office about the confusion and the need for land surveys before termination. She insisted that "if the tribe is to consider termination at its Feb[ruary 1958] meeting, we must assist them in every way possible to become acquainted with their tribal properties and assets."[40] Secondly, the existence of the Cayuga Treaty of 1788 with New York State, and with it annuity payments to the tribe, along with the long-delayed adjudication of their case before the Indian Claims Commission, complicated termination and set back the date of federal withdrawal. Thirdly, and perhaps most significantly, the question of who was legally the chief of the Seneca-Cayuga Tribe of Oklahoma, caused by the disputed election of 1955, went unresolved until the spring of 1957.

Almost immediately after the passage of the Ottawa-Peoria-Wyandotte termination bill in August 1956, Fickinger advised the Quapaw Area Field Office to pursue "terminal legislation" for the remaining four tribes.[41] Bureau personnel had to delay their efforts after Charloe's resignation in April 1956, and the subsequent tribal election of Peter Buck, an ally of Charloe, as chief of the Seneca-Cayugas. An Indian of Cayuga descent born at the Six Nations Reserve near Brantford, Ontario, Buck was able to push tribal divisions into the background and present a concerted Seneca-Cayuga stance against termination. Despite being in poor health, Buck, aided by his son-in-law, the attorney W. W. Works of Tulsa, and by Amelia Perry, tribal secretary-treasurer, succeeded in this difficult endeavor.

In 1956, during the internecine political battles between Charloe's and Splitlog's factions, there was considerable talk by tribal members favoring termination at tribal meetings.[42] Yet by the fall of 1957, few Seneca-Cayugas viewed termination as a desired goal.[43] When the BIA asked the tribe for a meeting to thoroughly discuss a proposed termination bill, Buck was already preparing his tribe to counter arguments put forth by Department of the Interior officials. In November 1957, Buck and Perry informed tribal members that a special meeting would be held on February 18, 1958, for the purpose of further discussion of the proposed bill for the termination of federal supervision over the trust and restricted property of the Seneca-Cayuga Tribe of Oklahoma.[44]

Even before the Indians held their showdown meeting on tribal termination, the Seneca-Cayugas were gathering information about the ramifications of the proposed legislation. At least one member of the newly constituted grievance committee went to Muskogee to

Chief Peter Buck of the Seneca-Cayuga Tribe of Oklahoma, 1958.
Photograph courtesy of Velma Nieberding.

get advance information from the BIA area office.[45] Other Seneca-Cayugas were informed by the Wyandottes that their neighbors were totally dissatisfied with being terminated in 1956 "since they [Wyandottes] understood that a promise was made that you would settle their claims and help them dispose of their [Kansas City] cemetery before you released them."[46] Furthermore, the Oklahoma Iroquois were witness to the bitter recriminations made by pro- and anti-terminationist political leaders of the Ottawas, Peorias, and Wyandottes.

The so-called "moccasin telegraph" operated at this time to keep Seneca-Cayugas posted about other Indian nations and their particular crises with the federal or state governments. The annual Seneca-Cayuga Green Corn ceremonial held in August at the tribal stomp grounds brought these Oklahoma Iroquois in contact with Indians on the powwow circuit from around the country. Menominees from Wisconsin were among the visitors to Green Corn in the 1950s bringing news of the troubles befalling their peoples after passage of the termination bill. The doings at Green Corn also attracted Indians from the Iroquois homeland in New York bringing news about plans for the massive Kinzua Dam along the Allegany River that would flood Seneca lands. As early as August 1957, militant Mohawks from Saint Regis (Akwesasne), infuriated by the development of the Saint Lawrence Seaway, the failure to recognize Iroquois claims to Barnhart Island, and the New York State Power Authority plans for a large reservoir at Tuscarora that would condemn Indian land, received front-page attention in the *Miami News Record* in their call for the return of millions of acres of New York to the Iroquois. These Indians, Standing Arrow and Wounded Buffalo, while attending the Green Corn ceremonial, attempted to win support for the building of a self-sufficient Iroquois community at Fort Hunter along the banks of Schoharie Creek in historic Mohawk country.[47] The Seneca-Cayugas, "the Iroquois at the end of the log" in the words of Chief Buck, had renewed their ties with other tribes and with kin from their original homeland in order to prepare themselves for the showdown meeting over termination.[48] In the process, they had learned about nationwide problems of and outrages toward Indian people.

When the meeting on termination finally took place on February 18, 1958, at the Seneca-Cayuga Council House, southwest of Wyandotte, Oklahoma, these Indians presented a united front against the proposed legislation. The meeting was attended by approximately seventy-five people, fifty-one tribal members, attorney Works, a minister, Lawrence Pickard, four representatives from the BIA, including Fickinger, Lamb, and two assistants, as well as fifteen to twenty in-

vited visitors. The bureau personnel had the unenviable task of trying to sell a proposed termination bill to the unfriendly gathering.
The four-hour meeting, which appears rather innocuous in the transcript, included threats of personal violence by at least one tribal member against the BIA personnel in attendance.[49] Despite the obvious
tension, Fickinger first reviewed the Ottawa-Peoria-Wyandotte termi-
nations and the overall policy directions of the bureau and Congress
under House Concurrent Resolution 108. He insisted that Congress
had mandated the BIA "to continue to work with the Indian people
in an effort to develop programs which would lead to the release of
supervision by the Federal Government over those tribes and individuals considered to be able to go on their own."[50]

Fickinger, fully aware of tensions within the Seneca-Cayugas over
the Cayuga claim, emphasized that the bill would revoke the incorporation, and with it the consolidation, under the Oklahoma Indian
Welfare Act. He also added that termination would become effective
only when all existing claims of the tribe against the United States
were settled before the Indian Claims Commission. Hoping to further induce the Seneca-Cayugas, the bill provided for a guarantee of
water rights for the tribe and its members even after termination, an
important concern expressed by the Indians at a meeting in 1954. As
in the Wyandotte case, Fickinger explained that the bill included "a
special program of education and training designed to help the members of the tribe to earn a livelihood, to conduct their own affairs, and
to assume their responsibilities as citizens without special services
because of their status as Indians." In summary, the BIA area director
added that the legislation was really aimed at freeing the Indians from
federal supervision, allowing Indians to dispose, sell, or transfer previously restricted trust property at will. Fickinger insisted that Congress was ready to pass legislation whether the Seneca-Cayugas wanted
it or not since consent was not required, although congressional leaders "would prefer that the Indian people agree that it is a good thing."[51]

The Seneca-Cayugas intensely cross-examined Fickinger for the
remainder of the meeting. Tribal members were incensed that the proposed bill did not deal with or even mention the retention of the tribal
ceremonial grounds and cemetery. Despite Fickinger's assurances that
the BIA would work with Oklahoma to retain the land under a non-
taxable status, the area director admitted that the land after termination could not be used to generate a profit for the tribe, even though
tribal concessions were located there during Green Corn. Other Indian concerns about land included suspicions about Section 6 of the
proposed bill. It dealt with heirship lands, allowing only one heir to

the land, going against the wishes of other heirs, known or unknown, to enter court and request partition of the land. Former chief Charloe, who dominated the cross-examination of Fickinger, questioned the supposed benefits of the legislation, especially what he claimed were the added tax burdens on tribal members; he then insisted that the United States government should first settle its claims with the tribe and then maybe the Indians would accept new congressional legislation. Another tribal member, Levi Spicer, insisted that the tribe needed an extension of restrictions on tribal trust lands, not what Fickinger was advocating.[52]

The Seneca-Cayugas also questioned Fickinger on termination's impact in the realms of education and health. Ruby Charloe Diebold posed the question whether funds for the promised educational program would be made available by Congress once the Seneca-Cayugas acquiesced to termination. The Muskogee area director responded by admitting that Congress might not fund the special program once the original moneys were depleted. One tribal member questioned whether Congress would continue to provide Johnson-O'Malley funds for Indian public school education even after termination. Another inquired about Indian access to bureau boarding schools and Indian Health Service hospitals after termination went into effect.[53]

Seneca-Cayuga suspicions about the bill were intensified by Fickinger's responses. Charloe's suggestion to hold a tribal referendum on termination, because "we have people scattered throughout the United States," was rejected by the area director.[54] Fickinger's insistence that no formal plebiscite was needed was met with skepticism by tribal members present. The common Indian view that the bureau was once again trying to slip something by the tribes was reinforced. Attorney Works then carefully summarized the bill for those in attendance, employing a definite anti-terminationist tone.[55]

The Seneca-Cayugas, after a final statement made against the bill by Diebold, then voted on the proposed legislation. Not one member of the tribe stood up in favor of the bill, while a majority of Seneca-Cayugas stood in opposition to the legislation.[56] Fickinger, although extremely frustrated by the Seneca-Cayugas' action on the proposed bill, wrote Commissioner Emmons about the rejection, suggesting that plans for termination should proceed without the consent of the tribe since we "can not [sic] go on indefinitely this way" attempting to secure approval. He suggested that the Department of the Interior "submit to the Congress a bill looking toward the termination of Federal supervision over this tribe." He continued, "It is probable you will not wish to do that this year [1958] it being an election year, but it does seem to me we need to know if Congress means business or whether they are going to insist upon the 'consent' of Indian tribes."[57] Commissioner Emmons agreed with the area director's conclusions that a unilateral legislative proposal be drawn up by the bureau and presented to Congress; however, the commissioner concluded that there was no likelihood of passage during this session.[58]

Although Indian tribes continued to be terminated in 1958, including the Catawbas of South Carolina and forty-one Indian *rancherias* in California, Secretary of the Interior Fred Seaton put an end to efforts at Seneca-Cayuga termination when he announced in September 1958 that no Indian tribe would be forced to end its relationship with the federal government unless it "concurs in and supports the plan proposed."[59] Even though talk of terminating Iroquoian nations continued right through the 1960s, they had fended off forcible attempts to bring them into the mainstream. Despite this victory, the Iroquois had now to face new and bigger challenges to their tribal existence, the large loss of their homelands in New York, Pennsylvania, Ontario, and Quebec, and two more aggressive enemies—the Army Corps of Engineers and Robert Moses.

6

Interiors

The Administration, as you know, has pledged itself to consult
with the Indian people of this country and to give them every opportunity for a full expression of their desires, suggestions, hopes
and aspirations.

> President Dwight D. Eisenhower
> Letter to the Commissioner of
> Indian Affairs, Glenn Emmons,
> September 2, 1953.

My mind and my heart still hurt.

> Richard JohnnyJohn (Seneca)
> At Seneca Nation memorial,
> "Remember the [Kinzua] Removal,"
> September 29, 1984

Despite the previous chapters' emphasis on congressional initiative
in formulating and implementing policies, the executive branch of
the United States government substantially shaped Indian affairs during the Eisenhower administration. Nowhere was its role more evident than in the area of public works projects that impinged upon
federal-Indian treaty relationships. Eisenhower's military-styled command structure in the executive branch efficiently coordinated efforts
at building public works projects, taking advantage of the already existing favorable climate for such efforts in Congress and in the country at large.[1] One such project, the Kinzua Dam, and the courageous
fight of the Seneca Nation of Indians and its allies to save tribal lands
has been written about before; however, no historian has attempted
to fit this particular project into the full context of how Indian poli-

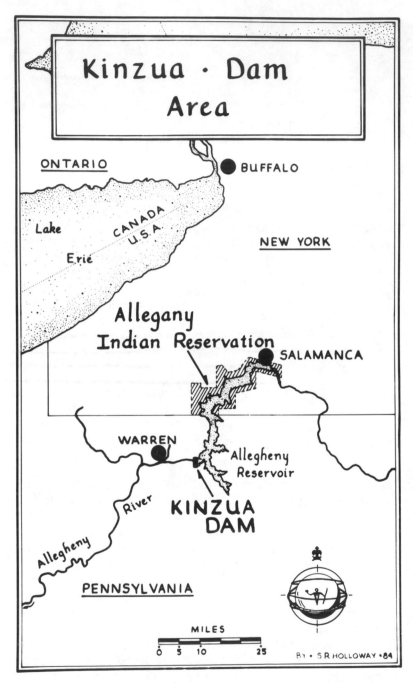

Kinzua Dam Area. Map by S. R. Holloway.

President Cornelius Seneca of the Seneca Nation (right) discusses legal strategy with attorney Edward O'Neill (left) concerning the fight over the Kinzua Dam, 1957. Photograph courtesy of Pauline Seneca.

cies and public works were interrelated during the Eisenhower administration.[2] From an analysis of the decision-making process, it is also clear that the Indians and their political allies were not privy to how and where policy was being formulated. Despite strong protests from the Senecas, from the Society of Friends, and from various conservation and Indian rights groups, policy initiators operated, in the main, far from public view. Unlike termination policies that were set rather openly in the committees of Congress, public works projects affecting Indians during the Eisenhower years had the official imprimatur of the executive branch and were made "backstairs" at the White House.

The Seneca Nation's unsuccessful fight to save their ancestral lands was the most tragic event of their contemporary history. The

Dr. Arthur E. Morgan, consulting engineer for the Seneca Nation.
Photograph courtesy of Arthur E. Morgan Papers, Antioch College.

building of the 125 million-dollar Kinzua Dam broke a federal-Iroquois
treaty, the Canandaigua Treaty of 1794; flooded more than 9,000 acres
of Seneca lands (all acreage below 1,365 feet elevation, including the
entire Cornplanter Tract); destroyed the old Cold Spring Longhouse,
the ceremonial center of Seneca traditional life; caused the removal
of 130 Indian families from the "take area"; and resulted in the relocation of these same families from widely spaced rural surroundings
to two suburban-styled housing clusters, one at Steamburg and the

The old Cold Spring Longhouse before its destruction for the Kinzua Dam project, October 1964. Photograph courtesy of Doctor Theodore Hetzel.

other at Jimersontown adjacent to the city of Salamanca. In compensation, Congress awarded the Seneca Nation 15,000,573 dollars by a law passed, belatedly, in 1964. This act provided 1,289,060 dollars for direct damages caused by land loss; 945,573 dollars for indirect damages, compensating the Indians for relocation expenses, loss of timber, and destruction of wildlife; 387,023 dollars for "cemetery relocation"; 250,000 dollars for Indian legal and appraisal fees; and 12,128,917 dollars for "rehabilitation," which was directed at meeting the Senecas' urgent need for community buildings, economic development, education, and housing.[3]

Even today, more than twenty years after the flooding of their homeland began, Seneca elders have difficulty speaking of this modern time of troubles. Going against Iroquois customary decorum, Seneca elders break down and cry, expressing their anguish in recalling the years 1957 to 1964. To them, the relocation and removal of Seneca families from the "take area" was their second "Trail of Tears," comparable only to these same Indians' loss of and removal from the Buffalo Creek Reservation in the first half of the nineteenth century.[4]

Senecas of all ages still ask themselves and their elders how this tragedy came about. In fact, the Senecas had attempted to stop the building of the dam from 1927 onward, frequently calling into play the Canandaigua Treaty; nevertheless, the federal courts dismissed their arguments in 1958, insisting that the doctrine of plenary power allowed Congress to unilaterally sever treaty guarantees, even by a one million-dollar line item in the 800 million-dollar House Public Works Appropriations Bill passed on June 19, 1957. Despite the heroic and massive attempt to sway public and political opinion against the 180-foot-high dam right to 1964, the Senecas and their friends had lost the battle long before the flooding occurred. Although many of the writings on the Kinzua Dam have centered on the presidency of John F. Kennedy, the critical period for the Seneca Nation was from 1955 to 1959.[5] The inclusion of the small but initial Kinzua line-item appropriation in the 1958 budget was not altogether the work of the Pennsylvania delegation in Congress. It was a command decision by President Eisenhower, his White House staff, and his cabinet.

Eisenhower's emphasis on organization is the key to understanding why Kinzua happened. Powerful politicians and special interests had urged the dam's construction since the 1930s; nevertheless, Kinzua did not come about until the right circumstances, organizational framework, and personalities were in place in the executive branch. The president's "hidden hand" in the decision was evident in his staff, cabinet, and sub-cabinet level appointments. Final decision making rested in Eisenhower's hands but the president also relied on his appointees in areas with which he was not familiar, such as Indian affairs. Assistant Secretary of the Interior Wesley D'Ewart has observed about Eisenhower and Indian policy: "He [Eisenhower] took his secretaries and heads of the Indian Bureau with what should be done and how it should be done, but never did he refuse to do anything that came up to him that looked reasonable."[6] Eisenhower, the commander-in-chief, diligently checked with his key field commanders, namely his Attorney General, his Secretary of the Interior, his Secretary of the Army, as well as his Special Counsel, Secretary and Special Assistant for Public Works Planning, about the Kinzua Dam project. As had not been true of previous administrations, all agencies now agreed about the feasibility and need for the project and never questioned the legal right of the United States government to violate a federal-Indian treaty through a pork-barrel appropriations bill. It is important to note that each of these offices and agencies were never impartial in their reviews of the project. Moreover, in *Seneca Nation v. Brucker*, the Indian's legal attempt to stop the dam, the Department of Justice intervened on behalf of the Department of the Army and the Army Corps of Engineers, the defendants in the case.[7]

The proponents of the dam manifested a near-total lack of concern for the Indians at every stage of the project's development. They made initial studies from 1908 to 1928 about the feasibility of flood-control projects on the upper Allegheny River without the Indian's knowledge. From 1928 to the mid-1940s, the Army Corps of Engineers, the Pittsburgh Chamber of Commerce, and the New York State Council of Parks prepared individual surveys, each of which called for the flooding of vast acreage of Indian lands, and in spite of Seneca tribal protests.[8] Moreover, in the late 1950s Congress sent pending legislation affecting the Senecas' treaty rights to subcommittees dealing with public works appropriations and not to those whose charge was Indian affairs. In addition, the federal government's condemnation proceedings and the Corps of Engineers' construction of the dam went ahead, well over three years before Congress passed the compensatory bill in 1964. Throughout the tragedy, the Army lacked sensitivity to Seneca mores and were often callous and intransigent in negotiating with the Indians; they bulldozed sacred sites, disturbed burials, and refused every alternative about the relocation of a separate Cornplanter cemetery.[9] Incredibly, the money from the compensatory bill became available only four months before the final deadline imposed by the Corps of Engineers for the removal of the last Indian families from the "take area."[10]

For nearly fifty years prior to the Eisenhower administration, a variety of interests had proposed an upper Allegheny River dam and flood-control project. The idea largely stemmed from the organization of the Flood Commission of Pittsburgh by the city's chamber of commerce in 1908. Headed by "Ketchup King" H. J. Heinz and composed of a special engineering committee, this commission attempted to work out a detailed plan for flood control at the "golden triangle," the confluence of the Allegheny and Monongahela Rivers which form the Ohio River at Pittsburgh. In 1912, the commission recommended the development of a series of reservoirs on the three-river system to provide flood control, and, at the same time, to encourage industrial growth for Pittsburgh and environs. The need for flood control in the

Ohio River systems was made clear in the following year when the tragic Dayton flood killed 200 people and destroyed 200 million dollars worth of property.[11]

The United States Army Corps of Engineers became involved in the plans for flood control from 1924 to 1928, issuing a special report in the latter year which apparently favored the idea of power development more than flood control by the construction of a series of dams for the Allegheny River. By the early 1930s, the Army engineers were working in tandem with various Pittsburgh companies—Jones and Laughlin, Carnegie Steel, Gulf Oil—and special interests groups such as the Pittsburgh Chamber of Commerce and the Allegheny River Improvement Association to promote the Kinzua Dam project.[12]

Hoping to secure available funding from the New Deal's Public Works Administration, the Corps of Engineers and its allies pushed throughout the 1930s for flood control. One Jones and Laughlin corporate executive, adding weight to the Army's position, insisted: "We employ an average of about 20,000 people, so that the interruptions . . . due to high water, and the delays due to low water periods, result in large losses to our employees and to the corporation."[13] Another lobbyist for the project in the early 1930s maintained that Allegheny River dams for flood control had been studied for a quarter of a century and that they were especially imperative during the Great Depression because they "will give employment to eight or ten thousand men for several years besides requiring large quantities of construction materials thus further increasing employment and purchasing power in the tri-state district."[14] It is clear that Pittsburgh industrialists were also interested in having the Allegheny River kept at a uniform level through Kinzua and other projects in order to reduce the pollution of the sulphurous drainage from the coal mines in the city's environs which were rusting boilers in their steel factories.

Impetus for flood control arose again in 1936. On Saint Patrick's Day in that year, a disastrous flood hit Pittsburgh, with most of the downtown area of the city inundated by waters that crested at a record forty-six feet. The need for flood control coincided with the joint efforts of industrialist Richard King Mellon and Mayor David Lawrence to create a "Pittsburgh renaissance." Even before the formal master plan for Pittsburgh rejuvenation was born at the Allegheny Conference on Community Development that took place in 1943, the city's political power was already weighty and influential. Congress passed three flood-control acts in 1936, 1938, and 1941 that dealt with Pittsburgh and environs. The 1936 act included the Kinzua Dam as part of nine flood-control reservoirs planned for the protection of Pittsburgh and for the reduction of flood heights in the Ohio River valley. This Allegheny project was also included in 1938 as part of a general comprehensive plan for flood control in the Ohio River basin. The 1941 act authorized a modification of the original plan to take into consideration the interests of pollution abatement and stream-flow regulation for navigation. In each case, no specific funds were appropriated by Congress for the construction of the dam, largely because of increasing foreign crises, military-preparedness spending, and significant opposition from the executive branch of government.[15]

Pittsburgh's and the Army Corps of Engineers' effort to implement the Kinzua Dam were stalled by Justice and Interior departments policies during the Roosevelt administration. In the 1940s, the Department of Justice, whose Public Lands Division under Aubrey Lawrence and C. C. Daniels assertively defended Seneca interests during the Forness case, did not support efforts at flooding Seneca lands. Secretary of the Interior Harold Ickes and his staff had also resisted these attempts to build the dam during the New Deal. At a meeting held in Harrisburg on December 22, 1936, at which Army Corps of Engineers and Bureau of Indian Affairs personnel were in attendance, Department of the Interior representatives rejected the project, insisting that they were "not prepared to commit either the Commissioner of Indian Affairs or the Secretary of the Interior on that matter."[16] Oscar Chapman, then Assistant Secretary of the Interior, writing to the Department of the Army in 1940, also rejected this course and emphasized the federal-Seneca treaty relationship. He insisted that the "desires of the Indians in the matter must be recognized and respected, and assuredly no invasion of their domain, without their consent, is lightly to be considered." Significantly, he added that even if consent were obtained in the taking of Indian lands, the "matter should be made the subject of further appropriate legislation by the Congress, preferably in the form of a *separate* bill."[17] (Emphasis added.) E. K. Burlew, the Acting Secretary of the Interior, also maintained in 1940: "No breach of the foregoing treaty stipulation should now be brought about, of course, without the consent of the Indians and certainly they should not be deprived of their property without full, adequate, and even generous compensation being made to them for the loss of such a valuable part of their original patrimony."[18] It should be noted that the Department of the Interior during the New Deal was not altogether opposed to supporting the building of dams that would flood Indian lands, but these projects were almost exclusively in the West and were largely the "pet projects" of Elmer Thomas, powerful chairman of the Senate Indian Affairs Subcommittee.[19]

President John F. Kennedy with Governor and Mrs. David Lawrence of Pennsylvania, 1963. Photograph courtesy of Pennsylvania Historical and Museum Commission.

| With the coming of peace in 1945, proponents of the Kinzua Dam once again pushed for the project. Congressional fiscal conservatism, and the costly foreign expenditures for the Marshall Plan and the Korean War pushed these efforts to the background until the early 1950s.[20] The presidential campaign of 1952 and the election of Eisenhower was a definite turning point on public works projects, among them the Kinzua Dam. Candidates Dwight Eisenhower and Adlai Stevenson went head-to-head on the issue of expanded public works and power development, with retiring President Truman insisting that only the Democrats would appropriate the necessary funds for dam construction. General Eisenhower, although wary of excessive spending by the Bureau of Reclamation and peeved by congressional waste

on public works projects, nevertheless took this challenge seriously. Significantly, in his memoirs Eisenhower proudly took credit for fifty-three major reclamation projects during his two terms.[21]

Most writers, in analyzing the origins and development of this specific upper Allegheny River flood-control project, emphasize the powerful role of the Corps of Engineers, the special interests of Pittsburgh industrialists and politicians, and the congressional pork-barrel system in the making of appropriations legislation.[22] One recent study of the formulation of public works projects and the congressional propensity for pork-barrel legislation stresses the interaction of all three groups in the form of an "iron triangle" of interests: the congressmen in the apex; the beneficiaries, the local users group and their lobbyists, in the right hand corner; and the federal agency which will construct the project in the lower left hand corner. Each section of the triangle bears an equal weight of the burden placed on it in securing the project. To the congressman, the public works project means reelection, namely votes from his constituency in the next election. The beneficiaries or local users groups need it because of the tremendous infusion of federal subsidy. The federal agency, in this case the Army Corps of Engineers, needs new projects in peacetime to justify its high level of congressional funding.[23] Moreover, as was true in the Kinzua Dam lobbying efforts, proponents of the project were aided by the strong sense of camaraderie that develops within the triangle, one that is "nice and tight, combining the desire for something (the lobby), the ability to provide it (the agency), and the ability to pay for it (Congress), and to those closed within the lines, there seems no need to look beyond them."[24] Significantly, congressmen frequently fail to challenge others' special legislation or Army Corps of Engineers projects because they themselves may someday be in need of the pork barrel and might require votes or studies endorsing their own projects from the Corps of Engineers. The iron triangle is also helped by the image of expertise perpetuated by the agency, the Army Corps of Engineers, and the factor of crossover employment from the agency to the private sector.[25] Eisenhower was fully aware of this powerful iron triangle of interests and recognized their influence in his memoirs:

> The subject of power involves energy of several kinds. Electric power is generated by falling water. . . . But the other power which charges the question is political-power exercised by lobbies and congressional blocs, power contesting with power, for motives sometimes obvious, sometimes obscure, with little of the seeth-

ing contest revealed fully and accurately to the public for whom the fight is presumably waged.[26]

The iron triangle, as was true of other special interests, used the exaggerated fears created by the Cold War to promote its own project, namely the Kinzua Dam. Maurice Goddard, the Secretary of Forests and Waters for the Commonwealth of Pennsylvania during the Leader-Lawrence administrations and former professor of forestry at Pennsylvania State University, served as a major proponent of the project from his Harrisburg office.[27] Kinzua was viewed as necessary not only for flood control, but also for economic development, and to protect the people and industry of the Allegheny River Valley. To Goddard, the dam was necessary "for the safeguarding of our economy and way of life." He added that Indians "are American citizens and like any other Americans, are subject to the same rights, freedoms, and laws as are some 171,000,000 other of our people."

Goddard saw the Kinzua Dam and other public works projects as inevitable. He insisted: "To date this will mean that some of our people may have to give up homes and land, in accordance with law, for the common good of the majority." In words that echoed nineteenth-century expansionist Thomas Hart Benton, he concluded that "in the march of civilization and progress, there must be sacrifice of a few for the protection and well-being of the many."[28] Goddard, along with Senator Joseph S. Clark and Congressman Leon Gavin, all allies of the powerful Lawrence machine of Pittsburgh, continued to push for the dam in congressional committees and hearings throughout the late 1950s and early 1960s.

Clark, a freshman senator, did David Lawrence's bidding in the upper chamber. A highly respected liberal Democrat with a strong commitment to civil rights, he never seemed to see the moral dilemma in his position in favor of the Kinzua Dam. In a statement prepared in May 1957, for presentation at a hearing of the House Public Works Subcommittee of the Committee on Appropriations, Clark criticized the delay in building a worthwhile dam whose merits had been debated for twenty years. He, like Goddard, viewed the loss of Indian lands as essential: "While we are all sympathetic with the problems of the American Indians and while they certainly deserve just and fair treatment by our Government, in cases such as this one, their interests, like those of any other citizens affected, are subordinate to the interests of the entire region."[29] Clark praised the expertise of the Army Corps of Engineers and, with Hugh Scott, his Republican colleague in the House, worked the floor for key votes to get approval each time the project arose in the late 1950s. Clark was especially aided by the presence of Allen Ellender, the chairman of the Senate Public Works Subcommittee, whose state of Louisiana was most dependent on levees built by the Corps of Engineers and on pork-barrel politics.[30]

Despite the immense power of the iron triangle in the 1950s, the Kinzua Dam would not have been built without the prominent role of the executive branch in its determination. The "hidden hand" of support from President Eisenhower and his White House staff contributed significantly to the iron triangle's successful push for upper Allegheny flood control. Most importantly, although the Kinzua was stopped immediately after World War II on economic grounds, the project gained powerful support during the Eisenhower years from two departments which had previously opposed it: the Interior and Justice departments.

Eisenhower, the organizational genius who helped construct and administer Operation Overlord, the Normandy invasion plan, and who had emphasized teamwork from his youth, brought a new command structure to the presidency. He intentionally and artfully constructed an elaborate maze of "buffer zones" that allowed him to be perceived as being above the fray of party politics. Cabinet officers, like his military aides during World War II, were expected to administer their departments without presidential interference. They knew the "outer limits of their assignments and had no fear of poachers."[31] Operational and procedural matters were out of the president's purview, although "his delegation practices were informed by a well-developed sense of whom he could entrust with what amount of decision-making power and of the need to be vigilant about possible failures by line and staff officials to adhere to their chief's policies."[32] Although the president made the final decisions, he made use of his cabinet as a policy body as well as a buffer zone. The cabinet served as a sounding board, contributed to the president's team concept of administration, and had a substantial bearing on the Kinzua Dam's outcome.[33]

The direct connection between Indian affairs and public works development was made clear by Interior personnel and their procedures during the Eisenhower administration. The Department of the Interior hierarchy was composed of westerners interested in the water and power development needs of their region. Eisenhower chose Douglas McKay, the retiring governor of Oregon, to be his first Secretary of the Interior. McKay, later dubbed "Giveaway" by his enemies for his controversial public lands, parks, and natural resources policies, resigned in 1956 to run unsuccessfully for a seat in the United States Senate. He was replaced by Fred Seaton, the former senator from Ne-

98   THE IROQUOIS STRUGGLE FOR SURVIVAL

braska who had served as an assistant staff member to Eisenhower's
chief of staff, Sherman Adams.[34] Yet, it is clear that Department of
the Interior policy was largely set at the deputy or assistant secretary
level during the 1950s, and not by Commissioner Glenn Emmons,
Assistant Commissioner Rex Lee, and the BIA. At a time when the
United States government was encouraging federal withdrawal and
shifting administrative functions out of the BIA, the Indian Service
personnel were largely focusing their attention on convincing Indian
nations to terminate their treaty relationships, relocating Indians to
cities, or administering educational programs.

In a summary report entitled "Accomplishments of the Department of Interior, 1953–1960," the Eisenhower administration insisted:
"The policies of this administration mark a turning point in the history of Indian affairs in the United States." In this report, prepared
in 1960, Indian policy, perhaps symbolically, received the least amount
of space and was the last subject considered. Significantly, reclamation and hydroelectric power development received the primary attention followed by recreational resources, fish and wildlife conservation, public land management, minerals and metals programs, water
management, and Alaskan and Hawaiian statehood. The Department
of the Interior briefing books follow the same pattern throughout
the period.[35]

McKay's appointment of Ralph Tudor to the post of deputy secretary, although short-lived, signaled a change in policy direction with
respect to Indian lands. Tudor was a former colonel in the Army Corps
of Engineers and a construction executive who built the gigantic Oak-
land Bay Bridge in San Francisco.[36] His appointment showed the growing alliance between traditional rivals, the Army engineers, and the
Department of the Interior Bureau of Reclamation. In the postwar era,
the Corps of Engineers, in cooperation with their former rival, Interior's Bureau of Reclamation, condemned sizeable parcels of Fort
Mohave, Chenchuevi Valley, Colorado River, Yuma, and Gila Bend
reservations in Arizona to harness the power and manage the water
of the Colorado River basin. Their joint Pick-Sloan plan, originally
conceived in 1944 for the Missouri River basin, took Chippewa, Man-
dan, Hidatsa, and Arapaho land in Wyoming; Crow, Cree, Blackfeet,
and Assiniboine land in Montana; while over 200,000 acres of Sioux
lands in North and South Dakota were also flooded for the building
of the Fort Randall, Oahe, and Big Bend dams. In each case, the federal government uprooted tribal peoples and relocated them from
their homelands, disturbed sacred sites, seriously affected the ecology of each region, and showed too little concern for treaty and human rights.[37]

The debate over what constituted compensation for Indian land loss was tied, as in the Seneca case, to the "prevailing arguments over 'termination' and other policies by which the federal government hoped in the 1950s to conduct its future Indian affairs."[38] Significantly, in Section 18 of the Seneca compensation bill of 1964, Congress required the Secretary of the Interior to submit to Congress within three years "after consultation with the Seneca Nation" a "plan for complete withdrawal of Federal supervision over the property and affairs of the Nation and its members."[39]

The prevailing attitude in Interior during the Eisenhower years was reflected by the views of two assistant secretaries, Wesley D'Ewart and Orme Lewis. D'Ewart, a former pro-terminationist congressman, was a frequent critic of Indian advocacy organizations and attorneys working for tribes, blaming them for perpetuating Indian dependence. The Montanan viewed Indians as capable of managing their own affairs and taking care of their people but resisting government efforts at "independence" because of their special tax status and because of the "generous" educational, welfare, and medical services provided by the federal government.[40] Lewis was equally direct:

> I think assimilation is what has happened throughout the world and I think it's the good thing now. We talk about all of this and what we are trying to do with the Negroes and with the Puerto Ricans and what not. . . . And yet with the Indians we put a fence around the place they live. Well, are we nuts?[41]

These attitudes contributed to termination and federal relocation policies which attempted to move Indians into mainstream America, and also led Department of the Interior officials to concede to Army Corps of Engineers demands about federal-Indian treaty breaking. Letters of protest against plans for Kinzua received by the Department of the Interior were referred to the Army for reply. Hatfield Chilson, the Deputy Secretary of the Interior serving as interim secretary in 1957, wrote President Eisenhower about Kinzua, outlining his department's position on the matter: "Jurisdiction over Indian affairs in New York has been assumed by that State. The proposed [Kinzua Dam] flood control project is entirely a Corps of Engineers project with which we have no connection."[42] Federal withdrawal policies put into place in 1948 and 1950 were now being used by Interior to "wash their hands of the entire matter." Later in 1957, Secretary Fred Seaton suggested an exchange of lands for those lost by the dam project, even though the Seneca Nation had rejected this alternative since

1946. It is noteworthy that Seaton, extremely sensitive to political matters as a result of his previous work with Sherman Adams, viewed some of the conservationist opponents of the Kinzua Dam as being similar to other administrative political enemies and called this to the attention of Eisenhower's Special Assistant for Public Works Planning. In Seaton's view they were the "same outfit" which had recently disrupted one of the secretary's speeches in western New York.[43]

The significant shift in Department of the Interior policies was also apparent in Interior-congressional relations during the Eisenhower years. The president's appointment of Congressman D'Ewart as Assistant Secretary and Elmer Bennett as Deputy Secretary of the Interior reflected his concern with the need to improve this connection. D'Ewart had served ten years on the House Indian Affairs Subcommittee and had been a deputy Republican whip. Bennett was an expert on mineral and water matters who had served as an aide to Senator Eugene Millikin of Colorado, the ultra-conservative head of the powerful Senate Finance Committee. Importantly, Bennett had been recommended for the Interior post by none other than Senator Hugh Butler of Nebraska. Their jobs were to improve Interior-congressional relations.[44] Interior had been, according to Bennett, "notoriously in default in responding to Congress on legislation and had been for years"[45] prior to the Eisenhower administration. Hence, as in the Kinzua Dam case, the Department of the Interior's non-involvement policy was an intentional response by the executive branch to accede to congressmen, in this instance the twenty-nine of thirty Pennsylvania representatives who favored the 1958 appropriations bill funding the Kinzua project.[46]

The Department of Justice was the other cabinet-level agency that supported efforts at building the dam. The shift from the New Deal years was especially evident in the department's responses to the controversy. Ironically, by intervening in the case on behalf of the Army Corps of Engineers, the Department of Justice found itself face-to-face with Edward O'Neill, the Seneca Nation's attorney who had worked for Aubrey Lawrence and the public lands division of the Department of Justice from the New Deal to 1953.[47]

On January 3, 1957, the Department of Justice filed a condemnation proceeding at the insistence of the Secretary of the Army in order to acquire the use of "certain Seneca lands for the purpose of making surveys and appraisals essential in the development of the project," citing eminent domain provisions of various flood-control statutes from 1888 to 1941.[48] Eight days later, the Federal District Court for the Western District of New York, in the first of a series of legal decisions, held that, despite the Treaty of 1794, the United States had the right to condemn any land essential for the purposes of the project. The court rejected the Seneca Nation's plea about the primacy of their treaty, by maintaining that Indian lands were subject to the power of eminent domain, just as are all lands privately held in the United States. The court added that a federal-Indian treaty could not rise above the power of Congress to legislate.[49]

This and later decisions repeated the arguments made by Department of Justice attorneys in their memoranda of law and briefs. Citing *Lone Wolf v. Hitchcock* (1903) and other key decisions, these attorneys questioned the power of treaties to control the power of Congress to legislate and insisted that "treaty rights do not forbid the taking, by the United States, of lands within the Allegany Reservation."[50] Department of Justice officials throughout Eisenhower's second term repeated this argument and, like Interior officials, never questioned the morality or the legality of the federal government's actions.

The legal battles between the Seneca Nation and the Army and its ally the Department of Justice raged until the United States Supreme Court denied the Indians a writ of *certiorari* in June 1959. In each of the lower federal courts, attorney O'Neill argued that general legislation earmarking congressional funds for construction of an Allegheny Reservoir project was not sufficient to overthrow the sanctity of the Treaty of 1794. Although recognizing the power of Congress under federal law to break treaties, he insisted that specific legislation, not pork-barrel appropriations, was needed for Congress to unilaterally change the federal-Indian treaty relationship.[51] At the district court level, Judge Joseph McGarraghy described the Senecas' contention: "The Seneca Nation *does* claim that the rights covenanted under such a treaty—especially one with an Indian tribe—cannot be destroyed by implication, innuendo, or unauthorized acts of the Executive. To destroy such rights Congress must specifically so say." McGarraghy then went on to maintain that the congressional intent in passing the Public Works Appropriation Act of 1958 was sufficiently clear to set aside a treaty consummated 163 years earlier.[52] On November 25, 1958, in what proved to be the last major rendering by a federal court in the Kinzua Dam matter, the three judges of the United States Court of Appeals for the District of Columbia unanimously affirmed McGarraghy's decision and denied the Senecas an injunction against the Army. Citing congressional testimony throughout 1958, the courts clearly found that the Congress was aware of what it was doing to Indians and their lands when it passed the Public Works Appropriation Act of 1958.[53]

The Justice and Interior departments' support for the Army's position and their shift away from New Deal philosophy were not the only reasons for the eventual reality of the Kinzua Dam. Eisenhower's White House staff was the last necessary ingredient to make Kinzua happen. Eisenhower strengthened the White House staff by adding aides who had the ability and stature of department secretaries. He gave them cabinet-level status but demanded of them more responsibility than such positions had carried in previous administrations. Eisenhower brought to the White House very definite notions of staff, based largely on the military model. He made skillful use of his staff, buffering himself from outside political pressures. His staff had more previous experience in government service than his cabinet officers but were appointed largely because of their "functional professionalism," namely past experience in similar positions or because of their particular expertise in rather specific fields. Sherman Adams played the role of Eisenhower's chief aide, a deputy almost in a military sense, and was followed by General Wilton "Jerry" Persons, a professional congressional lobbyist for the military's interest and a World War II associate of the president. Eisenhower's hidden hand in the decision-making process was always there. His White House staff was fully aware of the president's views and made the final decisions according to his determination.[54]

In 1956, Eisenhower appointed John Hamlin to the White House staff. Hamlin was an executive assistant to the President until 1959 and investigated special policy matters. He circulated weekly reports to the members of the Republican National Committee as well as to key staff members, including White House Chiefs of Staff Adams and Persons. The Hamlin reports outlined problem areas, showed the Republican policy differences with the Democrats, and suggested ways to handle the issues. In an undated weekly report in 1957, Hamlin focused on the Indians. He insisted that it was fortunate that "there are probably few national problems with which we as a Nation have dealt less successfully than with the Indians." After maintaining that the "problem" was not nearer a solution and "getting worse," Hamlin blamed the Indians and the Democrats for it—the Indians because they maintained a "separate, distinct, primitive culture and . . . show no uniform desire or talent for integration with our complex, fast-moving, materially rewarding, western civilization"; and the Democrats, except for a shift under Truman, for fostering dependence and paternalism.[55]

In this seven-page report, Hamlin elaborated on the need for a Republican assimilationist cost-efficient strategy. To Hamlin, the Republicans, in contrast to the Democrats, had always desired the Indians' integration into society and wanted to assist them "to make the transition from special status to equal status with all deliberate speed." Since the majority of Indians did not want to change, Hamlin argued that the Republican policy must not subsidize the "less productive" Indian culture:

> Either these two societies must be able to coexist or one must drive out the other. We Americans tend to assume that our way is so much more productive and so much better, that everyone will wish to emulate it. Under this circumstance, the only problem is how can they? But the Indians do not clearly *want* to change. What is to happen when the 'backward' society actively resists integration?

He continued by viewing the "Indian problem" in late nineteenth-century Social Darwinist terms:

> Well, it seems to be probable that the two kinds of culture cannot co-exist intimately indefinitely. The less competitive culture would have to adapt or die out, if it could not be effectively insulated geographically or otherwise. *This may seem a harsh conclusion, but it is probably a manifestation of that harsh law of nature, the survival of the fittest.* [Emphasis added.]

Hamlin added that while Indian culture has been increasingly "circumscribed and diminished" in America, Indian birth rates were increasing at alarming rates, adding to the acceleration of costs in the administering of Indian programs. In referring to these specific trends, Hamlin observed:

> Subsidizing of the backward group by the productive one is a possible temporary palliative and it is temporarily acceptable if the surplus of the productive group is considerable. But it is costly; it seems unfair to the productive people; and it aggravates the problem and postpones a solution. The backward population becomes constantly larger and poorer as it relies on primitive means of production, and hence more reliant, more costly, and more frustrated.

Hamlin pointed out that the federal subsidy per capita for Indians was "89% of the average per capita income of persons on farms and is nearly twice the average per capita income of U.S. Negroes." Despite praising the substantial efforts by the Eisenhower administration to advance education, industrial programs for the reservations, and relocation policies, Hamlin bemoaned a situation in which "Federal costs are steadily mounting. It is costing more and more merely to keep the problem from getting worse."[56]

Hamlin's lack of understanding of Indians reflected much more than the Eisenhower administration's attitude toward native peoples. Hamlin had pointed out that historically Americans "argued that a few savages could not stand in the way of the progressive development of this country."[57] Dams, reservoirs, and power development were part of the 1950s idea of progress and were seen as more important than Indians and the protection of their treaty rights. Consequently, Eisenhower was the first president to create a special assistant for public works planning on his White House staff. Eisenhower's interior design in creating this office sealed the fate of the Seneca Nation of Indians' lands.

7

Command Decision
General John S. Bragdon
and the Kinzua Dam

Now, the United States acknowledge all the land within the afore-
mentioned boundaries, to be the property of the Seneca nation;
and the United States will never claim the same, nor disturb the
Seneca Nation, nor any of the Six Nations, or of their Indian friends
residing thereon and united with them, in the free use and enjoy
ment thereof; but it shall remain theirs, until they choose to sell
the same to the people of the United States, who have the right
to purchase.

Article III of the Canandaigua Treaty of 1794

How long is forever?

George Heron, former President
of the Seneca Nation
West Chester, Pennsylvania
March 21, 1984

A "great fear" permeated American life in the 1950s and shook the
society at its foundations. Every Soviet success in the area of arma-
ments or public works had to be met in kind by the United States
to calm fears of an apprehensive American public and their representatives. As a result of this societal preoccupation and his army background, Eisenhower turned to military personnel to deal with the day-
to-day pressing administrative problems of his presidency. Accustomed
to working in a military group command situation, Eisenhower as
president surrounded himself with his military associates from World
War II and his years at the North Atlantic Treaty Organization Supreme Command in Europe, especially Generals Paul T. Carroll, Alfred Gruenther, Wilton B. Persons, and Walter Bedell Smith.

Dam construction, as was true of interstate highway projects in the mid-1950s, was substantially aided by this Cold War climate.[1] Moreover, funding for power development, flood control, and water programs was helped because the miltary gave its stamp of approval to these projects, had a special working relationship with key congressmen, and had a sympathetic ear in and direct channel to the decision-making command structure in the White House. Because of these pressures, Eisenhower created the Office of Public Works Planning in 1955 and appointed his former classmate at West Point, Major General John S. Bragdon, as his public works aide. In appointing him the first Special Assistant for Public Works Planning, Eisenhower maintained that Bragdon was to "advise him on public works and to coordinate 'as rapidly as possible' Federal, State, and local efforts in the field."[2]

Although Eisenhower was increasingly concerned about the excessive costs of public works projects, the president nevertheless viewed Bragdon's appointment as more to facilitate, not stall, the development of these efforts in the United States. In addition, Bragdon, a native of Pittsburgh, was the former deputy chief of the Army Corps of Engineers. He had been educated in engineering at Carnegie Institute in Pittsburgh, the city that would benefit most by the Kinzua Dam, and had been, after his retirement from the Army Corps in the early 1950s, vice president of Vermilya-Brown, a major construction company based in New York City.[3] Although the final decision maker, Eisenhower depended on Bragdon to abstract, coordinate, and filter information to him about the Upper Allegheny River flood-control project sent from the Department of the Army, the Justice and Interior departments, and from the Seneca Nation of Indians and their supporters. Eisenhower, the army hero of World War II, received information from Bragdon, another retired senior army officer, about a major flood-control project which was initiated and sponsored by the Army Corps of Engineers. It is also significant to note that General Lucius Clay, one of Eisenhower's key advisors, had served in the Pittsburgh District of the Army Corps of Engineers in the 1930s and had been an early proponent of Allegheny River dam projects.[4]

Eisenhower, who had known Bragdon for forty years, had complete faith in his abilities and gave him substantial responsibilities in the White House. At a news conference in early 1956, the president, in answering a question posed by the journalist Sarah McClendon about water resources policies, claimed, "I have a man now in this work, I believe as deeply as administrative action can place him, General Bragdon."[5] The major general also had substantial influence

General John Stewart Bragdon, chief of the White House Office of Public Works Planning.

in interstate planning from 1956 to 1959. When Eisenhower needed a representative to serve on his Joint Federal-State Action Committee to demarcate jurisdiction and prevent costly overlap, Bragdon was one of the three top staff members to be appointed by the president. Although Bragdon's expertise was in engineering, Eisenhower increasingly gave him responsibilities in the area of federal-state relations. It is important to note that Bragdon's work on the federal-state action committee brought him into contact with another committee member, George M. Leader, the Democratic governor of Pennsylvania and proponent of the Kinzua Dam.[6]

Bragdon's handling of the Kinzua Dam controversy is the key to how the whole project came about. He and his two assistants, Floyd Peterson and Donald Bower, dealt with every aspect of the project from July 1957 to the end of Eisenhower's presidency. From the beginning, the Office of Public Works Planning assumed the project was a worthwhile and justifiable action. After reading about it while at his Gettysburg farm, the president, on July 12, 1957, ordered Bragdon to look into the "Kinzua (Allegheny) Dam Project." Six days later, Bragdon replied, summarizing the reasons why the dam had to be built:

(a) On the basis of available data, the project is justified by its widespread benefits.
(b) Testimony in Congress to date is predominantly in favor of the project.
(c) The problem of taking Indian lands is capable of a fair solution.
(d) Paper mills, while objectionable, appear to be a matter for State regulation.
(e) Safety of the dam is not a valid objection; there are many other larger dams and reservoirs in the east.

Bragdon put one suggestion to Eisenhower: "(f) Further investigation is needed of the feasibility and economics of possible alternatives prior to the start of any construction. This investigation is under way by the Chief of Engineers."[7]

In a major policy decision, Bragdon added that there was no reason to strike the project out of the proposed 1958 budget, that one million dollars was an acceptable amount for further design and for initiation of construction, and that congressional support for Kinzua was overwhelming. He clearly spelled out to the president that the "Attorney General has pointed out that courts have ruled that the United States has the right to acquire Indian lands on payment of just compensation." He continued by maintaining that the Indians, as in other similar projects in the past, would be liberally compensated, but all within economic limits. Moreover, the Army would secure a legal assessment and the Indians would retain subsurface rights to land flooded.[8]

Bragdon's letter of the eighteenth of July is significant in several respects. He assumed from the start that the dam was going to be built because it was a popular, politically expedient project that could be rationalized in the name of progress. He also believed from the beginning that criticism of the project could be defused easily, either through monetary compensation to the Indians or through favorable legal opinions in the federal courts about treaty violations and environmental damage. Perhaps, most significantly, he rationalized the inclusion of one million dollars in the 1958 budget for the initiation of the project even while he was questioning the economics of the project. This line item in the 1958 budget was subsequently used by the federal courts to justify the breaking of the Canandaigua Treaty of 1794 by so-called "congressional action." In addition, Bragdon relied on the Corps of Engineers' expert opinion from the beginning, portending the near-incestuous relationship between his office and the federal agency in the months to come.

On July 22, 1957, President Eisenhower met with General Bragdon about the dam. Major John Eisenhower, who was also in attendance at the meeting, insisted that his father believed that construction of the "dam would be wrong if the Indians do not desire it, unless it is essential rather than merely desirable," and that it "is particularly essential that our word be kept with the Indians." The president told Bragdon to check with Secretary Seaton about "whether we are doing right by the Indians from the point of view of Interior." Bragdon informed Eisenhower that the attorney general had already given "his approval from a strictly legalistic viewpoint." The three also discussed the Corps of Engineers' estimate of costs and the recent alternative flood-control plans set forth by Arthur E. Morgan to save Seneca lands.[9]

Morgan, the former head of the Tennessee Valley Authority and a New Dealer, was to be instrumental in delaying the flooding of Indian lands. In 1956, at the urging of President Cornelius Seneca and members of the Society of Friends, Morgan, a self-educated genius and maverick in the civil engineering community, was hired by the Seneca Nation as an independent consultant. With his associate, Barton M. Jones, who had been chief designing engineer of the TVA, Morgan developed a proposal to make use of a great glacial depression in the Conewango basin as a natural reservoir site and to divert Allegheny River flood water into Lake Erie. This Conewango plan (also called the Conewango-Cattaraugus Plan) had various alternative components. Morgan and Jones designed it largely to protect Indian treaty lands and provide more flood-control protection along the Allegheny River than under the Army Corps of Engineers' plan.[10]

The Senecas' efforts to save their lands soon became intertwined with Morgan's longstanding war with the Corps of Engineers. Morgan had clashed with the Corps of Engineers as far back as 1913, ironically because of the military's early resistance to flood-control reservoirs after the Dayton flood. During the New Deal, Morgan helped write the bill creating the TVA which had excluded the Corps of Engineers from planning, chairing, or being the chief engineer of the massive project. In the 1930s, Morgan, as head of the TVA, chided the Army for its faulty plans for dam sites and control of the Tennessee River, for overspending beyond reasonable limits, and for being politically allied with the Water Resources Congress, formerly the Rivers and Harbors Congress, a registered lobby group. These past battles did not contribute to Morgan's ability to deal with the Corps of Engineers and its allies during the Kinzua fight.[11]

Morgan was one of the true intellectuals of twentieth-century America. A Renaissance man, he was largely self-educated in engineering, had risen to the presidency of Antioch College, had been the first president of the Progressive Education Association, and had served as a member of the executive committee of the League to Enforce Peace, which initiated the plan for the League of Nations. Although a first-rate scholar in rural sociology, community studies, and utopian thought, Morgan had virtually no contact with American Indians and their communities before 1956.[12] Yet, in his writings, he clearly reflected an abiding respect for "the vitality of the community spirit" in Indian communities in the face of what he called "the great American inquisition."[13] To him, the challenge was to preserve the small community from its progressive disappearance in present-day life, "one of the most disturbing phenomena of modern history," and a major historic crisis. Morgan firmly believed that the community need not disappear but that it could be recreated for greater possibilities. "But there is little time to lose, for with its passing some fine cultural traditions are being broken; and with human culture as with the human breed, if we have no children we cannot transmit our inheritance to grandchildren."[14]

Thus, Morgan saw the Conewango alternative as his planned experiment to reshape yet preserve the cultural integrity of the Seneca Nation and counter the efforts of the Army Corps of Engineers, his historic foe. Morgan's approach was totally against the Corps of Engineers' tradition, which inevitably resulted in his opposing the Kinzua Dam. As a utopian planner with little skill or interest in politics, he believed, as he later wrote, in the demands of "civilian human relations in planning and construction of public works program." To him, the Army Corps of Engineers—West Point engineers trained in war and military considerations which were "very different from the process of internal improvements"—had too little course work in the technical engineering required for civil engineering and flood control.[15]

On July 25, 1957, Bragdon reported to the president that Secretary Seaton believed that the United States had a "complete legal right to take the land," but in view of the "old treaty" the condemnation would be immoral without some consideration of substitute lands. Bragdon concluded that the Corps of Engineers were studying possible alternative approaches to the project and that when these studies were completed the Senecas' objections would be satisfied. After all, he insisted, "Chief Seneca" had earlier "stated that the Indians would not stand in the way of progress if it [the Army's plan] is the only economic and engineering solution for prevention of floods in the lower Allegheny River Valley." Importantly, Bragdon once again recommended that the president not delete the one million-dollar line item in the 1958 budget "since this money can be used for needed further engineering."[16]

By the late summer, the Army Corps of Engineers was systematically attempting to destroy various alternative flood-control plans. At a meeting on September 6, 1957, at the Executive Office Building, Army Chief of Engineers Emerson C. Itschner and Assistant Secretary of the Army Dewey Short indicated to Bragdon that the dam project had overwhelming bipartisan support in Congress. They observed that "Indians usually obtain more generous allowances than most non-Indian landowners" do in condemnation proceedings for federal public works projects. The Army officials then went on to consider alternative plans for flood control. Chief of Engineers Itschner belittled the idea of constructing a smaller dam and reservoir and insisted that this idea went "contrary to our national water resources policy" by not developing sites to their maximum potential. He rejected the idea of a system of smaller dams as not feasible and opposed the construction of one other alternative plan, the French Creek Reservoir, as not being economically feasible because it would require very expensive relocation work for the Pennsylvania Turnpike. Because Itschner could not completely counter the final alternative, the Conewango plan proposed by engineer Morgan, and there was wide disagreement about its costs, Itschner suggested hiring a consulting firm to make a systematic study of alternatives. Itschner had previously maintained that the Corps of Engineers had not undertaken a complete analysis of the Lake Erie diversion plan proposed by Morgan, arguing that "it was not customary to undertake detailed investigations and cost breakdowns until funds were on hand to start construction on a project." Now, because of Morgan's international reputation as an expert and his ability to generate headlines and support for his proposal, Itschner proposed hiring a consulting firm to make a six-month study at a cost of 70,000 dollars. Bragdon, Itschner, and Short all agreed that "a study developed by an outside firm would gain better public acceptance than a restudy by the local Corps of Engineers' office." They also agreed that the Army and Interior departments should coordinate their efforts in dealing with the Indians about a satisfactory settlement.[17]

In mid-September, at the urging of Bragdon and under direct authorization from President Eisenhower, the Corps of Engineers hired the firm of Tippetts-Abbett-McCarthy-Stratton (TAMS) of New York City to conduct what Bragdon deemed "an independent investigation" to check the Morgan plan and the costs and feasibility of other alternatives.[18] While the Senecas were fighting against the dam in courts, TAMS went about their research. Although both Morgan and the Army Corps agreed to and cooperated with this investigation, the independent judgment of the firm is suspect. Retired Brigadier General James H. Stratton, who had become a partner in the firm in 1949, had been director of civil works for the Army Corps of Engineers before his retirement. He had previously been in charge of engineering for water projects, such as the Dennison Dam, that had affected Indian lands.[19]

Crossover employment produced conflicts of interest at every stage of the Kinzua Dam controversy. Congressman James Haley, chairman of the House Indian Affairs Subcommittee, later pointed out to President Kennedy that this so-called "'independent' firm gets more business from the Army Engineers than from any other sources, and also that some of its principal partners were former Army Engineers."[20] Morgan observed in 1971 that the Army "did not tell me that the firm was founded by a man who was a member of the Corps until he resigned or retired to set up this firm, three were ex-Corps members, nor did he tell me that for twenty years or more the Corps had been by far the most important client of the firm." He added: "Since the Corps already had strongly condemned my proposal it might be embarrassing for this consulting firm to make a contrary finding."[21]

Even before the TAMS report was released to the press, Bragdon had written a memorandum indicating that the Morgan plan was feasible and that Morgan's estimate was accurate but "still largely in excess of the Corps' plan." He added that despite this fact, confirmed in the TAMS' draft report, the Corps of Engineers believed "that Morgan will die hard on this matter and continue to argue." Bragdon continued by mentioning that the Corps of Engineers were now ready to proceed to spend five million dollars in the next year on the project but that a war was now brewing between them and Morgan and the Senecas that would delay the project at least another year.[22]

On April 1, 1958, the Army Corps of Engineers, Ohio Division Office in Cincinnati, released TAMS' letter of transmittal to the press. This letter of transmittal was attached to the consulting firm's full report, which was not released. Although the TAMS report did not express any preference for either the Kinzua or Conewango plan, the Corps of Engineers and its allies presented this letter as proof positive that the report favored its plan. Despite a limited budget of 70,000 dollars, a six month time limit, and specific instructions that narrowed the focus of its research, the TAMS findings were presented as scripture. In the summary of major findings, the report maintained: "There is no engineering or construction reason why either the Authorized Project or any of the alternate plans cannot be built, and either the Authorized Project or any of the alternate plans could be operated to meet the requirements established by the Corps of Engineers for flood control and low-flow augmentation in the Allegheny River."[23] It conceded that Morgan's alternatives would store substantially more water by creating a pool 500,000 acre-feet larger than the Corps of Engineers' Kinzua plan and would be capable of producing cheaply 115,000,000 more kilowatt hours by diverting flood waters to Lake Erie. Nevertheless, the TAMS report concluded that Morgan's alternative plans would cost twenty-five percent to thirty-eight percent more, would require fifty-one percent to 108 percent more land, and would dislocate 150 percent to 180 percent more people than the Corps of Engineers' Kinzua project.[24]

The impression left from the report was that Morgan's alternatives were too expensive and too massive in scope, and that too many people, nearly all non-Indian, would be dislocated — unacceptable alternatives to politicians in Congress as well as to Eisenhower and his staff. Morgan had insisted that, since the storage capacity for the Conewango reservoir would be three times that of Kinzua, more people naturally would be displaced, but not without benefit to them. Four villages and a few small hamlets would be flooded, including Randolph, a town already seriously threatened by flooding because of severe rains. Morgan believed that the communities could have been relocated well above the water line, "where they would have been on the shore of a large lake with pleasantly sloping shores. They would become popular recreation centers."[25] Perhaps naively, both Morgan and his supporters believed that a time-honored federal-Indian relationship and the sacredness of Indian land made the continued maintenance of the Cornplanter Tract more important than several hamlets occupied by non-Indians. Charles C. Congdon, the Salamanca attorney, leading city elder, and shrewd authority on the politics of southwestern New York, perceptively observed in 1964: "Flooding the Conewango Valley would provide more water for Pittsburgh, but it would flood out white folks! They vote [unlike many Iroquois]. I told this to Arthur Morgan when he was at Cornplanter one summer and he became incensed. He simply did not understand."[26] A utopian planner with his band of Seneca Indians and their allies, wedded to historic and moralistic principles, were no match for the American Army and its allies in Congress and the White House during the 1950s.

Even before the release of the TAMS report, the Senecas had mounted a major lobbying effort. The Senecas, with little money for an all-out campaign, attempted to fight the dam as best they could. They channeled money gained through hastily made leases with the Pennzoil Corporation and money from easements for a natural gas pipeline and for the New York State Thruway extension.[27] From 1956 onward, President Cornelius Seneca and his successors George Heron and Basil Williams frequently alluded to the immorality of the United States' breaking the Canandaigua Treaty of 1794. Seneca attempted to explain the importance of the document at every turn. Pointing to the annual distribution of treaty cloth, he insisted in 1957: "Is this cloth, symbolic to the entire world that the policy of this government is to aid and defend the rights of minority peoples, to be kept clean — or is it to be ground into the dust in the construction of the proposed Kinzua Dam?"[28] Seneca steadily maintained that the Indians would cooperate to the fullest with the Army Corps of Engineers if the most competent engineering testimony showed there were no other alternatives for flood control. In the desperate effort to stop the Kinzua Dam, President Seneca attempted to win publicity by appearing in full Indian regalia as "Chief Seneca" on the nationwide television program, "To Tell the Truth."[29] Heron, first as treasurer in 1957 and 1958 and later as president of the Seneca Nation in 1959 and 1960, reiterated Seneca's moralistic objections to the Kinzua plan. A hero who had received three citations for battle valor in World War II, Heron added in congressional testimony in 1957, "Along with my fellow Indians, I fought to preserve and maintain this government in the full belief that this government would preserve and maintain my Indian homelands."[30] By the time Williams had assumed the Seneca presidency in 1961, these arguments had been well publicized along with Morgan's alternative plans for flood control.[31]

The Seneca Nation collaborated with a wide variety of supporters in order to try to stop the Kinzua project. The Indian Committee of the Philadelphia Yearly Meeting of Friends stood firmly behind the Indians.[32] The Senecas were also successful in convincing Governor Averell Harriman of New York to take a stand in their favor. In January 1957, Harriman urged the Army Corps of Engineers to consider alternatives "without forcing the Indians to leave their homes."[33] Unlike his successor Nelson Rockefeller, who assumed the governorship in 1959, Harriman and his aides Jonathan Bingham and Daniel Patrick Moynihan gave the Senecas some hope for reversal of the Corps' project. During the critical period from 1956 to 1958, the Senecas also received support from the Indian Rights Association and the Central Missionary Guild of the Presbyterian Church of America.[34] The Senecas and their attorney Edward O'Neill plotted strategy and collected ethnohistorical expert testimony on the Canandaigua Treaty of 1794 from anthropologist William N. Fenton, then serving as assistant commissioner for the New York State Museum and Science Service.[35] From 1959 onwards, the coalition broadened and the letter-writing campaign intensified as a result of the activities of Walter Taylor of the American Friends Service, the American Civil Liberties Union, and especially because of the influential writings of Brooks Atkinson in the *New York Times* and the publication of Edmund Wilson's *Apologies to the Iroquois*.[36]

Despite the failure of this lobbying effort, the dam controversy ultimately led to the beginnings of a new sense of Indian purpose. The Seneca Nation received significant support from other Indians and Indian nations. Although the Senecas withdrew from the Iroquois traditional council fire at the Onondaga Longhouse in 1848, the Six Nations Confederacy Council on February 21, 1957, adopted a resolution condemning the planned flooding of the Cornplanter Tract. The National Congress of American Indians, the American Indian Chicago Conference in 1961, the councils of the Cherokee and Oneida nations, as well as individual Indians from around the United States, expressed unanimous sentiments about the breaking of the Canandaigua Treaty of 1794 and the dispossession of native peoples from their homelands.[37] Most Indians agreed with the sentiments expressed by Eva Danforth, the Wisconsin Oneida tribal secretary, in a letter to President Eisenhower in early 1960:

Harry Watt (left) and Abner Jimerson (right) at the Kinzua Dam construction, September 1962. Photograph courtesy of Doctor Theodore Hetzel.

Protest against Kinzua Dam, early 1960s. Left to right: Don De Vault, Robert Euler, Abner Jimerson, Mamie Cavell, Patricia Mc-Mahon. Photograph courtesy of Buffalo and Erie County Historical Society.

In the interest of safe-guarding [sic] the treaty of the Seneca Nation, made in 1794, we as official members of the Oneida Tribe of Indians do here-by [sic] request your support in opposing appropriating any moneys for the construction of a federal-flood control dam at Kinzua, in northern Pennsylvania, until a fully impartial and competent examination be made in regards to an alternative plan, namely the Conewango Cattaraugus Plan. It is a matter of grave concern to us too, as a member of the original six nations that the United States government should have so little concern for one of America's oldest treaties. We as a Nation among Nations, who are constantly striving for and negotiating treaties with foreign countries for the preservation of our God-given Rights to life, liberty, and the pursuit of happiness, should be the last to pay so little honor to our treaties here, if we are to expect other nations to honor treaties with us.[38]

Long before these efforts had been organized and implemented, the hand had already been played by General Bragdon, his Office of Public Works Planning, and other Eisenhower staff members. They used the TAMS report to justify their already predetermined leanings in favor of the Corps of Engineers' plan. Realizing as he did earlier in March that Morgan and the Senecas would continue to protest even after the release of the report, Bragdon attempted to defuse the criticism of the Corps of Engineers, the dam project, and the consultants' findings. Before Bragdon gave the Department of the Army a complete authorization for construction, he arranged for a meeting between General Itschner, "Chief Seneca," and Morgan in order "to avoid the possibility of his [Morgan's] appealing to the President with the claim that they were not fairly considered before the decision was made."[39]

This meeting was finally held on July 29, 1958, at the office of Assistant Secretary of the Army Dewey Short. Morgan, Itschner, and Short were joined by Charles Okey, an engineer and assistant to Morgan from his days at TVA, Seneca attorney O'Neill, Floyd Peterson, Bragdon's assistant, and two staff members from the Army assistant secretary's office. Morgan was allowed to present his case for the Conewango alternative. Although Bragdon was not in attendance, Peterson reported the meeting in full, especially Morgan's criticism of the TAMS study. "The objections to the report are that it was made in accordance with specific instructions by the Corps and treated the same way one would call in a consulting engineer to comment on a specific plan. It has the same defects as the Corps record, i.e., it didn't study all the alternative plans."[40]

Before Bragdon and his Office of Public Works Planning could give their final stamp of approval and go-ahead for the Army project, the Congress, as a result of the actions of John Saylor of Pennsylvania, put a temporary roadblock in the way of Kinzua. In the fall of 1958, the House Appropriations Committee, at the congressman's urging, restricted further expenditures—one and a half million dollars had been appropriated in 1958 and 1959—until the pending settlement of the Indians' court case. Bragdon had to wait until the summer of 1959 before he could once again raise the issue of the Kinzua Dam.

When the Supreme Court refused the writ of *certiorari* to hear the Senecas' case, Bragdon's office once again began to push the Corps of Engineers' project. Even when the Corps of Engineers had temporarily suspended its lobbying efforts on behalf of the dam project, the Office of Public Works Planning resurrected it and encouraged cooperation between Interior and the Army in order to get it going again. Peterson, on July 27, 1959, penciled in on a memorandum to Bragdon: "General Bragdon. I think we ought to write a follow up letter to Dewey Short on this so that we can be prepared to act if House decides to withdraw from its contemplated study [of alternatives to Kinzua]."[41]

Bragdon, a month later, reported to Eisenhower that the matter was now virtually closed after Congress included 1.4 million dollars in the 1960 budget for the initiation of construction after "extensive consideration of Dr. Arthur E. Morgan's attacks against the engineering plans and estimates of the Corps of Engineers." Bragdon insisted that "I believe we should accept this as terminating that [Morgan's] line of argument." To ease Eisenhower's misgivings, Bragdon added that the Senecas were opposed to accepting substitute lands and that they will no doubt be handsomely paid by congressional legislation for their land loss. Bragdon then sealed the fate of the Cornplanter heirs and their Pennsylvania lands. In language remarkably similar to that used by President John F. Kennedy eighteen months later, the retired major general concluded:

> The controversial aspects of this project have received extensive review and have been resolved by the decision of the Court and by Congressional action. There is now no reason why this project should not proceed subject to budgetary considerations. I believe the situation concerning this project has developed sufficiently that you may consider the matter closed.[42]

In letters to the president in October 1959, and in later letters to opponents of the dam, Bragdon repeated this position and insisted that he did "not know of any overpowering new information which would justify any further action by the Executive Office at this time."[43] Bragdon's office turned its attention to other matters, while opponents and proponents of the project continued to discuss this *fait accompli*. Perhaps as a result of his trusted advisor's influence, Eisenhower in 1960 added 4,530,000 dollars to his 1961 budget request for the Kinzua project.[44]

In 1960, the Lawrence machine geared up for their final efforts

Representatives of the Army Corps of Engineers addressing the Seneca Nation about the impact of the Kinzua Dam, February 4, 1961, at the Jimersontown Presbyterian Church. Photograph courtesy of Doctor Theodore Hetzel.

to encourage Congress to release the already committed funds for the Kinzua project. They systematically appealed to the Pennsylvania congressional delegation. On May 25, 1960, the House of Representatives passed a four and one half million-dollar appropriation bill for the project by a vote of 398 to eighteen. Governor Lawrence personally directed the final assault when he testified on June 23, 1960, before James Haley's Subcommittee on Indian Affairs. Haley had attempted to delay construction moneys by insisting on further study of the alternatives to the Army Corps of Engineers' plan.[45] Lawrence repeated the proponents' arguments: the widespread benefits to six states; the need to "support one of the heaviest industrial concentrations in the world"; the expertise of the Army Corps of Engineers; the "24 years of studies and restudies, surveys and resurveys and investigations"; the legal decisions in federal court; and the independent finding that alternative plans were too expensive and would displace too many people. After all, Lawrence claimed, Indians in Idaho, Oregon, Montana, North Dakota, South Dakota, and Wyoming had acceded to the general American public interest in similar circumstances. Earlier flood-control efforts and the work of the Corps of Engineers had already helped "make the Pittsburgh Renaissance possible." To Lawrence, the Senecas should accede to this dam since the benefits of the new reservoir created by the project "will exceed by far those they currently derive from the river. New investment, new business and new job opportunities will inevitably be attracted to the region and will add to the general prosperity."[46]

Four months later, on October 22, 1960, Governor Lawrence delivered the major address at the groundbreaking ceremony for the Allegheny River Reservoir at Kinzua, Pennsylvania. He hailed the project as the "first giant stride to bring flood protection to millions of homes and thousands of industries in six states." He lauded Clark, Goddard, Gavin, and the Army Corps of Engineers, "who have studied the project objectively and have acted, I believe, with the interests of the citizens of this area at heart, at all times." He concluded that the project "will some day stand as a living, useful reminder of the first lesson of good government—the needs of human welfare come first and those needs can be answered when we work together and meet the challenge willingly."[47]

President John F. Kennedy, who had depended heavily on the Lawrence machine for his narrow election win in 1960, was in no way going to antagonize the governor or overturn a project whose construction had already started. Despite persistent appeals to halt the dam, the president and his advisors assumed the posture that the issue had already been determined. In a widely publicized letter to Seneca president Williams in 1961, Kennedy insisted that impounding funds appropriated by Congress after long review by Congress and legal determinations by the courts "would not be proper." In words that echoed those used by Major General John S. Bragdon from 1957 to 1960, Kennedy rested his case by once again bringing in the expert opinion of the Army Corps of Engineers and quickly dismissing Morgan's plans: "Moreover, I have been assured by the Corps of Engineers that all of the alternative proposals that have been suggested, including the so-called Morgan Plan Number Six, have been thoroughly and fairly examined and are clearly inferior to the Kinzua Project from the viewpoint of cost, amount of land to be flooded and number of people who would be dislocated." Kennedy ended by observing that further delay of the project would needlessly halt providing the "essential protection" for the people downstream on the Allegheny River.[48]

Historian Elmo Richardson, in *The Presidency of Dwight D. Eisenhower* (1979), raised the important question for future study of how Eisenhower's praiseworthy but deliberate style as president was translated into law. Richardson, seeing certain inconsistencies in the president's political behavior, observed that Eisenhower's concern for civil rights contrasted with his "apparent acquiescence in the termination of Indian reservations, a matter that also involved the social disruption and federal coercion that he abhorred." Richardson added: "Can the difference in degree of interest be ascribed to the influence of his advisors?"[49]

In examining the Kinzua Dam controversy, it is clear that Eisenhower's emphasis on organization and his specific appointments to key positions helped determine the outcome. Much responsibility for the eventual flooding of Seneca lands must rest with the powerful iron triangle of interests—Congress, Pittsburgh and its industrialists and politicians, and the Army Corps of Engineers. Yet Eisenhower's not-so-hidden hand was there in the budgetary process, in his key appointments at Interior and especially in his selection of Major General John S. Bragdon to be the first head of the Office of Public Works Planning in the Executive Office.[50] Although one can easily see how the climate of the Cold War and American society as a whole entered the picture, the Kinzua Dam, formally dedicated on September 16, 1966, was largely a command decision made by Eisenhower, his White House staff, and his cabinet.

As a result of the American Indian Chicago Conference of 1961 and the singer Buffy Sainte-Marie's song, "Now that the Buffalo's Gone," Kinzua was to symbolize a growing awareness by Indians that policy makers had to be stopped, one way or another, if they operated in the same high-handed and insensitive manner concerning native peoples in the future. The dawn of Red Power was slowly coming up in the East, almost ten years before it arose in the rest of Indian country. Nowhere was this phenomenon more evident than in the Iroquois communities of Tuscarora and Saint Regis (Akwesasne). Faced with a struggle created by the construction of the Saint Lawrence Seaway and the master plans of Robert Moses and the Power Authority of the State of New York, the Indians began militantly to assert themselves and fight back from 1958 onward. Although not immediately successful and losing substantial acreage, the Iroquois forged a new sense of nationalism across reservation and urban community lines that still shapes their polity and world outlook today.

8

Drums Along the Waterway

The Mohawks and the Coming

of the Saint Lawrence Seaway

We lost more than land with the coming of the seaway.

Julius Cook (Mohawk)
August 1, 1983

The Seneca Nation homeland was not the only Iroquois land sacrificed in the name of progress in the postwar years. Three other Iroquois communities—Saint Regis (Akwesasne), Caughnawaga, and Tuscarora—faced in rapid succession the trauma of tribal land loss and outside legislative interference in the years 1954 to 1961. The construction of the Saint Lawrence Seaway and the building of the reservoir at Tuscarora, two closely related endeavors, set in motion changes in Iroquoia that drastically affect Indian life today. By changing the course of the mighty Saint Lawrence and Niagara rivers, the Saint Lawrence Seaway Authority, the Saint Lawrence Seaway Development Corporation, the Hydro-Electric Power Commission of Ontario (Ontario Hydro), and the Power Authority of the State of New York (SPA) did more than condemn Indian lands. They industrialized the Saint Lawrence and Niagara frontier regions. By thus transforming this area, they also brought problems of environmental pollution which weakened Indian self-sufficiency and virtually destroyed the Indian fishing and dairy cattle industries.[1] Quite significantly, by expropriating Iroquois lands, these agencies contributed to a powerful Indian backlash which led directly to the rise of Red Power militancy. The seaway project affected the Saint Regis (Akwesasne) and Caughnawaga reservations dramatically, shaping the Indian economy, the politics, and the world view of the two communities down to the present day.

The Saint Lawrence Seaway was a product of a long series of historical forces. Although ocean-going vessels from Europe had made

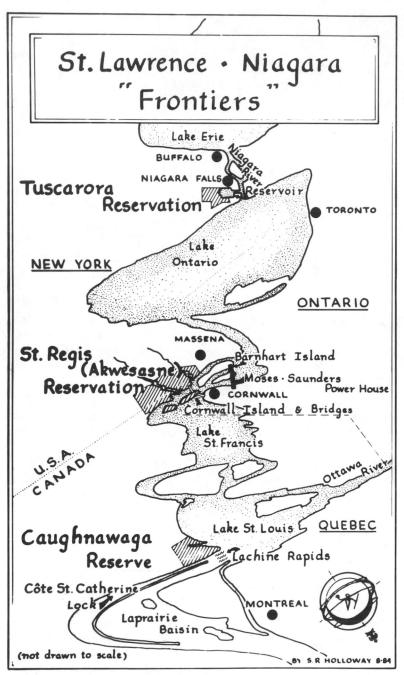

St. Lawrence–Niagara "Frontiers." Map by S. R. Holloway.

President Dwight D. Eisenhower signs the Saint Lawrence Seaway Bill, May 13, 1954. National Park Service photograph, courtesy of Dwight D. Eisenhower Library.

their way through the Saint Lawrence River to lake ports such as Chicago before the creation of the seaway, deep draft, ocean-going shipping was restricted because of the river's depth. Interestingly, it was
the Iroquois presence on the Saint Lawrence that, in part, first
motivated white men in New France to seek to improve the river. In
1700, Dollier de Casson, superior of the Sulpicians, attempting a defen-
sive move against the Iroquois, hired a contractor to dig a one-mile,
twelve-foot wide canal to bypass the Lachine Rapids. This attempt
ended when the contractor went bankrupt.[2] Proposals for the development of a major seaway were put forth in Canada and in the United
States throughout the nineteenth century, resulting in a series of piece
meal canal projects; however, joint international cooperation did not
come until 1895 when an international Deep Waterways Association

Governor Thomas E. Dewey addressing audience at groundbreaking ceremonies for the Saint Lawrence Seaway Project. Robert Moses seated on the right. August 10, 1954, Massena, New York. Photograph courtesy of the Thomas E. Dewey Papers, Department of Rare Books and Special Collections, the University of Rochester Library.

Mohawks greeted by Leslie Frost, Prime Minister of Ontario, and Robert Saunders, Ontario Hydro Chairman, at groundbreaking ceremonies for the Saint Lawrence Seaway Project, August 10, 1954. Photograph courtesy of the Thomas E. Dewey Papers, Department of Rare Books and Special Collections, the University of Rochester Library.

was formed. Despite lobbying by Midwestern farm and port interests, Eastern railway companies and transit ports such as Montreal, Quebec City, Buffalo, and New York City effectively blocked the seaway idea. In 1909, Canada and the United States signed the International Boundary Treaty which created an international joint commission to regulate construction in boundary waters. By that time, the seaway's potential as a shipping land had taken a back seat to its potential utilization for hydroelectric power.

In 1896, the New York State Legislature formed the Saint Law-

A dynamite charge on the water's edge at Barnhart Island deto-
nated by Governor Dewey, site of Long Sault Rapids Control Dam
at groundbreaking ceremonies for the Saint Lawrence Seaway Project, August 10, 1954. Photograph courtesy of the Thomas E. Dewey
Papers, Department of Rare Books and Special Collections, the
University of Rochester Library.

rence Power Company to develop the route as an energy source. That
eventually led the Aluminum Company of America (ALCOA) to locate
a plant at Massena. In Canada, Ontario Hydro was created in 1906
to safeguard the energy interests of the province and encourage the
extension of the Saint Lawrence system. The seaway idea was furthered when, in 1931, the New York State Legislature, urged on by
Governor Franklin D. Roosevelt, passed the Power Authority Act which
authorized full development of the International Rapids section by
a new public agency, SPA. This action was designed to stimulate cooperation between SPA and its Canadian counterpart, Ontario Hydro;
SPA was also given an exclusive right in New York to develop the

Saint Lawrence Seaway construction. The city of Cornwall, Ontario is on the right. Cornwall Island, Saint Regis (Akwesasne)
Reserve, is on the left in the foreground. Note that on the left in
the background, the International Bridge connecting Cornwall Island with the United States is under construction (7455-S). July 3,
1958. Courtesy of New York Power Authority and Dwight D. Eisenhower Library (80-21-308-G).

water power of the Saint Lawrence. Roosevelt, exploiting the populist
support for cheap hydroelectric power and the strong distrust for utilities caused by the onset of the Great Depression, was a firm supporter of the seaway.[3]

From the time of its creation, SPA, which had been charged
with the responsibility for developing and marketing the hydroelectric power of the Saint Lawrence, became the leading New York pressure group lobbying for a Canadian-United States accord on the seaway.
They hired numerous consultants to study production costs and
opened up negotiations with utility companies on rates for the private transmission of public power. Despite SPA's early lobbying efforts,

Moses-Saunders Power House, Barnhart Island. Photograph courtesy of New York Power Authority.

the Senate in 1934 rejected the United States-Canadian Saint Lawrence Seaway Treaty of 1932. Although President Roosevelt suffered a major setback on the seaway project, he bypassed Congress by signing an executive agreement with Canada in 1941 which provided for construction of improvements in the International Rapids section and completion of navigation improvements in other sections of the Great Lakes-Saint Lawrence areas within seven years.

World War II, the Cold War, and the Marshall Plan for European recovery shifted the United States away from its 1941 commitment to build the seaway jointly with its northern neighbor. Yet several factors resurrected the idea in the United States. In 1948, one of the richest sources of iron ore in the world was discovered in Labrador, a strike that was developed in part by the M. A. Hanna Company of Cleve-

House relocation, Saint Lawrence Seaway Project construction,
Caughnawaga Indian Reserve (PA 115336), August 21, 1956. Photograph courtesy of Public Archives of Canada.

land whose chief operating officer was George Humphreys, later named
Secretary of the Treasury by President Eisenhower. A year later, the
Great Lakes-Saint Lawrence Association was established as a major
lobbyist in Washington, D.C., headed by the capable N. R. Danielan,
a former official in the Department of Commerce.[4] When Congress
failed to take any action appropriating money for the seaway project,

Former President Truman, former Governor Poletti and Robert Moses admire mural painted by Thomas Hart Benton at Moses-Saunders Power House, March 26, 1958 (971 P). Courtesy of New York Power Authority and Dwight D. Eisenhower Library (80-21-267-G).

C. D. Howe, the Canadian minister of trade and commerce, announced in 1951 that his country would unilaterally build the seaway. In the same year, the Canadian Parliament, urged on by the powerful Minister of Transport Lionel Chevrier, a prominent attorney from Cornwall, passed a law creating the Saint Lawrence Seaway Authority, which would have the task of building, maintaining, and administering a Canadian seaway in Canadian waters of the Saint Lawrence River and Great Lakes. In 1952, President Truman and President-elect Eisenhower, spurred on by the Canadian sole effort, urged Congress finally to accept the seaway project. The same year, Ontario Hydro and SPA were accorded user rights for hydroelectric development. Finally, on

May 7, 1954, the Senate approved the Wiley-Dondero Act which established the Seaway Development Corporation, the counterpart of Canada's Saint Lawrence Seaway Authority. The act affirmed the United States' intention to cooperate in the construction of the seaway. Thus, after more than a half-century of debate and delay, North America's greatest canalization project was off the drawing board.[5]

The construction of the seaway began in the summer of 1954. The seaway, in reality, consisted of a twenty-seven-foot deep channel, dug through dry land and dredged lake bottoms, stretching from Montreal to Lake Erie, and capable of lifting ships about 600 feet above sea level as they sailed inland. The new waterway with its fifteen locks replaced a fourteen-foot deep system of canals and thirty time-consuming locks. The final product was a major transportation link in a 2,350-mile chain stretching from Duluth, Minnesota to the Atlantic Ocean, halfway across the North American continent. In the words of Chevrier, it "was one of the most ambitions and effective man-made alterations to the face of the earth ever completed. It outranks Suez or Panama in size."[6] The project entailed moving 210,515,000 cubic yards of earth, pouring 6,196,000 cubic yards of concrete, constructing forty-five miles of dikes and digging sixty-nine miles of channel. The process of construction included relocating 9,000 individuals, 650 families, forty-seven miles of highway, and forty miles of double-track railroad, and condemning nearly one hundred square miles of property. More than 22,000 workers were employed at the height of construction and more than one billion dollars was spent in building the seaway. Even more remarkable was that nine governmental agencies, representing four separate provincial, state, or national governments, cooperated to accomplish this construction feat in a little more than four years: Ontario Hydro, SPA, the Saint Lawrence Seaway Authority, the Saint Lawrence Development Corporation, the Saint Lawrence River Joint Board of Engineers (composed of representatives from the two nations which reviewed, coordinated, and approved plans and specifications as well as construction in the International Rapids section), and three separate Canadian and American agencies concerned with controlling water levels and water flow—the International Joint Commission, the International Saint Lawrence River Board of Control, and the International Lake Ontario Board of Engineers. Moreover, four separate construction agencies were involved in carrying out the engineers' plans—Uhl, Hall and Rich; the United States Army Corps of Engineers; Ontario Hydro; and the Canadian Department of Transport—making it, in the words of ex-President Hoover, an engineer himself, the biggest engineering job in the world.[7]

The Saint Lawrence Seaway project was only exceeded by the Grand Coulee Dam on the Columbia River in United States history. Almost all of the United States' commitment to the project, which was far less than Canada's in construction and in monetary allocation, was in the International Rapids section near Massena. Coordinated for the most part by the Seaway Development Authority, this massive effort consisted of building the Long Sault Canal (Wiley-Dondero Channel), a navigable channel ten miles in length, and the construction of two major locks, the Snell and Eisenhower locks, each of which had total lift up to ninety feet. In this same area around Massena, SPA and Ontario Hydro jointly constructed two power dams, the Moses-Saunders Power House and the Long Sault Spillway Dam, both of which were in the environs of lands historically claimed by the Mohawks. In addition, New York State Route 37 was rerouted and 130 acres of Mohawk lands on Cornwall Island were condemned in the building of the Cornwall-Massena International Bridge, a new high-level suspension structure, and the approaches to it. This massive construction in the Cornwall Island-Massena-Barnhart Island area was soon to become the focal point of a series of legal controversies that have raged for decades.[8]

In Canada, seaway construction began in Montreal. The Saint Lawrence Seaway Authority built a channel 300 feet wide, two turning basins, and two locks to bypass the Lachine Rapids. This construction was done to overcome a drop of fifty feet in the Saint Lawrence in an area two miles below Jacques Cartier Bridge and extending upstream about eighteen miles to the east end of Lake Saint Louis. It was the Mohawk community of Caughnawaga, founded in the seventeenth century as a Jesuit mission, just northwest of the Lachine Rapids, that was to be seriously affected in the construction of this channel and in the building of the new Côte Sainte Catherine Lock, two vertical lift bridges, a railway, and new approaches to the Honoré Mercier Highway. In order to bypass the rapids, the Saint Lawrence Seaway Authority, rejecting alternative proposals, expropriated 1,260 acres of Indian land.

Ontario Hydro, the Saint Lawrence Seaway Authority, SPA, and the Saint Lawrence Seaway Development Corporation were the agencies responsible for moving people out of the way of the project. The condemnation and relocation process began in 1954 while homes were relocated in stages from 1955 onward. After building a steel frame under the sills and load-bearing portions of the building, house-moving contractors used two U-shaped machines capable of lifting 200 tons. The machines backed up to the building, electric winches were attached, and it was hoisted up till the frame rested on the machine.[9] The building was then hauled to its new site where a new foundation had been prepared to fit it. Yet much more, it is clear, was uprooted than buildings.

This massive undertaking was not done without resistance, especially in those deep-rooted communities along the river. In a manner reminiscent of Appalachian folk faced with the coming of the TVA, many Indian and non-Indian Saint Lawrence residents resisted to the end efforts at relocation, even while massive construction of canals, dikes, dams, and locks was progressing toward their homes. Despite the resistance, the joint efforts led to completion of the seaway in a remarkably short time. On April 25, 1959, the first ships entered the waterway that had opened up the heartland of the continent to deep-draft ocean-going shipping for the first time.

The seaway was the last in a series of fundamental economic changes affecting two Mohawk communities since the colonial period. A highly adaptable and mobile people, the Mohawks have adjusted to rapid economic change for four centuries. In the seventeenth and eighteenth centuries, they adjusted to the coming of the fur trade. Their great prowess as canoemen led British and Canadian explorers of the Arctic and Africa to recruit their help in the nineteenth century. Many worked as timber rafters running oak and pine over the Lachine Rapids, while others became farmers and dairy men in the same period. Some Saint Regis (Akwesasne) and Caughnawaga Mohawks were the first Indians involved with the traveling circuses and medicine shows of the late nineteenth century. Because of their early exposure to bridge construction trades from the 1870s onward, Mohawks to this day are internationally famous as ironworkers. This skill in high steel has led Mohawks to seek employment in cities, to make adjustment to the urban life, and to play key roles in the Indian communities of Syracuse, Rochester, and New York City.[10]

Despite the fact that World War II had shifted both communities' attention in an outward direction, had ended the vestiges of the remaining barter economy, and had begun to undermine community cohesiveness through accelerated out-migration, the Mohawks of Saint Regis (Akwesasne) and Caughnawaga faced their first major modern-day crisis to their homeland with the coming of the Saint Lawrence Seaway.[11] Much of the responsibility for this crisis in Mohawk life belongs to two individuals: Lionel Chevrier and Robert Moses. Chevrier's role in the development of the seaway idea is the easier to comprehend. As a member of Parliament, cabinet minister, and later president of the Saint Lawrence Seaway Authority, Chevrier "was born by the river, brought up there and was always specially interested in it."[12] His family, French Canadians from Sainte Anne de Bellevue, Québec, had long been involved in canal transport of coal and lumber on the Saint Lawrence River. His father, who was elected mayor of Cornwall, had been an early proponent of the city's economic development as a river port. To Chevrier, the failure to utilize the Saint Lawrence River, this "huge marine highway" and source of "abundant cheap power" for industrial development, was an international travesty.[13] After completing his education and setting up his law practice in Cornwall, Chevrier became identified with "the drama and scope of the St. Lawrence River" and its vast potential for his home city and Canada at large.[14] However, it was not until 1951 that, as minister of transport, he helped forge an agreement to build the seaway between Canada's prime minister Saint Laurent, C. D. Howe, Ontario's prime minister Leslie Frost, and Ontario Hydro's chairman Robert Saunders. In that year, Saunders, the former mayor of Toronto who died in an airplane crash in 1955, agreed to proceed with the project with or without the United States' financial support.[15]

Chevrier's role as president of the Saint Lawrence Seaway Authority bore directly on promoting favorable publicity and countering criticism of the project. From 1954 onward, he was largely responsible for justifying the sizeable dislocations caused by the waterway. To Chevrier, the "seaway was the most controversial project the world has known." It was bitterly opposed and "inspired so many opinions, arguments, legal battles, treaties and inter-government memoranda." To him, the seaway story was "a chronicle of men fighting for self interest against nations fighting for national interests."[16] Chevrier especially did not understand the Indian mind. Despite living in Cornwall, which is in close proximity to the Saint Regis (Akwesasne) Mohawks, he insisted that the Caughnawagas' protest was motivated merely by "a chance to make some money out of the seaway," and they were "just having a lot of fun at the expense of the seaway." To him, the Indians who "staged war-dances against the seaway and captured big headlines in the Montreal newspapers" were in the minority and the vast majority "were satisfied with what we were doing."[17]

Despite Chevrier's contentions, the Mohawk community at Caughnawaga was in open rebellion against the seaway.[18] The Indians did not sit by passively and see their lands condemned by the Canadian government. The reserve, located at the western end of the seaway at Montreal just before it opens into Lake Saint Louis, is situated on a piece of land that juts out into the river due south of the entrance to the Lachine Canal. To these Indians, the Saint Lawrence

Seaway Authority's expropriation of their land was in direct violation of treaties made by the British crown and the Iroquois Confederacy. Furthermore, these Mohawks insisted that their land base had been protected by the British Proclamation Line of 1763 and by subsequent agreements.[19]

On March 30, 1955, Chief Angus Joseph K. Beauvais called a band meeting in response to the crisis, soon followed by a referendum on the issue of surrendering Indian land to the Saint Lawrence Seaway Authority. The Caughnawagas as a whole rejected doing so and refused to accede to the authority's demands; however, it is also clear that some of the Mohawks, economically hard pressed, were encouraged to make separate individual settlements signing releases provided by the authority offering them monetary advances pending final legal settlement. Despite the counsel of the legal adviser of the Department of Justice that the Indians should agree to the authority's demands because legal action would be futile and would waste their time and money, Chief Mike Montour and the new band council initiated suit, asking that the seaway evictions be stopped. The Indians' argument was eventually rejected in Montreal in a superior court decision of January 18, 1957. Although the Caughnawagas suffered this major setback, they continued to appeal for compensation, despite increased band political divisions from 1956 onward. Chief Councillor Matthew Lazare attempted to bring the matter, in typical Iroquois fashion, to international forums. As late as 1961, Lazare, encouraged by attorney Omar N. Ghobashy of New York City, petitioned the secretary general of the United Nations as well as the World Court in the Hague for a hearing. These efforts proved fruitless. Despite the hyperbole of many of Lazare's actions and statements and the ultimate loss of their cause, it is clear from the record that Caughnawaga lands were purposely undervalued and that the expropriation process was done without sensitivity to Indian culture, concepts of sovereignty, or views about homeland.[20]

Chevrier held three significant meetings at the Caughnawaga Reserve with band officials and community people in September 1955 and March and July, 1956. Meanwhile, the attorney general of Canada in Superior Court, District of Montreal in September 1955, had initiated condemnation proceedings.[21] After Chevrier detailed his plans at one of these conclaves, a Mohawk arose to reply, condemning the authority's plans as illegal. The dissenter eloquently insisted that the Caughnawagas "were members of the Six Nations who held their land by treaty with the British government. Since the treaty was concluded before the British North American Act [1867], Canada had no jurisdiction over these people or their land." Chevrier dismissed this position as legally untenable since no court would uphold putting "the seaway on the other side of the river—at an additional cost of many millions." The seaway president then attempted to sell his plan by telling the Indians what his agency was prepared to do for them: fill in low-lying lands; provide a water and sewage system; preserve old stone dwellings and build a wall to protect the Jesuit church; pay the Indians compensation equal to that paid to whites being displaced along the river; and award the Indians reversionary rights to lands not used by the Seaway Authority.[22]

After the July meeting, Chevrier believed he had silenced his Indian opponents by reaching a financial settlement under which a 4,200-foot section of the Overland Canal would be excavated, and by cementing an uneasy truce by symbolically smoking the calumet, which, much to his later embarrassment, he had puffed upside down; nevertheless, the crisis at Caughnawaga continued full blast.[23] The Mohawks insisted that they needed every acre because of rising population and claimed they would slap tolls on those ships that passed through their section of the seaway. The issue of taking Indian lands had even arisen in debate in the Canadian Parliament as early as 1955 with Member William Hamilton charging that the seaway channel could have been placed farther out in the river, which would mean no Indian land would be needed for the project. Despite Chevrier's insistence that the Indians would be paid just like other property owners—market value plus ten percent for inconvenience—Hamilton accused the authority of "callous disregard" of white communities and mistreatment of Indian people who had no one to protect their interests. Even the future Conservative Party prime minister, John Diefenbaker, raised the issue of whether Parliament had the right to set aside Indians' treaty guarantees. Another member of Parliament, D. S. Harkness of Calgary, chastised the Ministry of Citizenship and Immigration, which housed the administrative structure of native affairs in Canada at this time, of collusion with the seaway authority in the expropriation of Mohawk lands. Harkness, in radical fashion for the times, maintained that the manner in which Indian lands at Caughnawaga were expropriated gave further justification and need for the "setting up of a claims commission in order to settle those claims and numerous other claims of Indians across Canada in regard to their property rights in what they own and do not own."[24]

The Caughnawaga Mohawks who refused to move soon found out to what lengths the Seaway Authority would go. One lady, out in her yard hanging clothes, saw a bulldozer advance on her property and knock her house down. Another Mohawk, Louis Diabo, became an international celebrity by resisting almost to the very end. Diabo refused to move from his homestead and farm even after construction continued around his house; his well went dry, and his sixty-nine-year old wife had to haul drinking water two miles each day; yet he refused to budge. Excavation approached and dynamite blasts rocked the area around his home. In the end, Diabo accepted a monetary settlement of 70,000 dollars, which was personally presented to him by Chevrier. The authority later agreed to fill in swamps, build a beach, and pay the band, not just individuals such as Diabo, to compensate for land loss.[25]

The Mohawks to the southwest faced an equally determined foe. Although Robert Moses is generally associated with the Niagara power development that condemned a large chunk of the Tuscarora Reservation, his role in the Saint Lawrence Seaway project is less well-documented. In Moses' mind, the seaway and Niagara frontier power development had been inextricably tied together since the 1920s.[26] As chairman of the New York State Council of Parks, Moses had a "direct and active interest in the Niagara frontier and St. Lawrence River areas since 1924."[27] From this time until his appointment by Governor Thomas Dewey to head SPA in 1954, he pushed the seaway idea in order to further his grand design for an international waterway, public power, regional economic development, and the expansion of state parklands.

Despite never holding an elected office, Moses, the legendary master builder, wielded unrestrained power for well over forty years. Although associated in the main with transforming the face of New York City and Long Island, its beaches, parkways, and skyline, his influence extended far beyond—to Massena and Niagara Falls, as well as to the backroom political clubhouses of Albany. His critical biographer Robert Caro has observed: "In the shaping of New York, Robert Moses was comparable only to some elemental force of nature."[28] An arrogant, power-hungry individual, he intimidated governors as well as lesser politicians until his political demise under Governor Nelson Rockefeller.

Moses' involvement in Iroquois matters in the mid-1950s was not new. In 1945, as head of the New York State Council of Parks, he had commissioned Colonel William S. Chapin, an engineer who had helped build the famed Burma Road during World War II, to study the potential impact of the Kinzua Dam, especially its effect on Allegheny State Park. When the Chapin report was released in New York City in January 1946, it supported a federal plan to buy the entire Allegany Indian Reservation and remove all the Indians, in order to further flood control and develop the valley for recreational purposes.[29] To the then-chairman of the Allegheny State Park Commission, Charles C. Congdon, Moses had "cut a deal" with Pittsburgh industrialists by supporting their demands for Upper Allegheny flood control with the design of getting a *quid pro quo* sometime in the future.[30] Consequently, as early as 1946, Moses had begun to view Iroquois lands as regional sacrifice areas for his vision of America. Just as he dispossessed 250,000 people, mostly urban black poor, in his reshaping of New York City and environs, Moses' idea of progress had little place for Indians. His only involvement with Indians was his hiring of ironworkers on his many projects and in commissioning the famous artist, Thomas Hart Benton, to paint murals for SPA power houses nostalgically depicting Indians as background to Cartier's heroic "discovery" of the Saint Lawrence and Father Hennepin's "discovery" of Niagara Falls.[31]

Moses' work in the 1920s laid the blueprint for seaway development and regional planning of the Saint Lawrence frontier. His brother Paul had worked as an engineer for Consolidated Edison during this period and had been assigned to find ways to harness the vast hydroelectric potential of the Saint Lawrence River. The two brothers, who openly despised each other, nevertheless discussed the feasibility of the project.[32] In 1924, Moses wrote *A State Park Plan for New York*, which he drafted under the aegis of the New York State Association. This groundbreaking study was "a seminal document in the history of parks in America."[33] In this report, Moses helped shape the direction of park development by shifting the philosophy of parks away from merely conservation; he now combined it with the recreational needs of the masses and the means to get to the parks, namely parkway development. He added that the state should develop a park system divided into eleven regional administrations or commissions. The president of each of these regional commissions, Moses' later power base for his multifaceted projects, would sit as a state council of parks and coordinate and unify park policy. It is little wonder that at a time when Letchworth was the only state park of any appreciable size between the Palisades and Buffalo, Moses combined a definite need with a means of achieving the goal. Through this new body and as head of it, Moses' political alliances with municipal, county, and regional officials were sealed. Significantly, Governor Alfred Smith's appointment of Moses to be secretary of state of New York in 1928 gave the master builder membership on the state's Board of Commissioners of the Land Office. This seemingly minor post helped him acquaint himself with the entire history of state lands since 1784; it also gave him insight into problems arising in connection with state titles and ownership, a most important factor in his later dealings with the Mohawks and Tuscaroras. Thus, it is clear that to Moses, the seaway was conceived as not merely an international waterway, but in far larger terms.[34]

Moses' ideas for economic and energy development were the keys to his master plan and were to have the most impact on Mohawk life along the Saint Lawrence River. Although in the 1920s and 1930s, Moses had viewed the utility companies as the enemy in his insistence on public control of cheap hydroelectric power, by the postwar era he became convinced that these same utilities could be persuaded to reduce rates, improve services, and bring electric power to rural areas. Leland Olds, the first executive secretary of SPA and later chairman of the Federal Power Commission (FPC), frequently attacked Moses for subverting the original mandate of SPA, namely for failing to favor domestic consumers, small rural interests, and municipally owned power cooperatives.[35]

Instead of advocating a totally government-owned, government-controlled power industry, Moses believed his objectives could be achieved by an effective regulatory commission as well as by comprehensive regional planning. By developing public hydroelectric power along the Saint Lawrence and Niagara frontier regions, he would stimulate heavy industry, and, at the same time, seaway transport. By constructing a series of parks and parkways for tourist and recreational purposes, while providing special low rates for Saint Lawrence–Niagara frontier residents, he would counter any local opposition to the project. By improving the state's total economic picture, he would satisfy the utility companies' quest for increased profit margins.[36] By sacrificing Indian lands or those that were claimed by Indians, who were a small powerless racial minority largely outside of the American electoral process, he would not alienate white voters and their political representatives, especially in the economically depressed North Country of the state.

In fairness to Moses, although he originated the master plans for Saint Lawrence regional development, he reflected much of the economic climate and planning concepts of the Eisenhower years. On the national level, Army Corps of Engineers and Bureau of Reclamation pork-barrel projects, as in the Kinzua case, were a congressional way of life, usually accepted by the chief executive as well as the federal courts. The academic world also added weight to Moses' plans for the Saint Lawrence frontier. In a Maxwell School public policy analysis published by Syracuse University in 1956, two researchers,

Sidney C. Safrin and Edward E. Palmer, compared the seaway project's impact to that of the Erie Canal. Although suggesting that the early nineteenth-century waterway had raised the entire economic system, not just that of one region, it characterized the Saint Lawrence Seaway's potential impact in Turnerian terms. By transforming an underdeveloped "frontier," namely the Saint Lawrence River valley, the seaway would produce thousands of new jobs and vast and needed changes for "an area [in] which the full potential in its natural and human resources has never been approached." The survey added: "In this sense the area is one of the great frontiers of the state and the region. But it is particularly a frontier for American industrial expansion." Since neither "the human nor the natural resources of the special place referred to are being utilized in such a way as to create as rich and full a life for its people as the proper development and use of those resources could reasonably make possible," the authors rationalized the seaway construction:

> The almost unlimited possibilities of the St. Lawrence area may be more easily envisioned if one views it in a broader geographical context. It lies about halfway between the great population areas of "upstate" New York, that is, Schenectady, Albany, Utica, Syracuse, Rochester, and Buffalo, on the one hand, and the great population belt of Canada, in which is included the Montreal-Toronto industrial axis, on the other. A moderately well-developed network of roads and railroads, in addition to commercial airline routes, provides abundant connection to the industry and commerce of Canada and provides ready entry into the New York City-Chicago industrial axis, the present northern boundaries of which are just slightly to the south of the St. Lawrence area. The industrial East and the Middle West and Prairie Provinces are already connected by a water route, but the establishment of the Seaway will provide its full development. Moreover, the Seaway's construction will create and furnish the St. Lawrence area with an excellent connection with the whole wide world, for it does indeed bring the Great Lakes to the Atlantic Ocean and makes seaports of lakeports.

Indeed, the idea of progress had finally reached the North Country and the Indians were once again pushed aside as on earlier American frontiers. It is important to note that nowhere in this report did the authors deal with the social costs of the project, its possible effects on Indian and non-Indian, or the economic dislocations to the fishing industry in the region.[37]

Upon assuming the chairmanship of SPA and after the passage of the Wiley-Dondero Act in 1954, Moses promoted corporate relocations to the seaway area. As he over-optimistically wrote in 1956, the "St. Lawrence Power project and seaway will, we believe, attract much permanent business to the area."[38] Even with the support of the New York State Department of Commerce, the Rutland and New York Central railroads, and the Saint Lawrence Valley Association of Chambers of Commerce, SPA's efforts to attract industry proved a limited success. Reynolds, which was the second biggest producer of aluminum in the world, was one of two major new corporations induced to set up operations. Reynolds, a major "power hog," sought cheaper energy rates, and, at the same time, waterway access to bauxite brought up the Saint Lawrence River from the West Indies and South America. In 1956, the company signed a thirty-five year contract to buy power from SPA.[39]

Although the Reynolds plant never produced the number of jobs forecast in SPA projections or in seaway promotional films, New Yorkers in the North Country welcomed it because it was the first major industry to come into the area in fifty years, even though Saint Lawrence power was not supposed to be monopolized by industry. Reynolds' efforts to persuade the Chevrolet division of General Motors to establish a plant to cast auto parts from Reynolds' molten aluminum, and the personal interjection of Governor Averell Harriman contributed to the establishment of another major plant in the area. Yet one historian has observed that, with the coming of the two plants, "57 percent of the American share of St. Lawrence power was allocated to industry near the dam," a clear violation of New York State law that required preference to domestic and rural consumers.[40] Despite this fact, the vice president of Massena Banking and Trust Company urged Governor Harriman to name the new gigantic power house after Robert Moses, the "dynamic" chairman of SPA, whose many accomplishments had helped this part of the state.[41]

At the ceremony marking the first delivery of commercial power by SPA in 1958, Moses introduced members of the boards of Reynolds and General Motors and insisted that SPA's aim was not "to replace private utilities or to put them out of business. Our main function is to preserve, for the people of the State of New York, natural resources which produce power," and which "are inalienable and belong to the people themselves."[42]

Notwithstanding Moses' rhetoric, nothing whatsoever that he did was concerned with the wishes or needs of the Iroquois. He battled with federal authorities as well as with Canadian seaway agencies about the positioning and types of bridge construction in the International Rapids section because he opposed a proposal which would have been more accommodating to the Mohawks.[43] Nevertheless, Moses' steamrolling tactics won mostly praise from his Canadian counterparts. Moses insisted in July 1955, that it was "essential to speed up land acquisition in order to keep up with the schedules for both Power and Seaway construction." In typical fashion, the SPA head maintained that "personal feelings" and group pressures that look to "protecting present interests" should be ignored in the pursuit of this "great public undertaking." He added: "We recognize the human side of this problem but we do not propose to be cajoled, threatened, intimidated, or pressured into modifying sound engineering plans to suit selfish private interests."[44]

Most importantly for the Mohawks, SPA's designation of the Rooseveltown peninsula, non-Indian lands immediately adjacent to the Saint Regis (Akwesasne) Reservation, for the sites of the Reynolds and General Motors plants, did not take into consideration the long-range economic and health implications to the Indians. Although fluoride and other chemical emissions from these two plants have not been conclusively proven to be harmful to human beings, the tribal fishing and dairy cattle industries have virtually come to an end, in part as a result of pollution and in part because the seaway has changed the spawning areas for fish. Moreover, despite promises to the contrary, only a small percentage of Indians have been or are employed by Reynolds and General Motors at Rooseveltown.[45]

As early as 1941, the Mohawks protested against the proposed plans for the seaway. Surveyors, without tribal or band approval, came to Cornwall Island and other parts of the reservation studying the potential alternatives for future construction. Ernest Benedict, a Mohawk resident of the island, objecting to the seaway plans, wrote to the American Civil Liberties Union in that year, insisting that he had seen an "advance-publicity map" of the proposed project which called "for a great canal to be dug through the middle of an island which is part of our reservation." He added: "There was no mention of the fact that this was reservation or of how the land was to be obtained as was done with other affected areas." Although seaway plans at that time included constructing a canal through Cornwall Island, a heavily populated section of the Mohawk territory, later proposals and the actual construction beginning in 1954 did not include this idea.[46]

Instead, the four agencies involved in construction were to affect the Saint Regis (Akwesasne) Mohawks in several distinct ways. Although little land was lost in contrast to Caughnawaga, several

homesites were shifted with the widening of the channel and the re-
routing of Route 37. Moreover, the influx of over 20,000 construction
workers to the North Country to build the seaway awakened and transformed forever the sleepy little hamlets, Indian and non-Indian, to the
realities of the outside world.[47] Gigantic "cats," which were used to
bulldoze tons of earth to build cofferdams and permanent dams, shift
the course of the river, widen the waterway, or construct immense
power houses, became common features in Massena and environs.
Mohawk men, famous in the construction trades since the late nineteenth century, became part of the work crews in this massive project
and two of them lost their lives working on the seaway at Massena
and on SPA's related project at Niagara Falls.[48]

More important to the Mohawks was the total disregard of their
land claims. As early as February 1946, the FPC had commissioned
a study of Saint Lawrence River power potential. The report, which
never mentioned the Indian claims to the island, stated that the "Barnhart Island Powerhouse will be the largest single feature of the planned
hydroelectric project," one that would be 3,585 feet long and produce
2.2 million horsepower capacity for rural electric and municipally
owned utilities' needs.[49] Moses raised the idea of the Barnhart Island
power house in 1954, and, as in the earlier FPC report, he totally dis-
regarded the Indian claims within the area chosen for development.
He wrote about the Mohawk claim in a disdainful way two years later:

> This job has its humor. In addition to those who supervise the
> supervisors, execute the executives and watch the watchmen, we
> have to contend with St. Regis Indians, who ask the tidy little
> sum of $34 million for their pre-Revolutionary interest in Barn-
> hart Island, and assorted characters who are steaming up distant
> owners on the Great Lakes shorefront to sue us for the rise and
> fall of the tides.

Moses insisted that these "are merely little incidents that brighten
our days."[50] To the Mohawks, the Barnhart Island claim was and is
hardly an incidental matter and one that still receives serious attention at tribal meetings and in the reservation newspaper. To the over
10,000 members of the Akwesasne community that straddles a six-
mile square area along the Saint Lawrence River in Ontario, Québec,
and New York State, with all the attending problems of overlapping
jurisdiction, Barnhart Island is Mohawk territory.[51] Yet today, two
major power houses, high voltage power lines, two ship locks, and a
major beach-camp recreation area occupy the island.

In 1956, the Mohawks filed suit for 33.8 million dollars against New York in the Court of Claims to force the state to compensate the tribe for appropriating the island. The suit sought compensation for the state's appropriation of the land and water of Barnhart Island as well as the adjacent river bed and water power of the river. The case, conditioned by seaway development, was also an outgrowth of the failure of Mohawk efforts in the early 1950s to reclaim land in Vermont which it had been seeking for over 150 years.[52]

The resulting case, *St. Regis Tribe v. State of New York*, was fought in the courts for nearly two years and right up to the New York Court of Appeals. Although Court of Claims Judge Charles Lambiase agreed that the Mohawks had the right to bring such an action in state courts, the appellate division reversed the decision and dismissed the case.[53] On June 25, 1958, the court of appeals unanimously affirmed the appellate division. In its decision, Judge Charles W. Froessel pointed to the State of New York's 1796 treaty with the Seven Nations of Canada in which the so-called "St. Regis Tribe" allegedly ceded all of its lands, except for a tract six miles square. To Froessel, this treaty was a legal one since it was negotiated in the presence of a federal commissioner in accordance with the nonintercourse acts (Trade and Intercourse Acts of 1790 and 1793); however, one legal ambiguity remained, namely the uncertain border between Canada and the United States. The two countries' claims of ownership to the island were not settled until 1822 when an island exchange was made between the two countries. As in the appellate court decision, Judge Froessel, in finding against the Indians, pointed to an 1856 act of the New York State Legislature which appropriated 5,960 dollars "for the payment and in full of the claim of the St. Regis tribe of Indians, for the sale by the State of two certain islands in the river St. Lawrence, known as Barnhart's and Baxter's islands, which belonged to the said tribe." Citing the New York State Constitution, Froessel insisted that the state had the right to settle this dispute under the treaty through a legislative act. To Froessel, the 1856 act was not a new purchase of Indian land, which would have been a clear violation of the federal Trade and Intercourse Acts, "but rather the adjustment of a claim that had arisen as the result of the ambiguous language of the 1796 treaty."[54]

Because of the unique physical geography of Saint Regis (Akwesasne), Barnhart Island was not the only legal brouhaha caused by seaway development. This Mohawk reservation straddles both sides of what the non-Indian world refers to as the United States–Canadian border. Five major jurisdictions impinge on Mohawk life—the United

States, Canada, New York State, Ontario, and Québec. There are separate tribal governments at Hogansburg and on Cornwall Island, the former one to deal with Indian affairs in the United States and the latter with those in Canada. Yet, as Chief Lawrence Pyke has recently observed, "It doesn't matter which side of the border anyone lives on. You can live over there and be with us or you can live over there and be with them." According to one Mohawk attorney: "That border was made by white people. It has nothing to do with us."[55] Despite this view and the fact that the Mohawks today do not pay the toll on the bridge over the Saint Lawrence and whisk through separate customs lanes flashing their identity cards to Canadian and United States inspectors, the border has played a key and at times determinant role in Mohawk life.

As a result of the seaway project, highway approaches on Cornwall Island to the Cornwall-Massena International Bridge were built. This new construction soon led to increased tribal friction and protest. All Mohawk objections to the condemnation and expropriation of band lands, a total of 130 acres, for approaches across Cornwall Island, were directed to the Canadian government. When the Ministry of Transport and the Department of Citizenship and Immigration, which at the time was in charge of administering Indian affairs, supported the Saint Lawrence Seaway Authority's plan to expropriate these lands, the governor general of Canada approved it, without parliamentary action, on November 29, 1956.[56] Despite assurance by the Indian Branch of the Department of Citizenship and Immigration that "in no circumstance will any tolls be charged to Indians," the promise was soon broken. Moreover, nowhere in negotiations with the band council did any agencies or the Ottawa government reveal their full plans for toll gates, a customs house, garages, and offices on Cornwall Island.[57]

In September 1959, John Sharrow, a Mohawk resident of Cornwall Island and an elected band chief, threatened to cut off all traffic across the bridge unless the Saint Lawrence Seaway Authority paid 45,000 dollars to guarantee three years' rental for the new one and a half-mile road which traverses the all-Indian owned island. He insisted: "We mean business. If we don't get our money, we'll block off the road to traffic. It's our road and we can do what we want with it." Three weeks later, the dispute was settled when the authority acceded to Mohawk demands after the Indians threatened to collect fifty cents per car from all drivers using the road after the fourteenth of October.[58]

The issue of tolls and customs duties, nevertheless, continued to be a sore point. The Indian Defense League, which had many Mohawk members, had championed the issue since the 1920s. They pointed to Article III of the Jay Treaty (1794), later reaffirmed in the Treaty of Ghent (1814), which provided and assured the Indians free and unrestricted passage and trade across the border. This right, which had been recognized by the United States as a result of Tuscarora chief Clinton Rickard's efforts in the 1920s and after, had repeatedly been rejected by Canadian authorities.[59] Even before the seaway, Louis Francis, a Mohawk Indian residing on the so-called Canadian side of the reserve, had brought suit against what he viewed as the illegal seizure and imposition of 123 dollars in customs duties by Canadian authorities. Francis had purchased a washing machine, electric refrigerator, and an oil stove on the United States side of the international boundary. The goods were not reported to the customs office and were subsequently seized until Francis paid the duty. Francis then sued the Canadian government to obtain return of the moneys, claiming a violation of the Jay and Ghent treaties. The court dismissed Francis' action, maintaining that Indian rights under the Jay Treaty were never implemented or sanctioned by legislation and that the Indian Act of Canada was not applicable and could not, in any case, provide Francis immunity from the Customs Acts or Customs Tariff Act of Canada. The court also implied that the Jay Treaty, despite the Treaty of Ghent of 1814, had been abrogated by the War of 1812.[60]

The Mohawks' protests to Canadian and United States officials about this decision and its implications fell on deaf ears for the next ten years.[61] In the fall of 1968, Indians at Cornwall Island were required to pay customs duties on all goods, including food, of more than five dollars in value. On the eighteenth of December, after careful planning, approximately one hundred Mohawks, mostly women and teenagers, blocked the International Bridge with twenty-five automobiles in protest against these Canadian levies. The demonstration was planned from early November onward in Ernest Benedict's home on Cornwall Island. The fifty-year-old head of the North American Indian College had, as one Iroquois newspaper stated, "put aside his school work to assist the distraught St. Regis Indians" in protest against the Francis decision and Canadian violations of the Jay Treaty.[62] Charging that the Mohawk agreement with the Saint Lawrence Seaway Authority had been violated by the imposition of tolls and by the presence of a customs office, the Indians sat down or threw their bodies in front of tow trucks sent to clear away the wall of Mohawks and their automobiles. Letting the air out of their automobiles' tires and carrying placards reading "This is an Indian Reservation, No Trespassing," they confronted the Royal Canadian Mounted Police and the Ontario Provincial Police. The police seized and arrested forty-one Mohawks, including Kahn-Tincta Horn, a colorful Mohawk activist and former beauty queen from Caughnawaga. Eventually, after another sitdown in February 1969 and a prolonged series of negotiations, the Canadian government agreed to the duty-free status of the local Mohawks.[63] Since going from one part of Saint Regis (Akwesasne) to another frequently involves going into what non-Indians term another country, be it the United States or Canada, the final Canadian recognition of previously denied Indian rights under Article III of the Jay Treaty is considered by the Mohawks as a major victory. Quite significantly, the bridge blockage led directly to the founding of the major Iroquois newspaper, *Akwesasne Notes,* which has had immense impact on Indian communities throughout the United States and Canada.[64]

A decade before the blockade of the International Bridge, activists from the two Mohawk communities had predicted this new political strategy largely in response to the crisis caused by the Saint Lawrence Seaway. In August of 1957, approximately 200 Indians, led by Francis Johnson (Standing Arrow), a muscular twenty-four-year old Mohawk ironworker from the Saint Regis (Akwesasne) Reservation, occupied land off Route 5S on Schoharie Creek near Fort Hunter. The Mohawks protested the coming of the Saint Lawrence Seaway and the fact that some of them were "blasted from their homes" by the massive construction project. Standing Arrow, with typical bravado, boldly insisted that "more than 2,000 Indians from reservations in Québec, at Caughnawaga, Oka, and St. Regis, their life changed by the St. Lawrence Seaway," were considering his call to resettle their original homeland in the Mohawk Valley. Citing the Treaty of Fort Stanwix of 1784, the Mohawks claimed a fifteen-square mile territory and insisted that the New York State treaty of 1789 that ceded land was invalid because the state had no legal right to enter negotiations with the Mohawks after the formal adoption of the United States Constitution in 1788.[65]

These so-called "Seaway Indians," or "DPs" as they were referred to in some news articles, were eventually to disperse after a court ordered them evicted in March 1958; nevertheless, they were harbingers of a new militant position developing in Iroquoia from the late 1950s onward. Threatened by termination in Wisconsin, Oklahoma, and New York, and facing the harsh realities of land loss in four separate communities — Cornplanter, Caughnawaga, Saint Regis (Akwesasne), and Tuscarora — many Iroquois, conservative-minded, largely rural people, began to see no other alternative except to fight back. Losses in Congress in 1948 and 1950 and the series of detrimental court defeats in Canada and the United States between 1956 and 1958 raised the Iroquois frustration level to the boiling point by the late 1950s. Although Standing Arrow's leadership was short-lived, he did predict, as the bridge blockade in 1968 indicated, the strategy that the Iroquois and later other Indians nationwide would use in their fight to save their lands and way of life: more renewed assertions of sovereignty and treaty rights; more vocal calls for land claims; more and careful manipulation of the press to gain attention for Indian concerns; and more organized demonstrations and protests.

9

Moses Parts the Waters

The Reservoir at Tuscarora

We can do at Niagara what we have done on the St. Lawrence.

Robert Moses
September 28, 1957

The Federal Government by Treaty has given us assurance that
we can live undisturbed. We want to be left alone.

Chief Elton Greene (Tuscarora)
November 8, 1957

Robert Moses saw Niagara regional development as a direct outgrowth of his involvement in the promotion of the Saint Lawrence
Seaway. He envisioned them together as one of the most challenging
and important undertakings of his life. Today, the Niagara project alone
provides one-third of the power needs of New York State and the cheapest hydroelectric power rates in the nation. Yet, as did the Saint Lawrence project, Niagara regional development drastically impinged on
the Iroquois and their lands. SPA's construction of the "Tuscarora Reservoir" cost the Tuscarora Indians 550 acres, 495 acres for the power
project and fifty-five acres for an easement for transmission lines
through their reservation. Without question, the battle over the reservoir was the greatest threat that the Tuscaroras had faced in their
contemporary existence. The project also helped create a legal and
political reawakening among the Iroquois as a whole that still affects
Indian life today in New York State.[1]
    In this particular controversy, Robert Moses was even more de-
termined to win because of the unique power potential of Niagara Falls
and the "opportunity of developing to its fullest the most magnificent

recreational area in the East, if not in the entire country."² Although
Moses had had an interest in the Niagara frontier long before he was
appointed SPA chairman in 1954, the master builder's attention was
not primarily focused on the region until 1950. In that year, the United
States and Canada signed the International Niagara River Treaty to
promote the hydroelectric potential of the river, as well as the conservation, preservation, and enhancement of the falls and the Niagara
escarpment. The treaty also stipulated that the two nations maintain
a continuous minimum flow over the falls; each country would share
equally in the additional water. The 1950 agreement, however, contained a requirement that Congress pass on the manner of the disposition of additional water for power development made available to the
United States.

From the time the treaty was signed until 1957, SPA fought vigor-
ously for the exclusive right to develop this hydroelectric potential,
fighting off five separate private utilities. In typical fashion, Moses
saw the Niagara project, in his first annual report as head of SPA, in
grandiose terms, as part of a massive park and parkway development
south to the Ohio and Pennsylvania lines and north to the Canadian
border. He maintained that the present supply of power in New York
State was "not sufficient to promote growth in industrial production
and power use without interruption and curtailment" since an additional 3.8 million kilowatts would be required by 1965. It is important to note that as early as 1954, Moses had a detailed plan of action
for hydroelectric, park, and parkway development, including what became the Tuscarora reservoir, a "pumping-storage reservoir [of] 41,000
acre feet," which he expanded to 60,000 acre-feet capacity in 1957.³

Despite repeated congressional delays in sanctioning SPA's development of Niagara hydroelectric power, Moses took advantage of
an "act of God" in 1956 to win approval for his plans. Instead of the
Burning Bush in the Sinai desert, Robert Moses used the collapse of
the Schoellkopf power station caused by water seepage into rock crev-
ices between the lip of the Niagara gorge and a hydraulic canal feeding
the power house. On June 7, 1956, after a series of gigantic rockfalls,
two-thirds of this power station tumbled into the Niagara River gorge
one-half mile below Niagara Falls. The collapse of the power house,
the largest hydroelectric plant in the Niagara Mohawk power system,
resulted in the death of a thirty-nine-year old machinist as well as a
massive power outage in the city of Niagara Falls. Significantly for
the future of the Tuscarora Indians, the loss of a 360,000-kilowatt power
station gave impetus to Moses' already existing plans for Niagara power
development.⁴

Five days later, at a meeting of corporate and utilities executives at Massena, who were touring the construction of the Saint Lawrence Seaway, Moses confidently insisted that a new Niagara power project by the state could be started as early as 1959 if SPA received congressional approval. Although his audience included representatives of the same utilities which had fought bitterly against state development of Niagara power, the destruction of the Schoellkopf station led to a consensus. Moses, quickly seizing upon the opportunity, maintained that SPA and Ontario Hydro could guarantee to Niagara Mohawk the power it lost until SPA could build a 400,000,000-dollar plant at Niagara. Since replacement of the Schoellkopf station might cost Niagara Mohawk 100,000,000 dollars and the company's license had only fifteen years more to run, the giant utility, Moses logically argued, should be influenced by the economics of the situation and support state power development at Niagara. To further back up Moses' points and to emphasize the crisis situation affecting New York's industry caused by the loss of Schoellkopf power, G. J. Zimmerman, assistant to the president of the Carborundum Corporation, the major plant and employer in Niagara Falls, was one of those executives in attendance. Several days later, an editorial in the *New York Times* reiterated that a crisis was at hand and suggested the "promotion of state construction of a new power plant at Niagara and equitable distribution of electricity on a non-preference, non-discriminatory basis to customers of private companies and public-owned systems alike."[5] Soon, the AFL-CIO petitioned Governor Averell Harriman to act quickly and develop Niagara power because of the Schoellkopf disaster.[6]

On August 21, 1957, Congress, confronted with intensive lobbying by Congressman William Miller of Lockport and with the critical need for power caused by the destruction of the Schoellkopf plant, passed Public Law 85-159, the Ives-Javits-Miller bill. The act expressly authorized and directed the FPC to issue a license to SPA for the construction and operation of a power project with capacity to utilize all of the United States' share of the water of the Niagara River permitted by international agreement.[7] Subsequently, SPA, a municipal corporation created under the laws of New York State in 1931 to develop Saint Lawrence and Niagara power, applied to the FPC for a license. In its application SPA indicated that the proposal was estimated to cost 720,000,000 dollars and would be finished in 1963. After a series of hearings, the FPC on January 30, 1958, issued its order granting SPA a license. The FPC failed to decide on the Tuscarora Indian objection about the taking of their land; however, it directed SPA to revise its exhibit to show the area and acreage involved in the project.[8]

The Tuscarora Indians were Iroquois refugees from tidewater North Carolina, having suffered extreme losses in a bloody war from 1711 to 1713. In 1714, the Iroquois Confederacy had informed Governor Robert Hunter of New York Colony that some of the Tuscaroras, perhaps as many as 500 families, had come and taken shelter among them. By 1723, these Tuscarora refugees were formally adopted as the sixth nation of the confederacy. Although they were not admitted on a completely equal basis since their chiefs were not made sachems of the league, they participated in all the confederacy's councils. The Tuscaroras settled mostly along the upper Susquehanna River on the border of New York and Pennsylvania colonies under the watchful eyes of the Oneida. By 1776, the Tuscaroras were drawn into the conflict between Great Britain and the American colonies, most choosing, as the Oneida did, the patriot side — in part because of Reverend Samuel Kirkland's influence. Those that fought on the British side and many pro-patriot refugees from the war-torn Susquehanna ended up on the Niagara frontier by the end of the war.

The next two decades dramatically affected Tuscarora existence and shaped their later legal battles with Robert Moses and SPA. The Tuscaroras were parties to the major federal treaties of the period, including the Fort Stanwix (1784), Fort Harmar (1789), and Canandaigua (1794), which reinforced their Iroquoian outlook and concepts of sovereignty. About 130 Tuscaroras moved to the Six Nations Reserve along the Grand River after the American Revolution while the majority, perhaps three times the Canadian contingent, remained in New York. Even before the war, some Tuscaroras were apparently residing on Seneca lands along the Niagara River; however, during and after the American Revolution, their numbers quickly grew. By 1789, 110 Tuscaroras lived at Niagara Landing, their population increasing to 260 three years later. Because of the Treaty of Big Tree of 1797, the Seneca interest in the bulk of its Niagara lands was transferred to Robert Morris and ultimately to the Holland Land Company. In 1798, the company ceded a tract of 640 acres to the Tuscaroras, followed by another one of 1,280 acres the following year. Although these two cessions totaled significant acreage, these lands were never directly involved in the later litigation over the "Tuscarora reservoir." The Tuscarora legal controversy of 1958–60 involved lands of the so-called Dearborn Tract.

With the proceeds, 13,722 dollars from the sale of their remaining lands in North Carolina, the Tuscaroras purchased 4,249 additional acres. In 1809, these lands, held in trust by Henry Dearborn since 1804 after purchase from the Holland Land Company, were conveyed by

Dearborn and assigned in fee simple title to the "Tuscarora Nation of Indians." Thus, by 1809, the Tuscaroras had a total land base of 6,249 acres, or just under ten square miles. It is important to stress that the Tuscaroras were parties to many of the post-Revolutionary War treaty negotiations, were for the most part allies of the patriots, and that their fee simple title, gift, and/or purchases of Niagara lands occurred after the Treaty of Canandaigua had defined their territory; however, the lands they settled upon were initially Seneca lands which were guaranteed at the time of the three treaties.[9]

Despite their refugee status, the Tuscaroras adjusted to their new surroundings and to the changes they faced in the nineteenth and first half of the twentieth centuries. These included the establishment of two missions by the Baptists and the Presbyterians; the founding of a branch of the Iroquois Temperance Society; the rise and decline of agriculture; the growing encroachment of the city of Niagara Falls, only four miles southwest of the reserve, and of other smaller white communities such as Lewiston; and the growing economic integration of the Tuscaroras into the market economy and day-wage system of the outside white world. In addition, the Tuscaroras faced local prejudice as well as other major outside pressures. They were, as previously described, among the Iroquois leaders against the Selective Service Act of 1940 and New York State jurisdiction in Indian civil and criminal matters in 1948 and 1950.

While the white world steadily impinged on Indian life, the Tuscaroras retained a marked separation from Niagara Falls and its environs. The anthropologist Anthony F. C. Wallace, who did fieldwork among the Tuscaroras in the late 1940s, described this conscious separation:

> 'Off the reserve' is like the forest. One goes into it to earn money; for the 'excitement' of frequenting the 'Indian hangouts' in the cities; to acquire special powers by virtue of education, both religious and lay; for the thrill of conquest in sports, war, love; to escape difficult social situations. The reserve, and especially the clearing in the reserve, always remains 'home' and old men often return from the outside to die in the clearing.[10]

Moreover, the Tuscarora definition of success, as defined by Wallace's study, was in sharp contrast to that of the outside. Whites are generally guided by the individual's ideal of progress, namely socioeconomic mobility, and by the "progress of civilization as measured . . . by bigger and better refrigerators, cars, houses, bridges, factories, and so forth."

Although the white man's gadgetry was wanted by Indians, Tuscarora wants were not "guided and systematized and regimented by the ego ideal of success" or by an "inflexible level of achievement."[11] Thus, the battle over the Tuscarora reservoir was not simply a fight between two strong-willed leaders, Robert Moses and Elton Greene, but involved two definitions of land and the meaning of progress.

Tuscarora resistance to the reservoir plan began long before the approval of the Ives-Javits-Miller bill and the Tuscarora appearance at the FPC hearings. From early 1957 onward, SPA attempted to convince the Tuscaroras of the necessity of the project and sought surveying rights on the reservation. In March 1957, Moses sent William Latham, an SPA engineer, to address the Tuscarora General Council about the need to determine the soil depth down to bedrock in order to ascertain the cheapest way of building a water storage reservoir. The council then denied SPA engineers the right to carry out their survey, realizing that the agency was contemplating building the reservoir on Indian land.[12] Despite this earlier failure, Moses believed that the Tuscaroras could be bought off, insisting in September that SPA "shall fully compensate the Tuscarora Indians for land."[13]

On October 15, 1957, Moses first admitted having a problem in dealing with the Tuscaroras. On that date, he addressed the American Society of Civil Engineers in New York City on the topic of "St. Lawrence and Niagara Power." Moses, it is clear, was becoming concerned. At the Tuscarora Indian Reservation, as Moses described it, the "braves are whooping it up and attempting to block our survey parties." Yet, like Ol' Tom Benton, senator from Missouri in the 1840s, Moses minimized the problem and the Indians by insisting they occupied "uncultivated and unused land."[14]

Moses' growing problem with the Tuscaroras was in part a result of his selecting Latham and SPA attorney Thomas F. Moore, Jr. to negotiate with the Indians. Moses had full confidence in Latham, who had been in charge of Moses' field operations on other projects. Yet Latham was a brusque individual, who appeared to be solely concerned with engineering and hydroelectric power schedules. Consequently, he was strongly resented by the Indians from the outset. Moore, an arrogant individual who professed to be an expert on Iroquois history because he had been brought up in the Mohawk Valley and educated at Hamilton College, was combative in his approach to the Tuscaroras. Always seeking a good fight, he assured Moses that the Indian war could easily be won and at the right price. Both Moore's and Latham's assessments of the situation, namely that the Tuscaroras could be convinced to "sell" their lands, were well off the mark and contributed

Robert Moses in front of Robert Moses Niagara Power Plant (PA 7-25724), July 19, 1963. Photograph courtesy of New York Power Authority.

Tuscaroras protest against the New York (State) Power Authority's condemnation of their lands for a reservoir, 1958. Left to right: William Rickard, John Hewitt (standing), and Wallace "Mad Bear" Anderson (kneeling). Photograph courtesy of Buffalo and Erie County Historical Society.

to Moses' inability realistically to assess the size and scope of the Indian opposition to the project.[15]

Neither Moses nor the Indians were aided in resolving the controversy by the nature of Tuscarora politics of the 1950s. The Tuscaroras had severe political divisions that made negotiations difficult. Any leader seen as willing to settle with SPA was viewed as selling

Tuscaroras debating strategy in protest against the New York (State) Power Authority's condemnation of their lands for a reservoir, 1958. Photograph courtesy of Buffalo and Erie County Historical Society.

out. Although the general council of fifteen chiefs was the formal voice of negotiations, increased dissension weakened Tuscarora ability to deal with this great threat to their land base. While the Tuscarora General Council under Chief Elton Greene's highly controversial leadership focused their efforts at fighting SPA in the federal courts and tacitly, not openly, agreed to passive resistance to halt surveying and construction, other Tuscaroras came to the fore demanding more vociferous and militant action. These internal battles on the Tuscarora Reservation actually had surfaced as early as the fall of 1957. A dissident group, viewing Greene's leadership as dictatorial, went to the Tonawanda Reservation and attempted to have the Senecas depose five of the chiefs on the Tuscarora Reservation for allegedly considering an SPA settlement and sale of Indian lands.[16]

Moses also had to contend with the traditional Iroquois resentment and historical distrust of the State of New York. The Tuscaroras, as was true of all the Six Nations, viewed the state as the enemy. Instead of blaming Congress for the jurisdiction transfer bills of 1948 and 1950, the Tuscaroras saw it "as part of an insidious plot against Indian welfare" perpetrated by state lobbyists. As Wallace has pointed out: "*Anything* which the State plans to do with respect to the Indians is automatically resisted."[17] Thus, the SPA-Tuscarora conflict of the late 1950s had its antecedents in nearly 175 years of friction between Indian and white in the Empire State.

Moses met a formidable opponent in the person of Chief Greene. The Iroquois elder was well known in western New York and had generated good will in the non-Indian world because of his keen interest in and knowledge of Iroquois lore and his participation in the development of the Maid of the Mist Festival in the mid-1950s. A polite, soft spoken, articulate man before non-Indian audiences and quite photogenic with his Seminole shirts and western-styled hat, he helped generate favorable publicity for the Tuscarora cause in newspapers nationwide in the late 1950s. Despite his reserved image before the media, Greene was a skillful, shrewd, and, at times, ruthless Iroquois politician, realizing that the controversy threatened not only the Tuscarora Reservation, but also his power in council and in the eyes of his people.[18]

When SPA received its FPC license approval in September 1957 and announced that it was seeking 960 acres of Indian lands for the construction of a 2,400-acre reservoir, the Tuscaroras reacted immediately. Chief Greene wrote to President Eisenhower objecting to the SPA-planned reservoir and asserting Tuscarora treaty rights under the Fort Stanwix (1784) and Canandaigua (1794) treaties. Moses then called for a meeting with the council to discuss SPA's survey rights on the reservation, which would not bind the Indians in any way as to possible future acquistion or prices. Greene rejected the request, indicating that the council had decided it would serve no benefit. When Moses over-reacted and suggested that SPA would get a federal court order to grant access for survey purposes, the second great Tuscarora war (the first being the one in the early eighteenth century) erupted.[19]

By November, Moses had increased the stakes by declaring that 1,220 acres of Indian lands were needed for the reservoir and for the success of this 600 million-dollar project. At the FPC hearings in Washington and later in Buffalo, the Tuscarora delegation, which included

The Robert Moses Niagara Power Plant (foreground) and the "Tuscarora" Reservoir (background), June 8, 1983 (PA 7-46358). Photograph courtesy of New York Power Authority.

Chief Greene as well as Chief Harry Patterson, requested, much as
had the Seneca treaty contention in the Kinzua Dam controversy, that
the commission forbid SPA's taking Indian lands. In typical traditionalist fashion, they declared themselves to be independent of unilateral
action by Congress. Ignoring the Americal legal precedents and congressional plenary power over Indians, they reaffirmed their sovereignty. Declaring themselves to be part of the Iroquois Confederacy
which had a longstanding treaty relationship with the federal government, Greene insisted that these agreements could not be altered
without the consent of both parties. At this same hearing, thirty-nine-
year old William Rickard, a political opponent of Greene and the son
of the famous Tuscarora leader Clinton Rickard, added to Greene's

sovereignty position by describing why the reservoir was a threat to Iroquois traditionalist values: ". . . we do not feel that we own the land. It is only loaned to us to be saved for 'the ever coming faces' of the next generation of the Tuscarora. It is not ours to dispose of. We are only its custodians."[20] Although the Indians' argument did not win the day, the FPC hearings were shifted to Buffalo in spite of Moses' objections.

After the FPC provisionally granted a license to SPA on January 30, 1958, Moses took the offensive. Almost immediately SPA announced that it was seeking 1,383 acres, twenty percent of Indian lands, for its reservoir. In an open letter to the tribe, released to the press, he offered that SPA buy 1,200 acres since the acreage was necessary. He suggested that a "prompt friendly agreement on the generous terms the authority offers" would be most advantageous to the Indians. Even though condemnation proceedings would have to be formally filed, Moses determinedly added that "we must go ahead in any event." Losing patience, he stated that SPA had "no more time for stalling and debate"; the power broker stated that the total payment for prompt settlement might be as much as 1,000 dollars an acre, not including house values and extra compensation for possible inconvenience, for the reservoir and the transmission line. Moses was especially worried that further delays would undermine the sale of SPA bonds in the Wall Street financial market, causing economic shock waves. Insisting that obstructions "in the way of the project have already caused unconscionable economic loss to the whole Frontier community and to the entire western part of the state," he urged the Tuscaroras to accept the reality of a large storage reservoir since alternative plans would be too costly and more people, roads, and homes would have to be relocated. He added, rather callously, that the sale of this land "by you obviously will impose no hardship on your community" since only "about 15 houses are in the way" and because much of "your land is presently uncultivated and unused." He added that more than 5,000 acres would remain, or about eight acres of land per Indian, and that SPA would "respect your fishing rights" along the shore of the Niagara River even after completion of the reservoir. The money from the sale, the SPA chairman observed, could also provide money for needed educational scholarships and community improvements. Perhaps drawing on his days as secretary of state of New York, when he had done extensive research on land titles, Moses rejected Tuscarora claims to inviolate treaty rights, claiming that "the treaties you talk about have nothing to do with your reservation in Niagara County."[21]

The Indians quickly rejected the offer. Chief Greene, in an untypical manner, exploded: "We won't sell for 5 million, 10 million or 15 million. If we let any of our lands go, in a few years the Tuscaroras will be standing in the road."[22] The tribe then hired the law firm of Strasser, Spiegelberg, Fried, and Frank, whose attorneys Arthur Lazarus, Jr. and Richard Schifter were assigned to the case, to halt the Moses juggernaut.[23]

As Lazarus prepared the legal groundwork and sought an injunction to stop the reservoir, Tuscarora activism and resistance grew. Indians began in early March to post signs warning officials, surveyors, contractors, and employees of SPA's Niagara power project to stay off the reservation. The same month, Moses announced to the world that SPA had begun to build its new power house at Lewiston. SPA formally laid claim to 1,383 acres of Indian lands on the fifteenth of April by filing a map of the property at the Niagara county clerk's office in Lockport and planned to enter the reservation the next day.[24]

The long-brewing confrontation erupted on the sixteenth of April. A Tuscarora automobile cavalcade blocked two efforts by SPA surveyors. This dramatic protest, at a time of civil rights foment in the South, brought media attention for the first time to a young, unimposing merchant seaman, Wallace "Mad Bear" Anderson, who previous to this incident had lived largely in reservation obscurity. The media was soon focusing on the gregarious and dynamic Anderson rather than on the issues involved in the controversy. Anderson's role was magnified by the media's looking for a "good story," and seeking Indians in traditional garb to photograph. Despite the news stories to the contrary, Anderson was not at the time of the protests a political leader on the reservation. His role in the events of 1958–60 are much exaggerated, largely perpetuated by the writings of Edmund Wilson and Anderson's own skillful manipulation of the media.[25]

On the seventeenth of April the confrontation between SPA surveyors and Indians intensified with Tuscaroras once again foiling attempts at surveying the reservation. One hundred fifty Tuscaroras faced off with sixty-two New York State troopers, Niagara County deputy sheriffs, and plainclothesmen as well as SPA staff, workmen, and surveyors armed with riot equipment consisting of tear gas, revolvers, side-arms, and submachine guns. Three Indians, William Rickard, John Hewitt, and Mad Bear Anderson, and an SPA surveyor were arrested in a scuffling incident related to the tensions. After national media attention was focused on the protest, the cases were later dismissed.[26]

The protests continued with marked intensity. When Indians planted themselves in front of transits and milled around other equip-

Chief Harry Patterson (Tuscarora), August 1966. Courtesy of Dr. Theodore Hetzel.

Chief Elton Greene (Tuscarora) and grandson, July 1972. Courtesy of Dr. Theodore Hetzel.

ment in passive resistance to the project, SPA attorney Moore declared that "we're not going to pull any punches from here on in" and said that he would slap contempt citations on those Indians interfering with the project.[27] Tuscarora clan mothers organized much of the resistance. The women, among their other activities, huddled in front of SPA's surveying equipment blocking the sights with their bodies. They, along with their men, pulled out SPA stakes that marked off land to be condemned for the reservoir. One woman, Mrs. Harry Patterson, whose homestead was to be the largest parcel condemned by SPA, threw her entire body over a stake that was about to be hammered in outside of her driveway. Others joined in by making placards condemning Moses, SPA, and New York State for stealing Indian lands. When SPA attempted to do its work at night using special high intensity lights, the Tuscaroras shot the lights out. Faced with unfavorable headlines and organized Indian resistance in and out of the courts, Moses struck back. Later, the Tuscaroras found out that Moses had been well aware of the Indians' strategies, that Indians' telephones and homes were "bugged," and even that one of the chiefs on the general council was passing information to SPA.[28]

The SPA chairman also mounted a massive public relations campaign. On June 9, 1958, Moses, seeing a real battle on his hands, issued an SPA report challenging Tuscarora contentions. In his finely illustrated brochure, he emphasized SPA generosity. The Tuscaroras would be paid 1,100 dollars an acre for 1,380 acres, or 1,520,000 dollars; would be paid extra for condemnation of any buildings on the land; houses would be moved, new roads built, and a new community center provided on the reservation. The last item, the community center, was supposed to sweeten the deal and received much attention from Moses in his report.[29]

This "compromise" was discussed by SPA officials for months prior to its inclusion in the report. Charles Poletti, SPA's vice-chairman and former governor of New York, had as lieutenant governor been instrumental in pushing for the building of the Tonawanda Indian Community House from 1935 to its completion in 1939. It appears that the suggestion of a community house stemmed from Poletti's influence. Yet it is clear that Moses was not sincerely interested in compensating the Indians and was only attempting to sell the reservoir. His and SPA officials' disdain for Indians was reflected in a memorandum dated May 19, 1958, sent by Moses to an assistant:

> Bill Chapin talked to Bill Latham about the proposed community house for the Tuscaroras. Bill Latham feels that the preliminary plan by John Peterkin is fine, but too flimsy and not husky enough

for the Indians, *who are not likely to maintain anything very
carefully.* Please go over the plan and see what can be done in the
light of one experience to strengthen and toughen the structure
and *make it fairly fool proof against neglect and vandalism.* Maybe
we should switch from wood to brick, stone, metal. *I guess they
are right. No use giving the redskins something they won't take
care of.*[30] (Emphasis added.)

Moses clearly revealed his attitudes about the Indians throughout the June 1958 report. He insisted that SPA for two years had been
attempting to buy land from the Tuscaroras and had repeatedly made
overtures to explain its position and pay equitable compensation to
the nation and to individual Indians. Reiterating nearly the same arguments of nineteenth-century expansionists, Moses insisted that it
would be economically impractical to construct the reservoir anywhere
else since the Indian area was not built-up land like the surrounding
non-Indian areas; that the Tuscarora population, which he significantly
underestimated, had increased twenty-five percent while Niagara
County population had risen 350 percent in the period from 1889 to
1958; that whereas in 1889 the Indians had 3,500 acres under cultiva-
tion and many orchards, only 500 acres were farmed and no orchards
remained in 1958. Only two farms would be affected by the reservoir
since most of the Indians were employed in commercial establish-
ments in Niagara Falls and in construction. He added that only twenty-
five percent of the land condemned for the project would be Indian-
owned. Underestimating his foes, he also insisted that the trouble was
caused by merely "a small number of recalcitrants" who "have stirred
up some of their brothers and blocked the nation" from compromis-
ing with SPA. After all, Moses maintained, cheaper electrical power
and jobs would be made available to Indian and non-Indian alike,
because the loss of the Schoellkopf station was necessitating the purchase of higher-cost Canadian power as well as contributing to local
unemployment.[31]

In the report, Moses also brought up his legal contention for appropriating Indian lands. He asserted what became the SPA argument
throughout the controversy, namely that the Indian land in the controversy was not protected by any treaty. Moses insisted that it was
purchased by the Tuscaroras "ten years after the last of the three treaties
[Treaty of Canandaigua, 1794] which, the Tuscaroras say, forbid the
appropriation of their land by the State." Thus, Moses had outlined
the arguments that SPA was to make in federal courts from 1958
through 1960.[32]

Clinton Rickard, in reflecting later on the Tuscarora-SPA struggle, insisted that Moses and SPA officials clearly demonstrated their race prejudice towards Indians and general contempt for Indian life as a whole. The chief observed that a man like Moses, "who had spent his career dumping concrete over the landscape would, of course, not be able to see how people could be using land unless they did likewise." In Rickard's view, SPA attorneys determined to prove that "the extent of a people's civilization was determined by the number of flush toilets they had." What they tried to do before the FPC was to show that "since this Indian community did not amount to anything, it had no right to stand in the way of whites who wanted Indian land for their own purposes." He added that SPA "respected only power and wealth and might, and we had none of these. That such a seemingly insignificant people would stand up to Robert Moses and fight back was the thing that infuriated him most of all, as his hysterical press releases only too plainly revealed."[33]

From the late summer of 1958 onward, Moses began accusing the Indians of adding millions to the cost of construction: "We have been shunted about and jackassed around from court to court . . . and are faced . . . with postponement of permanent financing and perhaps stoppage of work, which has already reached the reservation." Uhl, Hall, and Rich, SPA's consultant engineers, had concluded that modifying plans would exchange the Indians for an entirely new set of opponents, namely those non-Indian residents and homeowners outside the reservation. This would "create more problems, delay the project in litigation as much as two years and make it impossible to sell SPA's bonds in the financial market."[34] Apparently, Moses hoped to drive a greater wedge between the Indians and their non-Indian neighbors, some of whom had earnestly supported the Tuscarora fight against SPA. Moses frequently stated, in the months that followed, that if his agency did not condemn Indian lands, SPA had no other choice but to expropriate the residences of non-Indians adjacent to the Tuscarora reservation. If neither plan were acceptable, he suggested that unemployment would rise and the sagging economy of the Niagara frontier would worsen.

Moses also was attempting to negotiate at the "lowest bottom line," to satisfy the demands of the bond market. His financial package required a minimal settlement. When white real estate speculators started buying up lands adjacent to the reservation in anticipation of an SPA land swap with the Indians for Tuscarora lands lost in the building of the reservoir, Moses rejected the idea of exchange as being too costly. When the Indians asked SPA to provide free electricity in partial compensation for land loss, Moses turned down this

Chief Clinton Rickard and William Rickard. Photograph by Karen
Rickard. Photograph courtesy of Barbara Graymont.

avenue of settlement also as being too expensive. Nevertheless, it should be emphasized that the Tuscaroras were unwilling to compromise at all until all their legal appeals had been exhausted.[35]

Indeed, both SPA and the Tuscaroras were "jackassing" each other around in courtrooms and commission hearings. After SPA commenced so-called expropriation proceedings under New York State law on April 15, 1958, Lazarus filed a complaint for the Tuscaroras in the United States District Court for the Southern District of New York. The complaint asked for a permanent injunction against the action, claiming SPA had no right or power to take any Tuscarora lands without the express consent of the federal government. The court then issued a restraining order. On June 24, 1958, after the case was transferred to the United States District Court for the Western District of New York, the Tuscarora suit was dismissed.[36] In a separate action, the United States Court of Appeals held on July 24, 1958, that SPA had improperly condemned Tuscarora land and ordered reservoir work halted pending final settlement. Although not questioning SPA's right to exercise the power of eminent domain, the court decided that the condemnation proceedings could only go forward under federal law in the district where the property is located and in the manner provided by Section 21 of the Federal Power Act.[37] Within two months, SPA had begun this condemnation procedure in federal courts and was already in possession of some eighty-six acres of Tuscarora land. Although a Tuscarora petition for a writ of *certiorari* was denied by the United States Supreme Court on October 13, 1958, the Indians, in a third separate action, soon scored a major courtroom victory in their legal struggle to retain their lands.[38]

The Tuscaroras had brought another legal action in May against the FPC, which questioned the legality of SPA's license issued by the commission on the thirtieth of January. On November 14, 1958, the United States Court of Appeals decided that the commission had overstepped its bounds by issuing a license and remanded the case back to the FPC. The court found that the FPC could not license a reservoir on tribal lands unless it could find a way around a proviso of the Federal Power Act restricting its jurisdiction over reservations. This decision invalidated still another decision made in September granting SPA the right to take over the land after depositing 1,800,000 dollars with the court as compensation for land and for damages.[39]

In his legal defense of the Tuscarora lands in this suit, Lazarus, a protegé of Felix Cohen, the noted expert on Indian law, argued that the Tuscarora lands to be condemned were part of a reservation within the meaning of the Federal Power Act and thus were specifically excluded from its purview.[40] Since Indian reservation lands could not be sold without the formal consent of the United States expressed in an act of Congress, the FPC had no legal right to grant a license to SPA which, in effect, through condemnation proceedings was attempting to buy part of the Tuscarora Reservation.[41]

As a result of this decision, the tide seemed to favor the Indians for the next six months. The FPC held new hearings beginning in December, at which time Lazarus, representing the general council, and Stanley Grossman, representing Tuscarora opponents of Chief Greene, argued the Indians' case, and Moore and former judge Samuel I. Rosenman represented SPA. On February 3, 1959, the FPC, in a three-to-two vote, ruled that the Tuscaroras could not be compelled under federal law to sell land to SPA. This decision came four days after the Tuscaroras rejected a "final" SPA offer of three million dollars for their land. The FPC ruling found that the use of non-Indian lands for the reservoir would result in great delay, severe community disruption, and unreasonable expense; and that SPA's plans to utilize fully the water of the Niagara River under Public Law 85–159 required the building of a reservoir of 60,000 acre-feet, which could be done only by taking Indian lands; nevertheless, the FPC concluded that taking the 1,383 acres of Tuscarora lands for the reservoir "would interfere and would be inconsistent with the purpose for which the reservation was created or acquired."[42] One month after the FPC ruling, SPA's board of directors agreed to modify its planned reservoir. Their plans called for a reservoir outside the Tuscarora Indian community and entirely within the town of Lewiston, one that would be taller (fifty-five feet instead of forty-five feet high) and hold three-fourths the water capacity (45,000 acre-feet instead of 60,000 acre-feet). It would produce 100,000 fewer kilowatts of hydroelectric power than the original design, resulting in increased costs for consumers. Thus, all survey work on Tuscarora lands, the source of much protest by Indians since the early spring of 1958, came to a halt in late winter of 1959.[43]

Despite the overt concession by SPA's board, Moses was not one to surrender to the Indians. Through his powerful connections in the Republican Party—he had been nominated by some key party leaders in 1952 to be Secretary of the Interior but did not meet the regional requirement of being a Westerner—Moses refused to call retreat. On March 12, the Department of Justice asked the United States Court of Appeals for permission to intervene on behalf of the FPC in a new legal action. The FPC had two weeks earlier asked the court to review its interpretation of the Federal Power Act. Although Moses' role in these events is not clear, he had a longtime admirer and ally in Herbert Brownell, Jr., the attorney general of the United States.[44] The court cases, *Federal Power Commission v. Tuscarora Indian Nation* and *Power Authority of State of New York v. Tuscarora Indian Nation*, proved the Indians' undoing and led to the loss of their tribal lands.

Before the Tuscarora case reached the United States Supreme Court, the Six Nations Confederacy Council at Onondaga, at the urging of Indians at Tuscarora and at Ohsweken, sent a delegation to Washington in March 1959. Encouraged by General Herbert C. Holdridge, a self-styled but largely ineffectual "friend" of the Indians, the Iroquois attempted to gain an audience with President Eisenhower in order to present him with a formal petition protesting against United States and Canadian Indian policies. After an incident that was widely played up by the media as an attempt to make a "citizen's arrest" of Commissioner Emmons, the Indians eventually presented the petition to Department of the Interior representatives and congressional leaders. Among other things, the Iroquois petition protested SPA's "invasion" of Tuscarora lands in violation of the Treaty of Fort Stanwix, the passivity of the Interior and Justice departments in protecting the Indians, excessive legal fees, the loss of fishing rights along the Niagara River, and the location of high-tension lines which damaged Indian orchards, vineyards, woods, and fields.[45]

The high court case stems from a decision of the United States Court of Appeals handed down on March 24, 1959. The court approved the FPC's license to SPA and once again remanded the case to the commission with instructions "to exclude specifically the power of the said Power Authority to condemn the said lands of the Tuscarora Indians for reservoir purposes." The FPC appealed the case, asking the United States Supreme Court for a final determination. At long last, the legal merry-go-round seemed to come to an end when the Supreme Court finally agreed to hear the case.

On March 7, 1960, the Supreme Court ruled four-to-three against the Tuscaroras. The decision rested on the interpretation of Section 3(2) of the Federal Power Act, 16 U.S.C. Section 2796(2):

> 'Reservations' means national forests, tribal lands, embraced within Indian reservations, military reservations, and other lands and interests in lands owned by the United States, and withdrawn, reserved, or withheld from private appropriation and disposal under the public land laws; also lands and interests in lands acquired and held for any public purpose; but shall not include national monuments or national parks.

Justice Charles Whittaker, who wrote the majority opinion, stressed "and other lands and interests in lands owned by the United States," analyzing it to mean unallotted tribal lands, thus excluding the Tuscarora land which was held individually in fee simple title. According to Whittaker:

> Inasmuch as the lands involved are owned in fee simple by the Tuscarora Indian Nation and no 'interest' in them is 'owned by the United States,' we hold that they are not within a 'reservation' as that term is defined and used in the Federal Power Act, and that a Commission finding under section 4(c) of that Act 'that the license will not interfere or be inconsistent with the purpose for which such reservation was created or acquired' is not necessary to the issuance of a license embracing the Tuscarora lands needed for the project.

Thus, SPA had a legitimate right as an FPC licensee to proceed with the condemnation of Tuscarora lands. Since the Tuscaroras had argued that the taking of their lands for the reservoir was prohibited without the express and specific consent of Congress, Whittaker's decision dealt directly with this contention. In an opinion similar to the federal decisions made in the Kinzua Dam case, the high court's majority held that "the federal eminent domain powers conferred by Congress" upon the FPC in Section 21 of the Federal Power Act gave SPA the right to take the lands and did "not breach the faith of the United States, or any treaty or other contractual agreement of the United States with the Tuscarora Indian Nation in respect to these lands for the conclusive reason that there is none." Thus, in reversing the court of appeals decision, Whittaker insisted that the lands in question were entirely freed from existing treaties, as Moses had earlier argued, since they were derived from the Holland Land Company and were never a subject of any treaty between the United States and the Tuscaroras.

Justice Hugo Black, joined by Chief Justice Earl Warren and Justice William O. Douglas, were the three dissenting voices on the court. Black stressed a different phrase in the Federal Power Act, "tribal lands embraced within Indian reservations," maintaining that the United States Senate had included it in a specific amendment to the House version of the act. He insisted that Tuscarora lands were included in this phrase and thus protected. He then disputed Justice Whittaker's contention that the section of the act exempted certain types of Indian-held land. Black did not question the legal right of the United States government to take the land or even unilaterally to break the federal-Indian treaty relationship. Recognizing the doctrine of plenary power over tribal relations, he stated that it "would be far better to let the Power Authority present the matter to Congress and request its consent to take these lands" than for the high court to imply congressional approval indirectly through the Federal Power Act. In an eloquent conclusion, Black understood that there were intangible factors in the case, that Indian tribal existence was at stake, and that one's ancestral homeland could not be adjudicated properly in even the highest court of the land. He suggested that some "things are worth more than money and the costs of a new enterprise." Regretfully, Black concluded that the Supreme Court "is to be the governmental agency that breaks faith with this dependent people." In words that are hallowed on the walls of at least one Iroquois museum today, he added: "Great nations, like great men, should keep their word."[46]

One of the sidelights of this bitter struggle was Moses' public relations war with the Indians. When Edmund Wilson published articles in the highly prestigious magazine, *New Yorker*, in 1959 that championed the Tuscarora cause and which later became *Apologies to the Iroquois*, Moses was clearly enraged since Wilson had dared to attack the master builder on his home turf of New York City. Although Wilson's account was riddled with factual errors and was overly romanticized, it did reach an influential audience and did make an impassioned plea on behalf of the Tuscaroras, Mohawks, and Senecas. Challenging Wilson on each issue, Moses published a pamphlet, *Tuscarora Fiction and Fact: A Reply to the Author of Memoirs of Hecate County and to His Reviewers*. He minimized the extent of the Tuscarora opposition, insisting that many Indians wished to accept SPA's offer from the beginning. Portraying himself as sensitive to the lot of the Indians, he emphasized how SPA redesigned the reservoir in a way to take less Indian land and fewer Indian dwellings. Stating that "among my very best friends" are the high-steel Mohawks who appeared in Wilson's book on the Iroquois, Moses added:

> They are employed on all our big projects and I am proud to know the rising third generation. They are working Indians. The sure-footed high level Mohawks I know live in South Brooklyn. They don't have a ghetto, pale or segregated village. They get along fine with their neighbors. Maybe some other Indians should join the United States.

In conclusion, Moses insisted that SPA was committed to treat the
Indians not as a loser in the court case, but "with scrupulous fairness
and do everything in our power to improve their lot."[47]

After Lazarus' motion for a rehearing was denied by the Supreme
Court in April, the Tuscaroras, realizing defeat, individually and col-
lectively, began negotiating with SPA and numerous meetings followed. Finally, on August 12, 1960, the Tuscaroras, although divided
in the general council, accepted an SPA offer of 850,000 dollars for
550 acres, 495 acres for the power project and fifty-five acres for an
easement for transmission lines through the reservation. Since land
was individually owned, SPA compensated individual Indians, built
new homes, or moved old ones to new locations. All enrolled Tuscaroras whose land was not taken received 800 dollars as a final settlement. The monetary settlement included a 250,000-dollar payment
in lieu of SPA's building the community center on the reservation.
Despite SPA's insistence that it required 1,383 acres of Indian land,
it settled for substantially less land. Yet it should be pointed out that
the Tuscaroras also settled for substantially less money than they had
been offered in January and February 1959—three million dollars.[48]

Refusing to regard the deal as a land sale, Chief Greene emphasized that the SPA agreement was a settlement for damages. He added:
"Yes, they are using it, but there has been no sale. They took it away
from us but we will get it back when it becomes obsolete."[49] As in
the Seneca Nation's Kinzua Dam controversy, the Tuscaroras retained
ownership but granted an easement to SPA. This careful distinction
made by Greene, that appears to outsiders as a semantic exercise, is
an essential ingredient of Iroquois identity. Yet the bitterness ran deep.
According to Chief Clinton Rickard, "The SPA got its reservoir and
we were left with the scars that will never heal."[50]

Even during the two-year legal confrontation, construction proceeded on three sides of the reservoir. Now, with the final legal determination by the Supreme Court and SPA's settlement with the Tuscaroras, construction on the eastern side of the project began in earnest.
Hoping to meet an early 1961 deadline, work was speeded up on the
project: final surveys to plan the building of this fourth side of the
reservoir, subterranean grouting to fill cracks in the rock down to
seventy-five feet and prevent underground seepage, and construction
of the embankments. Some of the excavation on the site went as fill
for the new Lewiston-Queenstown Bridge plaza and approach. Moses'
engineers met every deadline. By October, dike construction reached
the halfway mark; the same month, the contractor completed the clear-

ing of the reservoir. On December 31, one of the upper river intake gates was opened and gradual flooding of conduits and waterways was begun. By January 5, 1961, the water reached the minimum operating level.[51]

The Tuscaroras were directly affected by the construction in a variety of ways. The SPA built new homes for four families, moved six homes, and transplanted one family from one rented home in the reservoir to one outside. The four who chose new homes were chiefs Harry Patterson and Kenneth Patterson, Elmer Mt. Pleasant, and Tracy Johnson.[52] Chief Johnson and his wife, who had worked for the SPA during the controversy, were later accused of passing information to SPA about the Tuscarora-planned strategy of resistance. Subsequently, he was removed from office and both he and his wife were removed from the tribal rolls.[53]

Among those Tuscaroras whose houses or trailer homes were moved were Dorothy Crouse, Leander Patterson, Franklin Patterson, Charles Johnson, William Farnham, and Ethel Zomont. Crouse, refusing to budge, was removed along with her home. Although nearly every home was improved in some way by SPA through the addition of central heating, new lighting and plumbing fixtures, new house entrances and cellars, or through redecorating, interior finishing, or exterior landscaping, the Tuscaroras regretted the Supreme Court decision. To this day, Tuscaroras sarcastically refer to their home improvement as their "SPA bay window or entrance."[54] Elmer Mt. Pleasant, interviewed after entering his new home, commented, "We still feel the decision was wrong. We're sorry to lose our home, but we might as well make the best of it." It is also clear that the tribal elders were more disastrously affected by the decision than some of the younger Indians in the impact area. Although Chief Harry Patterson received a new ranch-style home with two large steel-framed cinder block barns and two structures for his chickens and pigs, he had to abandon his family homestead, his extensive outbuildings, and a productive 600-acre fruit farm.[55]

The Niagara Power Project was formally dedicated at Niagara University on February 10, 1961, with Robert Moses acting as master of ceremonies. Among the honored guests were Governor Nelson Rockefeller and James Duncan, the chairman of Ontario Hydro. Although Chief Greene made peace with SPA and Moses in 1962, no Indians formally participated in the ceremony. Earl Brydges, the powerful Republican state senator from Niagara Falls, hailed Moses as "undoubtedly the greatest builder of this or any other generation." Reciting Persian poetry, Brydges admiringly added: "The waters parted in the days gone by at Moses' back and that of Joshua, And those above were walled and could not break, while those below fell sterile to the sea."[56]

Today, the "Tuscarora reservoir," a name that has never been accepted by the Indians, dominates the Niagara landscape. Young Indians as well as non-Indians attempt to ride up its steep incline with revved-up motorcycles, with little understanding of the war that was fought on this battleground a quarter-century ago. Besides the real trauma of land loss and tribal dislocation, two other major results stemmed directly from the Tuscarora-SPA war. Out of the bitterness of this setback, Iroquois political strategies shifted in new directions. As from the Saint Lawrence Seaway construction, a new, more assertive Iroquois emerged. Two Tuscaroras, of quite distinct backgrounds and personalities, came to public attention in the Indian and non-Indian worlds in the late 1950s: William Rickard and Wallace "Mad Bear" Anderson. Thus, as Vine Deloria, Jr. has observed, "the Tuscarora people of the Iroquois Confederacy" helped initiate "the type of [Red Power] protests which have now become so common."[57]

Rickard, who was to die tragically in 1964 at the age of forty-six after a life-long bout with acute emphysema, was without doubt the most eloquent spokesman of Iroquois sovereignty in the late 1950s and early 1960s. Unlike his famous father Clinton, William was a Longhouse follower. Yet, like his father, he was an outstanding voice for Indian treaty rights and conservatism, and they both were "men of brilliance and native genius, easygoing nature, selfless devotion to others, and tenacious belief in the rightness of their actions." Both were anti-assimilationist, anti-citizenship, and pro-tribal sovereignty in their views, believing that their Tuscarora Nation as a member of the Six Nations was a sovereign nation, independent of outside interference from newcomers, namely white Americans. Both courageously defended the same sovereign rights for all other Indian nations as they did for the Tuscaroras, in the Indian Defense League of America.[58]

Wallace "Mad Bear" Anderson, in sharp contrast, with no position of tribal authority among his own Tuscarora people, became the first of a new generation of militant Indians to realize the power of the media. From 1958 through 1960, his name and picture appeared in more newspapers than any other Indian in the United States, as a result of his participation in demonstrations throughout the eastern United States and Canada and a visit to Castro's Cuba. His flamboyant style continued and newspapers considered him newsworthy until the early 1970s.[59]

The Iroquois also reacted to land loss in another important way. Although there had always been a movement by individual tribal councils of the Iroquois and by the Six Nations Confederacy council at Onondaga to regain lost land, the late 1950s and early 1960s were an historic turning point in the land claims movement. Just as the so-called Kellogg Party of the 1920s rekindled the land-claims movement earlier in the century, the Tuscarora and Barnhart Island controversies revived interest in the soundness of the claims. The two cases combined with the establishment of the Indian Claims Commission in 1946, the Seneca and Mohawk land loss of the 1950s, and Standing Arrow's occupation of historic Mohawk territory, leading Iroquois leaders and their attorneys to research and explore the historic and legal documents to defend the little land they had left. As George Shattuck, the attorney for the Oneidas in the 1960s to 1975, commented: "I read the legal briefs in the Tuscarora case which contained an admission by the New York State Attorney General that the title to central and western New York was clouded."[60] This fact was readily admitted in 1959 by the Joint Legislative Committee on Indian Affairs when it stated that New York State had violated the Congress's Trade and Intercourse Acts: "When it is remembered that between 1788 and 1845 the State [New York] negotiated more than fifty purchases of former Indian-held lands in only a few of which the Federal Government participated, the far-reaching implications of the Tuscarora decision are obvious."[61] Thus, out of the wrenching loss of Mohawk and Tuscarora lands came the hope for a new day for the Iroquois.

10

Unlocking the Door
The Oneida Land Claims Case, 1919–74

Are we ever going to get anything out of these claims they say
we have coming?

> Mrs. Anderson Summers (Wisconsin Oneida)
> Seymour, Wisconsin
> November 16, 1950

Iroquois efforts to reclaim part of their homeland began long before
the legal issues in the Tuscarora case were raised. Iroquois Indian land
claims date as far back as the eighteenth century. Land claims have
been the subject of countless council meetings and their settlement
was the stuff of family hopes during times of economic and political
despair. Moreover, the Iroquois have over the years inculcated in their
children the righteousness of their land claims and a belief in the
eventual favorable conclusion of this agonizing process.

Despite their meaning to the Iroquois, these claims were purposely ignored and/or discounted by the non-Indian world. As a result,
some Indians grew even more determined, while others channeled
their primary energies to the immediate needs of economic survival.
While there were always Iroquois leaders, some honest, others not,
able to exploit the issue for political leadership purposes, others increasingly saw land claims as the politics of despair and opposed their
excluding other tribal goals. Thus, a major side effect of the historic
land-claims movement has been the fractionating of Indian communities. Ironically, while the pursuit of homeland through land claims
has reinforced Iroquois identity, the process has torn apart those same
communities by intensifying factional political behavior.

No better example of this dichotomy can be found than the
most significant of these claims, that of the Oneidas. Although the

Mohawk—whose claims to Barnhart Island, Fort Hunter, and land in Vermont have previously been mentioned—and Cayuga claims are equally fascinating, the Oneida claim is unique among Eastern Indian land claims. The landmark United States Supreme Court Oneida decision of 1974 overturned 140 years of American case law; it is also the only case that has been "decided favorably on the issue of whether the tribe's rights to land have been violated and the only modern eastern land claim to date to be considered by the Supreme Court."[1]

New York State's efforts to extinguish Oneida Indian land title began in earnest after the American Revolution, even though these Indians had been allies of the patriot cause. On September 22, 1788, at a time when the federal government was negotiating treaties to keep the Iroquois from allying with the Ohio River valley Indians against the United States, New York State and the Oneidas concluded a treaty at Fort Schuyler (Fort Stanwix). The Oneidas released to the state six million acres of land for 4,500 dollars in cash and goods and for 600 dollars in perpetual annuity. The treaty recognized a 300,000-acre Oneida reservation around Oneida Lake. This treaty occurred two months after the formal ratification of the United States Constitution with its proscription on state treaty-making powers.[2]

Despite the United States Constitution and the Nonintercourse Acts of 1790 and 1793, New York State continued to negotiate with the Oneidas for Indian lands. The 1790 act, among other provisions, prohibited the transfer of Indian land except through a federal treaty:

> And be it enacted and declared that no sale of lands made by any Indians, or any tribe of Indians within the United States, shall be valid to any person or persons, or to any state, whether having the right of pre-emption to such lands or not, unless the same shall be made and duly executed at some public treaty, held under the authority of the United States.[3]

When the act failed to provide law and order on the frontier, the United States Congress amended it on March 1, 1793, by adding a stipulation that required the presence of a United States Indian commissioner who would preside over state negotiations for Indian land. Both of these federal acts were aimed primarily at lawless whites on the frontier "and sought to restrain them from violating the sacred treaties made with the Indians."[4] Yet, in complete disregard of these two acts, the United States Constitution, and three federal-Iroquois treaties, New York State concluded a "treaty" in 1795. By this agreement, the Indians allegedly ceded some 140,000 acres of their 300,000-acre reservation. The Oneida Indian land base in New York was further eroded in the nineteenth century by later agreements with the state government, by land pressures of white land companies and individual speculators, by federal and missionary enticements to move west, and by the New York State Legislature's allotment of Oneida lands in severalty.[5]

As a consequence, the major Oneida communities are today geographically divided, with the largest communities outside of the historic Oneida territory of central New York. By far the most populous community, founded between 1823 and 1838, is located at Oneida, near Green Bay, Wisconsin. Next in population size is Oneida, near London, Ontario, established between 1839 and 1842. Oneidas in New York are found mainly at the Onondaga Reservation; they are also located along Marble Hill Road in Oneida County and along West Road (Route 46) south of the city of Oneida in Madison County as well as in the environs of Rochester. Although as late as the 1840s they held two reservations in New York, they retain at present only thirty-two acres of tribal lands along West Road in Madison County near Oneida, a tract of Oneida homeland that is the source of much controversy between competing Oneida groups over the past decade.[6]

The Oneidas, however disparate and distant their communities may be from each other, have, as Jack Campisi has observed, a common "estate." These include "ties to a landbase, land claims against the dominant society, exclusive membership by ascription in a community, a unique history, language, ceremonials, and belief system." Campisi has emphasized that land claims are not simply important in bringing diverse communities together by hopes of imminent awards. By entry into the courts, Oneidas also "receive from white society recognition of their ethnic identity."[7] The commonality of their "estate" was rekindled by the legal, political, and religious activism of one Wisconsin Oneida at the beginning of the twentieth century.

Any study of the Oneida claim in the twentieth century must begin with the life of Minnie Kellogg, née Laura Miriam Cornelius, and her role in Iroquois life from 1911 to 1930.[8] Born into a prominent Wisconsin Oneida family in 1880, she influenced important events both in the national arena and on the local Iroquois community level in Canada and in the United States. Kellogg, a noted reformer and author, was one of the founders of the Society of American Indians and of the modern Iroquois land claims movement. Every scholar doing fieldwork among the Iroquois from the time of J. N. B. Hewitt onward encounters her name and her legacy in research on Iroquois

Laura "Minnie" Cornelius (Kellogg), 1911.

factionalism, land claims, religion and revitalization movements, and
Indian views of Washington and Ottawa politics.

Kellogg was a dynamic leader who could sway large audiences.

She was the dominant personality in a major Iroquois secular movement that had revitalizationist overtones. In an extraordinary way, Kellogg could transcend her highly educated background to convey her ideas to largely rural, isolated, uneducated Indians. To white audiences and to her well-educated colleagues in the Society of American Indians, she frequently quoted from Franz Boas, G. Stanley Hall, and William James to back up her points about Indian race equality and mental capacities. To reservation communities, she spoke in "ancient tongues," and with traditional metaphors—the glory of the League of the Iroquois, the lessons of Indian elders and their wisdom, and, of course, the overriding concern of Indian people to win back their lands.

Despite her exceptional gifts—a brilliant mind, beauty, self-confidence, unusual oratorical abilities, and her educational attainments—Kellogg is also the most controversial Iroquois leader of the twentieth century. It is clear from her many bizarre involvements that she misused her prodigious talents and/or was incapable of carrying out all the massive designs she had for her people's betterment. Although acknowledged today as a major force and brilliant person, she is accused by many Iroquois elders of swindling them out of hundreds of thousands of dollars in her abortive efforts to bring their land claims to fruition and of creating debilitating factionalism that impeded tribal development for decades. Unfortunately, because of her questionable ethics and her inability to carry out what she espoused, Kellogg is blamed today for all that went wrong in Iroquois history in the interwar period. Consequently, her life story had the feel of a Greek tragedy: she wanted to use her extraordinary abilities to help her people but ended up accused by them of being a common outlaw.

Kellogg, as many an Iroquois before and since, attempted to speak for indigenous peoples as a whole. This ethnocentric characteristic of expression has frequently led these Indians to presume to voice concerns of all Native Americans in international convocations from New York to Geneva, Switzerland. Consequently, in her career, she became involved not only in the affairs of the Six Nations but also of the Blackfeet, Brothertown, Cherokee, Crow, Delaware, Huron, Osage, and Stockbridge Indians.[9] Her crusading and relentless agitating, which led to trouble with the law and to arrests in Oklahoma in 1913 and Colorado in 1916, also prompted her to help reform-minded Indians found the Society of American Indians in 1911.[10]

Kellogg's grandest design of all was reserved for the Iroquois. At the heart of her plan was the winning back of between six and eighteen million acres of land which she insisted had been taken fraudulently by New York State and/or by land speculators between 1784 and 1838. Her strategy was to win a favorable decision in the courts which would allow the Iroquois a sizeable restored land base for economic development and for the political restoration of the league's ancient greatness. Her activities emphasized solidarity with traditionalist politics, culture, and values. Through her masterful oratorical skills in Oneida and English, she encouraged traditional approaches to Iroquois medicine, set up her headquarters at the Onondaga Reservation, the historic capital of the league, revived Oneida chiefly titles associated with matrilineages, brought longhouse leaders from Onondaga to Wisconsin for condolence council, and "arranged" for the installation of nine "sachems" by Iroquois traditionalists on a visit to New York.[11]

Two events gave Kellogg hopes of success. On March 3, 1920, the United States Circuit Court of Appeals for the Second Circuit, in *United States v. Boylan*, an ejectment proceeding involving the removal of Indians living on a thirty-two acre tract of land, the Oneida homeland, and the partition of it to non-Indians, found that these Indians were a federally recognized tribe and that New York State courts had no jurisdiction in disposing of the Indians' property without the consent of the United States.[12] This hard-won Indian victory gave Kellogg and the Iroquois hopes for other victories in the courts.

In August 1920, the Everett Commission, a New York State Assembly committee formed in 1919 to examine "the history, the affairs and transactions had by the people of the state of New York with the Indian tribes resident in the state and to report to the legislature the status of the American Indian residing in said state of New York" began holding hearings. After nineteen months that included on-site inspections of Iroquois reservations in Canada and the United States, Chairman Edward A. Everett of Potsdam issued a report in 1922, that largely reflected his opinion and that of the commission's stenographer, Lulu G. Stillman. The report concluded that the Iroquois as Six Nations were legally entitled to six million acres of New York State, having illegally been dispossessed of their title after the Treaty of Fort Stanwix in 1784. This report, however unrepresentative of the commission, helped revive the Iroquois effort to recover lands through legal means and brought Kellogg to the fore.[13]

In the 1920s, Kellogg took advantage of these stirrings in Iroquoia. She, her husband, and her many followers collected money in every Iroquois community—in New York, Oklahoma, Wisconsin, Ontario, and Quebec—with the intention of using it for a massive Iroquois claim to up to eighteen million acres of land in New York and Pennsylvania. The Indians were told that if they did not contribute, they

would not be eligible for the claims when awarded. Kellogg and her
followers had several methods of collection in pursuit of the claim.
They gave tax receipts or due bills which indicated the contributor
was entitled to ten percent interest and a forty percent bonus when
the money was "recovered in our claim against the State of New York."
They also formed claims clubs on nearly every Iroquois reservation
in the United States and Canada, charging dues for membership or
levying a tax of approximately a dollar and a quarter a month on each
individual.[14] In spite of her husband's legal background, much of the
money collected, a considerable sum especially from economically
hard-pressed Indians, never went for the intended purpose and was
never returned to the contributors.

Kellogg's role in bringing the momentous land-claims case, *James
Deere v. St. Lawrence River Power*, initiated in 1925, makes her a
significant individual worthy of study since she helped define what
has been one of the Iroquois positions in this matter well into the
1980s.[15] In November 1922, Kellogg attended a meeting of the Indian
Welfare League in Albany in which Assemblyman Everett was chastised by Indian and non-Indian reformers for his report, including his
allegedly stirring up false hopes about the land-claims issue among
Indians. Kellogg reacted to the meeting in a column in the *Knickerbocker News* by defending Everett and claiming she belonged to no
welfare societies "because they seem to me to leave the Indians in
a worse condition than they found them in." She added that the real
question was not the workings of the Everett Commission but the
legal status of the Six Nations. To her, the Treaty of Fort Stanwix of
1784 gave the Iroquois Confederacy independence; however, the "only
way to put the Six Nations on an economically sound footing was
to obtain "the rights inherent" in that treaty. Less than a week later,
Kellogg, her brother, and the soon-to-be prominent James Deere sent
Everett a letter endorsing his report, condemning the Indian Welfare League, and making an offer to retain his legal services in future
litigation.[16]

The Deere case was brought before the United States District
Court for the Northern District of New York. The litigation was a
test case, a class action suit, on behalf of the Iroquois Confederacy.
Everett and the New York City law firm of Wise, Whitney, and Parker,
Carl Whitney being Everett's nephew, represented James Deere, a
Mohawk, in his ejectment proceedings against the Saint Lawrence
River Power Company, a subsidiary of Alcoa, and seventeen other occu-
pants of this one-mile-square parcel of land. The power company hired
the eminent statesman Charles Evans Hughes to argue the motion.

Hughes soon maintained that the case should be dismissed on technical grounds, claiming there was no federal question involved and consequently the court had no jurisdiction in the matter. The plaintiffs insisted that an 1824 treaty between the Saint Regis (Akwesasne) Mohawk Indians and New York State, which allowed for the sale of the disputed land to the state, was null and void since no single tribe of the Six Nations Confederacy had such authority and since at that time only the federal government and the Six Nations Confederacy could write such agreements.[17] In October 1927, the United States District Court dismissed the Deere case because of what it insisted was the court's lack of jurisdiction in the matter.[18] Everett's death and fruitless later appeals in the Deere case proved fatal to Kellogg's grand design.

The New Deal era was the final death knell of the Kellogg Party. The federal government's work-relief programs increasingly tied the Indian for better or worse to far-off Washington. Instead of a few thousand dollars, as in the 1920s, the federal government poured hundreds of thousands of dollars into Iroquoia. The Kellogg vision of self-help and self-sufficiency expressed in her writings and speeches went out the window along with the rugged individualism views of Herbert Clark Hoover. The community action programs of the New Deal, although not accepted universally, had the blessing of the majority of the Iroquois. Pie-in-the-sky grand designs about reconstructing the ancient league or winning millions of acres back were to mean less to the Iroquois when they had an administration in Washington providing employment and allowing them to revive their arts, their language, and their pride in being Iroquois. By taking care of their immediate needs, the federal government actually contributed to the co-opting of the claims movement.[19] Although Kellogg continued to operate throughout the 1930s, opposing Commissioner Collier's policies and holding fast to her own rehabilitation program, few Iroquois listened. By 1947, she was a broken woman, who had outlived her time in history and dissipated both her fame and the money that had come with it. Kellogg died in obscurity soon after.[20]

Despite her sophistry and her inability to provide both moral stewardship and the total transformation of the Iroquois polity, she dealt with questions of Iroquois treaty rights and sovereignty as well as with other fundamental aspirations, needs, and values of her people. The Kellogg movement was no mere scam nor a fleeting episode in Iroquois history, but a revolution. Jack Campisi has perceptively observed:

Nevertheless, the actions of the Kelloggs encouraged Oneida identity and a sense that the various bands were one people, different in culture, history, and language from the other Indian groups.
The Kelloggs encouraged communication among the Oneida bands
and increased the awareness of their common heritage. And lastly,
the Kelloggs kept active a series of contacts with the state and
national governments relative to the status of the Oneidas. The
Oneidas existed as a problem because they made themselves
one.[21]

Kellogg indeed helped transform the Iroquois into major land-claims
litigants in twentieth-century America.

Even after the Kellogg movement had waned, some Iroquois, especially Oneidas, continued to believe in "the claim" and pushed for
it. Two Oneidas from New York, Mary Cornelius Winder and her sister Delia Cornelius Waterman were instrumental in keeping the
Oneida claim alive. These two powerful women, from their homes
at Prattsburg, New York and from the Onondaga Reservation, constantly badgered the federal government to intervene on the Oneidas'
behalf.

Actually, Mary Winder had pursued the Oneida claim since 1920.
On June 30 of that year, she wrote the Indian Bureau:

> Would you please tell me how much money the Oneida Indians
> have in Washington and when they will get it? New York State
> has never bought the reservations at Fish Creek and Oneida Lake.
> How can we get them back? Can I go there and camp and plant?
> By a treaty they rented those lands but the Oneidas has never seen
> any of the rent yet.[22]

Winder was especially influenced by her father, Wilson Cornelius,
who had been active in this issue since the turn of the century.
Moreover, her inclusion of "Canadian Oneidas" in her claims movement was no accident since her father for years had lived on the
Oneida-on-the-Thames Reserve in Ontario. One of Mary Winder's
daughters later married a leading artist from the Ontario community,
which further contributed to her view that the Oneidas had a common claim.[23]

By the 1940s, the Oneidas residing in New York were a hetero-
geneous people. Since the Onondaga Reservation is the historic Iroquois capital, the closest Indian community to the Oneida homeland,

Delia Cornelius Waterman and Mary Cornelius Winder (Oneidas), Onondaga Indian Reservation, 1949. Photograph courtesy
of Maisie Winder Schenandoah.

and the center of the Longhouse religion, many Oneidas had drifted
there after the loss of most of their reservation lands in the first half
of the nineteenth century. Other Oneidas, some enrolled, others not,
from the Ontario, Wisconsin, and Marble Hill communities married
Onondagas or earlier Oneida arrivals. Although frequently perceived
as outcasts, metaphorically "in the shadows of the Confederacy's council," these Oneidas were, nonetheless, given shelter in symbolic and
real terms under the "Great Tree of the Ancient League." Yet, at times
of crisis at Onondaga, these same Indians, having no rights to land,
were usually the losers. Although some Oneidas were allied, politically or otherwise, to the Grand Council and faithfully participated

in the Longhouse ceremonials at Onondaga, most never felt the reservation was their home.

William Rockwell, a moderate, was the recognized chief spokesman of these Oneidas for a half-century until his death in 1960, but was unable to fulfill the dreams of his followers to return to their homeland. It is important to point out that Rockwell's Oneidas could not even return to their thirty-two acre reservation in Madison County because of threats of white reprisals resulting from the Indian victory in the Boylan case of 1920. Many of the Rockwell-led group had migrated in the 1920s to Rochester, aided in their relocation by the prominent attorney George Decker.[24]

Because the legal activism of the 1920s produced few tangible beneficial results and led to increased intratribal feuding, Rockwell, who had been directly involved in the Boylan decision and who fought all his life to retain the remaining thirty-two-acre reservation, chose an even more conservative course from the early 1930s to his death in 1960. He had little sympathy for "returned Oneidas," those who had come back to central New York from Canada or Wisconsin. In the political vacuum caused by the bitter aftertaste from the Kellogg movement and Rockwell's conservative stewardship of the Oneida Nation, Winder carefully plotted the direction of the Oneida Indian claims movement. Since Rockwell was a man of advanced years by the late 1940s, Winder's strategy was largely to go around his leadership.[25]

Dictating a letter through her daughter Gloria to the Indian superintendent in New York, Winder insisted in April 1943, that the Oneidas were tired of being in a homeless situation, living on the hospitality and/or whims of the Onondagas. Citing the Oneida support of American military action since 1776 and the Treaty at Fort Schuyler which "reserved lands for their [Oneida] posterity forever," Winder requested federal intervention to help her people get back their lands. Incredibly, the New York superintendent, ignoring the historic Boylan case that restored federal recognition to these Indians, replied in May that the Oneidas had long since divided their lands in severalty and left the state. The superintendent concluded that he and the BIA were unable to intervene on the Oneidas' behalf.[26]

The Oneidas were soon encouraged by the passage of the Indian Claims Commission Act of 1946. Until the passage of this act, American Indians could not bring a claim against the United States government without special permission by an act of Congress. The act established the Indian Claims Commission and authorized it to hear and determine claims by Indian tribes, bands, or other identifiable groups of American Indians against the United States:

(1) claims in law or equity arising under the Constitution, laws, treaties of the United States, and Executive orders of the President; (2) all other claims in law or equity, including those sounding in tort, with respect to which the claimant would have been entitled to sue in a court of the United States if the United States was subject to suit; (3) claims which would result if the treaties, contracts, and agreements between the claimant and the United States were revised on the ground of fraud, duress, unconscionable consideration, mutual or unilateral mistake, whether of law or fact, or any other ground cognizable by a court of equity; (4) claims arising from the taking by the United States, whether as a result of a treaty of cession or otherwise, of lands owned or occupied by the claimant without the payment for such lands of compensation agreed to by the claimant; and (5) claims based upon fair and honorable dealings that are not recognized by any existing rule of law or equity.[27]

One historian has observed: "One wonders whether the belated act of reparation was motivated as much by concern for the victims of white action as by the desire to rub out the memory of that action on the part of those making the reparation." He added that like other post-World War II policies the act was motivated in part "by the desire to eliminate the Indian as a separate factor in American society."[28]

Although President Truman was seriously disturbed by the potential economic consequences of the act, fearing it, in his words, as "unloosening a Frankenstein" of claims actions, he was convinced by the Department of the Interior that it would save money in the long run by "streamlining" procedures and would put "many Indian tribes on a self-supporting basis and eliminate the need for further Federal gratuities." At a time when the United States had refused to ratify the United Nations Genocide Convention, the act proved valuable in other ways. Citing "international repercussions" of the act, the secretary of the Interior insisted that it would "be widely viewed as a touchstone of the sincerity of our national professions of fair and honorable dealings toward little nations. In abolishing a racial discrimination affecting resort to the courts, we will strengthen our moral position in the eyes of many other minority peoples."[29]

The passage of the Indian Claims Commission Act was hailed widely throughout Iroquoia, leading the Mohawks to write to President Truman thanking him for promoting and signing the bill.[30] The Oneidas were equally elated and initiated a new flurry of claims activity from 1946 to 1951.[31] Despite these renewed hopes, the Department of the Interior soon identified the Oneida Indians of New York State as not being an identifiable group within the meaning of the Indian Claims Commission Act.[32] Yet, Winder and Waterman persisted in their efforts, especially after the building of a dam at Onondaga in the late 1940s which forced many Oneidas off the reservation. Winder once again petitioned the BIA for help, insisting that her tribe of 350 Oneidas living on the Onondaga Reservation were seeking lands "that N.Y.S. never paid for." Claiming she and her sister, Delia Waterman, had already made two separate appeals, she poignantly described how the Oneidas, having no title to land at Onondaga, were forced off the reservation when a huge dam had been recently constructed on the Onondaga Reservation. She asked whether land claims would be furthered by tribal incorporation under the Indian Reorganization Act. Significantly, she inquired whether her group should join in with the Oneida Band of the Thames (Ontario) in a claims action since "we are not sure if they are still N.Y. Indians or not. Since they have a reservation of their own [sic]."[33]

By 1948, Winder had attempted to bypass Rockwell, the acknowledged Oneida spokesman, requesting that Ross Webster be recognized by the bureau as "chief of the Oneida Indians of New York."[34] Although the Oneidas had rejected the Indian Reorganization Act in a referendum held in 1936, she became increasingly concerned about her group's lack of official federal recognition since New York Indian Superintendent Benge and the bureau insisted that Winder's group had no standing to bring a claims action unless they joined in with the IRA-organized Wisconsin Oneidas. She and Milton Babcock, who she now referred to as president of the Oneida Nation, then hired an attorney to pursue the claims and made a formal alliance with the Oneida Tribe of Wisconsin to file a case before the Indian Claims Commission.[35]

Although it is not clear what authorization she had for her efforts from Rockwell or other prominent Oneidas, Winder attempted to unify the diverse Oneida communities from the 1930s onward. She and her sister had traveled to Wisconsin and addressed the Oneida Tribal Business Committee about the claim as early as 1938. A decade later, after repeated failures to persuade the BIA to aid her group, she hired an attorney and then held an Oneida unity meeting over the claim at Onondaga where thirty-five to forty Indians from Wisconsin, New York, and Canada discussed strategy. Despite the drafting of a charter or constitution of incorporation, New York Superintendent Benge quickly dismissed these legal doings. He ignored the Boylan case once again, suggesting that the Oneidas at Onondaga were not recognized as an IRA government or within the meaning of the Indian Claims Commission Act.[36]

Winder, however, was making some headway in her efforts. On January 19, 1948, she was given an audience in Washington with Acting Commissioner Zimmerman in which they discussed the 1788 New York State treaty at Fort Schuyler with the Oneida Indians. The agreement had provided that one-half-square-mile areas of land be set aside at a distance of every six miles on the North Bank of Oneida Lake and a one-half mile strip on each side of Fish Creek. These lands were to be "reserved for the Oneidas and their posterity" and "for the inhabitants of the said State [New York] to land and encamp on." Despite the treaty, the Oneida told Zimmerman that these lands were sold to private landowners, excluding the Indians from their use. Disturbed by the legal implications of what Winder was showing him, Zimmerman requested more information from the bureau's land division.[37] Two years later, the BIA finally approved the Oneida's attorney contract. They joined with their Wisconsin kin to hire Marvin Chapman of Aaron, Aaron, Schimberg, and Hess, a leading Chicago law firm, who in 1951 filed a case before the Indian Claims Commission.[38]

Through the 1950s, the Oneidas hoped for some quick resolution of the claims. With Winder's death in the mid-1950s, Delia Waterman took over leadership of the claim. She adopted her Mohawk son-in-law, Jacob Thompson, into the Oneidas and entrusted to him the information about the claim the sisters had collected. Thompson, a Syracuse ironworker, was perhaps the individual most responsible for getting the Oneida case heard by the United States Supreme Court in 1974. Although a highly controversial leader, his persistence produced positive results, drawing other Oneidas into his circle. Significantly, in the 1960s, he cemented legal and political alliances with several of these disparate groups, including the Oneidas in Wisconsin, Ontario and the Rockwell faction at Onondaga, then headed by Ray Elm. Although tireless in his pursuit of the claim, his style of keeping information tight-to-the-vest later contributed to the alliance's collapse in 1975.[39]

Thompson frequently testified at the hearings of the New York State Joint Legislative Committee on Indian Affairs. From 1961 onward, he participated at nearly every hearing, visibly keeping the claim alive. On November 17, 1961, he appeared at the hearings held at Tonawanda Indian Community House. Leighton Wade, still the council for the Interdepartmental Committee, ignored the Boylan case and insisted that under "treaties many years ago the lands comprising the then [Oneida] Nation were sold and for practical purposes, the tribal existence then terminated." Thompson, identifying himself as "president of the Oneida Nation" and a resident of Onondaga, quickly challenged Wade's statements: "You said the Oneida lands were sold. I think if you go back you will see there is a suit against the State of New York to have some of the lands brought back to the Oneida Indians." At this same hearing, the presence and remarks of Emily Johnson, a clan mother of another Oneida group, the Marble Hill Road Indians in Oneida County, also questioned Wade's statements.[40]

Thompson continued to exert a role in Interdepartmental Legislative hearings throughout the 1960s. At another hearing in 1963, he firmly advocated Iroquois fishing and hunting rights on and off reservations in New York, insisting that no formal license was necessary since these rights were guaranteed by treaty.[41] Always seeking to assert his adopted people's legal status and land contentions, he sought historical documents and maps at every turn. According to his former attorney, it was this intensity and determination that led Thompson into his office. In 1964, spurred on by the maps, shown him by Professor Robert Rayback of Syracuse University, demarcating the historic Oneida territory, Thompson began to seek out an attorney to take the Oneida case. After one suggested by Rayback indicated that his practice was too limited for this massive undertaking, Thompson was referred to one of the major law firms in central New York, Bond, Schoeneck, and King, whose office was in downtown Syracuse. Soon Thompson and Rayback met with the firm's attorneys. Thompson, "in salesmanship fashion," persuasively argued, employing maps and old documents, that the Oneidas had a legal case to recover land fraudulently taken over time. After long discussions by the firm's attorneys, whose legal staff and clientele owned land in the claims area, the firm accepted the case and assigned it to George Shattuck, Jr. According to Shattuck, "We accepted the case for monetary reasons only. We never came off as do-gooder reformer types."[42]

For the next two years, Shattuck, under Thompson's tutelage, got "his feet wet" about Indian concerns and the land claim itself. He met with tribal elders, including Ray Elm, and spelled out his motives for involvement in the case. He did extensive research, reading the legal briefs of the Boylan, Deere, and Tuscarora cases in order to piece together the Oneidas' position. Importantly, throughout this time of preparation, he had become aware of the long history of the claims movement. In the process, he learned that the Boylan decision was ignored and that the Deere case was argued in the wrong court and on the wrong premise. Upon reading one of the Tuscarora decisions at the appellate court level, Shattuck became convinced of the merits of his case, since the state had clearly admitted questionable title to lands obtained after the passage of the Trade and Intercourse Act of 1793.[43]

In 1965, a major Oneida legal brainstorming session was held at Shattuck's office. Besides Thompson, Oneidas from the Thames, including Longhouse members Irving Chrisjohn and George and Amos Elijah, who spoke only Oneida at the meeting; Oscar Archiquette and Norbert Hill, Sr. recognized tribal voices from Wisconsin; and Ray Elm, chief spokesman of the Oneidas at Onondaga, attended. Despite their divisive history, Longhouse, Episcopal, Catholic, and Baptist Oneidas came together, for this brief moment in history, to unite on behalf of the land claims. At this meeting, despite later insistence to the contrary, four groups of Oneidas agreed that Shattuck should first push for monetary compensation, rent value for two years, on Oneida lands taken illegally by the state, not by individual "owners." They also agreed that all parties in the room would share in any financial settlement. Oneida hopes were further raised when Robert L. Bennett, one of their own tribesmen from Wisconsin and classmate of Norbert Hill, Sr., the Wisconsin Oneida tribal chairman, became Commissioner of Indian Affairs in 1966. Bennett, a longtime BIA employee, encouraged the claim when he reestablished the BIA office in New York and met with Oneidas and Onondagas upon his visit to Syracuse soon after his appointment.[44]

Between 1965 and 1970, Thompson, with Shattuck's encouragement, attempted to set a favorable climate for the case. He sought key political support for the Oneida position. On a state-wide level, he petitioned Governor Rockefeller on behalf of the Oneidas, pledged support for his reelection, and asked him to intercede at the New York State Constitutional Convention to allow the Indians to seek redress in state courts. On June 12, 1967, in a "plea for justice" to the delegates of that Constitutional Convention, Thompson maintained that through the process of the white man's education, the Oneidas no longer were "stone-age" in their technology. They had also learned how to function effectively in an increasingly progressive world. In the process, they realized through their white man's education that they had been duped out of millions of acres of land. Appealing "within the framework of our own American Society and in the spirit of cooperation," Thompson insisted that his goals were twofold: (1) to reestablish a reservation of approximately 10,000 acres; and (2) to set up a capital fund to finance Indian agriculture, education, and industry as well as the "preservation of the enduring vestiges of our ancient culture including practice of its folkways, music, rituals, and arts and

Robert L. Bennett being sworn in at the White House as Commissioner of Indian Affairs by President Lyndon Johnson, April 28, 1966. Also shown are Bennett's family, Secretary of the Interior Stewart Udall, and Lady Bird Johnson. Photograph courtesy of the LBJ Library.

language." Hoping to settle the land dispute amicably by building intersocial understanding as Shattuck had suggested, Thompson urged this so-called "con-con" convention to change the New York State Constitution by passing a simple amendment to allow the Oneida Nation access to New York courts, which at that time was denied to Indian nations.[45]

Thompson failed in his efforts at changing the New York State Constitution after the New York State attorney general's office quickly dismissed the Oneida claim. Julius Sackman of the attorney general's office observed that the claim award for five million acres would be "astronomical," between 6 million and 858 million dollars. Incorrectly citing the legal findings in the Barnhart Island case, he argued that the Trade and Intercourse Acts did "not apply to the state of New York."

Wisconsin Oneida Tribal Chairman Norbert Hill, Sr. and Oneida
elder Ruth Baird present award to Oneida tribal member, Commissioner Robert L. Bennett, 1966, Green Bay, Wisconsin. Photograph courtesy of the Oneida Indian Tribal Museum.

Despite the New York State Attorney General's briefs in 1958 and
the 1959 report of the New York State Interdepartmental Committee
on Indian Affairs, Sackman insisted that the Tuscarora case was "firstly
obiter in character, and secondly, was rendered moot by subsequent
proceedings." Besides, Sackman concluded, the Oneidas have filed an
identical claim in the Indian Claims Commission and should pursue
their case there or obtain authorization for enabling legislation to
pursue the claim from the New York State Legislature.[46]
   Thus, the Oneidas found themselves in a "catch-22" situation.
A state could only be sued with its consent. Yet, the eleventh amendment of the United States Constitution barred suit against a state in

federal courts. Since New York courts had uniformly held that an Indian nation had no standing to sue in New York courts, the Oneidas had no forum in which to present their claims.

Stymied on the state level, Thompson and Shattuck sought to bring the Oneida case, with the aid of Congressman James Hanley of Syracuse, to the attention of President Lyndon Johnson. Writing to the president on January 19, 1968, Thompson asked for an audience to present a memorial to him, coyly suggesting that he sought "only the time it would take you to walk to the door and receive this petition." Subsequently, Thompson presented his petition to Commissioner Bennett at the Interior Department Building with Bennett, Matthew Nimitz, a presidential assistant, James Officer, and Clyde Martz in attendance.[47]

Exhibit III of this petition contained Shattuck's "Memorandum of Law and Fact," which detailed his arguments. In the appeal to President Johnson, Shattuck indicated that as attorney for three bands of Oneidas — New York, Wisconsin, and Ontario — he was presenting the case against New York for taking Oneida lands without fair and adequate compensation. Shattuck then recounted the history of the Oneidas, the Oneida treaties, and Oneida land loss, Oneida court cases, and state investigations of Oneida claims. Most significantly, in five pages of the twenty-five-page plea, Shattuck focused on the Tuscarora decision of 1958. Quoting from the brief of New York State Attorney General Louis Lefkowitz, Shattuck wrote: "Actually, a very large number of agreements were made with the New York Indians extinguishing their titles without the presence of a United States Commissioner." Lefkowitz had claimed that the Trade and Intercourse Act, in this case the one of 1802, was not applicable to any of the thirteen original states since land title was derived from the British crown. SPA attorney Thomas F. Moore, Jr. went even further, admitting the illegality of the state's dealings in Indian land deals:

> Except for the period from 1790 to 1793, New York made a practice of purchasing Indian rights of aboriginal occupancy without the intervention of the Federal Government. . . . While as our memorandum below shows, at pages 27, 49–52, New York purchased some Indian land rights at Federal treaties subsequent to 1793, in most instances when it purchased such rights it did so without Federal intervention. A vast part of the territory within the State was purchased by the State without such intervention. *The present day title to this area depends upon the validity of these purchases.* Invariably when such purchases were challenged the courts have sustained them.[48] (Shattuck's emphasis.)

This admission was further hinted at in the affidavit of Henry Manley who in 1958 had been working on behalf of SPA, leading Shattuck to conclude that the "implications of the *Tuscarora* decision are staggering." Shattuck added that the Oneidas were not challenging the ownership of any persons holding record title to the lands. After all, he concluded, the "people who now occupy the former Reservation should be left peacefully there, but the Oneida Nation should have justice too."[49]

Shattuck then recounted the history of the so-called Oneida–New York State Treaty of 1795, which was the first of a series of similar transactions in which the Oneidas lost a 300,000-acre reservation. To Shattuck, the 1795 agreement was a clear violation of the Indian Trade and Intercourse Act of 1793 since no federal commissioner was present to supervise and carry out the trust responsibility. Shattuck then urged the president to intercede with New York State for a fair monetary settlement of the claim. If that intercession failed, Shattuck urged "the United States to bring an action in the Supreme Court against New York State." Insisting that the Indians were restricted by a "maze of legal technicalities," the petition asked the federal government to "free the Oneidas from the legal bondage imposed on them by the courts of New York." Citing Article II of the Treaty of Fort Stanwix (1784), Article 3 of the Treaty of Fort Harmar (1789), Articles 2 and 7 of the Treaty of Canandaigua (1794), and the Oneida Treaty of 1794, Shattuck insisted that the federal government had a legal obligation to help their former Indian allies in time of need. Citing Justice Black's famous words—"Great nations, like great men, should keep their word"—Shattuck requested that "the United States keep its word to them given by George Washington in three formal treaties."[50]

Six weeks after presenting the petition, Thompson, Ray Elm, and Ruth Burr, officially identifying themselves as president, vice president, and secretary of the Oneida Nation of New York, once again pleaded for justice for the Oneidas under the "Iroquois Treaty of 1794." Reciting the words of George Washington, they criticized the federal government, especially the BIA, for stonewalling their pleas and failing to push the Oneida claim. Importantly, they challenged the position that their only redress was before the Indian Claims Commission. After insisting that the United States had denied liability in that forum too, the Oneidas revealed that their ulterior motives were not simply a monetary settlement: "We wonder also if the United States can abrogate its treaties by payment of money damages." Requesting a personal audience with the president, the Oneidas used traditional Indian-white metaphors to emphasize their point. "The Oneidas are hurt by this treatment as though a father had slapped his son across the face for no reason. We should know better by now! We will continue to keep our promises and we will continue to appeal to the conscience of the United States and New York State, rather than their fears."[51]

When the Department of Justice refused to intervene on behalf of the Oneidas in the fall of 1968, Thompson once again appealed directly to President Johnson: "'To clear the conscience of your peoples past and present, of their injustices and liabilities perpetrated against us, it would be a loyal and fitting act for you, to close your administration with an act of responsibility for the Oneida Indian Nation."[52] The Oneidas continued to lobby at the federal level into 1969 and 1970. They attempted to elicit the aid of the new commissioner of Indian Affairs, Louis Bruce, Jr., a Mohawk-Sioux Indian who had been raised at the Onondaga Reservation and who had longstanding friendships with Oneidas there.[53]

In the climate of increased Iroquois militancy in response to the International Bridge sitdown protest of December 1968, the takeover of Alcatraz in November 1969, the wampum return controversy, and the educational policies of New York State, the Oneidas once again attempted to push their case on the state level in the late fall of 1970. In November, Thompson, Shattuck, Ruth Burr and Robert "Skip" Burr, Jr., and Earl George appeared in downtown Syracuse before a tense special hearing of the New York State Subcommittee on Indian Affairs of the Standing Committee on Governmental Operation headed by Assemblyman Joseph Reilly of Nassau County. In the setting of "Red Power militancy," the Oneidas attempted carefully and moderately to present their case. Reacting to a public television broadcast in which Sackman indicated that the state's attorney general would not impede the Oneidas' efforts to convince the state legislature to pass enabling legislation allowing the Oneidas to sue New York, the Indians requested that Reilly's subcommittee endorse this idea.[54] Shattuck then explained how the Oneidas were systematically dispossessed of their four to six million acre estate by state violations of Section 177 of the Federal Indian Law, namely the Nonintercourse Acts. Although the state recognized the need for a federal commissioner's presence at land negotiations and purchase in 1798, no federal commissioner was present at the 1795 Oneida–New York State "treaty" or at twenty-four of twenty-six "treaties" made after 1798. According to Shattuck, "if you simply dismissed the Oneida argument as a 'clever legal technicality to go back 200 years,' you would ignore these Indians' longstanding pleas for justice." Shattuck then described how the Indians had been locked out from state and federal courts.[55] Without special enabling legislation allowing for the suit, the Indians' would be ignored again. Shattuck argued:

> So the State has done a very great job, they take away the land fraudulently from people who couldn't even sign their full names, then they conveniently make the law that says, 'We are sorry we have got your land, but you are not a person or a corporation or an entity which can bring a lawsuit to get it back, and furthermore the State has sovereign immunity and you can't sue us anyway.' So they were just locked out, they were just locked out, they had no recourse.[56]

Shattuck then insisted that the federal remedy was not satisfactory either since the Oneidas could only bring an action before the Indian Claims Commission against the United States for breach of fiduciary responsibility in allowing the state illegally to take Indian lands. Shattuck also pointed out that an Indian Claims Commission award also did not allow interest on the 175 years of damages which the Oneidas claimed. He later maintained that "if you take the capital from someone and you keep his capital for 175 years during which time you have gotten many benefits from it, we will say the Erie Canal, the railroad tracks, the Thruway, Route 5, Route 20, that maybe in equity you should pay someone a little interest on his capital." The Syracuse attorney then cited *Seneca Nation v. Christie* as a precedent for the legislature's passage of an enabling bill to allow the Indians to sue the state; yet, as Shattuck carefully pointed out, the Senecas were ultimately denied a fair settlement in this 1896 case because the legislature had placed a twenty-year statute of limitations and the event happened sixty years before the suit. He called for real relief, not a token bill that would be overturned by the New York Court of Appeals. He and Thompson concluded by once again reiterating that they did not intend dispossessing individual landowners but sought a fair monetary settlement to repurchase tribal lands.[57]

After a series of meetings with leaders of the Wisconsin Oneida community from 1968 to 1970 and with the failure to convince the federal or state governments of the seriousness of their claim, Shattuck in 1970 filed a test case in federal court.[58] He sued Oneida and Madison counties, challenging the validity of the Oneida–New York State "treaty" of 1795 and seeking trespass damages for a two-year period, 1968 and 1969. By suing the two counties and not New York directly, Shattuck attempted to circumvent the previous federal legal restrictions against such an action.[59] Hence, the case revolved around whether the federal courts had jurisdiction in this matter. In Shattuck's earlier stated metaphor, he was attempting to "unlock the door."

William L. Burke, the attorney for the two counties, supported by the New York State attorney general's office, argued that the federal courts had no jurisdiction in the matter. Burke and Assistant Attorney General Jeremiah Jochnowitz also emphasized the legal theory of laches, namely that the Indians had not brought "timely suit" but had waited 175 years to do so. Subsequently, the United States District Court for the Northern District of New York and the United States Court of Appeals for the Second Circuit dismissed the action, deciding that the Oneidas' complaint had indeed not raised a question under federal law as Burke and Jochnowitz had argued in their first contention.[60]

Oneida hopes, nevertheless, were soon raised when the United States Supreme Court granted a writ of *certiorari* and agreed to hear the case. In his arguments in November 1973 before the high court, Shattuck reiterated the long-held Oneida position that the 1795 state treaty was executed in violation of the Constitution, three federal treaties, and the Indian Nonintercourse Act. Using archeological, historical, and linguistic expert findings, Shattuck insisted that the Oneidas bringing suit were federally recognized successors in interest to the Oneidas of the 1790s and those of the pre-contact period. Bringing in further expert testimony, Shattuck maintained that the Oneidas who signed the 1795 instrument were not the recognized chiefs since the traditional leaders had rejected the state's offer a month earlier. Nowhere on the 1795 "treaty" did these traditional leaders affix their names. Moreover, through thousands of correspondences related to Indian policy in the period, nowhere was a federal commissioner's presence noted at the negotiations.

Shattuck maintained that the doctrine of laches did not apply since the Oneidas were prevented from previous action by poverty, illiteracy, and social barriers, and that the United States departments of the Interior and Justice from 1909 to 1965 failed to carry out the federal-Indian trust relationship by inhibiting the Oneidas from asserting their claims despite yearly letters from Oneidas petitioning for help. The Oneidas were not, as Shattuck observed, complaining of mere technical failures to comply with the letter of the law. In his exhibits, Shattuck clearly showed that federal officials responded by denying the merit of the claims and discouraging legal action; wrongly advised after 1920 that they had no federal tribal status in New York; advised them that Congress would retroactively ratify any illegal land sales even if they won in court; and indicated, even before the jurisdiction bills of 1948 and 1950, that the Oneidas were under state jurisdiction, which precluded any federal action of redress. Since the Indians were also barred from state courts, the Oneidas were in effect denied a legal forum. Thus, Shattuck argued, as their guardian, the United States had a constitutional, treaty, and congressional responsibility to provide the Oneidas with their day in court by allowing them to sue in federal courts.[61]

The Supreme Court rendered its decision on January 21, 1974. In a unanimous decision with eight justices participating, the court sustained the Oneidas' position and remanded the case back to the lower federal courts. In this landmark decision, by holding that the Nonintercourse Act was applicable to the original thirteen states including New York, the Supreme Court opened up the federal courts to the Oneidas as well as to other Indians seeking to get back land in these states. No longer would they be stymied by jurisdictional barriers placed in their path. According to Justice Byron White's written opinion of the court: "The rudimentary propositions that Indian title is a matter of federal law and can be extinguished only with federal consent apply in all of the States, including the original 13." White added that controversy arises under the laws of the United States sufficient to invoke the jurisdiction of federal courts and reversed the earlier federal court determinations, remanding the case for further proceedings to the federal District Court for the Northern District of New York.[62]

For the past decade since the United States Supreme Court ruling of 1974, the Oneidas have squabbled amongst themselves and with other Iroquois about the direction of the claim. Separate feuding groups have brought actions and counteractions that have drained energies and delayed a final settlement of any legal doings. They have been divided over who should be parties to the claim, who should lead the action, what is the role of the Iroquois Confederacy council in the suit, whether land or money or both are the goals, and even who are the rightful heirs in interest to the thirty-two acres of remaining tribal lands in New York. Although the door was unlocked by Shattuck in 1974 after over a half-century of lobbying efforts by three Oneida women and a Mohawk ironworker from Syracuse, the Oneidas still await their new day. Sadly, although they still are attempting to persuade the "Great White Father," they now have to convince each other that they have a mutual interest in the claim's conclusion.[63]

Despite these continuing divisions, the Oneidas, on March 4, 1985, won another legal battle in the United States Supreme Court.

In a five-to-four decision, in a test case involving fewer than 900 acres of the extensive Oneida tribal land claim, the court held that Oneida and Madison counties were liable for damages—fair rental value for two years, 1968 and 1969—for unlawful seizure of Indian ancestral lands. Associate Justice Lewis F. Powell, Jr. who wrote the majority opinion, insisted that the Indians' common law right to sue is firmly established and that Congress did not intend to impose a deadline on the filing of such suits. Since the counties had firmly maintained that the Indians had not made a timely effort to sue and thus had forfeited their legal rights, the decision nullified the major non-Indian argument and opened the door for further Oneida litigation involving their lost lands. The court also suggested that, because of the tremendous economic implications of the case, Congress should settle the New York Indian claims as it had done in Connecticut, Maine, and Rhode Island.[64]

11

The Iroquois on the Road
to Wounded Knee, 1958–73

The Six Nations Iroquois Confederacy stands in support of our
brothers at Wounded Knee. . . . The people at Wounded Knee are
making a statement. The question is not what damage or destruction of property has occurred, but why it becomes necessary for
our people to have to resort to such extremes to gain some recognition of our desperate situation.

The Six Nations Iroquois Confederacy
Resolution of March 9, 1973

Contemporary Iroquois political activism did not stem merely from
Indian battles over jurisdiction, termination legislation, or significant
loss of their homelands after World War II. Nor did Red Power just
suddenly appear in the late 1960s as another manifestation of domestic protest in this period of general discontent in American society.
According to Vine Deloria, Jr., the noted Standing Rock Sioux political theorist and professor of political science at the University of Arizona, instead of understanding "the protests [of the late 1960s and early
1970s] as a continuing struggle of Indians, the media characterized
them as a new development thereby missing the entire meaning of
the protest."[1]

From the 1920s onward, the Indian Defense League of America
(IDLA), organized by Clinton Rickard, David Hill, and Sophie Martin, had protested the lack of recognition of Indian treaty rights by
the Canadian and United States governments. The repeated refusal
to recognize the free and unrestricted passage of Indians across the
Canadian–United States border under the provisions of the Jay Treaty
and the Treaty of Ghent led Indians to protest. Many IDLA members
were jailed, having been arrested in demonstrations or for refusing to

pay customs duties. Although these Indians were not exclusively Long-house followers and operated quite independently of any central body of the Iroquois, their courageous efforts through passive resistance-style protest and annual Jay Treaty renewal ceremonies at Niagara Falls reaffirmed the separate rights and identity of Indians as well as the symbols of Iroquois existence.[2]

It was no coincidence that the issue of free and unrestricted passage across the international boundary promoted by the IDLA became one of the first major battlefields of Iroquois Red Power. The International Bridge protest by Mohawks on Cornwall Island in December 1968 was a direct outgrowth of the earlier consciousness-raising protests of the IDLA in the 1920s. Ernest Benedict, one of the organizers of the 1968 protest, had been active in the IDLA since the 1940s, as had his mentor, confidante, and relative, Ray Fadden, the director of the Six Nations Indian Museum of Onchiota, New York. The IDLA had chapters in each of the Iroquois reserves in Ontario, Québec, and New York, effectively tying these communities together. This network provided a base of operations for other Iroquois political and cultural activities.[3]

The Iroquois power movement of the 1960s and 1970s drew from the symbols and style of earlier Indian protests and consciously attempted ties to actions of earlier Iroquois folk heroes. The words of Deskaheh, the Oneida-Cayuga chief from the Six Nations Reserve, were constantly raised by the new Iroquois of the 1960s. Deskaheh had traveled on an Iroquois Confederacy-issued passport to Europe in the early 1920s as a delegate of the traditionalists at Six Nations Reserve to protest Canadian Indian policies. Accompanied by George P. Decker, the Rochester attorney for the Six Nations, Deskaheh tried to bring the Indian position before the British Secretary of State of the Colonial Office, King George V, and the League of Nations in Geneva. In these appeals, which proved fruitless except in their deeper meaning to the Iroquois themselves, Deskaheh insisted that the Iroquois Confederacy had never relinquished sovereignty, citing as support for his position the historic alliance known as the Covenant Chain established in the colonial period between the English and Indians, and treaties and land patents made between the British crown and the Iroquois after the American Revolution.

The enduring legacy of Deskaheh was not in what he did, but in the way he attempted to change non-Indians' policy. His words, metaphors, and tactics are still emulated by Iroquois leadership in their determined effort to conserve and protect their existence. Iroquois delegates of the league in 1977 and after have retraced Deskaheh's path to Geneva, Switzerland. Under Iroquois-issued passports, they have appealed to the United Nations on behalf of all native peoples or have taken part in international convocations such as the Russell Tribunal in their activist determination to publicize their grievances against both the United States and Canadian governments.[4]

Iroquois activism was also apparent during the interwar years in two other distinct areas. Minnie Kellogg's activities from 1911 to 1930, although largely directed at recovering tribal territory through land-claims suits, brought Iroquois into contact with other Indian peoples and their grievances. Kellogg championed the rights of traditional people, castigated the BIA, and sought its abolition, and demanded better education, economic opportunities, and health care for Indian peoples. Kellogg, as well as other prominent Iroquois of the period, was active in the Society of American Indians, both as founder and later critic of the organization. This Iroquois involvement in Indian nationalist organizations continued long after the Kellogg movement waned.[5]

In the 1930s, Iroquois Indians, especially those from western New York, were among the leaders against the Indian New Deal and the Indian Reorganization Act. Senecas such as Alice Lee Jemison and Tuscaroras such as Clinton Rickard objected to outside bureau involvement in Indian political systems and the increased regulation of Indian life which they believed would result from New Deal legislation. They opposed uniform legislation arguing that such an approach did not fit the individual and diverse needs of American Indians. For these reasons and because of the strong Iroquois sense of sovereignty conditioned by their beliefs in the sanctity of three federal treaties — Fort Stanwix (1784), Jay (1794), and Canandaigua (1794) — Iroquois such as Jemison took strong activist stands, testified repeatedly on Capitol Hill, and helped organize and coordinate the militant political activities of the American Indian Federation.[6]

Iroquois activism of the 1940s and 1950s was largely reflected in Indian protests against the Selective Service Act of 1940, jurisdictional changes, the attempt to abrogate federal-Indian treaties, and the construction of the Kinzua Dam, the Saint Lawrence Seaway, and the "Tuscarora reservoir." Moreover, Indian policies in Canada from 1959 to 1970 also contributed to increased Iroquois activist stands and reinforced the Iroquois' already existing suspicions about the motives of policy makers in both Canada and the United States. In March 1959, an Iroquois traditionalist revolt occurred at the Six Nations Reserve in Ontario. In that upheaval, Indians, largely Onondaga Longhouse people, seized the council house at Ohsweken, the seat of the Indian elected system imposed by the Canadian government in 1924; these Indians then declared themselves to be both the sole ruling body on the reserve and independent of Ontario and Ottawa authorities. The uprising ended when fifty Royal Canadian Mounted Police raided the Ohsweken council house and restored the Canadian-recognized elected system. A similar revolt, leading to an "Iroquois Declaration of Independence" as well as to the formation of the Association of Iroquois and Allied Indians, occurred in 1969–70 after the Trudeau government in Canada announced its "White Paper."[7]

The Trudeau White Paper's new policy, which was totally rejected by Indians and subsequently withdrawn, called for the achievement of Indian "equality" or "non-discrimination" by terminating the special legislation and bureaucracy of Indian administration in Canada and transferring to the provinces the responsibility for administering services to Indians. The Indian affairs bureaucracy, the Department of Indian Affairs and Northern Development, would be dismantled within five years except for trusteeship functions for Indian lands. After this period, Indians would receive the same services from the same sources as other Canadians. The noted Canadian anthropologist Sally Weaver has written: "By implication, the result of the policy would see Indians with 'Indian problems' become provincial citizens with regular 'citizens'' problems."[8]

The Canadian White Paper was "an abrupt departure from the traditional practice of dealing with Indians, even though the implicit long-range goal of terminating the special treatment of Indians had been a part of governmental policies since the 1830s." At a time when much attention was devoted to the failure of the United States policy of termination and its disastrous effects on certain Indian communities, the Canadian version seemed incongruous to the realities of Indian life in North America. Consequently, Indians, including the Iroquois, "responded to the policy with a resounding nationalism unparalleled in Canadian history, contributing to the founding and growth of native organizations in Canada."[9] Importantly, *Akwesasne Notes* devoted much of its press coverage after June 1969 to policies emanating from Ottawa and the negative reaction of native peoples to the White Paper. Moreover, Mohawks, such as Ernest Benedict, working through the National Indian Brotherhood, helped to lead the fight against the Trudeau government's version of termination.[10]

In the United States, the American Indian Chicago Conference of June 13–20, 1961, was a crossroads in the development of Iroquois involvement in Red Power. At least 420 Indians from sixty-seven tribes attended the historic sessions organized by anthropologists Sol Tax and Nancy Lurie at the University of Chicago. They voiced their opinions about and desires on a number of aspects of contemporary Indian affairs. The convocation drafted the Declaration of Indian Purpose which asked for a reversal of the government's termination policy, for increased educational programs and better health care delivery systems, and for the abolition of ten BIA area offices. The declaration concluded: "What we ask of America is not charity, not paternalism, even when benevolent. We ask only that the nature of our situation be recognized and made the basis of policy and action."[11] Although the conference passed a plank urging President Kennedy to reappraise his stand in support of the construction of the Kinzua Dam, Iroquois traditionalists from New York reservations found much of the proceedings irrelevant to their needs and their beliefs; nevertheless, their critical voices were not completely silenced.

At this meeting and in the events of the 1960s and 1970s, the Iroquois played an instrumental role in the emergence of Indian activism. William Rickard is a case in point. Although far different in background, substance, and tone from other Indian activists of the period,[12] Rickard was representative of sovereignty-minded Iroquois and a harbinger of future political actions. From the SPA protests of 1958 onward, Rickard helped shape a new direction in the Iroquois polity. Moreover, his contacts and friendships with Indian traditionalists in North America, especially Hopi Thomas Banyacya, cemented an important alliance between the Iroquois Longhouse and other Indian communities that was to prove significant in the future.

In mid-January 1961, Rickard became aware of the major Indian convocation to be held in Chicago in June. On January 26, Tax extended an invitation to him, explaining the goals and agenda of the meeting. Tax insisted that instead "of having 'experts' plan for communities of people, we have learned that people have to plan for themselves." He continued by indicating that any "plan for American Indians is a bad plan if the Indians who have to live with it do not understand it or do not want it," adding that improvement could not take place "unless the Indian point of view is fully expressed and honored." Tax, a founder of the subdiscipline of action anthropology in his applied work among the Fox in Iowa, assured Rickard that he was the coordinator, not the czar of the meetings, and that he was attempting to bring all Indian viewpoints together. Yet he conceded to Rickard that he had limited knowledge of the diversity of positions: "But who are 'all Indians' and how can such a national discussion be carried through?" Tax then appointed Rickard to the planning committee of "12 or 15 Indian leaders from all over the United States" to

Eastern Regional Meeting of the American Indian Chicago Conference, April 1961, Haverford College. Among those shown are Clinton and William Rickard, Tall Oak; Mimi Hines; David Hill; Louis Mofsie; Earl Mills; and Theodore Hetzel. Photograph courtesy of National Anthropological Archives, Smithsonian Institution.

meet with him at the University of Chicago for four days beginning the tenth of February.[13] Rickard, as representative of the IDLA and as a prominent Iroquois from the days of the SPA protest, was subsequently chosen as a member of the Indian steering committee of the planned Chicago conference and chairman of the eastern regional meeting at Haverford College leading up to the major convocation in Chicago. Rickard suggested prominent Iroquois and other Indian leaders to be invited and made his traditionalist presence felt from the beginning.[14]

From the inception of his involvement in the organizing of the conference, William was at odds with many of the sentiments expressed by other Indian representatives. Viewing the process as largely dominated by the National Congress of American Indians, which he as well as many Iroquois in New York considered too conservative and too non-traditional, Rickard was one of the stalwarts willing to speak his mind about the BIA and Congress, as well as about issues related to sovereignty.[15] After the February planning session, Rickard wrote: "I was not at all satisfied the way the Chicago meeting was conducted by the National Congress of American Indians, if their plan is to be followed, the venture is doomed to failure. They talk of a 'new frontier' but it is the same old muddle that has got our Indian people in such a deplorable state." In typical Iroquois fashion, he added that his aim was to "initiate the True [sic] course for our Indian people at Haverford" and obviously later at Chicago.[16] As a result he suggested that more of an effort be made to broaden the representation. He recommended that invitations be sent to Indians with non-federally recognized status, representatives of traditionalist perspectives such as Iroquois *Tadodaho* George A. Thomas, and other "non-NCAI types."[17]

At the regional meeting at Haverford College preparing for the eventual Chicago conclave, he served as chairman, working with Haverford engineering professor and Indian rights proponent, Theodore Hetzel. At this meeting, held in April, William expressed his concern that Indian sovereignty was being eroded by such actions as those by SPA. After discussing his spiritual reawakening caused in part by the powerful effect of his recent visit to the traditional people of the Hopi Nation, Rickard insisted: "Here [New York State] they are even talking about building bomb shelters for the survivors [of a nuclear holocaust]. I suggest that Indian ways are right — they are right because they are natural ways."[18] As a result of Rickard's influence, the Haverford meeting included federally recognized, non-recognized, reservation, and urban Indians. Besides Rickard, his father William, and other Iroquois, the registration list included Louis Mofsie and Mimi Hines, leaders in the New York City Indian community; Tall Oak, a future leader of the Red Power movement among the Narragansetts of Rhode Island, as well as prominent leaders of the Mashpee, Powhatan, and Schaghticoke tribes. Led by the Rickards, they spent three days talking about Indian nationhood, sovereignty, and common problems and grievances.[19]

In the months that followed, Rickard became increasingly alarmed by the emphasis on United States citizenship. Since many eastern Iroquois purposefully do not vote in state and national elections because of their concerns for maintaining tribal sovereignty and citizenship, Rickard strongly objected to the circulation of a pamphlet, "A Program for Indian Citizens," prepared by the Commission on the Rights, Liberties and Responsibilities of the American Indian and circulated by the NCAI. Nowhere in the planning discussions for the Chicago convocation was the traditionalist view expressed, namely that Indians were citizens of their individual Indian nations. Rickard, objecting, pointed out to Tax in typical Iroquois fashion: "As you well know, you cannot be a citizen of one and a national of another at the same time."[20] Seeing too little emphasis on Indian treaty rights and sovereignty at the approaching Chicago meeting, Rickard, as early as February, had observed: "My only hope now is that I can warn the Six Nations Confederacy up to act, as I do believe it is to be a good opportunity to exert themselves and *take their rightful place* in the affairs of our Indian people. If they do not, then the NCAI will continue to assume leadership and then it is too bad as it will be the case of the blind leading the blind."[21] In the context of the Iroquois traditional world view, Rickard saw himself and his people as bringing truth to Indian America. The Iroquois, in other words, were not just the symbolic eagle on the great pine tree screaming its warning to the people; they now had an activist responsibility to save the Indians from themselves by bringing their Great Binding Law into national convocations of native peoples.

Tax, an open-minded and well-meaning man well liked by the Indians, was at first startled by Rickard's points. Later, he reflected on Rickard's statements, concluding that the Tuscarora's position was logical and worthy of further discussion and clarification at the Chicago meeting:

> I am overwhelmed by some of the perplexing legal questions with which many Indian groups are attempting to deal. Such things as complicated problems of land rights, taxation, etc. I expected. But it comes as a shock to me to find some Indians who "reject" their status as citizens and who insist that the 1924 act which granted them citizenship was done quite without their consent. After some reflection, I must concede they may have a point! They feel that being "citizens" violates, in some ways, being Indian. This, of course, I don't agree with, but I do see how much the question of Indian citizenship and its derivation needs clarification.[22]

When the conference convened in mid-June 1961, Rickard quickly found the meeting unacceptable. The sessions were largely conducted by D'Arcy McNickle, one of the chairmen of the conference, and Clarence Wesley, president of the National Congress of American Indians, as well as by other NCAI officers. Even the format of the meeting rubbed Rickard and his supporters the wrong way. In untraditional

fashion, delegates restricted debate and limited the allocation of discussion time to five minutes per participant.[23]

During the conference, Rickard and six other Indians were interviewed on television. Seizing the opportunity, the Tuscarora spoke
longer than the other participants. Rickard, in traditionalist fashion,
insisted that the Indians of today had much to contribute to the American people: "If others live like the North American Indian, world peace
would be assured." If Americans gave thanks to the Creator more often
than just at Thanksgiving, as Indians did, and did not "base his whole
existence on a monetary system which demands constant competi-
tion with his fellow man," they would be better off. Then, unbeknownst to his fellow panelists and probably to their embarrassment,
Rickard attacked the Indian Citizenship Act of 1924 as a device "to
commit legalized robbery of millions of acres of our land and natural
resources" and as an act not recognized by the Iroquois Confederacy.[24]

Throughout the proceedings of the week-long meeting, Rickard
frequently raised objections. Rickard caused a commotion on the floor
of the convocation when, after hearing McNickle read the full text
of the significant "Declaration of Indian Purpose," the Tuscarora
pointed out that some Indians did not come to an American Indian
conference to be told that "ALL INDIANS ARE U.S. CITIZENS."
Rickard explained once again that Iroquois traditionalist views did
not recognize the 1924 Indian citizenship act and that there was
nothing wrong with the requirements before 1924 when an Indian
had to qualify, be educated, and become a citizen of his own free will
and accord. Moreover, he was also extremely annoyed that representatives of eastern Indian groups, some of whom were from tribes that
were not recognized by the BIA, were permitted to speak and serve
on various committees and discussion groups only after other Indians
spoke or only as a token courtesy. It is significant to note that Rickard
by 1961 headed a small organization entitled Long House League of
North America which included Delaware Indians from New Jersey,
Powhatans from Virginia, Wampanoags from Massachusetts, as well
as Indians from federally-recognized tribes throughout the East and
West who were committed to traditionalist values.[25]

Rickard concluded by blaming the NCAI, that "is influenced
mainly by white politicians and lobbyists and that . . . [has] not worked
for the best interests of the Indians," "Indian Bureau politicians," and
misguided academics, diplomatically excluding his hosts Tax and
Lurie. Yet the Tuscarora activist insisted, in Iroquois metaphorical
style, that the voice of eastern Indians, who are "supposedly assimilated, terminated or relocated and are not federally recognized" had,

despite efforts to silence it, been heard. They had questioned the dangerous parts of various proposals, "symbolically screaming a warning to other Nations and Tribes of Indians of approaching danger as is the duty of the eagle atop the Iroquois tree of peace." No longer, according to Rickard, could the NCAI ignore the existence of Indian groups and Indian organizations east of the Mississippi.[26] In the end, as a result of Rickard's objections, a few Indians began walking out of the Chicago proceedings. Some of the younger Indians in attendance, including Rickard's sister Karen, who were moved by the debate, soon founded the National Indian Youth Council in August 1961.[27] Red Power had now been born, stemming from many diverse elements in the Indian world, including the emergence of an Iroquois traditionalist revival movement led by a Tuscarora Indian.[28]

Rickard, a budding leader of this revival, continued his campaign against the NCAI and the bureau through 1962 and 1963. He visited the North Carolina Haliwas and other federally unacknowledged groups at this time, encouraging them in their pursuit of outside recognition. Nevertheless, Rickard's death in 1964 did incalculable damage to the growing eastern pan-Indian movement.[29]

Some of Rickard's work in these efforts was assumed by others, among them Alfred Gagne. A quiet, unassuming man of French-Canadian-Mohawk-Montagnais ancestry, Gagne had been a friend of William's father, Chief Clinton Rickard, and had been active in promoting Indian causes since the mid 1930s. From his home in Johnstown, Pennsylvania, Gagne took over much of Rickard's unity work. Through his organization, the League of Nations Pan-American Indians, which was devoted to protecting the civil and treaty rights of all native peoples in the Americas, Gagne encouraged the growing calls for Indian unity. Working with Iroquois traditionalists such as Tonawanda Seneca chief Beeman Logan, Gagne sponsored grievance meetings on Iroquois reservations and petitioned Congress and the president on behalf of these same Indians. This unity movement soon broadened with the inclusion of Onondaga traditionalists Leon Shenandoah and Irving Powless, Sr., Hopi traditionalist Thomas Banyacya, —Rickard's old friend—as well as Mohawks, Shoshones, and Senecas. By the mid-1960s, Mad Bear Anderson, seeing the media potential of the emerging unity movement, joined what soon became known as the North American Indian Unity Caravan. Despite the media's and politicians' focus on Mad Bear throughout the mid- and late 1960s as "chief" of this movement, Gagne and especially Chief Logan were the leaders of this emerging force in Indian circles.

By 1967 the caravan met with federal officials at the White House,

Chief Beeman Logan (Tonawanda Seneca), August 1969. Courtesy of Dr. Theodore Hetzel.

urging the Johnson administration to end termination efforts, especially those directed at the Seneca Nation of Indians, and asked for
the convening of a special White House conference on Indian affairs
to focus on better federal services to Indians and the infringement
of states, such as New York, on the federal-Indian treaty relationship.
Although the Indians failed to see President Johnson, they did present their grievances and a cassette tape both at the White House and
at the Interior Building to presidential advisors. Soon after, the caravan, led by Chief Logan, left Tonawanda Reservation in New York on
a cross-country effort to unify traditionalist Indians with a scheduled
powwow at Hoopa Valley.[30] In 1968, Gagne and Chief Logan urged Iroquois leaders to host an international convocation dealing with the
concerns of indigenous peoples throughout the Americas. As a result
of the Mohawks' International Bridge crisis on Cornwall Island in
December and the resulting strong reverberations in Indian communities throughout the United States and Canada, the Six Nations' Confederacy Council at Onondaga, under the leadership of new Iroquois
Tadodaho Leon Shenandoah, who had earlier been involved in this
unity movement, agreed to this convocation. Shenandoah, in describing his hopes for the Indian convocation, insisted it was not a powwow of twenty to one-hundred nations but one "to discuss plans for
uniting all one people for action." He expressed with typical Iroquois
pride that his people had their "own constitution, which the other
Indian nations don't have" and that the Iroquois must show others
the way. He added that he hoped other Indians "may come into the
Confederacy."[31]

The meetings, which were held in the summer of 1969, talked
about Indian consensus for preserving traditions and traditional values, discriminatory treatment of Indians, the maintenance of tribal
sovereignty, homelands, and treaty rights, as well as the immediate
Mohawk crisis with Canadian officials about the international boundary. Quite significantly, the over one hundred Indians from fifty-six
tribes who came to the meetings first met at Tonawanda, then went
to Onondaga, and finally ended up at Akwesasne before leaving for
a meeting near Québec City. In traditional symbolic form, the Indian
delegates entered the western door of the Iroquois Longhouse by first
meeting at Tonawanda, then followed the Iroquois path to Onondaga,
and left the Iroquois League in Mohawk country at the Confederacy's
eastern door.[32] Oscar Archiquette, the noted Wisconsin Oneida, who
attended these unity meetings, later described them in a 1970 interview with historian Robert W. Venables:

In 1969 I visited the Seneca Indian Reservation where there was a unity meeting of various tribes of Indians of the United States and Canada. . . . At this meeting Loretta Ellis and I witnessed the first Thanksgiving service in our time. White men were not permitted on the grounds. The ceremony started about 1 p.m. We formed a large circle by joining hands; young and old took part. The reason for joining hands is to make us into one heart and mind and we ask He who holds the Blue Sky to forgive us, in silence.

Then the speaker, a Seneca [Beeman Logan] who was standing in the center of our circle started talking in Indian language, thanking God for everything. There was a fire about a foot in diameter near the speaker. After about an hour, then I could understand when he said in Seneca, "Indian tobacco." He reached into a large paper bag and came up with a big handful of Indian tobacco and he spread it over the fire. Then he continued talking. So this is the way my people send their message of thanksgiving to God. . . .

This service lasted till 5 p.m. Then we had supper. I do not know who paid for it, but we ate. After supper was the powwow. And talk about Indian dancing, the best dancers I ever saw, and the Seneca Indian dancers I thought were the greatest.

I joined the original Five Nations religion, but at this meeting there were Indians from Canada, Oklahoma, Arizona, California, and South America.[32]

Archiquette, recalling the fiasco of the Kellogg traditional revival and claims movement of the 1920s, had only praise for the new unity effort. "I could not see any harm in joining my people's religion. We did not sign anything. We were not asked to donate or give money."[33]

Unlike his predecessor as *Tadodaho*, George A. Thomas, who had set a non-political inwardly religious tone for the Onondaga Longhouse in his decade of spiritual leadership, Shenandoah, almost from the beginning, tied his religious faith to the increasingly activist world of Indian politics. Now the metaphors of the Tree of Great Peace and the Great Binding Law were going to be used to sanction and legitimize a new political activism.[34] Between 1969 and 1973, the Onondagas took over much of the leadership, direction, and strategy of the unity caravan movement. Through the organizing and rhetorical talents of Lloyd Elm, Oren Lyons, Lee Lyons, and Irving Powless, Jr., all political activists under the age of forty, the Onondagas took the offensive in the Iroquois world.

Making use of their position as the capital of the historic Iroquois Confederacy, the Onondagas drew upon religious and cultural symbols to add legitimacy to their new activism. It was no coincidence that the new *Tadodaho*'s first formal protest was over the custody of several sacred wampum belts which are housed at the New York State Museum in Albany. Just prior to Thomas's death in 1968, he had also initiated the call to return the belts and had admitted that "it was wrong for our grandfathers to give away the wampum. The wampum tells of old, old agreements and passes on the thoughts of our grandfathers. We would like to see them. Our people want to touch them."[35] The "great wampum war," as it has been dubbed by one prominent anthropologist, still rages and has drastically affected the relationship of the Iroquois with the academic community and the New York State Museum.[36]

Wampum is a species of white and purple beads, from the plentiful whelk and the somewhat rarer quahog clam, drilled through from opposite ends with steel awls and strung into strings or woven into belts in geometric designs. Today, twenty-five of these belts are housed in the New York State Museum. The Iroquois did not invent wampum, since its source was out of these Indians' territory and its greatest historic supply was concentrated around Gardiner's Island and Oyster Bay, Long Island, and at Narragansett Bay in New England. Iroquois making of wampum appears to date from the late 1620s; nevertheless, the Iroquois helped endow the belts with meaning and employed "them in all ritually sanctioned transactions for which wampum belts were affidavits. It was they who taught the colonial governors the protocol of treaty making, and as these activities increased so did the demand for wampum." The ritual symbolism and protocol employed by the Iroquois in using the belts was much older than the belts themselves, and largely "derived from the Iroquois paradigm of condolence, a system that every colonial officer" doing business with them had to learn, especially by the middle decades of the eighteenth century, the apogee of British-Iroquois treaty-making.[37]

The Onondagas have argued their case for the repatriation of wampum in legislative hearings, in the media, and in numerous protest demonstrations. Stressing their traditional role as Iroquois wampum keepers, although other Iroquois nations held their own wampum, the Onondagas insisted upon the religious necessity of restoring the belts. The academic and museum community, although hardly united on the issue of return, insisted that there were few, if any, Iroquois who could read the wampum; focused on the special needs for preservation that only the museum could provide; pointed out that the

Chief Oren Lyons (Onondaga), May 1980. Courtesy of Dr. Theodore Hetzel.

Onondaga Council of Chiefs itself had agreed in 1898 at a meeting in Albany to allow the University of the State of New York, namely the State Museum, to hold the wampum for safekeeping; and stressed the legality of the contractual transfers of the belts to the museum as well as the New York State law of 1909 that validated the institution's role as custodians of the wampum. They also maintained that the wampum was not just a part of the Indians' cultural and religious life but part of the history of New York as a whole, and that returning the belts would establish a dangerous precedent for other groups trying to reclaim cultural and religious treasures.[38]

In the Onondagas' eyes, undergoing as they were a new activist and religious awakening, the belts were seen as a way to reconsecrate and restore their ancient role in the League of the Iroquois as keepers of the wampum and capital of the Confederacy. Vine Deloria, Jr. has pointed out the wampum controversy was part of a larger struggle involving not just the return of belts, but questions of treaty rights and sovereignty and even the return of part of the Iroquois homeland.[39] After all, as one Onondaga chief observed: "How could New York State pass a law making itself wampum keepers when it did not have jurisdiction to do so."[40] Thus, the belts' return is seen by Indians today as part of the larger issues involving jurisdiction, tribal sovereignty, and the nature of the federal-Indian relationship. Deloria, for one, has concluded that the Onondagas, in effect, were fighting, as he claimed, to "complete the reintegration of their League on its traditional basis."[41] For the Onondagas, the final insult was the Pisani bill, passed in 1971, which allowed the Indians to have possession of five of the belts only after a suitable museum for storage and security of the wampum was built at Onondaga. Because no museum was forthcoming and because the Onondagas disagreed with this caveat, the wampum war still rages.[42]

Wampum was only one of three controversies that has helped to shape the renewed Onondaga leadership role in the Iroquois polity. A second conflict centered on Onondaga community influence and control of Indian education in the off-reservation Lafayette Central Schools, to which Indian children were bussed. Led by Lloyd Elm, at that time a science teacher in the school system, and modeled to some degree on similar Mohawk protests at Saint Regis (Akwesasne) in 1969, the Onondagas held their children out of school in 1971 to call attention to their educational concerns. The Onondagas were reacting to the extremely high drop-out rates among Indian students, the lack of cultural enrichment programs including language instruction, and their limited voice in school district policy. Seeing the decline in

knowledge of the Iroquois ways by the younger generation and fear-
ful of the future of their Longhouse religion, they proposed extending
their own community school through the twelfth grade.[43]

The boycott led New York State Education Department officials
to negotiate at the Onondaga Longhouse. Although the boycott did
not lead to the creation of an expanded school system on the reservation, the existing Onondaga elementary school was expanded to the
seventh grade and more awareness of Onondaga cultural concerns became evident in the Lafayette School District. Furthermore, as a result
of the boycotts at Akwesasne and Onondaga, a new state philosophy
on Indian education emerged. A committee, which included Anna
Lewis and later Philip Tarbell, two Iroquois employees of the New
York State Department of Education, drafted a proposal that, although
not altogether accepted, helped shape this new philosophy.[44] By 1975,
the New York State Board of Regents, in a position paper, called for
an end to state educational assumptions that Indians "desired to
become assimilated into the dominant American society, while for-
saking their tribal heritages." In a major policy shift, the regents, admitting mistakes of past federal and state Indian policies, added that
they "now recognize that these people prefer to retain their specific
tribal cultural identities and life styles [sic] and that they wish to exercise the prerogatives of adopting only those components of the dominant American culture that meet their needs."[45]

The Onondagas, during this same period, did battle in a third
area when the New York State Department of Transporation decided
it needed to widen Interstate 81 south of Onondaga Reservation lands
near Nedrow in order to provide an acceleration lane and improve
highway safety. In 1952, the Onondagas had granted the state an easement of over eighty-nine acres of their land for 31,500 dollars. The
Onondagas argued that the easement agreement specified only repairs
and improvements, not additions, and that in any case the 1952 agreement with the state was illegal since it was not approved in advance
by the federal government. Thus, in August 1971, about one hundred
Indians, mostly Onondagas but including Oneidas, Mohawks, and Tuscaroras, went to the road site and sat down to protest the construction project. From mid-August through the end of October, tension
built. By early September over two hundred Indians were on the highway to make sure the construction was not resumed, and the situation appeared to be a stalemate.

Governor Nelson Rockefeller met with the Council of Chiefs
in late October to resolve differences, and a week later, a six-point agreement was reached. The state agreed to abandon plans for the construc-

tion of an acceleration lane on Indian lands, to drop charges against Indians arrested, and to consult with the Council of Chiefs at all stages of the highway improvement project. In return, the Onondagas consented to allow the resumption of construction in order to provide a six-and-one-half-foot wide highway shoulder, not a lane, with a three-foot wide gravel slope. Once again, the negotiations took place in the Onondaga Longhouse with an agreement signed by Shenandoah and state officials on October 30, 1971.[46]

Another major component of this new Iroquois power movement was to evolve at Saint Regis (Akwesasne). In the mid-1960s, Jerry Gambill (Rarihokwats), a young non-Indian employed by the Canadian Department of Indian Affairs (DIA) as a community development worker, came to the Mohawk reserve. Gambill, who had been influenced by Arthur Morgan's utopian writings about community, quickly became involved in learning Mohawk history, mores, and traditional religious beliefs. He soon learned about earlier efforts by Ray Fadden and his Akwesasne Mohawk Counsellor Organization to preserve and revive Iroquois lifeways. Along with Ernest Benedict, who had been profoundly influenced by Fadden's work, Gambill contemplated the possibility of resurrecting similar programs. Through Benedict and Alec Gray, he was introduced to the Longhouse religion and was even taken by Gray to the Onondaga Longhouse. Because of the increased friction between him and Canadian officials in DIA caused by a variety of factors, Gambill was fired from his position in 1967. Yet the Mohawks allowed him to live on Cornwall Island on the Mohawk Reserve, participate in Longhouse ceremonials, and advise on community development projects.[47]

In 1967 and 1968, Benedict, with Gambill's help, devised the idea of the North American Indian Travelling College, which is housed on Cornwall Island, and is still a major Indian educational force in Canada. The original idea of the college was to employ a mobile railroad car that would carry teachers of Indian traditions from one reserve to another, networking Canadian Indian communities, and fostering unity among native peoples. This railroad concept, based on the reality that more reserves in Canada had railroad access than paved road access, never got off the ground because railroad charges were excessive for a car stored on the track. Nevertheless, the college, employing vans, became a reality in 1968, after Benedict quit his job at Reynolds Aluminum and devoted full time to the project.[48]

Gambill's significance was also sizeable in two other areas. Within an eighteen-month period from 1967 to February 1969, he contributed to the founding of the White Roots of Peace and *Akwesasne*

Ray Fadden, August 1967. Courtesy of Dr. Theodore Hetzel.

Notes, the newspaper that he edited until the mid-1970s. Both were conceived as community development projects and both have shaped the Iroquois polity and Indian movements nationwide over the past two decades. *Akwesasne Notes* started out as an effort to bring news to Indian people about the International Bridge crisis by reprinting articles from diverse newspapers. Although largely the single-handed effort of Gambill in organizing, editing, and writing, Mohawks contributed their time and efforts in paste-up and mailing of the newspaper. The success of *Akwesasne Notes* was largely a result of the Indian art work of John Fadden and the newspaper's letters-to-the-editor feature. The letters "networked diverse Iroquois and other Indian communities," thus making Akwesasne, at the gateway between Canada and the United States, a communications center for Indians in North America.[49]

In the same period, Gambill helped revive Ray Fadden's Akwesasne Counsellor Organization, which had traveled far and wide inculcating Indian pride among Mohawk youth from the mid-1930s through the 1950s. Gambill, hoping to influence a group of young Mohawks such as Tom Porter and Francis Boots to take up leadership roles in the Mohawk Longhouse, founded the White Roots of Peace. Seeing the spiritual crisis caused by the death of key elders and that many young Indians were moving away from the faith, Gambill founded this organization, which was committed to the preservation of tradition by bringing the Great Binding Law through speaking engagements to Indian and non-Indian communities and school audiences. In the process of touring, Gambill, as Fadden earlier, was purposefully trying to develop oratorical and leadership skills among his Mohawk troupe; he was also attempting to inculcate Indian pride and self-worth among the members, as well as to convey a certain political-religious message to his audiences. This latter point is clear since Gambill has insisted that the White Roots of Peace was also strongly influenced by the earlier unity caravans.[50]

The troupe's influence was remarkable. Indians of different religious backgrounds, such as Oneidas in Wisconsin, soon were driving several hours to Milwaukee to hear and meet the members of the White Roots of Peace. The troupe was especially effective from 1969 onward. In June of 1969, Gambill and his young Mohawks reached the campus of San Francisco State College. There, they spent three or four days meeting with students in the newly created Indian Studies program, talking about the Longhouse religion, traditions, and values, performing Iroquois social dances, and discussing Indian activist concerns such as the events that transpired at the International Bridge protest.[51]

Among the people who received the Mohawk message was a twenty-seven-year old student and part-time bridge construction worker by the name of Richard Oakes, an Iroquois Indian who had been born at Akwesasne. Oakes, in an interview published posthumously in 1972, described his background:

> I grew up on the St. Regis Reservation in New York, near the Canadian border. It's a big reservation, six miles square, with three thousand people and three thousand problems. My growing up was hard, as it is for most Indians. The hopes were there, the promises were there, but the means for achieving them weren't forthcoming. I couldn't adjust. I went to the schools, went to high school until I was sixteen, but the system never offered me anything that had to do with being an Indian. . . . All they wanted me to do was to become a part of the machinery, to make me into what they wanted: a *white* [emphasis Oakes] Indian. I wanted to do something for my people. But I didn't know what.[52]

Oakes, who had spent most of his life in Syracuse and New York City, had been an ironworker for eleven years and had "made good money, but beyond that there was nothing." During his move to California, he had visited other reservations en route and had become aware of the difficult and "different conditions in which the tribes lived."[53] Oakes, in common with many other young Iroquois of the period, was influenced both by the Iroquois unity movement and the White Roots of Peace troupe in his conversion to activist politics. In fact, Oakes was to join the White Roots of Peace in the months prior to his death in 1972.[54]

The seizure of the abandoned federal penitentiary on Alcatraz Island, the "Rock," in San Francisco harbor was soon to occupy Oakes' days. In 1964, after the prison closed, the United Bay Area Indians, led by Adam Nordwall, Allen Cottier, and Dick Mackenzie, had unsuccessfully attempted the first Indian "invasion" of Alcatraz. After that fiasco, Nordwall had planned carefully and become sophisticated in understanding that the seizure would be a major media event. Attempting to reverse the "doctrine of discovery" in favor of the Indian, Nordwall, along with activist students in the Bay area, prepared for a landing in the summer of 1970.[55]

Two events sped up the timetable. In July 1969, Texas mogul Lamar Hunt presented his idea for the commercial development of Alcatraz—complete with refurbished cellblocks, shops, and restaurants —to the San Francisco Board of Supervisors. On the twenty-eighth of October of the same year, the American Indian Center in the Mission District burned to the ground, leaving the Bay area Indian community without a focal point for educational, health, job, and social services.[56]

On the ninth of November, Bay area Indians, hoping to attract newspaper attention by symbolically reclaiming Alcatraz in order to raise money for a new Indian center, chartered a boat. Oakes soon saw the potential of diverting from the planned course: "A lot of us were sick of doing things for the public, so when they sailed around the island, we decided to jump off . . . swim out to the island, and claim it. . . . So I . . . dove into the water. Four others followed. . . . Before jumping I felt a great sense of urgency. I felt I had to do it."[57] The Coast Guard soon removed them from the island but Oakes and fourteen other students from Berkeley, Santa Cruz, and San Francisco state universities returned that evening. Although they were coaxed from the island, Oakes encouraged more than eighty Indians to join him to stay when he landed again on Alcatraz on the twentieth of November. On the next day Oakes, as a spokesman for the "Indians of All Tribes," telephoned "non-negotiable" demands to the regional coordinator of the Department of the Interior, calling for funds for the establishment of a major all-Indian university and cultural center, without government participation in its administration. Later, the Indians of All Tribes demanded funds for the creation of an American Indian spiritual center, a center for Native American Studies, and an Indian center of ecology, as well as a job training school for native peoples. Thus began the first prolonged demonstration against federal Indian policy in the new age of Red Power, one that was initiated in part by a young charismatic Mohawk, broad-shouldered in his heavy Mackinaw lumber jacket, from Saint Regis (Akwesasne).[58]

Despite the Indians' demands, the Nixon administration refused to negotiate until the Indians had left the island.[59] Strong divisions surfaced between the more conservative Bay Area Indians and the younger, more militant Indians on Alcatraz. When his twelve-year old stepdaughter died on the eighth of January after falling through an open stairwell on the island, Oakes announced he would not return to Alcatraz. He went to help the Pit River Indians organize to fight the Pacific Gas and Electric Company to save their lands. On June 11, 1970, Oakes was clubbed nearly to death by two assailants using pool sticks during a brawl in one of the "Indian bars" in San Francisco. Although never fully recovering from this beating, he subsequently went to help sovereignty-minded Indians in Sonoma County. He also started plans for an Indian traveling college, undoubtedly modeled on the Mohawks' North American Indian Traveling College on Cornwall Island.[60] On September 21, 1972, Oakes was shot to death by a caretaker for a YMCA camp in Northern California who claimed that Oakes had menaced him with a hunting knife. Long before that time, on June 11, 1971, the marshalls had returned to Alcatraz and removed the few remaining Indians.

The events at Alcatraz were a major turning point in the history of Indian activism. The takeover at Alcatraz became the symbol to many young, disillusioned Indians like Oakes, stimulating a rash of similar protests. In June 1971, a group of Indians that included Tom Cook, the assistant editor of *Akwesasne Notes* and himself a student and a Mohawk ironworker, threatened to hold the Statue of Liberty "hostage" in a protest demanding better treatment for American Indians.[61] The following year, Onondagas, Mohawks, and Tuscaroras participated in the nationwide protest, the "Trail of Broken Treaties."

The Trail of Broken Treaties caravan came to Washington, D.C. on October 31, 1972, with a carefully prepared twenty-point proposal for fundamental changes in federal Indian policy. The protest caravan, barely held together because it was composed of an extremely diverse group of Indians, reached the Capitol one week before the presidential election. On the first of November, after the total breakdown of communications between the Indians and federal officials caused by Department of the Interior officials' attempts to undermine the caravan, by the uncompromising militancy of some of the American Indian Movement (AIM) members in the caravan, and by the lack of proper accommodations for the hundreds of Indians, AIM leaders, along with 350 Indians, seized the Bureau of Indian Affairs Building, occupying it until the sixth of November.[62] Commissioner Louis R. Bruce, Jr., a Mohawk-Sioux Indian, aware that 150 riot police were massing to retake the building and understanding that some of his Iroquois kinsmen were in the building, gave assurances to the Indians that they could stay and that all problems could be resolved. Bruce was subsequently fired by President Nixon for his willingness to negotiate and to act as a peacemaker. The final settlement to evacuate the building was worked out by Hank Adams, one of the key organizers of the caravan and head of Survival of American Indians. Adams was aided in keeping peace by Mohawk Francis Boots, one of the members of the White Roots of Peace.[63]

Thus, by the end of 1972, Iroquois presence and influence in nationwide Indian militancy was evident. On the takeover of Wounded Knee in February 1973, the Onondaga Council of Chiefs sent a delegation of fourteen Indians to the Pine Ridge Reservation with a proclamation in support of AIM's action. One of these delegates, Chief Oren Lyons, explained the reason for their support:

Louis R. Bruce, Jr., Mohawk-Oglala Sioux, Commissioner of Indian Affairs, 1969–72. Photograph courtesy of Louis R. Bruce, Jr.

We support the Oglala Sioux Nation or any Indian Nation that will fight for its sovereignty. We recognized immediately the implications of such a nation and its fight, so we responded. The issue here at Wounded Knee is the recognition of the treaties between the United States Government and the sovereign nations that were here before. . . . Sovereignty is freedom of a people to act and conduct affairs of its own nation. We the *Hotinonsonni* [sic] [People of the Longhouse], the Six Nations, have our sovereignty. We conduct on our territories and we act for our people. And so we have the Oglala Sioux, who should be conducting their affairs here because this is their territory, but who now has its government interfered with and who now have another form from another power acting within their territory.[64]

The Onondagas aided Indians involved in the Wounded Knee struggle with time, money, and moral support. Importantly, the Onondagas later gave sanctuary to the fugitive Dennis Banks, the AIM leader, from February 1983 to September 1984.[65]

Although beyond the scope of this study, Iroquois participation in Indian political activist circles is still apparent in New York and in the national arena. Their particular style of activism, which was reflected in the words of sovereignty-minded Iroquois such as William Rickard in the late 1950s and early 1960s, has continued. From the American Indian Chicago Conference of 1961, to Wounded Knee in 1973, the Iroquois, well beyond their numbers, have influenced the activist direction of the Indian world. Perhaps most importantly, *Akwesasne Notes* has been at the forefront of Red Power militancy since the newspaper's founding. Despite a language of protest that appears to be borrowed from the social-activist rhetoric of the late 1960s, Iroquois activism is significantly an outgrowth of these Indians' past cultural, historical, political, and religious life.

12

The Watchful Eagle

We [the Iroquois] are survivors.

> Gloria Tarbell Fogden (Mohawk)
> Mohonk Mountain House
> New Paltz, New York
> May 27, 1982

Despite growing nationalist trends and appeals to unity, the Iroquois by the mid-1970s appeared to be more divided than anytime since the Kellogg movement of the 1920s. Indian land claims such as those brought by individual Iroquois nations, namely the Oneidas and Cayugas, challenged the growing assertions of the Onondaga Council of Chiefs, which now, as they had in the 1920s, talked of a Six Nations Confederacy claim. Moreover, many Iroquois in New York, Oklahoma, Wisconsin, and Canada did not view Iroquois flirtations with Red Power politics and with the American Indian Movement as a positive development. AIM's protests, some of which have led to violence, property destruction, trespass, and acts of rioting, were seen as antithetical to traditional values. In Wisconsin and Oklahoma, Iroquoian communities which had tribal elected systems created in the 1930s, AIM attacks on the Indian Reorganization Act (1934) and the Oklahoma Indian Welfare Act (1936) were scoffed at and strongly resented by Oneida and Seneca-Cayuga people whose land base and government had been in part restored by these acts. To many members of the Seneca Nation of Indians, this Red Power activist politics was out-of-step with the directions of their Allegany and Cattaraugus communities. These Senecas in 1973, in fact, fought off attempts by young militant tribal members who sought to create a new tribal structure through an Ohsweken-styled revolt on the Cattaraugus Indian Reservation. Al-

231

Reverend W. David Owl and Pauline Seneca, Cattaraugus Indian
Reservation. Reverend Owl, a Cherokee Indian, was a minister to
the Seneca Nation for fifty years. Mrs. Seneca, a Cayuga Indian,
was a teacher at the Thomas Indian School until its closing in
the mid-1950s. Photograph courtesy of Doctor Theodore Hetzel.

though beyond the scope of this study, many Iroquois looked askance
at the violent confrontation that occurred in May 1974, when some
Mohawks "reclaimed" a 612-acre site near Moss Lake in the Adiron-
dacks which they referred to as "Ganienkeh." After a series of careful
negotiations, these Mohawks from Caughnawaga and Akwesasne re-
settled their community to another area near the town of Altona in
Clinton County. Moreover, in 1979 and 1980 at Saint Regis (Akwesasne), "traditionals," with the support of the Onondaga Council of
Chiefs, dramatized their longstanding objections to the existing three-
member elected tribal system by establishing an encampment at Rac-
quette Point on the reservation. The confrontation scene could have
exploded like Wounded Knee in 1973 since the Indians and numerous
New York State troopers were armed to the teeth. Eventually, in 1980,
the traditionals and their opponents agreed to a compromise, and to

this day, each side participates in the existing elected system, far different from the past when the traditionals boycotted the electoral process.[1]

The unity movement, nevertheless, has also had other results, especially in the promotion of the Longhouse religion and Iroquois arts. At Oneida, Wisconsin, the Longhouse was established in the 1970s for the first time since the Kellogg movement of the 1920s. A major artistic revival was also a direct outgrowth of this unity movement. Significantly, one of its major architects was Duffy Wilson, a Tuscarora sculptor who had been involved in the protests against SPA in the late 1950s. In May 1970, Wilson, along with prominent non-Iroquois Indians, Buffy Sainte-Marie, Rupert Costo, Arthur Junaluska, Lloyd Oxendine, Robert Spoonhunter, and John Trudell, established the Native American Center for the Living Arts in New York City. The center was devoted to countering racial stereotypes, promoting the preservation of the visual and performing arts of Native American peoples, and to the development of new forms of creative and cultural expression. In 1975, Wilson moved the center to Niagara Falls, New York. Five years later, as a result of a 4.9 million-dollar public works grant from the United States Department of Commerce, Wilson's concept of a museum, administered by Indians and devoted to educating and promoting the living arts, was finally realized. In May 1980, the Turtle, the Native American Center for the Living Arts, opened in downtown Niagara Falls.

In addition to the Turtle, the Iroquois have developed or expanded their own museums to house their cultural treasures. The Seneca-Iroquois National Museum, the Oneida (Wisconsin) Indian Tribal Museum, the Akwesasne Museum, and the Woodland Indian Cultural Centre Museum (Six Nations Reserve) are all administered and directed by Iroquois Indians—George Abrams, Robert Smith, Salli Benedict, and Tom Hill. This trend was in part a reaction to the museum world's position on sacred objects and the Iroquois' growing nationalistic feelings. Iroquois artists were not only networked by new museums devoted to preserving their art. In December 1976, influenced by this movement to bring Iroquois communities together, Huron Miller, Elwood Green, Michael Mitchell, Carson Waterman, Allen Jock, and Richard Hill founded the Association for the Advancement of Native North American Arts and Crafts. As a result of their efforts and the work of scholars Christina Johannsen and John P. Ferguson, the first directory of Iroquois art and artists—*Iroquois Art: A Directory of a People and Their Work*—was published in 1983.[2]

In sum, after two decades of attempting to counter threats to

Members of Indian Defense League cross Whirlpool Bridge to commemorate their rights under the Jay Treaty, July 20, 1969. Photograph courtesy of Buffalo and Erie County Historical Society.

their landed and tribal existence during and following World War II, the Iroquois Indians emerged to assume a major leadership role in the contemporary Native American world. Iroquois peoples have been at the forefront of intertribal reform and radical activities both in the United States and Canada, and have been involved in the founding and/or the operations of the National Congress of American Indians, the Assembly of First Nations (National Indian Brotherhood), National Tribal Chairman's Association, National Indian Health Board, and the American Indian Movement. Two Iroquois Indians, Robert L. Bennett, and Louis R. Bruce, Jr., held the commissionership of Indian affairs in the United States in succession from 1966 to 1973, the first American Indians to hold that post in nearly one hundred years. In the past five years in Canada, the Iroquois have been among the leaders in the debate over aboriginal rights in the new Canadian Constitution. Roberta Jamieson, a Mohawk attorney from Six Nations Reserve, was an ex-officio member on the special House of Commons committee that produced the major Penner Report on Indian self-government in Canada in 1983. Moreover, on Pope John Paul II's recent visit to Canada, Ernest Benedict was chosen by the Assembly of First Nations to present the symbolic eagle feather to the pontiff.[3]

Iroquois leadership in Native American affairs in the postwar period was also reflected in other areas. The Iroquois, especially the Tuscaroras and Mohawks, were instrumental in the emergence of Red Power in the late 1960s. Their highly influential newspaper, *Akwesasne Notes*, helped set the tone for this new Indian activism since its founding in early 1969. The Iroquois spread their influence also through the North American Indian Unity Caravan and later through the White Roots of Peace. They sent delegations to participate at the takeovers of the Bureau of Indian Affairs in 1972 and at Wounded Knee in 1973, the sessions of the Non-Governmental Organization of the United Nations in Geneva, Switzerland in 1977, and on the Longest Walk demonstration protesting proposed congressional legislation in 1978. Even before the term "Red Power" was coined, their activism had led them to be vocal participants as well as staunch critics of the historic American Indian Chicago Conference of 1961 which drafted the Declaration of Indian Purpose.[4] Furthermore, Richard Oakes, a leader of the major Alcatraz Island takeover in 1969, was a Mohawk.

Iroquois self-assertions and sense of leadership must be understood in relation to how these Indians perceive themselves and the rest of the Indian world. What many outsiders interpret as militancy is in part a strategy of cultural survival to protect a rather conservative way of life. As eloquent orators on behalf of treaty rights

Julius Cook, prominent ironworker, virtuoso of high steel construction, noted silversmith, and former Mohawk chief, adjust-
ing a grinding machine he built to grind welded joints on the
Unisphere at the New York World's Fair in 1963 or 1964. Photograph courtesy of Kay Olan.

and as self-appointed protectors of tradition, they frequently project
an air of self-confidence that is widely admired by other Indians,
however grudgingly, nationwide. As a more widely separated people
than most—their communities are located in New York, Oklahoma,
and Wisconsin in the United States and Ontario and Québec in Canada
—their "moccasin telegraph" stretches nearly two thousand miles
across North America, linked by their historic memorybank of their
original homeland, ceremonies, claims, kinship, language, and common treaties with the federal government.

This telegraph, which carries messages to Iroquois and other In-

Dr. Rosa Minoka-Hill, 1949. Dr. Hill, a Mohawk Indian, served
as a physician in Wisconsin for over fifty years. An 1899 graduate
of the Women's Medical College, she received a special certificate
of appreciation by the American Medical Association and the
University of Wisconsin in 1949. Photograph courtesy of the Archives and Special Collections on Women in Medicine, Medical
College of Pennsylvania, Philadelphia.

Teaching Iroquoian songs to their Seneca-Cayuga children: Reuben Dutch White (glasses) and Bob White (on his left), late 1960s. Photograph courtesy of Velma Nieberding.

dian communities, is also aided by the type of employment that many Iroquois seek out. Skill in ironwork has long been valued and considered one path to tribal leadership. In fact, many leaders previously mentioned or discussed, such as Cornelius Seneca and Richard Oakes, had this particular occupation. The constant movement of ironworkers from one job to another and from one part of the country to another has served as a definite vehicle in the spread of valuable information relating to Indian political, cultural, economic, and religious doings and news about policies emanating from Washington and Ottawa. It is no coincidence that Mohawks, who have the longest experience in ironwork, view their Saint Regis (Akwesasne) Reservation along the Saint Lawrence River as the communications link between Canadian and United States Indian communities.

This clearly defined role of leadership in the postwar Native American world resulted only after the Iroquois faced continuous threats in the two decades following United States entry into World War II. Outside challenges to Iroquois concepts of sovereignty actually began to intensify with the congressional passage of the Selective Service Act of 1940 and the conscription of American Indians into the armed services. Later, in 1948 and 1950, Congress handed over criminal and civil jurisdiction of the Iroquois to New York State, despite large-scale Indian opposition to the move. The Iroquois also lost significant acreage in the East beginning with a dam project at Onondaga in the late 1940s. By the mid-1960s, the Kinzua Dam had flooded the entire Cornplanter Tract in Pennsylvania and over 9,000 acres of Seneca lands. The building of the Saint Lawrence Seaway in the 1950s disrupted Mohawk traditional life in two of their communities with industrialization and its resulting pollution along the river, and ignored Indian land claims. In the same decade, the New York State Power Authority (SPA), under Robert Moses' leadership, helped condemn one-eighth of the existing Tuscarora Reservation with its plans for a reservoir and the harnessing of the Niagara River for hydroelectric power.

The new "Indian war" against the Iroquois took other forms. The Seneca-Cayuga Tribe of Oklahoma and the Oneida Tribe of Wisconsin were among the first Indian groups in the nation faced with fighting termination legislation in the 1950s. From 1947 to 1967, Congress considered proposals for the commutation of the Canandaigua Treaty of 1794, the major federal-Iroquois treaty. Moreover, as a result of postwar budgetary cutbacks, assimilationist pressures and the statewide movement for the centralization of smaller district schools, New York closed all but three of the state's Indian reservation schools in the two decades following World War II.

While facing off against New York State, the Army Corps of Engineers, and Robert Moses and SPA, the Iroquois were also undergoing a major spiritual crisis that was rapidly undermining traditional values and transforming Indian life. With the growing intrusion of the outside into their communities and the loss of parts of their homeland, the Longhouse religion, the core of Iroquois life despite its minority status on most reservations, found itself with fewer and fewer followers with the knowledge of the *Gaiiwio*, the Old Way of Handsome Lake, and fewer and fewer speakers of the Iroquoian languages, the ancient tongues required in the ceremonies. Because of Iroquois frustrations in clinging to tradition in the face of assimilationist pressures, much of their political activism and protest in the past two dec-

Teaching the Cayuga language to the Seneca-Cayugas, late 1960s.
The class is led by Ruby Diebold (standing). Josephine Cata is to
Diebold's left and Reuben Dutch White at far right. Photograph
courtesy of Velma Nieberding.

ades has been directed against educational administrators and institutions in the United States and Canada for historically "de-Indianizing"
them through assimilationist policies, ignoring the worth of their culture, and even denying them the sacred religious objects, such as wampum or medicine masks, housed in museums.

Much of the material covered in this book focuses on Iroquois
legal struggles over the past four decades. As highly legalistic people,
these American Indians have found themselves all-too-frequently waging their battles in federal court rooms. In *Ex Parte Green* in 1941,
the court insisted that an Onondaga was subject to the military draft
as an American citizen within the meaning of the Selective Service
Act of 1940, rejecting the contention that the federal-Indian treaty relationship recognized Iroquois independence and placed members of
the Six Nations outside of the purview of Washington. The same
federal court in 1942 in *United States v. Forness* upheld the right of

Eastern Iroquois traditionalists renew their contact with their western kin, Seneca-Cayuga Green Corn Ceremony, 1963, Oklahoma. Left to right: Harry Watt and Ed Curry (Cold Spring Longhouse); and Chief Vernon Crow (Seneca-Cayuga). Photograph courtesy of Velma Nieberding.

the Seneca Nation, with the aid of the United States Department of Justice, to cancel delinquent leases of non-Indians in Salamanca, a city on the Allegany Indian Reservation. In the 1950s, the federal courts turned their attention to two cases affecting Iroquois lands and treaty rights. The United States Court of Appeals for the District of Columbia Circuit in 1958 in *Seneca Nation of Indians v. Wilbur M. Brucker* declared that a 1957 congressional appropriations bill authorizing funds to the United States Army Corps of Engineers for flood control on the Upper Allegany River was sufficient legal justification for the breaking of the Canandaigua Treaty of 1794 and the taking of Seneca lands. The Iroquois soon suffered another setback when the United States Supreme Court in 1960 held that the Federal Power Commission's issuance of a license to the New York State Power Authority gave SPA sufficient federal eminent domain power to allow

Eastern Iroquois at the Seneca-Cayuga Green Corn Ceremony, 1977, Oklahoma. Left to right: Chief James Allen (Seneca-Cayuga) and Hubert Buck (Six Nations Reserve). Photograph courtesy of Velma Nieberding.

it to condemn a part of the Tuscarora Reservation, which the court insisted was not protected by the Canandaigua Treaty. Despite defeats in the Seneca and Tuscarora cases in the 1950s, the Iroquois achieved their greatest legal victory in 1974. In that year, the United States Supreme Court in *Oneida Indian Nation of New York State et al. v. County of Oneida et al.* unanimously overturned over 140 years of American law. The court awarded the Oneidas access to federal courts to adjudicate their land claims since it insisted that the Non-Intercourse Acts of 1790 and 1793 required the consent of the United States before New York's extinguishment of Oneida title in 1795.

These pressures contributed to a growing sense of Iroquois na tionalism; paradoxically, these same pressures also exacerbated some of the already existing divisions within the Iroquois polity. To a great extent, outside threats such as the Selective Service, the Army Corps of Engineers, SPA, the Saint Lawrence Seaway, and Congress' termination legislation, as well as a common perceived enemy, New York State, brought these diverse Indians—Baptist, Catholic, Episcopal, Longhouse, Methodist, Mormon, Presbyterian—together. Despite a significant Iroquois unity movement over the past twenty-five years, the Iroquois remain divided. Bitter family feuds weaken the Oneidas in pursuit of their land claim. The Mohawks to this day argue amongst themselves about strategies to pursue for reclaiming Barnhart Island and about environmental damage caused by the Saint Lawrence Seaway and Reynolds Aluminum. The Tuscaroras are still traumatized by the bitterness of the SPA controversy, split by the actions of their leaders, real or assumed, during the events of the late 1950s. The "non-status" position of the Cayugas living on the lands of the Seneca Nation, which was dramatized during the 1948–50 debate over New York State jurisdiction, continues to be a sore point, especially on the Cattaraugus Indian Reservation. Equally true, the debate over the acceptance or rejection of the leadership and policies of the Onondaga Council of Chiefs has led to increased fragmentation in the Iroquois world.

However divided, the Iroquois nonetheless have survived as culturally and politically distinct Indians through the process described in this book. As proud, politically savvy people with a sense of a common estate, a "nationhood," they will continue to serve the Indian world of North America as the symbolic eagle warning other native peoples about the dangerous and shifting winds of Indian policies.

Notes

Preface

1. "The Twentieth Century." In *Red Men and Hat Wearers*,edited by Daniel Tyler (Boulder, Co.: Pruett Publishing Co., 1976), p. 166.

2. The major exceptions are William H. Armstrong, *Warrior in Two Camps: Ely S. Parker, Union General and Seneca Chief* (Syracuse, N.Y.: Syracuse University Press, 1978); Barbara Graymont's excellent edited autobiography of Chief Clinton Rickard, *Fighting Tuscarora* (Syracuse, N.Y.: Syracuse University Press, 1973); and my *The Iroquois and the New Deal* (Syracuse, N.Y.: Syracuse University Press, 1981).

3. Bruce G. Trigger and William C. Sturtevant, editors, (Smithsonian) *Handbook of North American Indians* (Washington, D.C.: U.S.G.P.O., 1978), Vol. 15.

4. Edmund Wilson, *Apologies to the Iroquois* (New York: Alfred A. Knopf, 1959), p. 284.

5. Edmund Wilson, *Letters on Literature and Politics, 1912–1972*, edited by Elena Wilson (New York: Farrar, Straus and Giroux, 1977), p. 553.

6. I have previously written about my methodological approach. See my article, "Iroquois History of the Twentieth Century: Needs and Opportunities for Research," *New York State History Network* 3 (Fall 1981): 3–6. I have been especially influenced by Benjamin Cohn, "History and Anthropology: The State of Play," *Comparative Studies in Society and History* 22 (1980): 216; Vine Deloria, Jr., "The Twentieth Century," in *Red Men and Hat Wearers*, edited by Daniel Tyler (Boulder, Co.: 1976), pp. 155–66; and by Francis Paul Prucha, "American Indian Policy in the Twentieth Century," *Western Historical Quarterly* 15 (January 1984): 1–18.

1   One War Ends, Another Begins

1. Francis Paul Prucha, *The Great Father* (Lincoln, Neb.: University of Nebraska Press, 1984) II, pp. 999–1002; Laurence M. Hauptman, "The American Indian Federation and the Indian New Deal: A Reinterpretation," *Pacific Historical Review* 52 (November 1983): 378–402; Kenneth R. Philp, "Termination: A Legacy of the Indian New Deal," *Western Historical Quarterly* 14 (April 1983): 165–80.

2. Oswald Garrison Villard, "Wardship and the Indian,"*Christian Century* (March 29, 1944): 397–98; O. K. Armstrong, "Set the American Indians Free!" *Reader's Digest* (August 1945): 47–52.

3. For a full discussion on Iroquois concepts of sovereignty, see Laurence M. Hauptman, *The Iroquois and the New Deal*, chapter 1.

4. Aren Akweks (Ray Fadden), *Six Nation Iroquois Confederacy Record (World War II)* (Hoganburg, N.Y., n.d.); "Indians Send Many to War," *Rochester Democrat and Chronicle* (January 3, 1944); "Indians Erect Roll of Honor for 82 in U.S. Armed Services," *Salamanca Republican-Press* (May 10, 1943). For American Indian participation in World War II, see Tom Holm, "Fighting a White Man's War: The Extent and Legacy of American Indian Participation in World War II," *Journal of Ethnic Studies* 9 (Summer 1981): 69–81.

5. Harold Ickes, "Indians Have a Name for Hitler," *Collier's* (January 15, 1944): 58–65.

6. Interviews of Vernon Crow, June 29, 1983, Miami, Ok., and Chief James Allen, August 17, 1979, Miami, Ok. Chief Allen spent nearly two years as a prisoner of war after being captured by the Nazis in 1943. *Six Nation Iroquois Confederacy Record (World War II)*.

7. "Welcome Home Banquet for Returned Veterans," *Pine Tree Chief* (June 28, 1946).

8. "Salute to Great Britain," *Pine Tree Chief* (April 25, 1941).

9. Max King, "With the Indian Boys Overseas," *Pine Tree Chief* (January 2, 1942).

10. Editorial, *Pine Tree Chief* (October 2, 1942).

11. Hauptman, *The Iroquois and the New Deal*, pp. 159, 175–76.

12. *Ibid.*, pp. 136–63. See the following articles in the *Rochester Times-Union*: "Rochester to Lone Ranger: Tonto Was Iroquois Lacrosse Star Here in 1930's" (February 12, 1955); and "Iroquois Plan Indian Day Fete" (September 17, 1937). See the following articles in the *Rochester Democrat and Chronicle*: "Indians Honor School Head" (September 25, 1938); "Indian Day on Indian Soil" (September 12, 1939); "Indians Greet Palefaces at Ellison Park Ceremony" (September 24, 1939); and "Indians Present Poetic Drama Pageant in Ellison Park" (September 29, 1940). Interviews of Francis Kettle, July 27, 1977, Cattaraugus Indian Reservation; Ramona Charles, July 21, 1982, Akron, N.Y.; Keith Reitz, July 20, 1982, Rochester N.Y.

13. Harvey Flad, "The City and Longhouse: A Social Geography of American Indians in Syracuse, New York," Ph.D. dissertation, Syracuse University, 1973, pp. 139–40. New York, Buffalo, Syracuse, and Niagara Falls had larger Indian populations in 1940, although census figures for Indians, especially mobile urban communities, are historically inadequate and usually quite inaccurate.

14. "Indians on Warpath as Soldiers, Workers," *Rochester Democrat and Chronicle* (August 8, 1943).

15. "Many Indians Reported Busy at War Work," *Buffalo Courier-Express* (March 13, 1942).

16. Interviews of Chief Leon Shenandoah (*Tadodaho*), Onondaga Indian Reservation, May 15, 1979; Ernest Benedict, Saint Regis (Akwesasne) Mohawk Reservation, September 10, 1982; Chief Corbett Sundown, Tonawanda Indian Reservation, May 22, 1980, Chief Edison Mt. Pleasant, November 30, 1984, Tuscarora Indian Reservation, Joseph Keppler letter to Oliver LaFarge, April 18, 1941; Ernest Benedict to American Civil Liberties Union, March 27, 1941, ACLU MSS., Princeton University; John Collier to Chief of the Saint Regis Mohawk Nation, October 16, 1940, John Collier MSS., Part II, Series I, Box 29, Folder 66, Yale University, New Haven, Conn. See the following articles in the *New York Times*: "Indians Seek Draft Test" (October 10, 1940), p.14; "Mohawks Reject Draft" (October 12, 1940), p. 14; "Say 1794 Treaty Exempts Indians" (February 22, 1941), p. 8; "Indian Loses Draft Plea" (May 15, 1941), p. 14; "Indian Drops Se-

lectee Fight" (August 15, 1941), p. 22; "Indians on the 'Warpath' Over Selective Service Act" (October 21, 1941), p. 25. See also "5 Indians Fight Draft as Threat to Sovereignty," *New York Herald Tribune* (October 21, 1941), p. 11.

17. Barbara Graymont, ed., *Fighting Tuscarora: The Autobiography of Chief Clinton Rickard* (Syracuse N.Y.: Syracuse University Press, 1973), p. 127.

18. "Indians Register as Aliens Under Protest," *Niagara Falls Gazette* (December 27, 1940).

19. *Ex Parte Green*, 123F.2d.862 (1941).

20. *United States v. Claus*, 63F.Supp.433 (1944); *Albany v. United States*, 152F.2d.267 (1945).

21. Interview of Louis R. Bruce, Jr., June 30, 1982, Washington, D.C.

22. Resolution Date June 12, 1942, BIA Central Files, 1940–52, Acc. #53A-367, Box 1056, File #26556-1942-054 N.Y., RG 75, NA.

23. *Ibid.*

24. F.D.R. to Chiefs Louis David, Peter Oake, Ulysses G. Pierce, Hilton Nickless, W. H. Rockwell, Jesse Lyons (separate letters), June 15, 1942, F.D.R. MSS., PPF 2530, Franklin D. Roosevelt Library, Hyde Park, N.Y.

25. Wilfred Hoffman to William Zimmerman, Jr., May 25, 1942, BIA Central Files, 1940–52, Acc. #53A-367, Box 1056, File #30304-1942-061 N.Y., RG 75, NA. This information was confirmed by my interview with Louis R. Bruce, Jr., June 30, 1982.

26. William Zimmerman, Jr to Jesse Lyons, June 22, 1942, BIA Central Files, 1940–52, Acc. #53A-367, Box 1056, File #30304-1942-061 N.Y., RG 75, NA; Department of Interior Office of Indian Affairs News Release, June 12, 1942, BIA Central Files, 1940–52, Acc. #53A-367, Box 1056, File #26556-1942-054 N.Y., RG 75, NA.

27. James M. Mead to William Zimmerman, Jr., June 4, 1942; Eleanor Williams' Memorandum to Indian Office Employees, June 11, 1942; Assistant Commissioner Memorandum for Captain of the Guard, June 13, 1942, BIA Central Files, 1940–52, Acc. #53A-367, Box 1056, File #26556-1942-054 N.Y., RG 75, NA. Zimmerman to Lyons, June 22, 1942.

28. Department of the Interior News Release, June 12, 1942; "Six Nations Declare War on Axis," *Indians at Work* 9 (May–June 1942): 17–18.

29. *Annual Report* of the Commissioner of the Office of Indian Affairs to the Secretary of the Interior, 1942 (Washington D.C., 1942), p. 240; Ickes, "Indians Have a Name for Hitler," pp. 58–65.

30. See the following articles in the *Syracuse Post-Standard*: "Onondaga Indians Cling to Traditions of Ancestors Tho White Man's Civilization Presses on All Sides; Insist None Come Under Draft Law" (November 30, 1941), and "Iroquois Indians Declare War on Enemies of U.S." (June 11, 1942); "Chiefs of Iroquois Leave for Capital with War Papers" (June 13, 1942). See also article and photograph, Stephen V. Feeley, "Indian War Declaration Is Delayed by Muffins," *Buffalo Courier-Express* (June 16, 1942).

31. Stephen V. Feeley, "Indians of Six Nations to Declare War on Axis," *Buffalo Courier-Express* (May 9, 1942).

32. Ickes, "Indians Have a Name for Hitler." Interviews of Ernest Benedict, September 9, 1982; Louis R. Bruce, Jr., June 30, 1982.

33. See Donald L. Parman, *The Navajos and the New Deal* (New Haven, Conn.: Yale University Press, 1976); Kenneth R. Philp, *John Collier's Crusade for Indian Reform, 1920–1954* (Tucson, Ariz.: University of Arizona Press, 1977); Graham Taylor, *The New Deal and American Indian Tribalism: The Administration of the Indian Reorganization Act, 1934–1945* (Lincoln Neb.: University of Nebraska Press, 1980); and my *The Iroquois and the New Deal.*

34. S. Lyman Tyler, *A History of Indian Policy* (Washington, D.C.: U.S. Dept. of the Interior, 1973), pp. 139–48; Larry J. Hasse, "Termination and Assimilation: Federal Indian Policy, 1943 to 1961," Ph.D. dissertation, Pullman, Washington State University, 1974, pp. 38–56.

35. Philp, "Termination: A Legacy of the Indian New Deal," pp. 165–80.

36. Hauptman, *The Iroquois and the New Deal.*

37. United States Congress. House Committee on Indian Affairs, *Hearings on H. Res. 166 . . . Investigate Indian Affairs.* 78th Congress, 1st-2d sessions. (Washington, D.C., 1943–45), 1st session (March 23, 1943), pp. 5–6, 16–17; 2d session, part 2 (February 2, 1944), p. 61.

38. United States Congress. Senate Committee on Indian Affairs. *Survey of Conditions of Indian Affairs. Partial Report No. 310*, 78–1, serial 10756 (Washington D.C., 1943); United States Congress. Senate Committee on Indian Affairs. *Survey of Conditions of Indian Affairs, Supplemental Report* (Washington, D.C., 1944).

39. United States Congress. *House Report No. 2091*, 78–2, serial 10848 (Washington, D.C., 1945).

40. United States Congress. *House Hearings on H. Res. 166 . . . Investigate Indian Affairs.* 78th Congress, 1st session and 2d session. (Washington, D.C., 1944), 1st session, March 23, 1943, pp. 16–17; 2d session, part 2, February 2, 16, 1944, pp. 52–91.

41. *Ibid.*, 78th Congress 2d session, part 2, February 2, 1944, pp. 51–52.

42. Margaret Szasz, *Education and the American Indian: The Road to Self-Determination, 1928–1973* (Albuquerque, N.M.: University of New Mexico Press, 1974), pp. 106–22.

43. Philip Cowen, *Survey of Indian Schools, State of New York, 1940*, found in Records of the Native American Eduation Unit, New York State Department of Education, New York State Archives, Albany, N.Y.

44. Willard W. Beatty, *et al.*, *Report and Recommendations to the Commissioner of Education, Albany, New York, on New York State Indian Schools*, found in Records of the Native American Education Unit, New York State Department of Education, New York State Archives, Albany, N.Y.

45. Willard W. Beatty, *An Informal Report on the Thomas Indian School, 1946.* BIA Central Files, 1940–52 (N.Y.), #5874-1943-210, acc. #53A-367, Box 1057, RG 75, NA, Washington, D.C.

46. *The Public Papers of Governor Averell Harriman, 1956* (Albany, N.Y.: 1957), pp. 1129–30. See also "State Indian School to Close," *New York Times* (September 1, 1956).

47. Interviews of Pauline Seneca, July 17, 1982; Corline Campbell, July 14, 1982, Cattaraugus Indian Reservation; Louis R. Bruce, Jr., June 30, 1982, Washington, D.C.; and William N. Fenton, May 18, 1983, Slingerlands, N.Y. Seneca Nation Council Resolution, June 11, 1955, in possession of Mrs. Pauline Seneca, Cattaraugus Indian Reservation. Report of Governor's [Averell Harriman] Committee on Utilization of the Thomas Indian School. New York State Deputy Commissioner of Social Welfare to William N. Fenton, November 21, 1956, both found in records of the Assistant Commissioner of Education. New York State Department of Education. Correspondence, 1956. New York State Archives, Albany, N.Y.

48. Interview of Anna Lewis, June 10, 1983, Albany, N.Y.; Charles Russell, *Problems Affecting Centralization of New York State Indian Schools: Report of a Survey, Dec. 20, 1954*, found in Herbert H. Lehman MSS., "Indians," C67–31, Columbia University, New York. See also Russell's "Centralizing New York Indian Schools: Report of Survey 7" (1955): 45–54. Russell's report was sponsored by the Association on Ameri-

can Indian Affairs. Ruth Birdseye, *Indian Education in New York State* (1846–1970) (Albany, N.Y.: New York State Education Dept., 1970).

49. "Indians to Honor Own Heroic Dead," *Syracuse Post-Standard* (September 30, 1945); "All-Indian Post of Legion Formed," *Buffalo Courier-Express* (October 26, 1946); "Legion Has All-Indian Post," *New York Times* (October 26, 1946); "Soldiers Honoured at Remembrance Service," *Pine Tree Chief* (December 14,1945); "Welcome Home Banquet for Returned Veterans," *Pine Tree Chief* (June 28, 1946). Interviews of Jeanne Marie Jemison, Winifred Kettle, and Pauline Seneca, July 14–17, 1982, Cattaraugus Indian Reservation.

2 Forness

1. *U.S. v. Forness et al. (Salamanca Trust Co. et al., Interveners).* 37F.Supp.337 (February 14, 1941), 125 Fed. Rep., 2d Ser., 928 (January 20, 1942). "Our Indian Landlords Finally Get a Break," *New York Times* (January 21, 1942).

2. 125 Fed. Rep., 2d Ser., 931.

3. *Ibid.,* 940.

4. *Ibid.,* 938.

5. *Ibid.,* 932.

6. Laurence M. Hauptman, "Senecas and Subdividers: Resistance to Allotment of Indian Lands in New York, 1875–1906," *Prologue* 9 (Summer 1977): 106; Thomas S. Abler, "Factional Dispute and Party Conflict in the Political System of the Seneca Nation (1845–1895): An Ethnohistorical Analysis," unpublished Ph.D. dissertation, University of Toronto, 1969, pp. viii, 169–73; Thomas E. Hogan, "A History of the Allegany Reservation: 1850–1900," unpublished M.A. thesis, State University of New York, Fredonia, 1974, p. 8; and Hogan's "City in a Quandary: Salamanca and the Allegany Leases," *New York History* 54 (January 1974): 79–101.

7. *Ibid.*

8. Gerald Gunther, "Governmental Power and New York Indian Lands—A Reassessment of a Persistent Problem of Federal-State Relations," *Buffalo Law Review* 8 (Fall 1958): 9.

9. Hauptman, "Senecas and Subdividers," 107.

10. *Ibid.*

11. U. S. Congress, House, *Congressional Record*, 57th Congress, 2d session, 1902, 36, pt. 1: 337; Edward B. Vreeland to Merrill E. Gates, January 10, 1902, Records of the U.S. Board of Indian Commissioners, 1899–1918, RG 75, NA.

12. *Proceedings of the Twentieth Annual Meeting of the Lake Mohonk Conference of Friends of the Indian, 1902* (Lake Mohonk, N.Y.: Lake Mohonk Conferences 1903), pp. 57–61, 101–106.

13. New York State, *Assembly Document 51—Report of the Special Committee Appointed by the Assembly of 1888 to Investigate the "Indian Problem" of the State* (Albany, N.Y., 1889), pp. 59–79.

14. *Ibid.* Interview of Keith Reitz, May 3, 1983, New Paltz, N.Y.

15. Hauptman, "Senecas and Subdividers," 112.

16. U.S. Congress, House, *Congressional Record*, 57th Congress, 2d session, 1902, 36, pt. 1: 337.

17. Hauptman, *The Iroquois and the New Deal*, chapters 1, 3, and 4.

18. Arch Merrill, "Salamanca Lease Settlement," *American Indian* [New York City] 1 (Spring 1944): 3.

19. W. K. Harrison and William N. Fenton, Report: "The New York Agency Problem," December 30, 1936, William N. Fenton MSS. In Dr. Fenton's possession at Slingerlands, N.Y. (Indian Service Records, 1935–37). These records have been recently transferred to the American Philosophical Society Library in Philadelphia, Pa.

20. Felix Cohen, *Handbook of Federal Indian Law* (Washington, D.C.; U.S. Dept. of the Interior 1942; reprint edition, Albuquerque, N.M.: University of New Mexico Press, 1972). p. 419.

21. Gunther, "Governmental Power and New York Indian Lands," 1–26; James W. Clute, "The New York Indians' Rights to Self-Determination," *Buffalo Law Review* 22 (Spring 1973): 985–1019.

22. United States Congress. House Committee on Indian Affairs. *Hearings on H.K. 9720: Indians of New York.* 71st Congress, 2d session (Washington, D.C.; U.S.G.P.O., 1930), pp. 1, 19–20, 154–65, 199. For the 1940 attempt to transfer jurisdiction, see "Indians O.K. Wanted," *Buffalo Courier-Express* (April 18, 1940); David C. Adie to Senator Robert F. Wagner, March 25, 1940, BIA Central Files, 1940–52, acc. #53A 367, Box 1055, File #22649-1940-013 (N.Y.), RG 75, NA.

23. Graymont, *Fighting Tuscarora*, p. 95.

24. *Ibid.*; "Salamanca Seeks to Enjoin Indians from Taking Lands," *Buffalo Evening News* (August 28, 1942); "Defendants File Answers in Indian Lease Cases," *Salamanca Republican-Press* (November 25, 1942). For Reed, see Peter B. Bulkley, "Daniel A. Reed: A Study in Conservatism," Ph.D. dissertation, Clark University, Worcester, Mass., 1972.

25. Joseph L. Morrison, *Josephus Daniels: The Small-d Democrat* (Chapel Hill, N.C.: University of North Carolina Press, 1966), p. 195.

26. "Charles C. Daniels," *Asheville Citizen* (March 22, 1951), Josephus Daniels Collection, Charles C. Daniels MSS., #3630, Southern Historical Collection, University of North Carolina, Chapel Hill (SHC, UNCCH).

27. "Charles Daniels Dies in Gotham," *Raleigh News and Observer* (March 21, 1951); "C. C. Daniels, 86, Dies in New York," *Asheville Citizen* (March 21, 1951), Josephus Daniels Collection, Charles C. Daniels, MSS., #3630, SHC, UNCCH. C. C. Daniels to Attorney General Homer Cummings with Memorandum Relative to C. C. Daniels, August 19 and October 30, 1933, Josephus Daniels MSS., Microfilm Reel 4, Library of Congress, Manuscript Division, Washington, D.C.

28. New York State Assembly, (unpublished) *Report of the Indian Commission to Investigate the Status of the American Indian Residing in the State of New York Transmitted to the Legislature, March 17, 1922* (Albany, N.Y., 1922), pp. 2, 303–304, 324; Hauptman, *The Iroquois and the New Deal*, pp. 11–12; and Helen Upton, *The Everett Report in Historical Perspective: The Indians of New York State* (Albany, N.Y.: New York State American Revolution Bicentennial Commission, 1980).

29. *New York Indians*, Memorandum of C. C. Daniels, Special Assistant to the Attorney General, Relating to the Everett Report, November 21, 1934. Memorandum found in Everett Report file copy, Akwesasne Museum, Hogansburg, N.Y.

30. John Collier to W. K. Harrison, March 4, 1935, Records of the New York Agency, 1938–49, Box 7, #380, RG 75, NA.

31. W. K. Harrison to Commissioner of Indian Affairs, March 22, 1935, Records of the New York Agency, 1938–49, Box 7, #380, RG 75, NA.

32. Interview of William N. Fenton, June 28, 1978, Albany, N.Y. Dr. Fenton was W. K. Harrison's assistant from 1935 to 1937. "Shifts State Indian Agency," *New York Times* (June 28, 1939). Congressman Daniel Reed protested the action. Reed to Harold

Ickes, April 24, 1939, BIA Central Files, 1940–52, acc. #53A 367, Box 1055, File #22649-1940-013 (N.Y.), RG 75, NA.

33. Hauptman, *The Iroquois and the New Deal*, chapters 3 and 4.

34. "Indian Landlords Insist Palefaces Pay," *Rochester Times-Union* (March 10, 1939).

35. Wilford Crouse, Chairman, "Resolution of the Lease Committee of the Seneca Nation of Indians", May 23, 1939, Records of the New York Agency, 1938–49, Box 7, #380, RG 75, NA.

36. Seneca Nation Resolution of May 1940 attached to letter of C. C. Daniels to Charles E. Berry, May 27, 1940, Records of the New York Agency, 1938–49, Box 7, #380, RG 75, NA.

37. C. C. Daniels to Charles E. Berry, March 12, March 22, July 3, 1940, Records of the New York Agency, 1938–49, Box 7, #380, RG 75, NA.

38. Harold Ickes to the Attorney General, May 21, 1940, Records of the New York Agency, 1938–49, Box 7, #380, RG 75, NA.

39. C. H. Berry to John R. Reeves, February 12, 1940; to John Van Aernam, July 3, 1940, Records of the New York Agency, 1938–49, Box 7, #380, RG 75, NA.

40. C. C. Daniels to Charles H. Berry, March 19 and 28, 1940; Daniels to Frank A. Archambault, June 20 and 28, 1940, Records of the New York Agency, 1938–49, Box 7, #380, RG 75, NA.

41. 37F. Supp. 337.

42. C. C. Daniels to Charles H. Berry, November 14, 1941; Berry to Daniels, November 24, 1941, Records of the New York Agency, 1938–49, Box 7, #380, RG 75, NA.

43. 125 Fed. Reporter, 2d Series, 928.

44. *City of Salamanca et al. v. United States*, 316U.S.694 (June 1, 1942); "Defendants File Answers in Indian Lease Cases," *Salamanca Republican-Press* (November 25, 1942); "Knight Dismisses City Suit Against Seneca Nation," *Salamanca Republican-Press* (November 18, 1942); "Salamanca Seeks to Enjoin Indians From taking Lands," *Buffalo Evening News* (August 28, 1942).

45. C. C. Daniels quoted in Frank A. Archambault to William Zimmerman, Jr., August 5, 1942; Daniels to Attorney General, August 3, 1942; Records of the New York Agency, 1938–49, Box 8, #380, RG 75, NA. Daniels had been relentless in his crusade to help the Senecas. C. C. Daniels to C. McFarland, September 10, 1937; to Josephus Daniels, October 12, 1937, December 16, 1937, February 5, 1938, July 15, 1938, September 8, 1939, Josephus Daniels MSS., Microfilm Reel 4, Library of Congress, Manuscript Division, Washington, D.C.

46. "Local Indian Office Issues Statement Regarding Leases," *Salamanca Republican-Press* (November 5, 1942). William Zimmerman to Charles H. Berry, June 26, 1942, Records of the New York Agency, 1938–49, Box 8, #380, RG 75, NA.

47. See footnote 43 above. Daniels to Attorney General, August 3 and 12, 1942, Records of the New York Agency, 1938–49, Box 8, #380, RG 75, NA.

48. "5-Year Dispute Over Indian Land Leases Is Ended," *Buffalo Evening News* (April 5, 1944). Paul L. Fickinger to C. H. Berry, September 7, 1944, Records of the New York Agency, 1938–49, #380, RG 75, NA.

49. Daniels to Attorney General, August 3, 1942. Daniels' role in the proceedings ended on January 31, 1943. The Seneca Nation passed a resolution honoring him as "one of the unsung heroes in the crusade for righteousness and justice." Norman Littell to C. C. Daniels, January 1, 1942; Seneca Nation Resolution, undated but signed by President Cornelius Seneca and Clerk Mitchell Luke for the council, Josephus Dan-

iels MSS., Microfilm Reel 4, Library of Congress, Manuscript Division, Washington, D.C.

3 Backlash

1. William Zimmerman, Jr. to Charles H. Berry, July 20, 1942, Records of the New York Agency, 1938–49, Box 2, #063.1, RG 75, NA.

2. Upton, *The Everett Report in Historical Perspective*, p. 147.

3. United States Congress. Senate. Subcommittee of the Committee of the Interior and Insular Affairs. *Hearings . . . New York Indians.* 80th Congress, 2d session. (Washington, D.C.: U.S.G.P.O., 1948), pp. 79–82, 213–18. *KA-WEH-RAS* [It Thunders] 1, No. 2 (1947): 1. *KA-WEH-RAS* was a newspaper published by Ernest Benedict on the Mohawk Reservation in the late 1940s.

4. "Move to Stop All State Aid to Indians," *Salamanca Republican-Press* (November 20, 1942); C. C. Daniels to Commissioner of Indian Affairs, November 24, 1942, Records of the New York Agency, 1938–49, Box 8, #380, RG 75, NA.

5. "They Never Will Be Missed," *Salamanca Republican-Press* (April 16, 1943).

6. *Ibid.* See also "The War on the Salamanca Front," *Salamanca Republican-Press* (November 18, 1942); "Sued by U.S. Government He Is Helping to Defend," *Salamanca Republican-Press* (November 17, 1942).

7. "Another Indian Outlook Is Given on Leases," *Salamanca Republican-Press* (date not known, 1943), Newsclipping found in Records of New York Agency, 1938–49, Box 8, #380.0, RG 75, NA.

8. "State Gets Taxes on Indian Lands, Seneca Contends," *Buffalo Evening News* (November 27, 1942); "Supervisors' Move Draws Criticism of Seneca Leader," *Buffalo Evening News* (December 27, 1942).

9. Nora Henhawk to Eleanor Roosevelt, November 25, 1942; Walter V. Woehlke to Henhawk, February 9, 1943, BIA Central Files, 1940–52, Acc. #53A-367, Box 1059, File #14726-1951-926 (N.Y.), RG 75, NA.

10. New York State. *Legislative Document #52* (Albany, N.Y., 1944), p. 32.

11. U.S. Senate. *Hearings, 1948*, p. 195.

12. John Reeves, Memorandum to Mr. Zimmerman, August 11, 1943, BIA Central Files, 1940–52, Acc. #53A 367, Box 1055, File #22649-1940-013 (N.Y.), RG 75, NA.

13. New York State. Joint Legislative Committee on Indian Affairs, *Public Hearing Held at Salamanca . . . September 7, 1943* (Buffalo, N.Y., 1943), pp. 3, 7–18, 23.

14. Interview of Pauline Seneca, July 17, 1982, Cattaraugus Indian Reservation. For the earlier Seneca political upheaval, see Thomas Abler, "Friends, Factions, and the Seneca Nation Revolution of 1848," *Niagara Frontier* 21 (Winter 1974): 74–79.

15. C. H. Berry to William Zimmerman, Jr., November 25, 1943; Zimmerman to William H. Mackenzie, December 11, 1943, BIA Central Files, 1940–52, Acc. #53A 367, Box 1055, File #22649-1940-013 (N.Y.), RG 75, NA.

16. Thomas H. Dowd to Norman M. Littell, August 12, 1943; Dowd to Martin McIntyre, August 14, 1943, Franklin D. Roosevelt MSS., Box 296, "Indians," Franklin D. Roosevelt Library, Hyde Park, N.Y.

17. "The Indian Lease Problem," *Salamanca Republican-Press* (September 11, 1943).

18. New York State. *Joint Legislative Committee Report, February 25, 1944* (Albany, N.Y.: 1944). "Forness Case Decision Termed 'Reproach to State and Nation,'" *Salamanca Republican-Press* (August 5, 1944).

19. Arch Merrill, "Salamanca Lease Settlement," *American Indian* 1 (Spring 1944): 7.

20. Quoted in *Ibid.*

21. Upton, *The Everett Report in Historical Perspective*, p. 145.

22. Abe Fortas to Leighton Wade, January 2, 1945, BIA Central Files, 1940–52, Acc. #53A 367, Box 1055, File #22649-1940-013 (N.Y.), RG 75, NA.

23. New York State Joint Legislative Committee, *Hearings, January 4, 1945* (Albany, N.Y.: 1945), pp. 89–90; New York State Joint Legislative Committee, *Report, 1946* (Albany, N.Y., 1946), p. 12; J. C. McCaskill, Memorandum to Mr. Zimmerman, January 9, 1945, BIA Central Files, 1940–52, Acc. #53A 367, Box 1055, File #22649-1940-013 (N.Y.), RG 75, NA; Lulu Stillman to Commissioner John Nichols, February 7, 1950, BIA Central Files, 1940–52, Acc #53A 367, Box 1055, File #28860-1947-013, 3B (N.Y.), RG 75, NA.

24. Mohawk Petition to Secretary of the Interior and Commissioner of Indian Affairs, August 9, 1943; William Zimmerman, Jr. to C. H. Berry, February 13, 1943; Archie Phinney, "A Study of Tribal Government of the St. Regis (Mohawk) Indians of New York, 1942," BIA Central Files, 1909–39, #9506-1936-066 (N.Y.), RG 75, NA; John Reeves, Memorandum to Mr. Collier, June 1, 1942, BIA Central Files, 1940–52, Acc. #53A 367, Box 958, File #68972-1940-351 (N.Y.), RG 75, NA; C. H. Berry to Commissioner of Indian Affairs, September 5, 1942, Records of the New York Agency, 1938–49, Box 2, #064.0, RG 75, NA. Interviews of Chief Julius Cook, May 27 and June 1, 1982, New Paltz, N.Y.; Ernest Benedict, September 10 and 11, 1982, Saint Regis (Akwesasne) Indian Reservation; and Ray Fadden, September 11, 1982, Onchiota, N.Y.

25. C. H. Berry to Albert Adams, April 2, 1945; Berry to Sylvester Sundown, April 2, 1945; Berry to Everett Parker, August 21, 1944; William Zimmerman to Berry, August 17, 1944, Records of the New York Agency, 1938–49, Box 2, #062.1, RG 75, NA; Chiefs' Council of the Tonawanda Band of Seneca Indians, Memorandum in Opposition to Senate Bill 192, July 6, 1949, J. R. McGrath MSS., Box 28, "Indian Legislation—Proposed," Legislation Senatorial, 1947–1949, Truman Library, Independence, Mo. Interview of Ramona Charles, July 21, 1982, Akron, N.Y.

26. Leighton Wade to William Zimmerman, Jr., February 8, 1945, BIA Central Files, 1940–52, Acc. #53A 367, Box 1055, File #22649-1940-013 (N.Y.), RG 75, NA. U.S. Senate, *Hearings, 1948*, pp. 79–82, 213–18.

27. New York State. Legislature. *Report* of Joint Legislative Committee on Indian Affairs, March 15, 1945 found in New York State. *Legislative Document 51* (Albany, N.Y.: 1945), pp. 3–5.

28. *Ibid.*

29. Daniel Reed to William H. Mackenzie, March 5, 1946; Reed to Senator James H. Mead, April 10, 1946; Leighton Wade to Reed, April 10, 1946; Wade to Senator Irving Ives and Wade to Reed, January 22, 1947; Reed to Wade, June 6, 1947; Wade to Reed January 27, 1948, Daniel Reed MSS., Cornell University Library, Ithaca, N.Y.

30. Buckley, "Daniel A. Reed," pp. iv–vii, 2–10, 24–27, 113–35, 305–11, 410–18.

31. Reed to Wade, June 6, 1947.

32. Donald L. Fixico, "Termination and Relocation: Federal Indian Policy in the 1950s," unpublished Ph.D. dissertation, University of Oklahoma, Norman, Oklahoma 1980, pp. 10–39; Hasse, "Termination and Assimilation . . . ," pp. 73–107.

33. William A. Brophy to Kenneth B. Disher, September 20, 1946, Brophy MSS., Box 2, Chron. File, Sept., 1946, Truman Library, Independence, Mo.

34. "Clarification of Indians' Status Is Goal of Agent," *Buffalo Courier-Express* (November 5, 1946).

35. United States Senate. Committee on the Post Office and Civil Service. *Hearings on S. Res. 41: Officers and Employees of the Federal Government.* 80th Cong., 1st sess. (Washington, D.C., 1947), pt. 3, p. 547.

4 Termination: The Iroquois in New York

1. Prucha, *The Great Father*, II, 1013–59; Charles F. Wilkinson and Eric R. Biggs, "The Evolution of the Termination Policy," *American Indian Law Review* 5 (1980): 139–84.

2. Bess Furman, "Campaign Pushed to 'Free' Indians," *New York Times* (July 22, 1947).

3. For Butler's career, see Justin F. Paul, *Senator Hugh Butler and Nebraska Republicanism* (Lincoln, Neb.: Nebraska State Historical Society, 1976).

4. The three bills can be found in Hugh Butler MSS., Box 260, Nebraska State Historical Society, Lincoln, Neb.

5. See the quotation at the beginning of this chapter. *United States Statutes at Large* 67 (August 15, 1953): 588–90.

6. *KA-WEH-RAS* 1 (April 17, 1948): 3.

7. *Ibid.* 1 (April 3, 1948): 2.

8. *Ibid.*

9. *Ibid.*, pp. 2–3.

10. Hugh Butler, "It is time to give serious consideration to setting Indians free." Speech reprinted from *Congressional Record* of July 21, 1947, Hugh Butler MSS., Box 211, Nebraska State Historical Society, Lincoln, Neb.

11. *Senate Hearings* (1948), p. 36.

12. *Ibid.*, p. 24.

13. *Ibid.*, pp. 39–46.

14. William Benge to Commissioner of Indian Affairs, November 5, 1947, BIA Central Files, 1940–52, acc. #53A367, Box 1055, #28856-1947-013 (N.Y.), RG 75, NA. Nearly every one of the elders interviewed made disparaging comments about Benge.

15. See, for example, chapter 3, footnote 26.

16. *Senate Hearings* (1948), pp. 5–9.

17. *Ibid.*, pp. 106–109; Elon Eels to President Truman, August 24, 1947, Harry S. Truman MSS., OF 296, Box 937, Truman Library, Independence, Mo.

18. William Benge to Commissioner of Indian Affairs, January 2, 1948, BIA Central Files, 1940–52, acc. #53A367, Box 1056, #36-1948-061 (N.Y.), RG 75, NA. See also "State Court Jurisdiction in Indian Cases Opposed," *Buffalo Courier-Express* (December 5, 1947).

19. Hauptman, *The Iroquois and the New Deal*, pp. 7–8, 45–46.

20. *U.S. Code Annotated* (St. Paul, Minn.: West Publishing, 1963), XXV, 185–86.

21. Julius Cook to Mrs. F. D. Roosevelt, January 24, 1948, BIA Central Files, 1940–52, acc. #53A367, Box 1055, #3040-1948-052 (N.Y.), RG 75, NA.

22. Elmer Thompson to William Zimmerman, Jr., Acting Commissioner, February 21, 1948, BIA Central Files, 1940–52, acc. #53A367, Box 1055, #28856-1947-013 (N.Y.), Part 3B, RG 75, NA. Thompson earlier had written to U.S. attorney George Grobe, September 10, 1947, BIA Central Files, 1940–52, acc. #53A367, Box 1055, #28856-1947-013 (N.Y.), Part 3B, RG 75, NA.

23. Oscar Chapman to Hugh Butler, March 1, 1948, BIA Central Files, 1940–52, acc. #53A367, Box 1055, #28853-1947-013 (N.Y.), Part 3B, RG 75, NA. For Zimmerman's comments, see *Senate Hearings* (1948), p. 15.

24. *Senate Hearings* (1948), pp. 130–138.

25. Nick Bailey to Daniel Reed, July 5, 1949, Reed MSS., Cornell University. For more of Bailey's views, see Bailey to Arthur Watkins, April 17, 1948, Records of the New York Agency, 1939–48, Box 1, "Jurisdiction," RG 75, NA.

26. *Senate Hearings* (1948), pp. 113–15. For Moses White, see pp. 74–77.

27. *Ibid.*, pp. 27–29. Interview of Louis R. Bruce, Jr., June 30, 1982, Washington, D.C.; Hauptman, *The Iroquois and the New Deal*, pp. 122–26. For Parker's testimony and Louis R. Bruce, Sr.'s positions on jurisdictional transfer, see their letters filed with the Senate Subcommittee, *Senate Hearings* (1948), pp. 29–30, 224.

28. See for example "Indians Split on Wisdom Value of New Legislation," *Buffalo Courier-Express* (March 11, 1948). "Indians Disagree on State Control," *New York Times* (June 12, 1949).

29. *Senate Hearings* (1948), p. 15

30. *Ibid.*, pp. 189, 219–22.

31. *Ibid.*, pp. 213–14.

32. *Ibid.*, pp. 30–37.

33. *Ibid.*, pp. 47–63.

34. *Ibid.*, pp. 80–81.

35. *Ibid.*, pp. 46–47.

36. *Ibid.*, pp. 184–92.

37. Reva Cooper Barse to Theodore Haas, May 12, 1948, BIA Central Files, 1940–52, acc. #53A367, Box 1055, #28860-1947-013 (N.Y.), RG 75, NA.

38. *Senate Hearings* (1948), pp. 39–47, 109–11.

39. *Ibid.*, pp. 169–71.

40. *Ibid.*, pp. 63–74. Stillman continued to push this argument well after passage of S. 1683. Stillman to Commissioner John Nichols, February 7, 1950; Stillman to Attorney General Tom Clark, March 8 and May 9, 1950; BIA Central Files, 1940–52, acc. #53A367, Box 1055, #28860-1947-013 (N.Y.), Part 3B, RG 75, NA; Stillman to Assistant Attorney-General for Public Lands, May 1, 1949, BIA Central Files, 1940–52, acc. #53A367, Box 1055, #28853-1947-013 (N.Y.), Part 3B, RG 75, NA.

41. *Senate Hearings* (1948), pp. 166–67.

42. *Ibid.*, pp. 142–43, 183–84.

43. Tillie John to Daniel Reed, June 15, 1948, Reed MSS., Cornell University Library.

44. "Congress Kills 2 Bills Affecting Indians," *Buffalo Courier-Express* (June 16, 1948). "State Gets Indian Jurisdiction," *New York Times* (July 3, 1948).

45. See for example the following articles in the *Buffalo Courier-Express*: "Indians Fight Against State Custody Bill" (March 25, 1949); "Indians Protest U.S. Payment in Lump Sum" (April 25, 1949); "Indians Oppose Lump Payment of Old Treaties" (June 9, 1949); "Indians Firm in Defense of Tribal Laws" (July 4, 1949).

46. Graymont, *Fighting Tuscarora*, pp. 134–37 and three photographs, pp. 98–99. "By the Shores of the Potomac; Senecas Say State's on Warpath," *New York Times* (June 10, 1949).

47. Albert Abrams and Everett Parker, Memorandum of Chief's Council of the Tonawanda Band of Seneca Indians, July 6, 1949, J. R. McGrath MSS., Box 28, "Indian Legislation—Proposed Legislation, Senatorial, 1947–1949," Truman Library, Independence, Mo.

48. Reverend Glenn Coykendall to Harry Truman, May 6, 1948, BIA Central Files, 1940–52, acc. #53A367, Box 1055, #28853-1947-013 (N.Y.), Part 3B, RG 75, NA; Reverend Emery Koesis to Harry Truman, Truman MSS., OF296, Box 937, Folder 1948-June 1949, Truman Library, Independence, Mo. "Indian Self-Government," *New York Times*

(September 9, 1950), letter to the editor; "Indian View Explained," *New York Times* (July 9, 1949), letter to the editor.

49. Reverend Glenn Coykendall and LeRoy Snow to Senator Joseph O'Mahoney, July 29, 1949, Daniel Reed MSS., Cornell University.

50. Hugh Butler to George E. Newton, September 16, 1949; William Zimmerman, Jr., to Robert T. Lansdale, March 25, 1949, Hugh Butler MSS., Box 211, Nebraska State Historical Society, Lincoln, Neb.; interviews of Julius Cook, May 27-June 1, 1982, New Paltz, N.Y.

51. Quoted in "Indians Fight House Bill to Extend States' Power," *Buffalo Courier-Express* (April 29, 1949).

52. Matthew Connelly to Vice President Alben Barkley, August 2, 1950, with attached petition submitted (by Lulu Stillman) to the House Subcommittee on Indian Affairs Hearing, July 14, 1950, Washington, D.C., Harry Truman MSS., OF296, Box 937, Folder July 1949–50, Truman Library, Independence, Mo.

53. Maxwell Garrow to Honorable Members of the Eighty-first Congress, August 18, 1950, Herbert H. Lehman MSS., "Indians" (American) A-H, C-100, 13, Lehman Collection, Columbia University.

54. Jesse J. Cornplanter to Herbert Lehman, July 25, 1950, Lehman MSS., "Indians" (American) A-H, C-100, 13, Lehman Collection, Columbia University.

55. For Ives' role, see "Statement of U.S. Senator Irving Ives Re S. 192 . . . " Irving M. Ives MSS., Box 45, Cornell University. For Whipple and Dowd, see Burdette Whipple to Daniel Reed, February 21, 1948, Reed MSS., Cornell University; Herbert Lehman to Thomas H. Dowd, August 14, 1950, Lehman MSS., "Indians" (American) A-H, C-100, 13, Lehman Collection, Columbia University.

56. Leighton Wade to Hugh Butler, February 5, 1949, Butler MSS., Box 211, Nebraska State Historical Society, Lincoln, Neb.

57. Daniel Reed to J. Hardin Peterson, August 10, 1949, Reed MSS., Cornell University.

58. New York State Legislature Joint Legislative Committee on Indian Affairs, *Report, 1949.* In: *N.Y. Legislative Document No. 39* (Albany, N.Y., 1949), pp. 3–8. "State Laws Urged to Benefit Indians," *New York Times* (May 22, 1949). Leighton Wade to Hugh Butler, February 5, March 30, 1949; March 3, June 16, July 31, 1950; Butler to Wade, March 10, April 5, 1949; May 2, June 19, July 27, 1950, Butler MSS., Box 211; Wade to Butler, September 14, 1950, Butler MSS., Box 265, Nebraska State Historical Society, Lincoln, Neb.

59. Congressional debate quoted in Wilcomb Washburn, ed., *The American Indian and the United States: A Documentary History* (Westport, Conn.: Greenwood Publishers 1973) III, 2013–14.

60. *Ibid.,* pp. 2019–21. Other congressional critics of the bill were Congressmen Martin Gorski and Anthony Tauriello of New York.

61. "Bill on Indians Voted," *New York Times* (August 15, 1950); "Bill on Indians Voted," *New York Times* (September 2, 1950).

62. "Indian Ct. Bill Signed," *New York Times* (September 14, 1950).

63. New York State Legislature, Joint Legislative Committee on Indian Affairs, *Report, 1953,* found in *New York Legislative Documents, No. 74* (Albany, N.Y. 1953), p. 3.

64. *United Statutes at Large* 67 (August 1, 1953): B132.

65. Bess Furman, "Senate Bill Would End 1794 Pact Giving Cloth Handout to Indians," *New York Times* (February 3, 1954).

66. Hauptman, *The Iroquois and the New Deal,* chapter 3.

67. *The First American* 2 (February 3, 1954): 3.

68. Douglas McKay to Mr. Stephens, July 1, 1954, Eisenhower MSS., Central Files, Box 618, OF121, Indians (1), Eisenhower Library, Abilene, Kan. "Senator Butler of Nebraska Dies," *New York Times* (July 1, 1954). See chapters 6 and 7.

5 Termination: The Wisconsin Oneidas and the Oklahoma Seneca-Cayugas

1. Hauptman, *The Iroquois and the New Deal*, chapters 5 and 6.
2. Interview of Norbert Hill, Sr., July 28, 1982. In October 1978, I attended a meeting of the Oneida Tribal Business Committee with the late Mr. Hill in which the BIA and tribal representatives were still dealing with the question of heirship lands.
3. Oscar Chapman to Harry Truman, March 18, 1950, Truman MSS., OF 6-C, Truman Library, Independence, Mo.
4. Fixico, "Termination and Relocation," pp. 49–69; Larry W. Burt, *Tribalism in Crisis* (Albuquerque, N.M.: University of New Mexico Press, 1982), pp. 1–13.
5. Report of the Committee on Indian Affairs of the Hoover Commission, Philleo Nash MSS., Box 44, Truman Library, Independence, Mo.
6. Quoted in "Indian Commissioner Sees Tribes Treated Like Other American Citizens in Future," *New York Times* (May 5, 1949).
7. Quoted in Hasse, "Termination and Assimilation," p. 127.
8. Quoted in *Ibid.*, p. 114.
9. Dillon S. Myer to Senator Herbert H. Lehman, Lehman MSS., "Indians" (American), J-WO-100-14, Columbia University.
10. United States Congress, House of Representatives, *House Report No. 2503* (Washington, D.C., 1952), pp. 2–3.
11. United States Congress, House of Representatives, *House Report No. 2680: Report with Respect to the House Resolution Authorizing the Committee on Interior and Insular Affairs to Conduct an Investigation of the Bureau of Indian Affairs.* 83rd Congress, 2d session. (Washington, D.C., 1954), pp. 3–4.
12. Burt, *Tribalism in Crisis*, pp. 15–30.
13. *United States Statutes at Large* 67 (August 15, 1953): 588–590. The origins of this act dated to at least 1949. United States Congress, House of Representatives, *House Report No. 1362: Subjecting Indians and Indian Reservations in the State of Wisconsin to the Laws of the State, With Certain Exceptions* (Washington, D.C., 1949), with attached bill H.R. 2736, Alexander Wiley MSS., Box 50, "Indians," State Historical Society of Wisconsin, Madison. Interviews of Norbert Hill, Sr., July 28, 1982, Oneida, Wis.; Ruth Baird, June 23, 1983, Green Bay, Wis.; Loretta Ellis Metoxen, June 22, 1983, Oneida, Wis.
14. Report to Committee on Interior and Insular Affairs on Oneida Reservation, September 25, 1952, made by Great Lakes Area Field Office, Ashland, Wis., submitted, June 19, 1953, "Withdrawal Programming Report for Oneida Tribe of Wisconsin," BIA Central Files, 1949–56, acc. #68H4937, Box 108, File #17112-1952-077, Great Lakes Consolidated AFO, RG 75, NA.
15. Oneida Executive Council to Dillon Myer, November 18, 1952, BIA Central Files, 1949–56, acc. #68H4937, Box 108, File #17112-1952-077, Great Lakes Consolidated AFO, RG 75, NA.
16. Dillon S. Myer to Oneida Tribal Executive Council, February 10, 1953; Don C. Foster to E. J. Riley, February 19, 1953; Foster to W. Barton Greenwood, May 21, 1953; Foster to G. Warren Spaulding, June 25, 1953; Greenwood to Congressman John W. Byrnes,

October 19, 1953, BIA Central Files, 1949–56, acc. #68H4937, Box 108, File #17112-1952-077, Great Lakes Consolidated AFO, RG 75, NA.

17. Dillon Myer to Senator Joseph McCarthy, March 19, 1953, BIA Central Files, 1949–56, acc. #68H4937, Box 108, File #17112-1952-077, Great Lakes Consolidated AFO, RG 75, NA.

18. Reply (of May 15, 1953) to House Committee on Interior and Insular Affairs, "Questionnaire on Tribal Organization, etc., Supplement to Withdrawal Programming Report of Aug. 5, 1952," BIA Central Files, 1949–56, acc. #68H4937, Box 108, File #17112-1952-077, Great Lakes Consolidated AFO, RG 75, NA.

19. "Oneidas Again Face Problem of Annuity; Reject Offer," *Green Bay Press-Gazette* (December 18, 1953).

20. Orme Lewis to Richard M. Nixon, January 4, 1954, Box 43, Philleo Nash MSS., Truman Library, Independence, Mo.; United States Congress, *Congressional Record*, 83rd Congress, 2d session, (January 18, 1954): 100, 322–23, 407, 410. For the Menominee termination, see Nicholas Peroff, *Menominee Drums* (Norman, Okla.: University of Oklahoma Press 1982):

21. Interviews of Norbert Hill, Sr., July 28, 1982; Ruth Baird, June 23, 1983; and Nancy Lurie, June 20, 1983, Milwaukee, Wis. For an early academic portrait of the Milwaukee Indian community, see Robert Ritzenthaler and Mary Sellers, "Indian in an Urban Setting," *Wisconsin Archeologist* 36 (1955): 147–61.

22. Interviews of Norbert Hill, Sr., July 28, 1982, and Ruth Baird, June 23, 1983.

23. See my *The Iroquois and the New Deal*, chapters 5 and 9. Interviews of Norbert Hill, Sr., July 28, 1982; Ruth Baird, June 23, 1983; Loretta Metoxen, June 22, 1983; Nancy Lurie, June 20, 1983.

24. Oscar Archiquette to Commissioner of Indian Affairs, February 1, 1954 with attached resolution of the Oneida Fact Finding Board, 1952; Glenn Emmons to Archiquette, February 23, 1954; Archiquette to Emmons, November 20 (?), 1956; Chief, Branch of Credit Memorandum to Peter Walz, December 10, 1956; Thomas Reid to Oscar Archiquette, January 7, 1957, BIA Central Files, 1949–56, acc. #68H4937, Box 108, File #17112-1952-077, Great Lakes Consolidated AFO, RG 75, NA.

25. Minutes of "Indian Affairs Conference, Minneapolis Area, Des Moines, Iowa, October 18–20, 1956," with attached notes, resolutions (copies in author's possession).

26. Interviews of Ruth Baird, June 23, 1983 and Norbert Hill, Sr., July 28, 1982; Robert Venables; transcribed interview of Oscar Archiquette, July 9, 1970, Shell Lake, Wis.

27. Interviews of Gordie McLester, June 21–23, 1983, Oneida, Wis.; Robert Smith, June 21, 1983, DePere, Wis.; Loretta Metoxen, June 22, 1983; and Nancy Lurie, June 20, 1983.

28. For background on tribal incorporation of 1937, see my *The Iroquois and the New Deal*, chapter 6.

29. Hauptman, "The American Indian Federation and the Indian New Deal," 378–402.

30. Report on Withdrawal Programming, Seneca-Cayuga Tribe of Oklahoma, 1952, Records of the Muskogee Area Office, #327, Office Files of the Tribal Affairs Officer, 1947–65, Box: Quapaw Agency Termination Tribal OPS, RG 75, Federal Records Center, Fort Worth, Tex.

31. *Ibid.*, appendix document D, September 15, 1952.

32. Grover C. Splitlog to Paul L. Fickinger, August 12, 1955; Lawrence K. Pickard affidavit, July 29, 1955; Roy Fisher affidavit, July 30, 1955; Chester Armstrong affidavit, July 30, 1955; David Charloe to Fickinger, June 17, 1955; Fickinger to Charloe, June 16, 1955; Splitlog to Muskogee Area Office, June 8, 1955 (with attached petition);

Petition of "Western Band of Cayuga Tribe," October 9, 1954; Splitlog to Fickinger, April 30, 1956; Fickinger to Senator Robert S. Kerr, April 12, 1956; Chester Armstrong and Elnora Enyart to congressmen and senators, March 19, 1956; Summary Report of Annual Meeting of the Seneca-Cayuga Tribe of Indians Held at the Tribal Stomp Grounds Near Miami, Okla., June 5, 1956, Muskogee, #327, Office Files of the Tribal Affairs Officer, 1947–65, Box: Seneca-Cayuga Tribal OPS, RG 75, FRC, Fort Worth. "Indian Meeting Lacks Authority Chief Declares," *Miami News Record* (August 29, 1957).

33. Summary Report of Annual Meeting, June 5, 1956; interviews of Ruby Diebold, June 24–25, 1983; and Velma Nieberding, June 25 and 29, 1983, Miami, Okla.

34. Homer Jenkins to William O. Roberts, March 25, 1954, Muskogee, #327, Office Files of the Tribal Affairs Officer, 1947–65, Box: Quapaw Agency Termination Tribal OPS, RG 75, FRC, Fort Worth.

35. Narrative Report of Assignment of Administrative Assistant, Muskogee Area Office to Quapaw Subagency, Miami, Okla., September 22–October 1, 1954; Field Trip to Muskogee Area Office and to Quapaw Subagency, Miami, Okla., September 20–30, 1954; Development of terminal plan for tribes in Quapaw Subagency, Muskogee, #327, Office Files of the Tribal Affairs Officer, 1947–65, Box: Quapaw Agency Termination Tribal OPS, RG 75, FRC, Fort Worth.

36. Narrative Report, September 22–October 1, 1954.

37. *Ibid.*; Field Trip to Muskogee Area Office . . . September 20–30, 1954.

38. Velma Nieberding, "Wyandotte and Peoria Leaders View Progress," *Miami News Record* (August 6, 1956). Interview of Velma Nieberding, June 29, 1983.

39. Fixico, "Termination and Relocation," 132.

40. Marie L. Hayes to E. E. Lamb, December 4, 1957, Muskogee, #327, Office Files of the Tribal Affairs Officer, 1947–65, Box: Tribal Operations, RG 75, FRC, Fort Worth.

41. Paul L. Fickinger to E. E. Lamb, August 9, 1956, Muskogee, #327, Office Files of Tribal Affairs Officer, 1947–65, Box: Quapaw Agency Termination, Quapaw Area, 1956, RG 75, FRC, Fort Worth.

42. Summary Report of Annual Meeting . . . June 5, 1956.

43. Minutes of the Regular Business Meeting of the Seneca-Cayuga Tribe of Oklahoma . . . October 1, 1957, Muskogee, #327, Office Files of the Tribal Affairs Officer, 1947–65, Box: Seneca-Cayuga Tribal OPS, File: Seneca-Cayuga Tribal OPS, RG 75, FRC, Fort Worth.

44. Amelia Perry (Secretary-Treasurer, Seneca-Cayuga Tribe of Oklahoma), to Seneca Tribe of Oklahoma, January 20, 1958; Perry to Marie Hayes, January 30, 1958, Muskogee, #326, Office Files of Tribal Affairs Officer, 1947–65, Box: Modocs, Wyandotte Tribal OPS, RG 75, FRC, Fort Worth.

45. Interview of Amanda Bearskin Harjo (Greenback), June 25, 1983, Miami, Okla.

46. Report of Special Meeting of the Seneca-Cayuga Tribe of Indians Held at the Council House Church, Southwest of Wyandotte, Oklahoma, February 18, 1958, Muskogee, #326, Office Files of Tribal Affairs Officer, 1947–65, Box: Modocs, Wyandotte Tribal OPS, RG 75, FRC, Fort Worth.

47. "Want It Back" (photo and caption), *Miami News Record* (August 19, 1957); interviews of Velma Nieberding, June 25 and 29, 1983, Ruby Diebold, June 24–25, 1983, and Vernon Crow, June 29, 1983, Miami Okla.

48. "Annual Green Corn Festival Nears for Seneca-Cayugas," *Miami News Record* (August 3, 1958).

49. Interviews of Jake Whitecrow, May 5, 1980, New Paltz, N.Y.; Velma Nieberding, June 25 and 29, 1983.

50. Report of Special Meeting of the Seneca-Cayuga Tribe . . . February 18, 1958. . . .

51. *Ibid.*

52. *Ibid.*

53. *Ibid.*

54. *Ibid.*

55. *Ibid.*

56. *Ibid.*

57. Paul L. Fickinger to Commissioner of Indian Affairs, March 31, 1958, Muskogee, #326, Office Files of the Tribal Affairs Officer, 1947–65, Box: Modocs, Wyandottes Tribal OPS, RG 75, FRC, Fort Worth.

58. Glenn Emmons to Paul L. Fickinger, May 8, 1958, Muskogee, #326, Office Files of the Tribal Affairs Officer, 1947–65, Box: Modocs, Wyandottes Tribal OPS, RG 75, FRC, Fort Worth.

59. United States Department of the Interior, *Annual Report of the Commissioner of Indian Affairs*, 1959 (Washington, D.C.: U.S.G.P.O., 1959), p. 231.

6 Interiors

1. For the organization of the Eisenhower presidency, see Fred I. Greenstein, "Eisenhower as an Activist President: A Look at New Evidence," *Political Science Quarterly* 94 (Winter 1979–80): 575–99. Greenstein has developed this theme further in *The Hidden-Hand Presidency: Eisenhower as Leader* (New York: Basic Books 1982). I have also benefited from reading Stephen Ambrose, *Eisenhower* (New York: Simon and Shuster 1984), vol. 2; Stephen Hess, *Organizing the Presidency* (Washington, D.C.: Brookings Institution, 1976), pp. 59–77; Richard T. Johnson, *Managing the White House* (New York: Harper and Row, 1974), pp. 74–119; Sherman Adams, *Firsthand Report* (New York: Harper, 1961); and Eisenhower's own memoirs, *The White House Years: Mandate for Change, 1953–1956*, and *Waging Peace, 1956–1961* (Garden City, N.Y.: Doubleday, 1963), 2 vols. The best study of Eisenhower's Department of the Interior in the period is Elmo Richardson, *Dams, Parks and Politics: Resource Development and Preservation in the Truman-Eisenhower Era* (Lexington, Ky.: University Press of Kentucky, 1973).

2. One significant study of how public works and Indian policies were interrelated in the period is Michael Lawson, *Dammed Indians* (Norman, Okla.: University of Oklahoma Press, 1982).

3. Public Law 88-533. 78 *United States Statutes at Large* 738 (August 31, 1964).

4. I participated with the Seneca Nation in its twenty-year memorial, "Remember the Removal, 1964–1984," held on September 29, 1984. The memorial included a six and a half-mile walk tracing the path of the removal, addresses by Senecas and Quakers involved in fighting the dam, and a panel discussion on the history of the project, in which I participated. I saw adult Senecas, choked up with emotion, unable to continue to speak about these events. I also had the opportunity and privilege to speak with the following: Rovena Abrams, Cornelius Abrams, Jr., George Heron, Carol Moses, and Walter Taylor, on September 29, 1984, at the Allegany Indian Reservation.

5. See for example, Alvin M. Josephy, Jr., *Now that the Buffalo's Gone: A Study of Today's American Indians* (New York: Alfred A. Knopf, 1982), pp. 127–50.

6. Wesley D. Ewart Oral History, Eisenhower Library, Abilene, Kan.

7. 360 U.S. 909 (1959); 262 F. 2d 27 (1958); 162 F.Supp. 580 (1958) (*Seneca Nation of Indians v. Wilbur M. Brucker, et al.*)

8. Interview of Merrill Bowen, August 26, 1983, Allegany Indian Reservation. Petition of the Seneca Nation to the President of the United States, *et al.*, May 9, 1938, BIA Central Files, 1907–39, #48662-34-066 (N.Y.), RG 75, NA. Elmer Thompson to President Harry Truman, June 23, 1945, BIA Central Files, 1940–52, acc. #53A-367, Box 1059, File #26702-1945-377 (N.Y.), RG 75, NA. "Indians Say Dam to Cost Them White Man's Gift," *Buffalo Courier-Express* (March 15, 1946). CEC (Charles E. Congdon) to William N. Fenton, December 4, 1964, William N. Fenton MSS., Box: Kinzua Dam III, American Philosophical Society Library, Philadelphia, Pa.

9. Interviews of Doctor Theodore Hetzel, January 17, 1984, Kennett Square, Pa., Edward O'Neill, January 10, 1984, Washington, D.C.; George Abrams and Merrill Bowen, August 26, 1983, Allegany Indian Reservation; Pauline Seneca, August 25, 1983, Cattaraugus Indian Reservation. Merrill W. Bowen, Sr. to Cornplanter Heirs, September 8, 1963, to Colonel de Melker, October 10, 1963, to President John Kennedy, October 21, 1963, to Governor William N. Scranton, October 21, 1963, to de Melker, November 12, 1963; and de Melker to Bowen, August 28 and October 2, 1963; and Lee C. White (Special Counsel to J.F.K.), December 4, 1963, Merle Deardorff MSS., Box 3, Pennsylvania Historical and Museum Commission, Harrisburg, Pa.

10. William N. Fenton, "From Longhouse to Ranch-type House: The Second Housing Revolution of the Seneca Nation," in *Iroquois Culture, History, and Prehistory*, edited by Elisabeth Tooker (Albany, N.Y., 1967), pp. 7–22.

11. Arthur E. Morgan, *Dams and Other Disasters: A Century of the Army Corps of Engineers in Civil Works* (Boston: P. Sargent, 1971), pp. 310–311.

12. *Ibid.*, 311–12; George Laughlin (Jones & Laughlin) to Harold Ickes, September 9, 1933; Major General Lytle Brown to Congressman Robert Ramsay, September 13, 1933; Frank C. Harper (Secretary-Manager, Pittsburgh Chamber of Commerce) to Brown, September 6, 1933 with attached petition, and to George Dern (Secretary of War), September 6, 1933; I. Lamont Hughes (Carnegie Steel) to Brown, September 1, 1933; Captain Lucius Clay to Hughes, September 6, 1933; J. F. Drake (Gulf Oil) to Brown, September 2, 1933; Clay to Drake, September 6, 1933; Nathan Strong (Allegheny River Improvement Association) to Brown, September 1, 1933; Clay to Strong, September 6, 1933; Senator James J. Davis (Pennsylvania) to Brown, September 6, 1933; Brown to Davis, September 12, 1933; John S. Fisher (President, Pittsburgh Chamber of Commerce), August 31, 1933; Clay to Fisher, September 5, 1933; Records of the Office of the Chief of Engineers, Civil Works, 1923–42: Rivers and Harbors Files, Allegheny River, RG 77, NA, Suitland, Maryland.

13. Laughlin to Ickes, September 9, 1933.

14. Strong to Brown, September 1, 1933.

15. Roy Lubove, ed., *Pittsburgh: A Documentary History* (New York: 1976), pp. 197–218; and Roy Lubove's *Twentieth Century Pittsburgh: Government, Business and Environmental Change* (New York; New Viewpoints, 1969), pp. 106–41. For the Lawrence machine, see Bruce M. Stave, *The New Deal and the Last Hurrah: Pittsburgh Machine Politics* (Pittsburgh: University of Pittsburgh Press, 1970). United States Congress, House of Representatives, House Document 300: *Allegheny River, N.Y. and Pa.-Allegheny Reservoir.* 76th Congress, 1st session. (Washington, D.C.: U.S.G.P.O. 1939).

16. John D. Reeves and A. D. Wathen to Commissioner of Indian Affairs, December 30, 1936, BIA Central Files, 1907–39, #2691-29-052 (N.Y.), RG 75, NA.

17. Oscar L. Chapman to Louis Johnson (Assistant Secrretary of War), June 6, 1940, BIA Central Files, 1907–39, #2691-29-052 (N.Y.), RG 75, NA.

18. E. K. Burlew to Secretary of War, May 2, 1940, BIA Central Files, 1907–39, #2691-29-052 (N.Y.), RG 75, NA.

19. Elmer Thomas, "Forty Years of Legislation," pp. 105–111, unpublished MSS., Elmer Thomas MSS., Unnumbered Box, Western History Collection, University of Oklahoma, Norman, Okla.

20. Interview of Edward O'Neill, January 10, 1984.

21. Dwight D. Eisenhower, *Mandate for Change, 1953–1956,* pp. 388–90.

22. Josephy, *Now that the Buffalo's Gone,* pp. 127–50. Morgan, *Dams and Other Disasters,* pp. 310–367. Wilson, *Apologies to the Iroquois,* pp. 190–197.

23. William Ashworth, *Under the Influence: Congress, Lobbies and the American Pork-Barrel System* (New York: Hawthorn/Dutton, 1981), pp. 105–45.

24. *Ibid.,* p. 142.

25. *Ibid.,* pp. 130–145.

26. Eisenhower, *Mandate for Change,* p. 394.

27. Reed M. Smith, *State Government in Transition: Reforms of the Leader Administration, 1955–1959* (Philadelphia: University of Pennsylvania Press, 1961), pp. 97n, 204–205.

28. Maurice K. Goddard to Congressman Clarence Cannon (Chairman, House Appropriations Committee), May 6, 1957, David Lawrence MSS., Box 40, Pennsylvania Historical and Museum Commission, Harrisburg, Pa.

29. Senator Joseph S. Clark News Release of Statement to be presented to the House Public Works Subcommittee of the Committee on Appropriations, May 15, 1957, John S. Bragdon MSS., Box 51, Eisenhower Library, Abilene, Kan.

30. Clark to Editor, *Washington Post* (June 24, 1957, January 26, 1960). David Lawrence MSS., Box 40, Pennsylvania Historical and Museum Commission, Harrisburg, Pa.; Morgan, *Dams and Other Disasters,* pp. 362–67.

31. Hess, *Organizing the Presidency,* p. 65.

32. Greenstein, "Eisenhower as an Activist President," p. 581.

33. William B. Ewald, Jr., *Eisenhower the President: Crucial Days, 1951–1960* (Englewood Cliffs, N.J.: Prentice-Hall, 1981), pp. 66–73. Ewald, White House staffer and assistant to Secretary of the Interior Fred Seaton in the Eisenhower years, has insisted that the President had a "feeling for organization."

34. Richardson, *Dams, Parks and Politics,* pp. 81–86, 185–201.

35. "Accomplishments of the Department of the Interior, 1953–1960," Ann Whitman Files: Administrative Series, Box 36, "Fred Seaton (1)," Eisenhower Library, Abilene, Kan.

36. Richardson, *Dams, Parks and Politics,* pp. 91–92.

37. Lawson, *Dammed Indians,* pp. xxi–xxii, 179–200.

38. *Ibid.,* p. xxii.

39. 78 *United States Statutes at Large* 738 (August 31, 1964).

40. D'Ewart Oral History.

41. Orme Lewis Oral History, Eisenhower Library, Abilene, Kan.

42. Hatfield Chilson to President Eisenhower, April 11, 1957, Fred Seaton (Subject Series) MSS., Box 17, "Kinzua Dam" (Seneca Indians), Eisenhower Library, Abilene, Kan.

43. John S. Bragdon, Memorandum for the Record, July 23, 1957, John S. Bragdon MSS., Box 51, Eisenhower Library, Abilene, Kan. The Senecas had rejected swapping lands since 1946; "Senecas Don't Want to Swap Reservation Lands for Park Lands," *Salamanca Republican-Press* (August 14, 1946).

44. Elmer Bennett Oral History, Eisenhower Library, Abilene, Kan.

45. *Ibid.*

46. See John S. Bragdon Notes, "Congressional Comment Re: Kinzua Dam" (Statements in Congressional Record on House or Senate Committee Hearings), 7/18/57, John S. Bragdon MSS., Box 51, Eisenhower Library, Abilene, Kan. Republican Congressman John Saylor was the lone dissenter in the Pennsylvania delegation.

47. O'Neill interview, January 10, 1984; Harold H. Healy, Jr. (executive assistant to the Attorney General), Memorandum for Bernard M. Shanley (Secretary to the President), May 8, 1957, Fred Seaton MSS., Subject Series, Box 17, Subject Series File—Kinzua Dam (Seneca Indians), Eisenhower Library, Abilene, Kan.

48. *Ibid.*

49. *Ibid.*

50. Excerpts from Department of Justice Memorandum of Law with respect to taking of Indian lands for the Allegheny Reservoir, July 15, 1957, John S. Bragdon MSS., Box 51, Eisenhower Library, Abilene, Kan. Eisenhower, through Bernard Shanley, requested legal opinions about the breaking of the Treaty of 1794 from Attorney General Brownell. Shanley Memorandum for Herbert Brownell, April 23, 1957, Eisenhower MSS., Central Files, Box 837, OF 155-E, 1957 (2), Eisenhower Library, Abilene, Kan.

51. Interview of Edward O'Neill, January 10, 1984.

52. *Seneca Nation of Indians v. Wilbur M. Brucker, et al.*, 162 F.Supp. 580 (March 24, 1958).

53. *Seneca Nation of Indians v. Wilbur M. Brucker, et al.*, 262 F.2d 27 (November 27, 1958).

54. Greenstein, "Eisenhower as an Activist President," pp. 582–84; Greenstein, *The Hidden-Hand Presidency*, pp. 138–50; Hess, *Organizing the Presidency*, pp. 67–71. Ewald, *Eisenhower the President*, pp. 66–73. According to Robert Griffith: "Eisenhower was a product of the organizational revolution that had transformed American life in the twentieth century, a member of the new managerial class that led the nation's great public and private bureaucracies." "Dwight D. Eisenhower and the Corporate Commonwealth," *American Historical Review* 87 (February 1982): 88.

55. Hamlin Reports (2), 1957, "Indians," Undated, James M. Lambie MSS., Box 36, Eisenhower Library, Abilene, Kan.

56. *Ibid.*

57. *Ibid.*

7 Command Decision
General John S. Bragdon and the Kinzua Dam

1. For the development of the interstate highway system, see Mark H. Rose, *Interstate: Express Highway Politics, 1941–1956* (Lawrence, Kan.: University Press of Kansas, 1979).

2. "Eisenhower Names Public Works Aides," *New York Times* (August 13, 1955). Letter to Major General John S. Bragdon Appointing him as Special Assistant to the President to Coordinate Public Works Planning, August 12, 1955, *Public Papers of the Presidents: Dwight D. Eisenhower, 1955* (Washington, D.C.: 1955), pp. 792–94.

3. "Major General John S. Bragdon, 70, of Civil Aeronautic Board Dies," *New York Times* (January 8, 1964); Eisenhower, *Mandate for Change*, p. 390; General John S. Bragdon Cullom File, Alumni Office, United States Military Academy, West Point, N.Y.

4. See chapter 6, note 12.

5. President's News Conference, January 19, 1956, *Public Papers of the President: Dwight D. Eisenhower, 1956* (Washington, D.C.: U.S.G.P.O., 1956), pp. 162–63.

6. *Ibid.* (1957), pp. 562–64; Rose, *Interstate*, pp. 72–98.

7. John S. Bragdon, Memorandum for the President, July 18, 1957, John S. Bragdon MSS., Box 41, Eisenhower Library, Abilene, Kan.

8. *Ibid.*

9. John S. D. Eisenhower, Memorandum of Conference with the President, July 22, 1957, Ann Whitman DDE Diary Series, Box 25, July, 1957 Staff Memos (1), Eisenhower Library, Abilene, Kan.

10. Morgan, *Dams and Other Disasters*, pp. 317–66.

11. Arthur E. Morgan, *The Making of the TVA* (Buffalo, N.Y.: Prometheus, 1974), pp. 18–19, 26–27, 50, 75, 93–94, 98, 100, 104, 129–30.

12. Morgan, *Dams and Other Disasters*, p. 317.

13. Arthur E. Morgan, *The Community of the Future and the Future of the Community* (Yellow Springs, Oh.: Community Service, 1957), pp. 156–59. Morgan was the author of more than sixteen books, including two on Edward Bellamy.

14. Arthur E. Morgan, *The Small Community: Foundation of Democratic Life* (New York: Harper and Brothers, 1942), p. 13.

15. Morgan, *Dams and Other Disasters*, p. 342.

16. John S. Bragdon, Memorandum for the President, July 25, 1957, John S. Bragdon MSS., Box 51, Eisenhower Library, Abilene, Kan.

17. Minutes of a meeting to discuss Allegheny Dam and Reservoir, Pa. . . . , September 6, 1957, John S. Bragdon MSS., Box 51, Eisenhower Library, Abilene, Kan.

18. John S. Bragdon, Memorandum for Assistant Secretary of the Army, Dewey Short, July 23, 1957, and Bragdon, Memorandum for the President, September 18, 1957, John S. Bragdon MSS., Box 51; Gerald D. Morgan (special counsel to the President) to Mr. (Cornelius) Seneca, D. D. Eisenhower MSS., Central Files, Box 837, OF 155-E, 1957 (2), EisenhowerLibrary, Abilene, Kan.

19. "General James H. Stratton, Flood-Control Specialist," *New York Times* (March 21, 1984).

20. James A. Haley to President John F. Kennedy, undated, James A. Haley MSS., Florida Southern College, Lakeland, Fla.

21. Morgan, *Dams and Other Disasters*, p. 321.

22. John S. Bragdon, Memorandum for the Record, March 27, 1958, John S. Bragdon MSS., Box 51, Eisenhower Library, Abilene, Kan.

23. Quoted in Morgan, *Dams and Other Disasters*, p. 332.

24. Tippetts, Abbett, McCarthy, Stratton, *Report: Plans 1, 2, 3: Allegheny River Reservoir: A Review of Authorized Plan and Alternatives for the U.S. Army Corps of Engineers Division, Ohio River, April, 1958.*

25. Morgan, *Dams and Other Disasters*, p. 338.

26. CEC (Charles E. Congdon) to William N. Fenton, December 4, 1964, William N. Fenton MSS., Box: Kinzua Dam III, American Philosophical Society Library, Philadelphia, Pa.

27. Interview of Arthur Lazarus, Jr., July 17, 1982, Buffalo, N.Y.

28. President Cornelius Seneca, "The Allegheny Reservoir Project: Statement in Opposition to Construction of the Proposed Kinzua Dam," 1957. Transcript in possession of Mrs. Pauline Seneca, Cattaraugus Indian Reservation.

29. Cornelius Seneca to Dwight D. Eisenhower, March 26, 1957, Eisenhower MSS., Alpha Series, Box 1699, File: Kinzua Dam (3); Seneca to Eisenhower, June 26, 1957,

Eisenhower Central Files, Box 837, OF 155-F, 1957 (2), Eisenhower Library, Abilene, Kan.; Interviews of Edward O'Neill, January 10, 1984; Pauline Seneca, July 17, 1982.

30. Treasurer George Heron, "The Allegheny Reservoir Project: Statement in Opposition to the Construction of the Proposed Kinzua Dam," 1957. Transcript in possession of Mrs. Pauline Seneca, Cattaraugus Indian Reservation.

31. Basil Williams to John F. Kennedy, February 22, 1961, William N. Fenton MSS., Box: Kinzua I, American Philosophical Society Library, Philadelphia, Pa. For typical examples of pro-Seneca news coverage, see "Second Look at Kinzua," *Washington Post*, Editorial (January 24, 1960); and the following articles in the *Rochester Democrat and Chronicle*: Floyd King, "Pledge to Cornplanter" (May 12, 1957); John Koenig, Jr., "Drowning of a Reservation" (November 22, 1959).

32. Interviews of Doctor Theodore Hetzel, January 17, 1984, Kennett Square, Pa., and Lawrence Lindley, June 25, 1981, Media, Pa. Sarah Stabler to Congressman Hugh Scott, December, 1956; Charles J. Darlington to Fred Seaton, March 31, 1960; Darlington to Dwight D. Eisenhower, March 31, 1960; AA3.10 Philadelphia Yearly Meeting of Friends MSS., Indian Committee, 1956–66, File: Kinzua Dam, Haverford College, Haverford, Pa. Mrs. Stabler's letter on its heading had the following words penciled in: "As a sample letter for the Indian Comm. Minutes." The letter was the model used in the Friends' campaign and showed up almost verbatim in letters written by other Kinzua opponents in 1956 and 1957. See also Philadelphia Yearly Meeting of Friends, Kinzua Project of the Indian Committee, *The Kinzua Dam Controversy: A Practical Solution—Without Shame* (Philadelphia, Pa.: Philadelphia Yearly Meeting of Friends, 1961).

33. Governor Averell Harriman, News Release, January 18, 1957, Averell Harriman MSS., Box 252, Syracuse University, Syracuse, N.Y. "Support for Senecas," *Rochester Democrat and Chronicle* (June 19, 1957).

34. Theodore Hetzel to President Eisenhower, July 3, 1957; Lawrence Lindley to Eisenhower, June 29, 1957; Leo Conner to Eisenhower, June 27, 1957; Mrs. Edwin B. Lefferts to Eisenhower, June 30, 1957, Eisenhower MSS., Alpha Series, Box 1699, File: Kinzua Dam (2), Eisenhower Library, Abilene, Kan. Arthur Morgan tried to use his influence with Ann Whitman, President Eisenhower's personal secretary and a graduate of Morgan's Antioch College. Ann Whitman to Doctor Morgan, June 13, 1958, Arthur E. Morgan MSS., Seneca Nation/Kinzua, Antioch College, Yellow Springs, Ohio.

35. William N. Fenton to Cornelius Seneca, October 8, 1957; Fenton to Congressman James Haley, July 4, 1960; Fenton to Walter Taylor, with attachments, March 17, 1961; Fenton To Edmund Wilson, March 28, 1961, William N. Fenton MSS., Box: Kinzua Dam I; Fenton to Nelson Rockefeller, May 2, 1960; Fenton to Arthur Schlesinger, Jr., May 16, 1961; Edward O'Neill to Fenton, September 16, 1958, William N. Fenton MSS., Box: Kinzua Dam II, American Philosophical Society Library, Philadelphia, Pa. Fenton, a classmate of Nelson Rockefeller, was unable to use his personal influence to open the doors to the Governor's Mansion. Interview of William N. Fenton, May 18, 1983, Slingerlands, N.Y. Nevertheless, Fenton was almost singlehandedly responsible for encouraging Edmund Wilson to take up the Senecas' cause. See Wilson, *Apologies to the Iroquois*, pp. vi, 198–200; and Wilson, *Letters on Literature and Politics, 1912–1977*, pp. 406, 552–61.

36. Wilson, *Apologies to the Iroquois*, pp. 169–251, 286–89; Wilson, *Letters on Literature and Politics*, pp. 552–61. For Brooks Atkinson, see his *Tuesdays and Fridays* (New York: 1962); "Brooks Atkinson, 89, Theatre Critics for the Times for 31 Years, is Dead," *New York Times* (January 15, 1984), for an example of Atkinson's strong stand against Kinzua, see his "Critic at Large: Proposed Dam that Would Violate Treaty with

the Senecas Poses Moral Question," *New York Times* (April 21, 1961). Walter Taylor of the American Friends Service was, without question, the most important non-Indian lobbyist on behalf of the Senecas from 1961 to 1964 and deserves credit for mobilizing the nationwide effort on behalf of the Seneca Relocation Bill of 1964. He helped establish the *Kinzua Planning Newsletter*. Interview of Walter Taylor, September 29, 1984, Allegany Indian Reservation. For his views, see Taylor to Senator Joseph S. Clark, April 14, 1961, American Friends Service Archives, CRD—American Indian Program, 1961, Program Projects, Kinzua Dam, Pa., Philadelphia. Patrick M. Malin (ACLU) and Burt Aginsky to the President, October 14, 1958, John S. Bragdon MSS., Box 51, Eisenhower Library, Abilene, Kan.

37. Memorandum by Sherman Adams, February 27, 1957 (Re: Resolution adopted by the Six Nations Confederacy, February 21, 1957), Eisenhower MSS., Alpha Series, Box 1699, Kinzua Dam (1); Eva Danforth to President Eisenhower, April 25, 1960; Mildred Garlow (Seneca) to Eisenhower, June 3, 1957; Fred Redeye (Seneca) to Eisenhower, August 12, 1959; Beverly Wheeler (Seneca) to Eisenhower, February 16, 1957, Eisenhower MSS., Alpha Series, Box 1699, Kinzua Dam (3), Eisenhower Library Abilene, Kan.; Clarence Wesley (NCAI) to Congressman Sidney R. Yates, April 15, 1960, Sidney R. Yates MSS., Truman Library, Independence, Mo.; Del Barton (Seneca) to Senator Lyndon Johnson, November 28, 1958, LBJ Senate Papers, 1949–61, Subject Files, Box 680; Ralph A. Dungan to Secretary of the Interior, April 17, 1964, with letter from Earl B. Pierce, Cherokee General Counsel—Muskogee, March 15, 1964, WHCF, 1963–69, Indian Affairs, Box 4, LBJ Library, Austin, Tex.; American Indian Chicago Conference, *The Declaration of Indian Purpose*, p. 37, Appendix 4: "Resolution on the Kinzua Dam," June 16, 1961, found in American Indian Chicago Conference MSS., Box 2, National Anthropological Archives, Smithsonian Institution, Washington, D.C.

38. Danforth to Eisenhower, April 25, 1960.

39. John S. Bragdon to Dewey Short, June 24, 1958, Fred Seaton MSS., Subject Series, Box 16, Indians (2), Eisenhower Library, Abilene, Kan. It appears Bragdon was not motivated by Morgan's direct appeal to the president. Morgan to Ann Whitman, June 4, 1958, John S. Bragdon MSS., Box 51, Eisenhower Library, Abilene, Kan.

40. F. D. Peterson Office Memorandum on Meeting on Allegheny (Kinzua) Dam Project to General Bragdon, July 29, 1958, John S. Bragdon MSS., Box 51, Eisenhower Library, Abilene, Kan.

41. F. D. Peterson to General Bragdon, July 27, 1959, penciled in note on memorandum from Walter G. Sutton to General Bragdon, July 23, 1959, John S. Bragdon MSS., Box 51, Eisenhower Library, Abilene, Kan. Sutton was still exploring the long-rejected idea of "substitute lands for Indians at Kinzua Reservoir."

42. John S. Bragdon, Memorandum for the President, August 24, 1959, Ann Whitman File, DDE Diary Series, Box 43, Staff Notes, August 1959 (1), Eisenhower Library, Abilene, Kan.

43. John S. Bragdon to Mrs. Whitman, October 17, 1959; John S. Bragdon to Reverend Donald Harrington, December 4, 1959, John S. Bragdon MSS., Box 51, Eisenhower Library, Abilene, Kan.

44. Phillip S. Hughes (Bureau of the Budget) to Secretary of the Interior, June 22, 1960, D. D. Eisenhower MSS., Central Files, Box 837, OF 155-E, 1957 (2), Eisenhower Library, Abilene, Kan.

45. Richard Hardtine to Governor David Lawrence, June 21, 1960; Lawrence Draft Telegram to Pennsylvania Congressional delegation, June 21, 1960; News Release: Statement of Governor David Lawrence Before the House Committee on Interior and Insular Affairs, June 23, 1960, David Lawrence MSS., Box 40, Pennsylvania Historical and Museum Commission, Harrisburg, Pa.

46. News Release: Statement of Governor David Lawrence, June 23, 1960.

47. News Release: Remarks of Governor David Lawrence at Groundbreaking, Allegheny River Reservoir, Kinzua, Pa., October 22, 1960, David Lawrence MSS., Box 40, Pennsylvania Historical and Museum Commission, Harrisburg, Pa.

48. John F. Kennedy to Basil Williams, August 9, 1961, William N. Fenton MSS., Box: Kinzua Dam 1, American Philosophical Society Library, Philadelphia, Pa.

49. Elmo Richardson, *The Presidency of Dwight D. Eisenhower* (Lawrence, Kan.: University Press of Kansas, 1979), pp. 210–211.

50. John Ferejohn, a political scientist, in his study of rivers and harbors legislation from 1947 to 1968, has maintained that the critics and supporters of pork-barrel politics would agree that Congress molds public works appropriations bills "to a great extent." The Kinzua Dam controversy counters Ferejohn's underlying assumption by illustrating the key role of the executive branch in this process. Ferejohn, *Pork Barrel Politics: Rivers and Harbors Legislation, 1947–1968* (Stanford, Ca.: Stanford University Press, 1974), pp. 1–2.

8 Drums Along the Waterway
The Mohawks and the Coming of the Saint Lawrence Seaway

1. Interviews of Julius Cook, August 1, 1983, and Ernest Benedict, July 30, 1983, Saint Regis (Akwesasne) Reservation. The Canadian government clearly chose the path to develop hydroelectric power, transport oil, gas, and iron ore, and strengthen its military defense by building the Saint Lawrence Seaway. Canada and the United States government clearly were less interested in protecting Indians, fisheries, and wildlife. See Robert W. Coates to Robert Henry Winters (Canadian Minister of Resources and Development), July 3, 1952; J. Smart (Director of Resources and Development) to Acting Deputy Minister, December 12, 1951; Ferdinand N. Menefee (engineer) to Hugh Keenleyside (Deputy Minister Mines and Resources), October 18, 1950; "Confidential Draft Memorandum for the Cabinet Committee on Economic Policy," undated, all found in Records of the Deputy Minister, Volume 615, File 31-2-13, Part 3, RG 22, Public Archives of Canada, Ottawa. "Significance of Seaway Outlined by Chevrier," *Ottawa Citizen* (February 22, 1951).

2. William R. Willoughby, *The St. Lawrence Waterway: A Study in Politics and Diplomacy* (Madison, Wis.: University of Wisconsin Press, 1961), p. 4.

3. For the relation of seaway transportation to power development, see Charles Poletti, "Confidential Report, 1931: St. Lawrence Seaway Power Project, 1930–1938," Charles Poletti MSS., 197, S 194, Herbert Lehman Collection, Columbia University. For the creation and earlier history of SPA, see Bernard Bellush, *Franklin D. Roosevelt as Governor of New York* (New York: Columbia University Press, 1955), pp. 208–42; Robert P. Ingalls, *Herbert H. Lehman and New York's Little New Deal* (New York: 1975), pp. 224–26; Frank Freidel, *Franklin D. Roosevelt: The Triumph* (Boston: Little, Brown, 1956), pp. 111–12.

4. Willoughby, *The St. Lawrence Waterway*, pp. 221–22; N. R. Danielian Oral History, Eisenhower Library, Abilene, Kan.

5. Willoughby, *The St. Lawrence Waterway*, pp. 233–63; Angelika Roemer, *The St. Lawrence Seaway, Its Ports and Its Hinterland* (Tübingen, Germany: In Selbstverlag des Geographischen Instituts der Universität, 1971), pp. 10–25.

6. Lionel Chevrier, *The St. Lawrence Seaway* (New York: St. Martin's Press, 1959), p. 5.

7. Willoughby, *The St. Lawrence Waterway*, pp. 264–66; Mabee, *The Sea-*

way Story, pp. 172–73; SPA, *Report: St. Lawrence Power, Aug. 10, 1954* (New York, 1954).

    8. Interview of Douglas George, July 29, 1983, St. Regis (Akwesasne) Indian Reservation. See George's article, "Barnhart Island," *Indian Time* (July 1, 1983): 6–7.

    9. Carleton Mabee, *The Seaway Story,* pp. 204–222.

    10. See William N. Fenton and Elisabeth Tooker, "Mohawk," in *Handbook of North American Indians,* edited by Bruce G. Trigger and William C. Sturtevant (Washington, D.C.: U.S.G.P.O., 1978) XV, 476–78; Jack A. Frisch, "Iroquois in the West," in *Handbook of North American Indians,* 15, pp. 544–46; and Frisch's "Revitalization, Nativism and Tribalism Among the St. Regis Mohawks," unpublished Ph.D. dissertation, Indiana University, Bloomington, 1970; David S. Blanchard, *Kahnawake: A Historical Sketch* (Caughnawaga: Kanien'kehaka Raotitiohkwa Press, 1980); Blanchard, "Entertainment, Dance and Northern Showmanship," *American Indian Quarterly* 7 (1983): 2–26; and Blanchard, "High Steel! The Kahnawake Mohawk and the High Construction Trade," *Journal of Ethnic Studies* 11 (Summer 1983): 32–60; Morris Freilich, "Cultural Persistence Among the Modern Iroquois," *Anthropos* 53 (1958): 473–83; Harvey Flad, "The City and the Longhouse: A Social Geography of American Indians in Syracuse, New York," unpublished Ph.D. dissertation, Syracuse University, Syracuse, N.Y., 1973, pp. 186–200.

    11. Interview of Gloria Tarbell Fogden, June 21, 1984, New Paltz, N.Y.

    12. Chevrier, *The St. Lawrence Seaway,* p. 5.

    13. *Ibid.,* p. 4.

    14. *Ibid.,* pp. 2–6.

    15. *Ibid.,* pp. 42–50.

    16. *Ibid.,* p. 5.

    17. *Ibid.,* pp. 105–107.

    18. For a different view, see Blanchard, *Kahnawake,* p. 26.

    19. Notes of Meeting . . . July 19, 1956, by the Superintendent General of Indian Affairs with the newly elected council of the Caughnawaga Band: Caughnawaga Band Council Resolution, July 13, 1956; Open letter to Queen Elizabeth II by Chief Tawistawis, undated (1955 or 1956?), 373/34-1-1, Vol. 4, Land Sales, Caughnawaga, St. Lawrence Seaway, Montreal District, Records of the Department of Indian Affairs, Department of Indian and Northern Affairs, Hull, Québec; "Iroquois Say Seaway Usurps Indian Land," *New York Times* (August 22, 1956). See for example, W.C. Bethune to Director, Indian Affairs Branch, November 2, 1956, 373/34-1-1, Vol. 5; Michael Rowe to L.A. Couture, February 6, 1956, 373/34-1-1, Vol. 1; H.T. Vergette to J.W. Churchman, October 17, 1968, 373/34-1-1, Vol. 13; Vergette Memorandum to File, 373/34-1-1, Vol. 14; Cyril E. Schwisberg to J. Pickersgill, May 15, 1956, Schwisberg to Laval Fortier, June 7, 1956, 373/34-1-1, Vol. 1, Land Sales, Caughnawaga, St. Lawrence Seaway, Montreal District, Department of Indian and Northern Affairs, Hull, Québec. Omar Z. Ghobashy, *The Caughnawaga Indians and the St. Lawrence Seaway* (New York: Devan-Adair, 1961), pp. 44–69, 115–26; "Wants Indians Paid by Canada," *New York Times* (October 2, 1961).

    20. Chevrier, *The St. Lawrence Seaway,* pp. 102–108.

    21. Chevrier, *The St. Lawrence Seaway,* p. 106.

    22. Lionel Chevrier Memorandum, September 7, 1955, J.H. Gordon Memorandum to Acting Deputy Minister, October 3, 1963, 373/34-1-1, Vol. 11, Land Sales, Caughnawaga, St. Lawrence Seaway, Montreal District, Records of the Department of Indian Affairs, Department of Indian and Northern Affairs, Hull, Québec; Chevrier, *The St. Lawrence Seaway,* pp. 107–108; "Vital Contract Let," *New York Times* (March 23,

1956); "Chevrier Puffs Peace Pipe, Says Compensation Just," *Montreal Gazette* (July 27, 1956).

23. Chevrier, *The St. Lawrence Seaway*, pp. 107–108.

24. Parliament of Canada, *House of Commons Debates*, 1955, pp. 5307–13; 1957, pp. 2635–38.

25. Mabee, *The Seaway Story*, pp. 208–209; "Indians Accept Seaway," *New York Times* (March 24, 1956).

26. Robert Moses, *Working for the People: Promise and Performance in Public Service* (New York: Harper, 1956), pp. 167–90; "St. Lawrence and Niagara Power, Address by Robert Moses . . . New York City, Tuesday, Oct. 15, 1957"; "Statement on Niagara Power by Robert Moses . . . Over Stations WBEN . . . and WNYC . . . Sept. 5, 1957"; Box 6, Bound Volume: Reports, 1957, Robert Moses MSS., Syracuse University; Robert Moses to Earle J. Machold, May 6, 1955, Box 4, Bound Volume: Reports, 1955, Robert Moses MSS., Syracuse University.

27. Moses, *Working for the People*, p. 167.

28. Robert A. Caro, *The Power Broker: Robert Moses and the Fall of New York* (New York: Random House, 1974), p. 830.

29. "State Control of Parks Backs Federal Plan to Buy Reservation and Remove Indians: Proposal Linked with Kinzua Dam; Would Develop Allegany Valley for Recreation," *Salamanca Republican-Press* (January 21, 1946).

30. CEC to Fenton, December 4, 1964.

31. The famous Benton murals are located at the Moses-Saunders Power House on Barnhart Island and at the Robert Moses Niagara Power Plant at Niagara Falls. Benton was also a descendant of the nineteenth-century expansionist senator from Missouri.

32. Caro, *The Power Broker*, pp. 580–581.

33. *Ibid.*, p. 166.

34. *Ibid.*, pp. 1–21, 163–68, 262–82.

35. Statement of Leland Olds at Governor's Hearing on Proposed New York Power Authority Aluminum Co. Contract for St. Lawrence Power, Albany, N.Y., June 14, 1955, Leland Olds MSS., Box 69, FDR Library, Hyde Park, N.Y.

36. Moses, *Working for the People*, pp. 181–90.

37. Sidney C. Sufrin and Edward E. Palmer, *The New St. Lawrence Frontier: A Survey of the Economic Potential in the St. Lawrence Area of New York State* (Syracuse, N.Y.: Syracuse University Press, 1956), pp. viii–x, 1–10, 58, 72.

38. Moses, *Working for the People*, p. 187. See also "Remarks of Robert Moses . . . Presiding at the Groundbreaking Ceremonies for the Reynolds Aluminum and General Motors Plants at Rooseveltown . . . , June 14, 1957, Bound Volume: Reports, 1957, Box 6, Robert Moses MSS., Syracuse University.

39. Mabee, *The Seaway Story*, pp. 230–32.

40. *Ibid.*

41. C. J. Ward to Governor Averell Harriman, June 25, 1958, Name File: Robert Moses, Box 586, Averell Harriman MSS., Syracuse University. See also "Massena to Honor Robert Moses," *Ogdensburg Journal* (May 6, 1960).

42. "St. Lawrence Power Ceremony Marking the First Delivery of Commercial Power at the St. Lawrence International Dam, Sept. 5, 1958," Bound Volume: Reports, 1958, Box 7, Robert Moses MSS., Syracuse University.

43. Chevrier, *The St. Lawrence Seaway*, pp. 77–78; Willoughby, *The St. Lawrence Waterway*, p. 269; L. L. Brown Memorandum to the Deputy Minister, April 25, 1955, 481/34-1-1, Vol. 1, Land Sales, St. Regis, St. Lawrence Seaway, Kingston District,

Records of the Department of Indian Affairs, Department of Indian and Northern Affairs, Hull, Québec.

44. SPA, *Report: Land Acquisition on the American Side for the St. Lawrence Seaway and Power Project, July 18, 1955* (New York: 1955); "The Other Side of the Seaway," *Montreal Gazette* (August 8, 1955).

45. Irving Selikoff, E. Cuyler Hammond, Stephen M. Levin, *Environmental Contaminants and the Health of the People of the St. Regis Reserve* (New York: Mt. Sinai College of Medicine, 1984); Benedict interviews, September 10–11, 1982, July 30, 1983; Peter Matthiesson, *Indian Country* (New York: 1984), pp. 160–61; the following issues of *Indian Time:* July 15, 1983, p. 1; January 27, 1984, p. 1; February 10, 1984, p. 1; March 23, 1984, p. 1; April 20, 1984, p. 1; June 15, 1984, p. 1; and *Akwesasne Notes* 14 (Early Spring): 4–6. The problem also includes PCB, mercury pollution, and acid rain. The seaway is also a source of Mohawk land erosion. The wakes of speeding ships create waves which erode the shoreline. In some places on Cornwall Island, Mohawks claim as much as six feet of the shoreline has been lost. See *Indian Time* (April 6 and 20, 1984), p. 1.

46. Ernest Benedict to ACLU, March 27, 1941.

47. Fogden interview, June 21, 1984.

48. Cook interview, August 1, 1983.

49. United States, Federal Power Commission, Bureau of Power, "Power Market Report for United States Portion of the Barnhart Island Project," St. Lawrence River, Feb., 1946, Rev. May, 1947, Leland Olds MSS., Box 141, FDR Library, Hyde Park, N.Y.

50. Moses, *Working for the People*, p. 186.

51. George, "Barnhart Island."

52. "Indians Press Claim to Isle," *New York Times* (March 27, 1956); "Tribe's Power Claim Argued," *New York Times* (April 17, 1956); Bill Ringle, "Barnhart Background: Indians' Indian Suit Puts History in Review," *Rochester Times-Union* (April 16, 1956). For the Vermont claim in the 1950s, see the following articles in the *New York Times:* "Indians Claim Up Again" (March 28, 1954); "Indians on Their Way" (April 9, 1954); "Vermont Repels Indian Invasion" (April 10, 1954); "A Little Slice of Vermont" (October 24, 1954).

53. "Indians Get Right to Push Land Suit," *New York Times* (January 3, 1957); 4 Misc. 2d 110 (1956); "Indians Lose Suit," *New York Times* (December 20, 1957); 168 N.Y.S 2d 894.

54. 177 N.Y.S. 2d 289 (1958). The Canadian government was also interested in the progress of the Mohawk Barnhart Island claim. N. F. Ogden to W. C. Bethune, June 11, 1956; L. A. Couture to C. I. Fairholm, June 7, 1956; H. M. Jones to Deputy Minister, June 11, 1956, Records Relating to Indian Affairs, Volume 7157, File 1/3-11-6, Part 1, RG 10, Public Archives of Canada, Ottawa. Canadian officials insisted there was no need for a joint United States-Canadian commission, as in the case of the Cayuga Indians in the 1920s, to arbitrate the Mohawk claim.

55. Chief Pyke and the Mohawk attorney are quoted in Michael T. Kaufman, "To the Mohawk Nation, Boundaries Do Not Exist," *New York Times* (April 13, 1984).

56. P.C. 1956-1761, November 29, 1956, reprinted in *Akwesasne Notes* (April 1969). The Mohawks also lost acreage on Stanley and Sheek Islands because of seaway construction.

57. W.C. Bethune to J.M. Pauze, September 18, 1956, reprinted in *Akwesasne Notes* (April 1969). See also St. Regis Band Council Resolution, December 8, 1956,

481/34-1-1, Vol. 2, Land Sales, St. Regis, St. Lawrence Seaway, Kingston District, Records of the Department of Indian Affairs, Department of Indian and Northern Affairs, Hull, Québec.

58. "Mohawks Threaten a Traffic Blockade," *New York Times* (September 30, 1959); "Indians Seek $45,000 as Rent from Seaway," *New York Times* (September 30, 1959); "Indians to Lease Road Again," *New York Times* (October 10, 1959).

59. See Graymont, *Fighting Tuscarora,* entire.

60. *Francis v. The Queen* (1956) S.C.R. 618; Malcolm Montgomery, "Legal Status of the Six Nations in Canada," *Ontario History* 55 (1965): 93–105; "Canadian Indian Loses Fight Against Tariff," *New York Times* (June 12, 1956).

61. (Undated) Statement of Grievances Submitted by the Six Nation Indian Confederacy of America, attached to letter of Jacob A. Javits to President Dwight Eisenhower, March 24, 1959, Eisenhower MSS., Eisenhower Central Files, Box 618, OF 121 Indians (3), Eisenhower Library, Abilene, Kan.

62. "Benedict Wants Indian Justice," *Tekawennake* (February 19, 1969).

63. The Mohawks recorded this incident in a film: "You Are On Indian Land," which is obtainable from the National Film Board of Canada. "Indians Define Problems," *Massena Observer* (December 17, 1968); "Indians to Seek MP, Threaten Blockade," *Cornwall Standard-Freeholder* (December 16, 1968); "Red Faces for Palefaces," *Ottawa Citizen* (December 20, 1968); "Chiefs From Six Nations Meet; Discuss Duty Problems with Canadian Customs," *Watertown Daily Times* (December 20, 1968). See also the following articles in the *New York Times:* "41 Mohawks Seized in Protest at Border Bridge" (December 19, 1968); "Indians and Canada Report Accord in Customs Dispute" (December 21, 1968); "Canada Is Seeking a Mohawk Accord" (December 29, 1968). Interviews of Ernest Benedict, September 10–11, 1982; Salli Benedict, September 11, 1982, Brasher Centre, N.Y. "They're Winning Some Battles: Vocal, Demonstrating Indian [Kahn-Tineta Horn] Emerging," *Rochester Democrat and Chronicle* (December 23, 1968). (Kahn-Tineta Horn) "Speaks with Sharp Tongue," *New Yorker* (May 27, 1972): 28–31.

64. The current newspaper *Akwesasne Notes* was originally founded and edited by Jerry Gambill (Rarihokwats), a non-Indian social worker, at Ernest Benedict's home on Cornwall Island. It grew out of two earlier publications which came out of the bridge demonstration, including *Akwesasne News,* a paper that merely reproduced Indian-related articles from other publications. See chapter 11.

65. "Seaway Indians Urged to Settle in State," *Niagara Falls Gazette* (August 23, 1957). See also Wilson, *Apologies to the Iroquois,* pp. 39–57. See the following articles in the *New York Times:* "Mohawks Invade Upstate Area; Assert Treaty Gives Them Land" (August 17, 1957); "Mohawks Insist on Claim to Land" (August 26, 1957); "Indians Defy Eviction" (January 18, 1958); "Mohawks Defy Order to Break Camp Upstate" (February 16, 1958); "Mohawks Ordered Out" February 21, 1958); "Mohawks Are Adamant" (March 2, 1958); "Indians Get Land Grant" (March 6, 1958); "Eviction Hearing Set for Mohawks" (March 9, 1958); "Mohawks Quit Camp" (March 22, 1958). "Indian Population Doubles at New Site Near Thruway," *Rochester Democrat and Chronicle* (June 26, 1957); "Legal Tomahawk Over City: Mohawks May Set Up Little White Teepee," *Rochester Democrat and Chronicle* (August 18, 1957); "Thruway Indians Defying Eviction," *Rochester Democrat and Chronicle* (February 16, 1958); "Standing Arrow Skedaddles, Too: Indian Squatters Quit Settlement," *Rochester Democrat and Chronicle* (April 1, 1958), Besides Standing Arrow, the following Indians played a role in the takeover: Wounded Buffalo, Peter Beauvais, Moses David, Eddie Delaronde, Ivor Benedict, Frank Diabo, John Cook, Nick and Theodore Thomas, and Two Arrows.

9 Moses Parts the Waters
The Reservoir at Tuscarora

1. Moses, *Working for the People*, p. 173; Graymont, *Fighting Tuscarora*, p. 138.

2. Moses, *Working for the People*, p. 179.

3. New York State Power Authority [SPA], *Annual Report, 1954* (New York, 1954), p. 9.

4. Robert Moses, "Statement on Niagara Power" . . . over Stations WBEN . . . and WNYC, September 5, 1957, Box 6, Bound Volume: Reports, 1957, Robert Moses MSS., Syracuse University; SPA, *Report, Sept. 28, 1956: Niagara Power Park and Arterial Development* (New York, 1956), pp. 4–8; SPA, *Report, July 25, 1957: As a Result of the Destruction in 1956 of the Schoellkopf Power Plant . . . the Niagara Area Is Faced with an Emergency* (New York, 1957), pp. 1–2; "3 Niagara Rockfalls Tumble Power Plant Into the River's Gorge and Kill a Worker," *New York Times* (June 8, 1956); "Utilities Study Accord on Power," *New York Times* (June 13, 1956).

5. "Nature and Niagara Power," *New York Times* (June 14, 1956).

6. AFL-CIO Petition to Governor Averell W. Harriman, April 5, 1957, Leland Olds MSS., Box 68, FDR Library, Hyde Park, N.Y.

7. 16 U.S.C.A. 836.

8. "FPC Approves Niagara Plan; Moses' Protest Expected Today," *New York Times* (January 31, 1958).

9. David Landy, "Tuscarora Tribalism and National Identity," *Ethnohistory* 5 (1958): 250–84; and his "Tuscarora Among the Iroquois," in *Handbook of North American Indians* XV, pp. 518–24; Douglas W. Boyce, "Tuscarora Political Organization, Ethnic Identity, and Sociohistorical Demography, 1711–1825," unpublished Ph.D. dissertation, University of North Carolina, Chapel Hill, 1973; and his "Iroquoian Tribes of the Virginia-North Carolina Coastal Plain," in *Handbook of North American Indians*, 15, pp. 282–89; for the Tuscaroras in the American Revolution, see Barbara Graymont, *The Iroquois in the American Revolution* (Syracuse, N.Y.: Syracuse University Press, 1972), which is a masterful study; Anthony F. C. Wallace, *The Death and Rebirth of the Seneca* (New York: Random House, 1970), pp. 179–218; William Chazanoff, *Joseph Ellicott and the Holland Land Company: The Opening of Western New York* (Syracuse, N.Y.: Syracuse University Press, 1970), pp. 74–75.

10. Anthony F. C. Wallace, *The Modal Personality Structure of the Tuscarora Indians as Revealed by the Rorschach Test*, Smithsonian Institution, Bureau of American Ethnology, *Bulletin 150* (Washington, D.C., 1952), p. 25.

11. *Ibid.*, p. 28.

12. Graymont, *Fighting Tuscarora*, p. 139.

13. Moses, "Statement on Niagara Power . . . Sept. 5, 1957."

14. Moses, "St. Lawrence and Niagara Power . . . Oct. 15, 1957."

15. Interviews of Cliff Spieler, Indian Point 3 Nuclear Power Plant, Buchanan, N.Y., December 10, 1984; Gary Patterson, Elma Patterson, Ruth Mt. Pleasant, Edison Mt. Pleasant, Beulah Rickard Lillvick, Tuscarora Indian Reservation, November 29 through December 1, 1984.

16. "5 Tuscarora Chiefs Are Reported Deposed," *Niagara Falls Gazette* (November 9, 1957); "Ouster Illegal Greene Claims," *Niagara Falls Gazette* (November 10, 1957); interviews of Duffy Wilson, April 11, 1985, Niagara Falls, N.Y. and David Richmond, March 22, 1985, Washington, Conn.

17. Wallace, *The Modal Personality*, pp. 33–34. See also Graymont, *Fighting Tuscarora*, entire.

18. Spieler interview, December 10, 1984. Spieler was the major reporter covering the SPA story for the *Niagara Falls Gazette* in the late 1950s. He was also a "stringer" for the *New York Times*. Greene's "image" was far different among his own people. Duffy Wilson interview, April 11, 1985.

19. "Indians Protest Niagara Project," *New York Times* (September 27, 1957), "Indians Charge Land Grab, Snag Niagara Power Plan," *Rochester Democrat and Chronicle* (September 27, 1957); John Felso, "Tuscaroras Rap SPA Land Plan," *Niagara Falls Gazette* (November 8, 1957).

20. Quoted in "Indians Protest a Niagara Plan," *New York Times* (November 9, 1957).

21. Robert Moses, *Open Letter to the Tuscarora Indian Nation, Feb. 11, 1958* (SPA, New York, 1958).

22. Quoted in Joe Higgins, "Embattled Tuscaroras Fight Moses," *Niagara Falls Gazette* (February 16, 1958).

23. Interview of Arthur Lazarus, Jr., July 17, 1982; Graymont, *Fighting Tuscarora*, p. 141.

24. Graymont, *Fighting Tuscarora*, pp. 141–42; "Indian Land Claimed," *New York Times* (April 16, 1958). Lillvick interviews, June 6, 1978 and November 29, 1984.

25. Hauptman Field Notes, 1971–84. "Tuscarora Braves Repel Surveyors," *New York Times* (April 17, 1957); "Tuscarora Brave Is Fed by Hand He Would Bite," *New York Times* (May 14, 1958). Wallace "Mad Bear" Anderson is adept at "pulling the leg" of reporters and men of letters. See the following fanciful accounts of his exploits: "Gandhi Student [Mad Bear Anderson] Leads the Braves," *Rochester Times-Union* (April 19, 1958); Wilson, *Apologies to the Iroquois*, pp. 126–68; Roy Bongartz, "The New Indian," *Esquire* (August 1970): 20–22; Peter Matthiessen, *In the Spirit of Crazy Horse* (New York: Viking Press, 1983), p. 37, and his *Indian Country* (New York: Viking Press, 1984), p. 136; Vine Deloria, Jr., *Behind the Trail of Broken Treaties* (New York: Dell Publishing, 1974), p. 21. Anderson was hired as a laborer for Merritt-Chapman and Scott, the largest contractor on the SPA project.

26. "Tuscaroras Stop Surveyors Again," *New York Times* (April 18, 1958); Graymont, *Fighting Tuscarora*, pp. 142–44; "Two Tuscaroras Freed in Land Dispute," *Rochester Times-Union* (May 23, 1958).

27. Quoted in "U.S. Seizes Leader [Mad Bear Anderson] of Indian Uprising," *Rochester Times-Union* (May 8, 1958).

28. Spieler, Ruth Mt. Pleasant, Edison Mt. Pleasant, Lillvick interviews. Ruth Mt. Pleasant is Mrs. Harry Patterson's daughter. To this day, some Tuscarora elders have their radios on in their homes while talking to outsiders because of the "bugging" of their homes during the SPA controversy. See also Graymont, *Fighting Tuscarora*, pp. 138–52. League of North American Indians, special issue of *Indian Views*: "N.Y. State Attempts Land Grab, Tuscarora Reserve," undated; William Rickard, undated, "Report on State Power Authority Activities on Tuscarora Reservation After the Supreme Court Decision." I should like to thank Barbara Graymont for copies of these two reports. Moses later denied that he "bugged" Tuscarora homes. "Tuscaroras Call Truce; Survey Crews Go to Work," *Rochester Times-Union* (May 9, 1958); "Indian Women Protest Niagara Power Survey," *Rochester Democrat and Chronicle* (July 2, 1958); "Tuscaroras in Protest," *New York Times* (July 2, 1958).

29. SPA, *Report, June 9, 1958: Niagara Desperately Needs More Power and the Potential Is Right Here to Produce Electrical Energy; Twice as Much Firm Power Can Be Produced by Storing Water in the Tuscarora Reservoir* (New York, 1958)

30. Robert Moses Memorandum to Stuart Constable, May 19, 1958, "Power Au-

thority," January–May, 1958, 197S180, Charles Poletti MSS., Columbia University. For Poletti, see Hauptman, *The Iroquois and the New Deal*, p. 132.

31. SPA, *Report, June 9, 1958.*

32. *Ibid.*

33. Graymont, *Fighting Tuscarora*, pp. 147–48.

34. Quoted in "Moses to Blame for Litigation Over Reservoir," *New York Times* (September 12, 1958).

35. Spieler, Ruth and Edison Mt. Pleasant, Gary Patterson interviews.

36. 164 F.Supp. 107 (*Tuscarora Nation v. SPA*).

37. 257 F.2d 885 (*Tuscarora Nation v. SPA*).

38. 79 S.Ct. 66 (*Tuscarora Nation v. SPA*); "Review Refused on Indian Lands Taken by the Project," *Rochester Democrat and Chronicle* (October 14, 1958).

39. 265 F.2d 338 (Tuscarora Nation v. FPC and SPA); "State vs. Indians Court War Stalls," *Rochester Times-Union* (September 10, 1958).

40. Interview of Arthur Lazarus, Jr., July 17, 1982.

41. 16 U.S.C.A. 836.

42. "Final Bid Rejected by Tuscaroras," *Rochester Times-Union* (January 30, 1959); "Indians Say 'No' to Niagara Deal," *Rochester Democrat and Chronicle* (January 30, 1959). See also "Indians Win FPC Decision on Reservoir," *Rochester Democrat and Chronicle* (February 3, 1959); "Tuscaroras Win; State Drops Fight," *Rochester Times-Union* (February 11, 1959).

43. "Power Authority Would Build Dam Off Indian Land," *Rochester Democrat and Chronicle* (February 27, 1959).

44. Caro, *The Power Broker*, pp. 361–62.

45. See chapter 11. Edward A. McCabe to Senator Jacob Javits, March 30, 1959; Javits to President Eisenhower, March 24, 1959, with attached undated "State of Grievances Submitted by the Six Nation Indian Confederacy of America," Eisenhower Central Files, Box 618, OF 121 Indians (3), Eisenhower Library, Abilene, Kan. "Indians Determined to Present Grievances Personally to Ike," *Syracuse Herald-Journal* (March 19, 1959); "General Helps Indians to Map White House March," *Syracuse Post-Standard* (March 14, 1959). Cf. Deloria, *Behind the Trail of Broken Treaties*, p. 21. The Iroquois traditionalists were embarrassed by the whole affair since they do not accept the idea that they are "citizens" of the United States.

46. 80 S.Ct. 543 (1960) (*FPC v. Tuscarora Indian Nation; SPA v. Tuscarora Indian Nation*).

47. Wilson, *Apologies to the Iroquois*, pp. 126–68; Robert Moses, *Tuscarora Fiction and Fact: A Reply to the Author of Memoirs of Hecate County and to His Reviewers* (New York: no publisher listed, 1960).

48. "Tuscaroras Accept $850,000 SPA Offer," *Niagara Falls Gazette* (August 13, 1960); "Tuscarora Tribe Ends Long Fight, Votes Sale of Land to Power Unit," *Rochester Democrat and Chronicle* (August 14, 1960).

49. Quoted in "Tuscaroras Vote to Yield Land to State, Ending 2-Year Fight," *New York Times* (August 14, 1960).

50. Graymont, *Fighting Tuscarora*, p. 152.

51. Tom Hewitt, "SPA Free to Build Indian Side of Dike," *Niagara Falls Gazette* (March 8, 1960). For the Herculean problems of construction, see Cliff Spieler and Tom Hewitt, *Niagara Power* (Lewiston, N.Y.: Niagara Power Publishers, 1959). For a final summary history of the construction, see "Litigation Complicates Building Reservoir," *Niagara Falls Gazette* (February 3, 1961). SPA, *Report: Niagara-St. Lawrence Power Projects: Construction Progress, Nov., 1959* (New York, 1959); SPA, *Report: Niagara Power*

Project: Construction Progress, Nov., 1960 (New York, 1960); SPA, *Report: Niagara Power Project Construction, Jan., 1961* (New York, 1961).

52. Bill Branche, "Indian Families Find SPA Generous Winner," *Niagara Falls Gazette* (July 31, 1960).

53. "Chief Is Convicted of Treason for Aiding the Power Authority," *Niagara Falls Gazette* (May 4, 1960); "Tuscaroras Move to Ostracize Chief Over a State Deal," *New York Times* (May 4, 1960); "Ouster of Tuscarora Upheld," *New York Times* (May 28, 1960).

54. Beulah Lillvick, Ruth and Edison Mt. Pleasant, Gary and Elma Patterson interviews; Branche, "Indian Families Find SPA Generous . . ."

55. *Ibid.*

56. Quoted in SPA, *Niagara Power Project First Power Ceremony, Niagara University, Lewiston, New York, Feb. 10, 1961* (New York, 1961), pp. 10–13.

57. Deloria, *Behind the Trail of Broken Treaties*, p. 20.

58. Graymont, *Fighting Tuscarora*, pp. 138–55. See also chapter 11.

59. Interview of David Richmond, March 22, 1985. Also see chapter 11.

60. Interview of George Shattuck, August 25, 1983, Syracuse, N.Y.

61. New York State, *Legislative Document No. 15: Report of the Joint Legislative Committee on Indian Affairs, 1959* (Albany, 1959), p. 4.

10   Unlocking the Door
The Oneida Land Claims Case, 1919–74

1. United States Commission on Civil Rights, *Indian Tribes: A Continuing Quest for Survival* (Washington, D.C.: U.S.G.P.O., 1981), pp. 109–10.

2. Jack Campisi, "New York–Oneida Treaty of 1795: A Finding of Fact," *American Indian Law Review* 4 (Summer 1976): 71–82.

3. *U.S. Statutes at Large* 1 (July 22, 1790): 137–38.

4. Francis Paul Prucha, *American Indian Policy in the Formative Years: The Indian Trade and Intercourse Acts, 1790–1834* (Cambridge, Mass.: Harvard University Press, 1962), p. 48.

5. For the best discussion of this process of dispossession, see Campisi, "Ethnic Identity and Boundary Maintenance in Three Oneida Communities," pp. 74–102. See also Philip Otto Geier, "A Peculiar Status: A History of Oneida Indian Treaties and Claims: Jurisdictional Conflict Within the American Government, 1775–1920," unpublished Ph.D. dissertation, Syracuse University, Syracuse, N.Y. 1980, pp. 83–191.

6. See Jack Campisi, "Oneida" in *Handbook of North American Indians* XV, 481–90.

7. Campisi, "Ethnic Boundary Maintenance . . . ," pp. 488–90.

8. For the career of Minnie Kellogg, see my chapter, "Designing Woman: Laura Minnie Cornelius Kellogg, Iroquois Leader," in *Indian Lives*, edited by Raymond Wilson and L. George Moses (Albuquerque, N.M.: University of New Mexico Press, 1985), pp. 159–88.

9. Laura Kellogg, *Our Democracy and the American Indian* (Kansas City, Mo., Burton, 1920), p. 17 passim; Janey B. Hendrix, "Redbird Smith and the Nighthawk Keetowahs," *Journal of Cherokee Studies* 8 (Fall 1983): 83–84.

10. Society of American Indians, *Report of the Executive Council on the Proceedings of the First Annual Conference, Oct. 12–17, 1911* (Washington, D.C., 1912), pp. 8–15, 46–50; and her "Some Facts and Figures on Indian Education," *Quarterly Journal* 1 (April 15, 1937): 36–46; William A. DuPuy, "Looking for an Indian Booker T.

Washington to Lead Their People," *New York Tribune* (August 27, 1911); Hazel W. Hertzberg, *The Search for an American Indian Identity: Modern Pan-Indian Movements* (Syracuse, N.Y.: Syracuse University Press, 1973), p. 61.

11. Ramona Herdman, "A New Six Nations: Laura Cornelius Kellogg Sees the Old Iroquois Confederacy Re-established on a Modern Business Basis," *Syracuse Herald* (November 6, 1927). See my article, "Designing Woman"; also see Campisi, "Ethnic Identity and Boundary Maintenance," pp. 442–43.

12. *U.S. v. Boylan*, 265 F. 165 (1920).

13. New York State Assembly (unpublished MSS. version), *Report of the Indian Commission to Investigate the Status of the American Indian Residing in the State of New York, Transmitted to the Legislature, March 17, 1922*, pp. 303–304, 324.

14. See my *The Iroquois and the New Deal*, pp. 74–77, 204–205 n. 21.

15. 32 F.2d 851 (1927).

16. Upton, *The Everett Report*, pp. 77–104, 114–15.

17. *Ibid.*, pp. 124–29. Upton fails to understand Kellogg's central role in these events.

18. "$2,000,000,000 Suit of Indians Rejected," *New York Times* (October 25, 1927).

19. Hauptman, *The Iroquois and the New Deal*, pp. 1–18, 30, 70–87, 177–83.

20. Hauptman, "Designing Woman."

21. Campisi, "Ethnic Identity and Boundary Maintenance," p. 443.

22. Quoted in Greer, "A Peculiar Status," p. 272.

23. *Ibid.* One of Winder's daughters married Chief Richard Chrisjohn.

24. Interview of Keith Reitz, May 2–4, 1982, New Paltz, N.Y. Reitz, "Urban Native Americans of Western New York," paper delivered at the Conference on New York History, June 9, 1984, Buffalo and Erie County Historical Society; Reitz, "George P. Decker and the Oneida Indians," unpublished MSS. in Reitz's possession.

25. Interview of Keith Reitz, July 21, 1982, Rochester, N.Y.

26. Mary Winder to Charles Berry, April 15, 1943; Berry to Winder, May 14, 1943, Records of the N.Y. Agency, 1939–48, 067 Tribal Relations, Box 3, RG 75, NA. Interview of Gloria Halbritter, April 21, 1985, Syracuse, N.Y.

27. *U.S. Statutes at Large* 60 (August 13, 1946): 1049–55.

28. Wilcomb E. Washburn, *Red Man's Land/White Man's Law* (New York: Scribner, 1971), p. 104.

29. President Harry Truman to Director of the Budget, February 25, 1946; Secretary of the Interior to President Truman, August 1, 1946, OF6-AA, Indian Claims Commission, Harry Truman MSS., Truman Library, Independence, Mo.

30. William and Andrew Cook to President Harry Truman, undated telegram, OF-6AA, Indian Claims Commission, Harry Truman MSS., Truman Library.

31. Mary Winder to Mr. Haas, June 7, 1948; Winder to William Benge, March 25, 1949, August 24, 1948, Records of the New York Agency, 1939–48, 067 Tribal Relations, Box 3, RG 75, NA; Winder to Benge, Feb. 6, 1951, BIA Central Files, 1940–52, #00-1951-260 (N.Y.), acc. #53A-367, Box 1058, RG 75, NA.

32. T. W. Wheat to William Benge, August 2, 1948, Benge to Commissioner of Indian Affairs, August 10, 1948, Records of the New York Agency, 1939–48, 067 Tribal Relations, Box 3, RG 75, NA.

33. Winder to Mr. Haas, June 7, 1948.

34. BIA Central Files, 1940–52, #00-1951-260 (N.Y.), acc. #53A-367, Box 1058, RG 75, NA: Nora Anderson to Milton Babcock, May 13, 1949, Records of the New York Agency, 1939–48, 067 Tribal Relations, Box 3, RG 75, NA.

35. Michael T. Smith to Director of Indian Services, Memorandum: Report on

the History of the New York Oneidas, February 24, 1982, copy in Keith Reitz's possession, Pittsford, N.Y.

36. Benge to Commissioner of Indian Affairs, August 10, 1948; Oneida Tribe of Wisconsin, Minutes of the Tribal Business Committee, 1938, in possession of Jack Campisi, Red Hook, N.Y.

37. William Zimmerman, Jr. to Land Office, February 2, 1948, BIA Central Files, 1940–52, #15030-1943-3074 (N.Y.), Box 1058, acc. #53A-367, RG 75, NA.

38. William Benge to Mary Winder, March 2, 1951, BIA Central Files, 1940–52, #00-1951-260 (N.Y.), Box 1058, acc. #53A-367; interview of Norbert Hill, Sr., July 28, 1982, Oneida, Wis. *Docket 301: The Oneida Nation of New York, the Oneida Tribe of Wisconsin, the Oneida Nation by Julius Danforth, Oscar Archiquette, Sherman Skenandore, Mamie Smith, Milton Babcock, Beryl Smith and Amanda Pierce v. U.S.A.*

39. Memorandum to the Files, 091 File; Minutes of Oneida Indian Nation Meeting, August 10, 1975, 058 File, James Hanley MSS., Hartwick College, Oneonta, N.Y.

40. New York State Legislative Document No. 6, *Report of the New York State Joint Legislative Committee on Indian Affairs, 1962* (Albany, 1962), p. 37.

41. New York State, *Minutes of Public Hearing of the Joint Legislative Committee on Indian Affairs . . . Nov. 9, 1963* (Albany, 1963), pp. 93–96.

42. Interviews of Jacob Thompson, April 15, 1972 and May 6, 1976, New Paltz, N.Y. Thompson, on each occasion, also presented a history of his involvement in the claim to a SUNY audience. Thompson, "The Oneida Case" (taped lecture). Interview of George Shattuck, August 25, 1983, Syracuse, N.Y.

43. Shattuck interview, August 25, 1983.

44. *Ibid.*; Hill interview; interview of Loretta Ellis Metoxen, June 22, 1983, Oneida, Wis. For Bennett's commissionership, see Richard N. Ellis, "Robert L. Bennett," in *The Commissioners of Indian Affairs, 1824–1977,* edited by Robert M. Kvasniska and Herman J. Viola (Lincoln, Neb.: University of Nebraska Press, 1979), pp. 325–32. Oral histories of Robert L. Bennett and Stewart Udall, LBJ Library, Austin, Tex. "Oneidas Hail a New Chief," *Milwaukee Journal* (June 19, 1966).

45. Exhibit I: Oneida Indian Nation to the Constitutional Convention of New York State, June 12, 1967, contained in petition of February 9, 1968, attached to letter of Joseph Califano to Jacob Thompson, February 28, 1968, Lyndon Johnson MSS., White House Central Files, Box 3, IN/A-Z, LBJ Library, Austin, Tex.

46. Exhibit II: Julius L. Sackman Memorandum prepared for Louis J. Lefkowitz, August 3, 1967, contained in petition of February 9, 1968 . . . (see footnote 45 above).

47. Jacob Thompson to Lyndon Johnson, January 19, 1968, Harry R. Anderson to Thompson, February 2, 1968, James H. Hanley to Barefoot Sanders, January 31, 1968, Thompson to Hanley, January 23, 1968, Thompson to LBJ, February 12, 1968, Lyndon Johnson MSS., White House Central Files, Box 3, IN/A-Z, LBJ Library, Austin, Tex.; Barefoot Sanders to Hanley, February 7, 1968, James Hanley MSS., File 270, Hartwick College.

48. Quoted in Exhibit III: Memorandum of Law and Fact, undated, contained in petition of February 9, 1968 . . . (see footnote 45 above).

49. *Ibid.*, pp. 16–17.

50. *Ibid.*, pp. 21–27.

51. Jacob Thompson, Raymond Elm, and Ruth Burr to President Johnson, March 26, 1968, Lyndon Johnson MSS., White House Central Files, Box 101, Name File: Thompson, Ja, LBJ Library, Austin, Tex.

52. Jacob Thompson to President Johnson, November 26, 1968, Lyndon John-

son MSS., White House Central Files, Box 101, Name File: Thompson, Ja, LBJ Library, Austin, Tex.

53. Interview of Louis R. Bruce, Jr., June 30, 1982, Washington, D.C.; Joseph H. Cash, "Louis Rook Bruce," in *The Commissioners of Indian Affairs, 1824–1977*, pp. 333–40; Hauptman, *The Iroquois and the New Deal*, pp. 122–26.

54. New York State Subcommittee on Indian Affairs of the Subcommittee on Governmental Operation, *Public Hearings, Nov. 18, 1970* (Albany, 1970), pp. 15–16.

55. *Ibid.*, p. 41.

56. *Ibid.*, pp. 41–42.

57. *Ibid.*, pp. 35–76; George Shattuck to Laurence M. Hauptman, August 26, 1983, letter in Hauptman's possession; *Seneca Nation of Indians v. Christie*, 126 N.Y. 122 (1896).

58. Metoxen interview, June 22, 1983; Hill interview, July 28, 1982; Robert W. Venables, p.c., July 25, 1984.

59. Shattuck interview, August 25, 1983; Jack Campisi, "Oneida Case," paper presented at the 5th Annual Eastern Regional Conference on the Native American, New Paltz, N.Y., May 6, 1976.

60. *Oneida Indian Nation of New York, et al. v. County of Oneida, New York, et al.*, 464 F.2d 916 (1972).

61. 94 S.Ct. 772 (1974); *Plaintiff's Post-Trial Memorandum on the Issue of Liability, Civil No. 70-CV-5, Oneida Indian Nation, et al. v. County of Oneida, et al.*

62. 94 S.Ct. 772 (1974).

63. Hauptman, field notes, 1972–84. The Hanley MSS. at Hartwick College, the best source on the Oneida claims since 1974, but which is largely closed for researchers, confirms these observations. The author would like to thank Carolyn Wolf of Hartwick College and Armand La Potin of the State University of New York at Oneonta for bringing this noteworthy collection to his attention.

64. *Oneida Indian Nation v. County of Oneida.* 83-1065; 83-1240-opinion. "Supreme Court Upholds Claim by Oneida Indians." *New York Times*, March 5, 1985.

11 The Iroquois on the Road to Wounded Knee, 1958–73

1. Deloria, *Behind the Trail of Broken Treaties*, p. 4. Interviews of Adam Nordwall, May 4, 1973, New Paltz, N.Y.; Vine Deloria, Jr., May 4, 1983, New Paltz, N.Y.; and Oren Lyons, Lee Lyons, Rick Hill, September 8, 1984, Syracuse, N.Y.

2. See Graymont, *Fighting Tuscarora*. Interview of Keith Reitz, June 8–9, 1984, Pittsford, N.Y.

3. *Ibid.* Interview of Ernest Benedict, July 30, 1983, Cornwall Island; Ray Fadden, September 11, 1983, Onchiota, N.Y.

4. Interviews of Keith Reitz, June 8–9, 1984; Ray Fadden, September 11, 1982. Hauptman, *The Iroquois and the New Deal*, chapter 1; *Basic Call to Consciousness*; *Native Peoples in Struggle: Cases from the Fourth Russell Tribunal and Other International Forums*, edited by Ismaelillo and Robin Wright (Bombay, N.Y.: Akwesasne Notes, 1982), pp. xiv–xv, 111–19, 156–57.

5. For Minnie Kellogg, see my forthcoming article, "Designing Woman: Minnie Kellogg, Iroquois Leader."

6. See my *The Iroquois and the New Deal*, chapters 2–4. See also my "The American Indian Federation and the Indian New Deal: A Reinterpretation," *Pacific Historical Review* 52 (November 1983): 378–402.

7. "Indian Chief Revolt, Start New Country," *Rochester Democrat and Chronicle*

(March 6, 1959); "Ontario: War on the Reservation," *Newsweek* (March 23, 1959): 66;
"An Iroquois War on White Man's Law," *Life* (March 30, 1959): 38–39; "Iroquois Declaration of Independence," November 29, 1969, Canadian Indian Rights Collection, Box 82,
National Library of Canada, Ottawa. Sally Weaver, "Election Behavior Under the Threat
of Termination," paper delivered at the American Anthropological Association annual
meeting, San Diego, Calif., November 20, 1970, and her "Schismatic Factional Behavior Among the Grand River Iroquois Under Threat of Federal Administrative Termination," paper delivered at the Central States Anthropological Conference, Bloomington,
Ind., April 24, 1970; and her *Making Canadian Indian Policy: The Hidden Agenda,
1968–1970* (Toronto: University of Toronto Press, 1981). The 1969–70 revolt is easily
followed in *Tekawennake* (June 25, 1969), pp. 2–6; (Sept. 3, 1969), p. 1; (January 13, 1970),
p. 1; (July 14, 1970), pp. 1–3; (July 28, 1970), pp. 1–5; see also *Akwesasne Notes* (June
1969): 1.

    8. Weaver, *Making Canadian Indian Policy,* p. 4.

    9. *Ibid.,* p 5

    10. See for example "End Special Status of Indians, Canada's Decision," *Akwesasne Notes* 1 (June 1969): 1.

    11. Quoted in Edward H. Spicer, *A Short History of the Indians of the United
States* (New York: Van Nostrand, 1969), p. 310.

    12. Barbara Graymont, *Fighting Tuscarora,* pp. 138–52; interviews of Beulah
Rickard Lillvick, Tuscarora Indian Reservation, June 6, 1978; November 29, 1982.

    13. Sol Tax to William Rickard, January 26, 1961, American Indian Chicago Conference MSS., Box 10, "Rickard," National Anthropological Archives, Smithsonian Institution, Washington, D.C. (hereafter cited as AICC, NAA). D'Arcy McNickle, *Native
American Tribalism: Indian Survivals and Renewals* (New York: Oxford University
Press, 1973), pp. 116–18.

    14. Interviews of Nancy Lurie, June 20, 1983, Milwaukee, Wis.; Theodore Hetzel, January 17, 1984, Kennett Square, Pa.

    15. Rickard to Mrs. Welch, January 25, 1961; Rickard to Tax, February 22, March
6, 8, and 14, 1961; Rickard to Nancy Lurie, February 16, 1961; AICC, Box 10, "Rickard,"
NAA.

    16. Rickard to Tax, March 23, 1961, AICC, Box 10, "Rickard," NAA.

    17. Tax in an interview proudly insisted that the American Indian Chicago Conference gave impetus to the modern movement for acknowledgment among tribes not
recognized by the federal government. Interview of Sol Tax, December 5, 1982, Philadelphia, Pa.

    18. Reports on Preliminary Eastern Seaboard Conference of the American Indian Chicago Conference held at Haverford College, April 8–11, 1961, AICC, Box 2,
"East Regional Meeting," NAA.

    19. *Ibid.* See photograph of Haverford College meeting of American Indian Chicago Conference. Interviews of Theodore Hetzel, January 17, 1984; and Trudie Lamb
Richmond, August 28, 1974, Meriden, Conn. Registration List, Haverford College Meeting, American Indian Chicago Conference, April, 1961, AICC MSS., Box 2, "East Regional Meeting," NAA.

    20. Rickard to Tax, February 22, 1961, AICC, Box 10, "Rickard," NAA.

    21. William Rickard, "Meeting of Indian Leaders," with copy of Rickard's letter
to Mrs. Welch, February 16, 1961, AICC, Box 10, "Rickard," NAA. Commission on the
Rights, Liberties, and Responsibilities of the American Indian, "A Program for Indian
Citizens," Gardner Jackson MSS., Box 39, FDR Library, Hyde Park, N.Y.: Sol Tax to Sophie
Aberle, March 30, 1961, AICC, Box 4, "A," NAA.

    22. Sol Tax to Richard Schifter, April 24, 1961, AICC, Box 10, "A," NAA.

23. William Rickard, "Report of American Indian Chicago Conference . . . ," June 13–20, 1961, AICC, Box 10, "Rickard," NAA. For the official report on the conference, see Nancy Lurie, "The Voice of the American Indian: Report on the American Indian Chicago Conference," *Current Anthropology* 2 (1961): 478–500.

24. Rickard Report of American Indian Chicago Conference, June 13–20, 1961.

25. *Ibid.*

26. *Ibid.*

27. Lurie interview, June 20, 1983.

28. Vine Deloria, Jr. has recognized the role of Tuscaroras in the emergence of Red Power: "In the last two decades it was the Tuscarora people of the Iroquois Confederacy who began the type of protests which have now become common." *Behind the Trail of Broken Treaties,* p. 20. Although Deloria is correct on this point, he, as other writers before him, has overemphasized the role of Wallace Mad Bear Anderson and totally ignored William Rickard's important role.

29. William Rickard to William Richardson, July 5, 1962; Rickard "to whom it may concern," April 8, 1963; Resolution from Haliwa Indian Tribe to Tuscarora Tribal Council, undated. All in possession of Jack Campisi, Red Hook, N.Y. (copies presented to him by Haliwa Indians, November 1984).

30. Interviews of Ramona Charles, July 15, 1982, Tonawanda Indian Reservation; Edison Mt. Pleasant and Ruth Mt. Pleasant, November 30, 1984, Tuscarora Indian Reservation; Beulah Rickard Lillvick, Tuscarora Indian Reservation, November 29, 1984. Alfred A. Gagne to U.S. Senate and House Committee on the Interior and Insular Affairs, June 30, 1967; "Mad Bear" to Lyndon Johnson, July 14, 1967; Mike Manatos to "Chief Mad Bear," July 27, 1967, LBJ Central Files, Box 74, Legislation/Indian Affairs, LBJ Library, Austin, Tex. "Mad Bear Anderson Leads California 'Unity' Trek," *Niagara Falls Gazette* (September 3, 1967). Mad Bear, despite his skill at getting publicity, was not the founder, "brains," or leader of this unity movement of the 1960s.

31. Quoted in "Pow-wow Planned by Disturbed Indians," *Syracuse Post-Standard* (January 6, 1969).

32. Herbert G. Pelkey, "National Parley Here: Indians Mull Single Longhouse," *Syracuse Herald American* (February 16, 1969); Charles Russo, "Unity Hope of Indians," *Syracuse Post-Standard* (August 20, 1969); see also Michael O'Toole, "Indians Issue Protest, End Council on Unity," *Syracuse Post-Standard* (August 25, 1967).

33. Venables' Archiquette interview, July 14, 1970.

34. Pelkey, "National Parley Here."

35. "Wampum Belts Asked: Chief [Thomas] Demands State Return Them," *Syracuse Herald Journal* (March 25, 1967).

36. Interviews of Oren Lyons and Lee Lyons, September 8, 1964; interview of William N. Fenton, May 18, 1983, Slingerlands, N.Y. For a portrait of George A. Thomas, see William N. Fenton, "The Funeral of Tadodaho," *Indian Historian* 3 (Spring 1970): 43–47.

37. William N. Fenton, "The New York State Wampum Collection: The Case for the Integrity of Cultural Treasures," *Proceedings of the American Philosophical Society* 115 (December 1971): 440, 442, 446. For a physical description of the wampum collection, see Noah T. Clarke, "The Wampum Belt Collection of the New York State Museum," *New York Museum Bulletin* 288 (July 1931): 85–124.

38. *Ibid.,* pp. 437–61. William N. Fenton, "Albany's Side of the Issue: State Expert on Indian Affairs Says Belts Belong in Albany," *Syracuse Herald American* (March 28, 1971); Richard Case, "Indians v. New York State: Wampum Belt Dispute Has Wide Ramifications," *Syracuse Herald American* (March 28, 1971). The 1909 law making the state

custodian of the wampum can be found in *The Indian Historian* 3 (Spring 1970): 11–12. The history of wampum acquisition at the museum can be followed in Charles Gillette, "Wampum Beads and Belts," *The Indian Historian* 3 (Fall 1970): 33–38; Committee on Anthropological Research in Museums (CARM) to Governor Nelson Rockefeller, February 23, 1970, reprinted letter in *Indian Historian* 3 (Spring 1970): 13–14; Bruce Detlefsen, "Indians Fail in Attempts to Obtain Wampum Belts," *Watertown Daily Times* (April 22, 1970); Richard G. Case, "Onondaga Indians a Nation and Want to Be Treated That Way," *Syracuse Herald-Journal* (September 2, 1970). New York State Legislature, Subcommittee on Indian Affairs, *Hearings* at the Onondaga Longhouse, September 1, 1970, pp. 13–66 (transcript available at New York State Library).

39. Vine Deloria, Jr., *God Is Red* (New York: Dell, 1973), pp. 19–20.

40. Interview of Oren Lyons, September 8, 1984.

41. Deloria, *God Is Red*, p. 20.

42. "Rocky Signs Bill Giving Wampum Belts to Indians," *Syracuse Herald-Journal* (July 2, 1971).

43. Lloyd Elm, "Educating the Native American: The Lollipop of Self-Deceit," talk at Herkimer Community College, December 1972; Gene Goshorn, "Chief Shenandoah Opposes School Proposal for Indians," *Syracuse Herald-Journal* (June 5, 1969). Richard Case, "Onondaga's Petition State: Unusual School Plan," *Syracuse Herald-American* (April 25, 1971); and his "Onondagas Concerned about School Hassle," *Syracuse Herald-American* (October 15, 1972).

44. Anna M. Lewis and Lilliam T. Samuelson, *"We Shall Live Again": A Positive Approach for Survival of a People: Proposal for Indian Education in New York State.* Interview of Anna Lewis, June 10, 1983, Albany, N.Y. For the Mohawk boycott, see Minerva White, "The St. Regis Boycott," in *Educating the Educators: The American Indian Student in Higher Education, St. Lawrence University, July 12–30, 1971,* edited by Roy Sandstrom, (Canton, N.Y.: St. Lawrence University, 1971), pp. 30–36. New York State Legislature, Assembly Standing Committee on Governmental Operations, Subcommittee on Indian Affairs, *Hearings* at the Saint Regis Reservation, September 19, 1970, pp. 6–82 (transcript available in New York State Library, Albany).

45. Regents of the University of the State of New York, "Native American Education," Position Paper, No. 22 (Albany, 1975), p. 4.

46. Harvey Flad, "The City and the Longhouse: A Social Geography of American Indians in Syracuse, New York," unpublished Ph.D. dissertation, Syracuse University, Syracuse, N.Y., 1973, pp. 162–73; *Akwesasne Notes* 3 (Autumn 1971): 1–6; "Onondagas, State Reach Accord on Route 81 Controversy," *Syracuse Herald-American* (October 31, 1971).

47. Gambill interview, August 22, 1984.

48. *Ibid.*; Benedict interview, July 30, 1983. For Fadden's remarkable work, see my *The Iroquois and the New Deal*, pp. 122–26.

49. Gambill interview, August 22, 1984.

50. *Ibid.*

51. McLester interview, June 24, 1984; Gambill interview, August 22, 1984.

52. Richard Oakes, "Alcatraz Is Not an Island," *Ramparts* (December 1972): 35.

53. Steve Talbot, "Free Alcatraz: The Culture of Native American Liberation," *Journal of Ethnic Studies* 6 (Fall 1978): 95 n. 2.

54. Gambill interview, August 22, 1984. Despite the claims of Peter Matthiessen, Mad Bear was not directly involved in the seizure of Alcatraz in the first "invasion," in the formation of Indians of All Tribes, or in the coordination of the protest. *In the Spirit of Crazy Horse*, p. 37. Nordwall, Oakes, Earl Livermore, Stella Leach, Grace Thorpe,

and John Trudell appear to have been the leaders. Indians of All Tribes General Fact Sheet, January 1970, National Council on Indian Opportunity MSS., Box 4, File: Alcatraz II, January–February, 1970, RG 220, NA. See also the Minutes of Regional Council Meeting with Indian Representatives on January 15, 1970, in same file.

55. Interviews of Adam Nordwall, May 4–5, 1973 and October 20, 1983, New Paltz, N.Y. Deloria, *God Is Red*, p. 15; Rupert Costo, "Alcatraz," *Indian Historian* 3 (Winter 1970): 4–12.

56. Richard DeLuca, "The Indian Attempt to Reclaim Alcatraz Island," *California History* 62 (1963): 10–12.

57. Oakes, "Alcatraz Is Not an Island," p. 38.

58. "Alcatraz Proclamation, Nov., 1969," *Indians of All Tribes Newsletter* (January 1970). DeLuca, "The Indian Attempt to Reclaim Alcatraz Island," p. 14. See also Peter Blue Cloud, ed., *Alcatraz Is Not an Island* (Berkeley, Ca.: Wingbow Press, 1972).

59. Walter Hickel to Leonard Garment, March 10, 1970, National Council on Indian Opportunity MSS., Box 4, File: Alcatraz, March–October, 1970, RG 220, NA.

60. "Leader's Daughter: Girl Dies After Fall on Alcatraz," *San Francisco Chronicle* (January 9, 1970); Tim Findley, "Alcatraz Dissension Grows," *San Francisco Chronicle* (January 7, 1970); and his "Factionalism and Feuds," *San Francisco Chronicle* (January 8, 1970); "Federal Officials Hope to Reach Indian Leaders," *San Francisco Chronicle* (January 8, 1970). Eleanor Dumas, "Richard Oakes Renews Cause in East; Saved by Medicine Man," *Watertown Daily Times* (October 15, 1970). Gambill interview, August 22, 1984.

61. Daniel Hays, "Indians Await Ellis Island 1-Hour As Officials Eye Invasion Threat," *Newark Evening News* (March 17, 1970). See also "Alcatraz: Indian War," *Akwesasne Notes* (November 1969).

62. Evelyn Pickett to Bob Robertson, October 17, 1972; C. D. Ward Memorandum, "Trail of Broken Treaties Caravan," October 30, 1972, National Council on Indian Opportunity MSS., Box 16, File: Caravan 10/30–11/7/72, RG 220, NA; Robert Burnette and John Koster, *The Road to Wounded Knee* (New York: Bantam, 1974), pp. 119–219; Deloria, *Behind the Trail of Broken Treaties*, pp. 43–62; Jack D. Forbes, *Native Americans and Nixon: Presidential Politics and Minority Self-Determination, 1969–1972* (Los Angeles, Ca.: American Indian Studies Center, UCLA, 1981), pp. 75–102.

63. Bruce interview, June 30, 1982; Hank Adams, "Trail of Broken Treaties" Information and Fact Sheet, November 20, 1972, National Council on Indian Opportunity MSS., Box 16, File: Caravan 10/30–11/7/72, RG 220, NA. *Akwesasne Notes* soon after published a "commemorative" booklet on the episode, *BIA: I'm Not Your Indian Anymore* (Rooseveltown, N.Y., 1974).

64. Quoted in *Akwesasne Notes*, comp., *Voices from Wounded Knee: The People Are Standing Up* (Rooseveltown, N.Y., 1974), p. 96. See the Six Nations Iroquois Confederacy resolution of March 9, 1973 reprinted in *Akwesasne Notes* (Early Spring 1973).

65. Richard D. Lyons, "Fugitive Indian Leader Seeks a Refuge Upstate," *New York Times* (February 4, 1983); "Indian Leader, 9 Years a Fugitive, Surrenders for Jail Term in Dakota," *New York Times* (September 14, 1984).

12 The Watchful Eagle

1. This concluding chapter is largely based upon my fieldwork since 1972. For the Ganienkeh takeover, see Gail H. Landsman, "Ganienkeh: Symbol and Politics in

an Indian/White Land Dispute," unpublished Ph.D. dissertation, American University, Washington, D.C., 1982.

2. Christina Johannsen, "Efflorescence and Identity in Iroquois Arts," unpublished Ph.D. dissertation, Brown University, Providence, R.I., 1984, pp. 209–13; Christina Johannsen and John P. Ferguson, eds., *Iroquois Arts: A Directory of a People and Their Work* (Schoharie, N.Y.: Association for the Advancement of Native North American Arts and Crafts, 1983); Rick Hill and Jim Wake, "The Native American Center for the Living Arts in Niagara Falls," *American Indian Art* 3 (Summer 1980): 22–25.

3. Robert M. Kvasnicka and Herman Viola, eds., *The Commissioners of Indian Affairs, 1824–1977* (Lincoln, Neb.: University of Nebraska Press, 1979), pp. 325–40; Canada, Parliament, House of Commons, *Issue No. 40: Indian Self-Government in Canada: Report of the Special Committee* (Penner Report), 32nd Parliament, 1st session (Ottawa, Ontario, 1983). Roberta Jamieson, "First Nations of Canada: A Question of Sovereignty," *Indian Time* (September 21, 1984); Billy Two Rivers, "First Ministers' Conference on Aboriginal Constitutional Matters," *Akwesasne Notes* (Early Spring 1984). Interview of Roberta Jamieson, May 28, 1984, Six Nations Reserve. "Protect Cultural Diversity," *Cornwall Standard-Freeholder* (September 17, 1984).

4. See *Akwesasne Notes, Basic Call to Consciousness* (Rooseveltown, N.Y., 1978).

Bibliography

Manuscript Collections

American Civil Liberties Union MSS. Princeton University. Princeton, N.J.

American Friends Service MSS. American Friends Service. Philadelphia, Pa.

American Indian Chicago Conference MSS. National Anthropological Archives. Smithsonian Institution. Washington, D.C.

Assembly of First Nations [formerly called National Indian Brotherhood] Collection. National Library of Canada, Ottawa, Ontario.

Association on American Indian Affairs MSS. Princeton University. Princeton, N.J.

Elmer F. Bennett MSS. Eisenhower Library. Abilene, Kan.

Ezra Taft Benson MSS. Eisenhower Library. Abilene, Kan.

Adolph A. Berle MSS. Franklin D. Roosevelt Library. Hyde Park, N.Y.

John Stewart Bragdon MSS. Eisenhower Library. Abilene, Kan.

William A. Brophy MSS. Truman Library. Independence, Mo.

Bureau of Indian Affairs. Record Group 75, National Archives. Washington, D.C.

    1. Central Files, 1940–56

    2. Records of the New York Agency, 1938–49

    3. Records of the Great Lakes Consolidated Agency, 1949–56

    4. Fred Daiker Records

    5. John Herrick Records

    6. William Zimmerman Records

Hugh Butler MSS. Nebraska State Historical Society. Lincoln, Neb.

Canada. Department of Indian Affairs and Northern Affairs Records (Saint Lawrence Seaway Expropriation—Caughnawaga and St. Regis Files—373/34-1-1 and 481/34-1-1. Department of Indian and Northern Affairs. Hull, Qué.

Canadian Indian Rights Collection. National Library of Canada. Ottawa, Ont.

John M. Carmody MSS. Franklin D. Roosevelt Library. Hyde Park, N.Y.

Oscar L. Chapman MSS. Truman Library. Independence, Mo.

O. Hatfield Chilson MSS. Eisenhower Library. Abilene, Kan.

Clark Clifford MSS. Truman Library. Independence, Mo.

John Collier MSS. Yale University. New Haven, Conn.

C. C. Daniels MSS (in Josephus Daniels and Daniels Family MSS). Library of Congress, Manuscript Division. Washington, D.C.

Josephus Daniels MSS. Southern Historical Collection. University of North Carolina. Chapel Hill, N.C.

Merle Deardorff Papers MSS. Pennsylvania Historical and Museum Commission. Harrisburg, Pa.

Thomas E. Dewey Collection. Rush Rhees Library. University of Rochester. Rochester, N.Y.

Dale E. Doty MSS. Truman Library. Independence, Mo.

Doris Duke American Indian Oral History Project. Western History Collection. University of Oklahoma. Norman, Okla.

Dwight D. Eisenhower MSS. Records as President. Eisenhower Library. Abilene, Kan.

    1. White House Central Files, 1953–61
        a. Official File
        b. General File
        c. President's Personal File
        d. Confidential File
        e. Alphabetical File
    2. Ann Whitman Files
        a. Administration Series
        b. Diary Series
        c. DDE Diary Series
        d. Name Series

Charles Fahy MSS. Franklin D. Roosevelt Library. Hyde Park, N.Y.

William N. Fenton MSS. American Philosophical Society. Philadelphia, Pa.

Frederic Fox MSS. Eisenhower Library. Abilene, Kan.

Howard Gansworth Collection. Buffalo and Erie County Historical Society. Buffalo, N.Y.

Warner Gardner MSS. Truman Library. Independence, Mo.

Homer H. Gruenther MSS. Eisenhower Library. Abilene, Kan.

James A. Haley MSS. Florida Southern College. Lakeland, Fla.

James Hanley MSS. Hartwick College. Oneonta, N.Y.

Bryce Harlow MSS. Eisenhower Library. Abilene, Kan.

Averell Harriman MSS. Syracuse University. Syracuse, N.Y.

Oveta Culp Hobby MSS. Eisenhower Library. Abilene, Kan.

Harold L. Ickes MSS. Library of Congress, Manuscript Division. Washington, D.C.

Indian Claims Commission MSS. Truman Library. Independence, Mo.

Indian Rights Association MSS. Historical Society of Pennsylvania. Philadelphia, Pa.

Irving Ives MSS. Cornell University. Ithaca, N.Y.

Gardner Jackson MSS. Franklin D. Roosevelt Library. Hyde Park, N.Y.

Lyndon B. Johnson MSS. Lyndon B. Johnson Library. Austin, Tex.
   1. Senate Files, 1952–61
   2. White House Central Files, 1963–68
Kenneth B. Keating MSS. University of Rochester. Rochester, N.Y.
John F. Kennedy MSS. John F. Kennedy Library. Boston, Mass.
   1. Pre-presidential files (Senate).
   2. President's Office Files
   3. White House Central Files
Robert F. Kennedy MSS. Attorney General Files. John F. Kennedy Library. Boston, Mass.
Joseph Keppler Papers. Heye Foundation. Museum of the American Indian Library. Bronx, N.Y.
J. A. Krug MSS. Library of Congress, Manuscript Division. Washington, D.C.
Oliver LaFarge Papers. Humanities Research Center. University of Texas. Austin, Tex.
James M. Lambie MSS. Eisenhower Library. Abilene, Kan.
David Lawrence MSS. Pennsylvania Historical and Museum Commission. Harrisburg, Pa.
Herbert H. Lehman MSS. Columbia University. New York, N.Y.
J. R. McGrath MSS. Truman Library. Independence, Mo.
Miami Agency Records. Bureau of Indian Affairs. Miami, Okla.
Arthur E. Morgan MSS. Antioch College. Yellow Springs, Oh.
Robert Moses MSS. Syracuse University. Syracuse, N.Y.
Muskogee Area Office (BIA). Office Files of the Tribal Affairs Office, 1947–65. Federal Records Center, Fort Worth, Tex.
Dillon S. Myer MSS. Truman Library. Independence, Mo.
Philleo Nash MSS. Truman Library. Independence, Mo.
National Congress of American Indian Collection. National Anthropological Archives. Smithsonian Institution. Washington, D.C.
National Council on Indian Opportunity Records (RG 220). National Archives. Washington, D.C.
New York State Department of Education. Assistant Commissioner for the New York State Museum MSS. New York State Archives, Albany, N.Y.
New York State Department of Education. Native American Education Unit. New York State Archives. Albany, N.Y.
   1. Johnson O'Malley Project Files, 1971–//
   2. Regents Position Paper No. 22—Background Files, 1974–75
   3. Native American Indian Education Unit, 1964–75 [materials predate World War II]
Gaylord Nelson MSS. State Historical Society of Wisconsin. Madison, Wis.
Leland Olds MSS. Franklin D. Roosevelt Library. Hyde Park, N.Y.
Oneida Tribe of Wisconsin, Inc. Minutes of the Tribal Business Committee 1937–57. [Copies in possession of Dr. Jack Campisi, Red Hook, N.Y. and of the author.]
Arthur C. Parker MSS. University of Rochester. Rochester, N.Y.

Philadelphia Yearly Meeting of Friends. Indian Committee MSS. Haverford
    College. Haverford, Pa.
Charles Poletti MSS. Columbia University. New York, N.Y.
Public Archives of Canada.
    1. RG 10 Indian Affairs
    2. RG 22 Deputy Minister Files, 1953–58
    3. RG 52 St. Lawrence Seaway Authority
    4. RG 89 Water Resources Files, 1926–54
Daniel Reed MSS. Cornell University. Ithaca, N.Y.
Robert Ritzenthaler Field Notes. Milwaukee Public Museum. Milwaukee,
    Wis.
William P. Rogers MSS. Eisenhower Library. Abilene, Kan.
Eleanor Roosevelt MSS. Franklin D. Roosevelt Library. Hyde Park, N.Y.
Franklin D. Roosevelt MSS. Franklin D. Roosevelt Library. Hyde Park, N.Y.
    1. Papers as Governor
    2. Papers as President, Alphabetical File
    3. Papers as President, Official File
    4. Papers as President, President's Personal File
    5. Papers as President, President's Secretary's File
Samuel I. Rosenman MSS. Franklin D. Roosevelt Library. Hyde Park, N.Y.
Fred Seaton MSS. Eisenhower Library. Abilene, Kan.
Seneca Family Records (Pauline and Cornelius Seneca). In possession of Pauline
    Seneca, Cattaraugus Reservation.
    1. Kinzua Dam
    2. Thomas Indian School
Stephen J. Spingarn MSS. Truman Library. Independence, Mo.
John Taber MSS. Cornell University. Ithaca, N.Y.
Elmer Thomas MSS. Western History Collection. University of Oklahoma.
    Norman, Okla.
Harry S. Truman MSS. Truman Library. Independence, Mo.
    1. Papers as President
        a. Bill File
        b. President's Secretary's File
        c. White House Central Files
United States Advisory Committee on Government Organization MSS. Eisen-
    hower Library. Abilene, Kan.
United States. Army Corps of Engineers (RG 77). Records of the Office of the
    Chief Engineer. Washington National Records Center. Suitland, Md.
United States Commission on Intergovernmental Relations MSS. Eisenhower
    Library. Abilene, Kan.
United States Military Academy. Cullum File of General John S. Bragdon. West
    Point, N.Y.
United States President's Committee on Civil Rights, 1946–47 MSS. Truman
    Library. Independence, Mo.
United States President's Commission on the Health Needs of the Nation,
    1951–52 MSS. Truman Library. Independence, Mo.

United States Department of the Interior. Office Files of the Secretary of the Interior (RG 48). National Archives. Washington, D.C.
1. Harold I. Ickes
2. Oscar Chapman
James J. Wadsworth MSS. Library of Congress, Manuscript Division. Washington, D.C.
Robert F. Wagner MSS. Georgetown University. Washington, D.C.
Paul A. W. Wallace MSS. Pennsylvania Historical and Museum Commission. Harrisburg, Pa.
Alexander Wiley MSS. State Historical Society of Wisconsin. Madison, Wis.
Lee White MSS., John F. Kennedy Library, Boston, Mass.
Joel D. Wolfson MSS. Truman Library. Independence, Mo.
Sidney R. Yates MSS. Truman Library. Independence, Mo.

Interviews
(Conducted by Laurence M. Hauptman)

Cornelius Abrams, Jr., September 29, 1984, Allegany Indian Reservation.
George Abrams, August 26, 1983, Allegany Indian Reservation.
Rovena Abrams, September 29, 1984, Allegany Indian Reservation.
Chief James Allen, August 17, 1979, Miami, Okla.; May 4–5, 1980, New Paltz, N.Y.
Marilyn Anderson, May 4–5, 1977, New Paltz, N.Y.
Ruth Baird, June 23, 1983, Green Bay, Wis.
David Bartholomew, May 3, 1975, August 4, 1978, New Paltz, N.Y.
Ernest Benedict, September 10–11, 1982, July 30, 1983, Akwesasne Indian Reservation.
Salli Benedict, September 11, 1982, Brasher Center, N.Y.
Roy Black, October 30–November 1, 1983, May 2–5, 1984, New Paltz, N.Y.
Merrill Bowen, August 26, 1983, Allegany Indian Reservation.
Louis R. Bruce, Jr., June 30, 1982, Washington, D.C.
Corline Campbell, July 14, 1982, Cattaraugus Indian Reservation.
Josephine Cata, June 25, 1983, Miami, Okla.
Ramona Norma Charles, July 21, 1982, Akron, N.Y.
Richard Chrisjohn, September 4, 1984, Hunter Mountain, N.Y.
Julius Cook, May 27–June 1, 1982, New Paltz, N.Y.; August 1, 1983, Akwesasne Indian Reservation.
Vernon Crow, June 29, 1983, Miami, Okla.
Vine Deloria, Jr., May 4, 1982, New Paltz, N.Y.
Ruby Diebold, June 24–25, 1983, Miami, Okla.
Ray Elm, October 20, 1984, Rome, N.Y.; April 21, 1985, Syracuse, N.Y.
John Fadden, September 11, 1982, Onchiota, N.Y.
Ray Fadden, September 11, 1982, Onchiota, N.Y.
Olive Fenton, October 13, 1984, Rensselaerville, N.Y.
William N. Fenton, June 28, 1978, May 18, 1983, Slingerlands, N.Y.

Gloria Tarbell Fogden, June 21, 1984, New Paltz, N.Y.
Jerry Gambill (Rarihokwats), August 22, 1984, Ottawa, Ont.
Elwood Green, April 11, 1985, Niagara Falls, N.Y.
Gloria Halbritter, April 21, 1985, Syracuse, N.Y.
Ray Halbritter, October 22, 1984, Rome, N.Y.
Amanda Bearskin Harjo Greenback, June 25, 1983, Miami, Okla.
George Heron, September 29, 1984, Allegany Indian Reservation.
Theodore Hetzel, January 17, 1984, Kennett Square, Pa.
Norbert Hill, Sr., July 28, 1982, Oneida, Wis.
Rick Hill, September 8, 1984, Syracuse, N.Y.; May 28, 1984, Six Nations
    Reserve.
Tom Hill, May 28–29, 1984, Six Nations Reserve.
Roberta Jamieson, May 28–29, 1984, Six Nations Reserve.
Jeanne Marie Jemison, July 14–17, 1982, September 8, 1984, Cattaraugus In-
    dian Reservation.
Hazel V. Dean-John, July 16, 1984, Albany, N.Y.
Norma Kennedy, May 4–5, 1977, New Paltz, N.Y.
Francis Kettle, July 27, 1977, June 4, 1978, Cattaraugus Indian Reservation.
Chief Ron La France, October 30–November 1, 1983, New Paltz, N.Y.
Arthur Lazarus, Jr., July 17, 1982, Buffalo, N.Y.
Anna Lewis, June 10, 1983, Albany, N.Y.
Beulah Rickard Lillvick, June 6, 1978, November 29, 1984, Tuscarora Indian
    Reservation.
Lawrence Lindley, June 25, 1981, Media, Pa.
Nancy Lurie, June 20, 1983, Milwaukee, Wis.
Lee Lyons, September 8, 1984, Syracuse, N.Y.
Chief Oren Lyons, September 8, 1984, Syracuse, N.Y.; May 6, 1985, Queens, N.Y.
Gordie McLester, June 24, 1983, Oneida, Wis.
Loretta Ellis Metoxen, June 22, 1983, Oneida, Wis.
Carol Moses, September 28, 1984, Allegany Indian Reservation.
Chief Edison Mt. Pleasant, October 20–21, 1984, November 30, 1984, Rome,
    N.Y. and Tuscarora Indian Reservation.
Ruth Mt. Pleasant, November 30, 1984, Tuscarora Indian Reservation.
Velma Nieberding, June 25 and 29, 1983, Miami, Okla.
Adam Nordwall, May 4, 1973, October 20, 1983, New Paltz, N.Y.
Rachel Sequoyah O'Connor, June 20, 1984, New York, N.Y.
Edward O'Neill, January 10, 1984, Washington, D.C.
Elma Patterson, November 30, 1984, Tuscarora Indian Reservation.
Gary Patterson, November 30, 1984, Tuscarora Indian Reservation.
Genevieve Plummer, July 28, 1977, Allegany Indian Reservation.
Tom Porter, May 5–6, 1982, New Paltz, N.Y.
Chief Irving Powless, Jr., October 21, 1984, Rome, N.Y.
Keith Reitz, May 2–4, 1982, New Paltz, N.Y.; July 21, 1982, June 8, 1984,
    Rochester, N.Y.
David Richmond, March 22, 1985, Washington, Conn.

Trudie Lamb Richmond, August 28, 1974, Meriden, Conn.
Maisie Schenandoah, October 22, 1984, Rome, N.Y.
Pauline Seneca, July 15–17, 1982, Cattaraugus Indian Reservation.
George Shattuck, August 25, 1983, Syracuse, N.Y.
Chief Leon Shenandoah (*Tadodaho*), May 15, 1979, Onondaga Indian Reservation.
Robert Smith, June 21, 1983, Oneida, Wis.
Cliff Spicler, December 10, 1984, Buchanan, N.Y.
Chief Corbett Sundown, May 22, 1980, Tonawanda Indian Reservation.
Chief Jake Swamp, April 25, May 6, 1985, New Paltz, N.Y.
Walter Taylor, September 29, 1984, Allegany Indian Reservation.
Sol Tax, December 5, 1982, Philadelphia, Pa.
Jacob Thompson, April 15, 1972, May 6, 1976, New Paltz, N.Y.
Lincoln White, July 1, 1982, Washington, D.C.
Jake Whitecrow, May 5, 1980, New Paltz, N.Y.
Duffy Wilson, April 11, 1985, Niagara Falls, N.Y.

Oral Histories
(Conducted by Others)

Clinton Anderson, copy on file at Lyndon Baines Johnson Library.
Oscar Archiquette, July 14, 1970, Shell Lake, Wis. (Conducted by Robert W. Venables; copy in author's possession)
Elmer Bennett, copy on file at Eisenhower Library.
Robert L. Bennett, copy on file at Lyndon Baines Johnson Library.
Ezra Taft Benson, copy on file at Eisenhower Library.
Herbert Brownell, copy on file at Eisenhower Library.
O. Hatfield Chilson, copy on file at Eisenhower Library.
N. R. Danielson, copy on file at Eisenhower Library.
Wesley D'Ewart, copy on file at Eisenhower Library.
Marion Folsom, copy on file at Eisenhower Library.
Warner Gardner, copy on file at Truman Library.
Carl Hayden, copy on file at Truman Library.
Jacob Javits, copy on file at Eisenhower Library.
Kenneth Keating, copy on file at Eisenhower Library.
Walter Kohler, copy on file at Eisenhower Library.
David Lawrence, copy on file at Eisenhower Library.
Orme Lewis, copy on file at Eisenhower Library.
Dillon Myer, copy on file at Truman Library.
Gladys Seaton, copy on file at Eisenhower Library.
Stewart Udall, copy on file at Lyndon Baines Johnson Library.
James Wadsworth, copy on file at Eisenhower Library.
Earl Warren, copy on file at Truman Library.
Arthur Watkins, copy on file at Eisenhower Library.

Court Cases

Ex Parte Green. 123F.2d.862 (1941).

Ex Parte Ray. 54F.Supp.218 (1943).

Federal Power Commission v. Tuscarora Indian Nation; Power Authority of (the State) of New York v. Tuscarora Indian Nation. 80S.Ct.543 (1960).

Francis v. The Queen. 1956 SCR618.

Richard Isaac v. Ackland Davey. 2RCS897 (1977).

Lonewolf v. Hitchcock. 187 U.S.553 (1903).

Oneida Indian Nation of New York, et al. v. County of Oneida, New York, et al. 94S.Ct.772 (1974); 464F.2d.916 (1972); and also U.S. Sup. Ct.—83-1065; 83-1240-opinion (March 4, 1985).

People v. Redeye. 358NYS2d.632 (1974).

St. Regis Tribe v. State of New York. 4 Misc.2d.110 (1956); 168 N.Y.S.2d.894 (1957); 177 NYS2d.289 (1958).

Seneca Nation of Indians v. Wilbur M. Brucker, et al. 360 U.S.909 (1959); 262F.2d.27 (1958); 162F.Supp.580 (1958).

Tuscarora Nation v. Federal Power Commission and Power Authority of (the State) of New York. 265F.2d.338 (1958).

Tuscarora Nation v. Power Authority of (the State) of New York. 164F.Supp.107 (1958); 257F.2d.885 (1958); 79S.Ct.66 (1958).

United States v. Boylan. 265F.165 (1920).

United States v. Claus. 63F.Supp.433 (1944).

United States v. Forness. 125Fed.Rep.2d.Series, 928 (1942); 37F.Supp.337 (1941).

United States v. National Gypsum. 141F.2d.859 (1944).

Newspapers and Periodicals

Akwesasne Notes
Albany Knickerbocker News
Albany Times-Union
American Indian
American Indian Journal
Asheville Citizen
Atlantic Monthly
Baltimore Sun
Batavia News
Brooklyn Daily Eagle
Buffalo Courier-Express
Buffalo Evening News
Christian Century
Commentary
Commonweal
Conservationist
Cornwall Standard-Freeholder (Cornwall, Ont.)

Daily Oklahoman (Oklahoma City)
De Pere Journal Democrat (De Pere, Wisc.)
Empire State Report (Albany, N.Y.)
The First American (Washington, D.C.)
Green Bay Press Gazette
Harlow's Weekly (Tulsa, Okla.)
Indians at Work (Washington, D.C.)
Indian Historian (San Francisco)
Indian Time (Mohawk Nation, via Rooseveltown, N.Y.)
Indian Truth (Philadelphia, Pa.)
KA-WEH-RAS (Akwesasne Reservation)
Kingston Freeman
Kinzua Planning Newsletter (Salamanca, N.Y.)
Life
Massena Observer
Miami Daily News-Record
Milwaukee Indian News
Milwaukee Journal
Milwaukee Sentinel
Montreal Gazette
Nation
Native American Rights Fund Announcements (Washington, D.C.)
Newark Evening News
Newburgh News
New Republic
Newsweek
New York Herald Tribune
The New York Times
Niagara Falls Gazette
Ogdensburg Journal
Olean Times Herald
Ottawa Citizen
Pine Tree Chief (Six Nations Reserve, Ohsweken, Ont.)
Progressive
Raleigh News and Observer
Rochester Democrat and Chronicle
Rochester Times-Union
Salamanca Republican Press
San Francisco Chronicle
Saturday Review
Si Wong Geh (Cattaraugus Reservation, Irving, N.Y.)
Syracuse Herald American
Syracuse Herald-Journal
Syracuse Post-Standard
Talking Leaf (Brooklyn, N.Y.)
Tekawennake (Six Nations Reserve, Ohsweken, Ont.)

Time
Tulsa Daily World
Tulsa Tribune
Warren Observer
War Whoop (Akwesasne Reservation)
Washington Post
Wassaja (San Francisco, Ca.)
Watertown Daily Times
Wisconsin State Journal (Madison, Wisc.)

Government Publications

American Indian Policy Review Commission. *Bureau of Indian Affairs Management Study.* Washington, D.C.: U.S.G.P.O., 1976.
American Indian Policy Review Commission, Task Force One. *Report on Trust Responsibilities and the Federal-Indian Trust Relationship.* Washington, D.C.: U.S.G.P.O., 1976.
American Indian Policy Review Commission, Task Force Three. *Report on Federal Administration and Structure of Indian Affairs.* Washington, D.C.: U.S.G.P.O., 1976.
American Indian Policy Review Commission, Task Force Five. *Report on Indian Education.* Washington, D.C.: U.S.G.P.O., 1976.
American Indian Policy Review Commission, Task Force Six. *Report on Indian Health.* Washington, D.C.: U.S.G.P.O., 1976.
American Indian Policy Review Commission, Task Force Eight. *Report on Urban and Rural Non-Reservation Indians.* Washington, D.C.: U.S.G.P.O., 1976.
American Indian Policy Review Commission. *Final Report.* 2 vols. Washington, D.C.: U.S.G.P.O., 1977.
Beatty, Willard W., comp., *Education for Cultural Change: Selected Articles from Indian Education, 1944–1951.* Washington, D.C., 1951.
Birdseye, Ruth A. *Indian Education in New York State, 1846– 1953–1954.* Albany, N.Y., 1954.
Canada. House of Commons. *House of Commons Debates*, 1951–59.
Canada House of Commons. *Minutes of the Proceedings of the Special Committee on Indian Self-Government* (Penner Report). Ottawa, 1983.
Cohen, Felix S. *Handbook of Federal Indian Law.* Washington, D.C.: U.S. Dept. of the Interior, 1942; Reprint, Albuquerque, N.M.: University of New Mexico Press, 1971.
Haas, Theodore H. *Ten Years of Tribal Government Under IRA.* Washington, D.C.: U.S. Dept. of the Interior, 1947.
Hoover Commission. *Report on Organization of the Executive Branch of the Government.* New York, 1949.
Kappler, Charles J., comp. *Indian Affairs: Laws and Treaties.* 5 vols. Wash-

ington, D.C., 1904–41. (Volume 2 has been reprinted as *Indian Treaties, 1778–1883*, New York: Interland, 1972).

New York State Governor. *Public Papers of Hugh L. Carey.* New York 1982.

New York State Governor. *Public Papers of Thomas E. Dewey.* 12 vols. Albany, N.Y., 1944–57.

New York State Governor. *Public Papers of Averell Harriman.* 4 vols. Albany, N.Y., 1958–61.

New York State Governor. *Public Papers of Herbert H. Lehman.* 10 vols. Albany, N.Y., 1934–47.

New York State Governor. *Public Papers of Malcolm Wilson.* Albany, N.Y., 1977.

New York State Governor. *Public Papers of Nelson A. Rockefeller.* 13 vols. Albany, N.Y., 1959–72.

New York State. Interdepartmental Committee on Indian Affairs. *Reports, 1959–1974.* Albany, N.Y., 1959–74.

New York State Legislature. Assembly Document No. 51. *Report of the Special Committee to Investigate the Indian Problem* (Whipple Report). Albany, N.Y., 1889.

New York State Legislature. Joint Legislative Committee on Indian Affairs. *Reports, 1944–1959.* Albany, N.Y., 1944–59.

New York State Legislature. [Everett Report] Assembly. *Report of the Indian Commission to Investigate the Status of the American Indian Residing in the State of New York . . . March 17, 1922.* (Unpublished.)

New York State Legislature. Joint Legislative Committee on Indian Affairs. *Public Hearings, 1943.* Buffalo, N.Y., 1943.

New York State Legislature. Joint Legislative Committee on Indian Affairs. *Minutes of Public Hearing . . . November 9, 1963.* Albany, N.Y., 1963.

New York State Legislature. Subcommittee on Indian Affairs of the Subcommittee on Governmental Operation. *Public Hearings, 1970–1971.* Albany, N.Y., 1970–71.

New York (State) Power Authority. *Annual Reports, 1931–1983.* New York, 1931–83.

New York (State) Power Authority. *Report, July 18, 1955: Land Acquisition on the American Side for the St. Lawrence Seaway Project.* New York, 1955.

New York (State) Power Authority. *Report, Sept. 28, 1956: Niagara Power Park and Arterial Development.* New York, 1956.

New York (State) Power Authority. *Report, July 25, 1957: As a Result of the Destruction in 1956 of the Schoellkopf Power Plant . . . the Niagara Area Is Faced with an Emergency.* New York, 1957.

New York (State) Power Authority. *Robert Moses' Open Letter to the Tuscarora Indian Nation, Feb. 11, 1958.* New York, 1958.

New York (State) Power Authority. *Report, June 9, 1958: Niagara Desperately Needs More Power and the Potential Is Right Here to Produce Electri-*

cal Energy; Twice as Much Firm Power Can Be Produced by Storing Water in the Tuscarora Reservoir. New York, 1958.

New York (State) Power Authority. Niagara Power Project First Power Ceremony, Niagara University, Lewiston, New York, Feb. 10, 1961. New York, 1961.

New York State. Regents of the University of the State of New York. Position Paper No. 22: Native American Education. Albany, N.Y.: New York State Education Dept., 1975.

(Smithsonian) Handbook of North American Indians. Vol. 15. Edited by Bruce G. Trigger and William C. Sturtevant. Washington, D.C.: U.S.G.P.O., 1978.

Thompson, Hildegard and associates, comp. Education for Cross-Cultural Enrichment: Selected Articles from Indian Education, 1952–1964. Washington, D.C.: U.S. Dept. of the Interior, 1964.

United States Commission on Civil Rights. Indian Tribes: A Continuing Quest for Survival. Washington, D.C., 1981.

United States Congress. Congressional Record, 1940–84.

United States Congress. House Committee on Indian Affairs. Hearings on H.R. 9720: Indians of New York. 71st Congress, 2d session. Washington, D.C.: U.S.G.P.O., 1930.

United States Congress. House Document No. 300: Hearings: Allegheny River, N.Y. and Pennsylvania, Allegheny Reservoir. 76th Congress, 1st session. Washington, D.C.: U.S.G.P.O., 1939.

United States Congress. House Rivers and Harbors Committee. Report No. 880: Investigation of St. Lawrence Waterways Project. Washington, D.C.: U.S.G.P.O., 1941.

United States Congress. House Committee on Indian Affairs. Hearings on H.R. 1198 and 1341: Creation of the Indian Claims Commission. 79th Congress, 1st session. Washington, D.C.: U.S.G.P.O., 1945.

United States Congress. House Committee on Indian Affairs. Hearings on H.R. 3680, H.R. 3681 and H.R. 3710: Removal of Restrictions on Indian Property and for the Emancipation of Indians. 79th Congress, 2d session. Washington, D.C.: U.S.G.P.O., 1946.

United States Congress. Senate Committee on Indian Affairs. Hearings on S. 1093 and S. 1194: Removal of Restrictions on Property of Indians who Served in the Armed Forces. 79th Congress, 2d session. Washington, D.C.: U.S.G.P.O., 1946.

United States Congress. House Subcommittee on Indian Affairs of the Committee on Public Lands. Hearings on H.R. 2958, H.R. 2165 and H.R. 1113: Emancipation of Indians. 80th Congress, 1st session. Washington, D.C.: U.S.G.P.O., 1947.

United States Congress. House Committee on Public Lands. Report No. 2355: Conferring Jurisdiction on State of New York with Respect to Offenses Committed on Indian Reservations with Such State. Washington, D.C., 1948.

United States Congress. House Committee on Public Lands. Report No. 2720:

Conferring Jurisdiction on Court of New York with Respect to Civil Actions Between Indians or to which Indians Are Parties. Washington, D.C., 1950.

United States Congress. House of Representatives. *House Report No. 2680: Report with Respect to . . . Conduct an Investigation of the Bureau of Indian Affairs.* 83rd Congress, 2d session. Washington, D.C., 1954.

United States Congress. House and Senate. *Joint Hearings before the Sub committees of the Committees on Interior and Insular Affairs . . . pursuant to H. Con. Res. 108: Termination of Federal Supervision Over Certain Tribes of Indians.* 83rd Congress, 1st session. Washington, D.C.: U.S.G.P.O., 1954.

United States Congress. *House Report No. 2635: To Authorize the Construction of Certain Works of Improvement in the Niagara River for Power and Other Purposes.* 84th Congress, 2d session. Washington, D.C., 1956.

United States Congress. House Committee on Public Works. *Report No. 862: Authorizing Construction of Certain Works of Improvement in Niagara River for Power.* Washington, D.C., 1957.

United States Congress. House Subcommittee on Indian Affairs. *Hearings on H.R. 1794, H.R. 3343 and H.R. 7354: Kinzua Dam (Seneca Indian Relocation).* 88th Congress, 1st session. Washington, D.C.: U.S.G.P.O., 1964.

United States Congress. House. *Conference Report No. 1821: Seneca Indian Nation.* Washington, D.C., 1964.

United States Congress. House Committee on Interior and Insular Affairs. *Report No. 1128: Authorizing Acquisition of and Payment for Flowage Easement and Rights-of-Way within Allegany Indian Reservation. . . .* Washington, D.C., 1964.

United States Congress. House Committee on Interior and Insular Affairs. Information on Removal of Restrictions on American Indians. 88th Congress, 2d session. Washington, D.C., 1964.

United States Congress. House Subcommittee on Indian Affairs of the Committee on Indian Affairs. *Hearings: Seizure of Bureau of Indian Affairs Headquarters.* 92d Congress, 2d session. Washington, D.C.: U.S.G.P.O., 1973.

United States Congress. Senate Committee on Civil Service. *Hearings on S. Res. 41: Officers and Employees of the Federal Government.* 80th Congress, 1st session. Washington, D.C.: U.S.G.P.O., 1947.

United States Congress. Senate Subcommittee of the Committee on Interior and Insular Affairs. *Hearings on S. 1683, S. 1686, S. 1687: New York Indians.* Washington, D.C., 1948.

United States Congress. Senate Committee on Interior and Insular Affairs. *Report No. 1139: Commuting Annuities, Seneca and Six Nations of New York.* Washington, D.C., 1948.

United States Congress. Senate Committee on Interior and Insular Affairs. *Report No. 1489: Conferring Jurisdiction on Courts of New York Over Offenses Committed by Indians.* Washington, D.C., 1948.

United States Congress. Senate Committee on Public Lands. *Report No. 1362: Subjecting Indians and Indian Reservations in Wisconsin to Laws of the State.* Washington, D.C., 1949.

United States Congress. Senate Committee on Interior and Insular Affairs. *Report No. 1836: Conferring Jurisdiction on Courts of New York with Respect to Civil Actions Between Indians or to which Indians Are Parties.* Washington, D.C., 1950.

United States Congress. Senate Committee on Interior and Insular Affairs. *Hearings: Nomination of Glenn L. Emmons.* 83rd Congress, 1st session. Washington, D.C.: U.S.G.P.O., 1953.

United States Congress. Senate Subcommittee of the Committee on Interior and Insular Affairs. *Hearings on H.R. 303: Transfer of Indian Hospitals and Health Facilities to Public Health Service.* 83rd Congress, 2d session. Washington, D.C.: U.S.G.P.O., 1954.

United States Congress. Senate Committee on Public Works. *Hearings on S. 512 and S. 1037: Development of Power at Niagara Falls, N.Y.* 85th Congress, 1st session. Washington, D.C.: U.S.G.P.O., 1957.

United States Congress. Senate Committee on Public Works. *Report No. 539: Development of Power at Niagara Falls, N.Y.* Washington, D.C., 1957.

United States Congress. Senate Committee on Interior and Insular Affairs. *Report No. 969: Authorizing Acquisition and Payment for Flowage Easement and Rights-of-Way Over Lands within Allegany Indian Reservation. . . .* Washington, D.C., 1964.

United States Congress. Senate Subcommittee on Indian Affairs of the Committee on Interior and Insular Affairs. *Hearings on S. 1836 and H.R. 1794: Kinzua Dam (Seneca Indian Relocation).* 88th Congress, 2d session. Washington, D.C.: U.S.G.P.O., 1964.

United States Congress. Senate. *Indian Education: A National Tragedy—A National Challenge.* Senate Report No. 501. Report of the Special Subcommittee on Indian Education, Committee on Labor and Public Welfare. 91st Congress, 1st session. Washington, D.C.: U.S.G.P.O., 1969.

United States Congress. Senate Subcommittee on Indian Affairs of the Committee on Interior and Insular Affairs. *Hearings on S. 1017 and Related Bills: Indian Self-Determination and Education Program.* Washington, D.C.: U.S.G.P.O., 1973.

United States Congress. Senate Subcommittee on Indian Affairs of the Committee on Interior and Insular Affairs. *Hearings: Occupation of Wounded Knee.* 93rd Congress, 1st session. Washington, D.C.: U.S.G.P.O., 1974.

United States Congress. Senate Subcommittee to Investigate the Administration of the Internal Security Act and Other Internal Security Laws of the Committee on the Judiciary. *Hearings: Revolutionary Activities Within the United States: The American Indian Movement.* 94th Congress, 2d session. Washington, D.C.: U.S.G.P.O., 1976.

United States Congress. Senate Select Committee on Indian Affairs. *Hearings on S. 2084: Ancient Indian Land Claims.* 97th Congress, 2d session. Washington, D.C., 1982.

United States Congress. House and Senate. *Joint Hearings Before Subcommittees of the Committees on Interior and Insular Affairs: Termination of Federal Supervision Over Certain Tribes of Indians.* 83rd Congress, 2d session. Parts 1–12. Washington, D.C.: U.S.G.P.O., 1954.

United States Department of Commerce. Bureau of the Census. *U.S. Census of Population: 1970. Subject Report: American Indians.* Washington, D.C.: U.S.G.P.O., 1973.

United States Department of Commerce. Bureau of the Census. *1980 Census of Population, Supplementary Reports: Race of the Population by States, 1980.* Washington, D.C.: U.S.G.P.O., 1981.

United States Department of Health, Education and Welfare. Indian Health Service. *The Indian Health Program.* Washington, D.C.: U.S.G.P.O., 1978.

United States Department of Health, Education and Welfare. Indian Health Service. *Indian Health Program, 1955–1980.* Washington, D.C.: U.S.G.P.O., 1980.

United States Indian Claims Commission, August 13, 1946–September 30, 1978. *Final Report.* Washington, D.C.: U.S.G.P.O., 1979.

United States Department of the Interior. Secretary of the Interior. *Annual Reports, 1940–1984.* Washington, D.C.: U.S.G.P.O., 1940–84.

United States Department of the Interior. *Indian Health: A Problem and a Challenge.* Washington, D.C.: U.S.G.P.O., 1955.

United States Department of the Interior. *Annual Report of the Commissioner of Indian Affairs.* 1941–73. Washington, D.C.: U.S.G.P.O., 1941–73.

United States Department of the Interior. *News Releases,* 1968–84.

Books and Pamphlets

Abbott, Frank. *Government Policy and Higher Education: A Study of the Regents of the University of the State of New York, 1784–1949.* Ithaca, N.Y.: Cornell University Press, 1958.

Abrams, George. *The Seneca People.* Phoenix, Ariz.: Indian Tribal Series, 1976.

Adams, Sherman. *Firsthand Report; the Story of the Eisenhower Administration.* New York: Harper, 1961.

Akwesasne Notes, Basic Call to Consciousness. Rooseveltown, N.Y.: Akwesasne Notes, 1978.

Akwesasne Notes. BIA: I'm Not Your Indian Anymore. Rooseveltown, N.Y.: Akwesasne Notes, 1974.

Akwesasne Notes, comp. *Voices from Wounded Knee: The People Are Standing Up.* Rooseveltown, N.Y.: Akwesasne Notes, 1974.

Alexander, Charles C. *Holding the Line: The Eisenhower Era, 1952–1961.* Bloomington, Ind.: Indiana University Press, 1975.

Ambrose, Stephen E. *Eisenhower.* 2 vols. New York: Simon and Schuster, 1982–84.

American Indian Studies Center, UCLA. *New Directions in Federal Indian*

Policy: A Review of the American Indian Policy Review Commission.
Los Angeles: American Indian Studies Center, UCLA, 1979.

Ashworth, William. *Under the Influence: Congress, Lobbies and the American Pork-Barrel System.* New York: Hawthorn/Dutton, 1981.

Atkinson, Brooks. *Tuesdays and Fridays.* New York: Random House, 1962.

Baird, W. David. *The Quapaw Indians.* Norman, Ok.: University of Oklahoma Press, 1980.

Barsh, Russel L. and James Y. Henderson. *The Road: Indian Tribes and Political Liberty.* Berkeley, Ca.: University of California Press, 1980.

Beauchamp, William M. *A History of the New York Iroquois.* New York State Museum Bulletin 78. Albany, N.Y.: University of the State of New York, 1905.

Bellush, Bernard. *Franklin D. Roosevelt as Governor of New York.* New York: Columbia University Press, 1955.

Benjamin, Gerald and Robert H. Connery. *Rockefeller of New York: Executive Power in the Statehouse.* Ithaca, N.Y.: Cornell University Press, 1979.

Benson, Ezra Taft. *Cross Fire: The Eight Years with Eisenhower.* Garden City, N.Y.: Doubleday, 1962.

Berkhofer, Robert F., Jr. *The White Man's Indian.* New York: Alfred A. Knopf, 1978.

Berman, William C. *The Politics of Civil Rights in the Truman Administration.* Columbus, Oh.: Ohio State University, 1970.

Blanchard, David S. *Kahnawake: A Historical Sketch.* Caughnawaga: 1980.

————. *Seven Generations.* Caughnawaga: Kanien'kehaka Raotitiohkwa Press, 1980.

Bornet, Vaughn D. *The Presidency of Lyndon B. Johnson.* Lawrence, Kan.: University Press of Kansas, 1983.

Brauer, Carl M. *John F. Kennedy and the Second Reconstruction.* New York: Columbia University Press, 1977.

Brophy, William A. and Sophie D. Aberle, eds. *The Indian, America's Unfinished Business: Report of the Commission on the Rights, Liberties and Responsibilities of the American Indian.* Norman, Ok.: University of Oklahoma Press, 1966.

Burner, David and Thomas R. West. *The Torch is Passed: The Kennedy Brothers and American Liberalism.* New York: Atheneum, 1984.

Burnette, Robert and John Koster. *The Road to Wounded Knee.* New York: Bantam, 1974.

Burt, Larry W. *Tribalism in Crisis.* Albuquerque, N.M.: University of New Mexico Press, 1982.

Carmer, Carl L. *Dark Trees to the Wind.* New York: W. Sloane Assoc., 1949.

Caro, Robert A. *The Power Broker: Robert Moses and the Fall of New York.* New York: Alfred A. Knopf, 1974.

————. *The Years of Lyndon Johnson: The Path to Power.* New York: Alfred A. Knopf, 1982.

Carter, Jimmy. *Keeping Faith: Memoirs of a President.* New York: Bantam, 1982.

Caute, David. *The Great Fear: the Anti-Communist Purge Under Truman and Eisenhower.* New York: Simon and Shuster, 1977.

Chazanoff, William. *Joseph Ellicott and the Holland Land Company: The Opening of Western New York.* Syracuse, N.Y.: Syracuse University Press, 1970.

Chevrier, Lionel, *The St. Lawrence Seaway.* New York: St. Martin's Press, 1959.

Cochran, Bert. *Harry Truman and the Crisis Presidency.* New York: Funk and Wagnalls, 1973.

Collier, John. *From Every Zenith.* Denver, Co.: Sage, 1963.

Congdon, Charles E. *Allegany Ox-Bow.* Little Valley, N.Y.: n.p., 1967.

Cuomo, Mario M. *Diaries of Mario M. Cuomo.* New York: Random House, 1984.

Deardorff, Merle. *The Religion of Handsome Lake: Its Origin and Development.* Bureau of American Ethnology. Bulletin 149. Washington, D.C.: U.S.G.P.O., 1951.

Deloria, Vine, Jr. *Behind the Trail of Broken Treaties: An Indian Declaration of Independence.* New York: Dell Publishing, 1974.

———. *Custer Died for Your Sins: An Indian Manifesto.* New York: Macmillan, 1969.

———. *God is Red.* New York: Grosset and Dunlap, 1973.

———. *We Talk, You Listen: New Tribes, New Turf.* New York: Macmillan, 1970.

Deloria, Vine, Jr. and Clifford M. Lytle. *American Indians, American Justice.* Austin, Tex.: University of Texas Press, 1983.

———. *The Nations Within: The Past and Future of American Indian Sovereignty.* New York: Pantheon, 1984.

Divine, Robert, ed. *Exploring the Johnson Years.* Austin, Tex.: University of Texas Press, 1981.

Donovan, Robert J. *Conflict and Crisis: The Presidency of Harry S. Truman, 1945–1948.* New York: Norton, 1977.

———. *Eisenhower: The Inside Story.* New York: Harper, 1956.

———. *Tumultuous Years: The Presidency of Harry S. Truman, 1949–1953.* New York: Norton, 1982.

Eisenhower, Dwight D. *The Eisenhower Diaries.* Robert H. Ferrell, ed. New York: Norton, 1981.

———. *The White House Years.* 2 vols. New York: Doubleday, 1963.

Ewald, William B., Jr. *Eisenhower the President: Crucial Days, 1951–1960.* Englewood Cliffs, N.J.: Prentice-Hall, 1981.

Fairlie, Henry. *The Kennedy Promise: The Politics of Expectation.* Garden City, N.Y.: Doubleday, 1973.

Fausold, Martin L. *James W. Wadsworth, Jr.: The Gentleman from New York.* Syracuse, N.Y.: Syracuse University Press, 1975.

Fenno, Richard, Jr. *The President's Cabinet: An Analysis of the Period from Wilson to Eisenhower.* Cambridge, Mass.: Harvard University Press, 1959.

Fenton, William N. *An Outline of Seneca Ceremonies at Coldspring Long-*

house. Publications in Anthropology, 9. New Haven, Conn.: Yale University, 1936.

———. *The Iroquois Eagle Dance: An Offshoot of the Calumet Dance.* Bureau of American Ethnology Bulletin 156. Washington, D.C.: U.S.G.P.O., 1961.

———, ed. *Symposium on Local Diversity in Iroquois Culture.* Bureau of American Ethnology Bulletin 149. Washington, D.C.: U.S.G.P.O., 1951.

Fenton, William N. and John Gullick, eds. *Symposium on Cherokee and Iroquois Culture.* Bureau of American Ethnology Bulletin 180. Washington, D.C.: U.S.G.P.O., 1961.

Ferejohn, John. *Pork Barrel Politics: Rivers and Harbors Legislation, 1947–1968.* Stanford, Ca.: Stanford University Press, 1974.

Forbes, Jack D. *Native Americans and Nixon: Presidential Politics and Minority Self-Determination, 1969–1972.* Los Angeles: American Indian Studies Center, U.C.L.A., 1981.

Foster, Michael, Jack Campisi, and Marianne Mithun, eds. *Extending the Rafters: Interdisciplinary Approaches to Iroquoian Studies.* Albany, N.Y.: SUNY/Press, 1984.

Fuchs, Estelle and Robert J. Havighurst. *To Live on This Earth: American Indian Education.* Garden City, N.Y.: Doubleday, 1972.

Ghobashy, Omar Z. *The Caughnawaga Indians and the St. Lawrence Seaway.* New York: Devin-Adair, 1961.

Goldman, Eric F. *The Tragedy of Lyndon Johnson.* New York: Alfred A. Knopf, 1969.

Goswell, Harold Foote. *Truman's Crises: A Political Biography of Harry S. Truman.* Westport, Conn.: Greenwood, 1980.

Gossett, Thomas F. *Race: The History of an Idea in America.* Dallas, Tex.: Southern Methodist University Press, 1963.

Graham, Frank. *The Adirondack Park: A Political History.* New York: Alfred A. Knopf, 1978.

Graymont, Barbara. *The Iroquois in the American Revolution.* Syracuse, N.Y.: Syracuse University Press, 1972.

———, ed. *Fighting Tuscarora: The Autobiography of Chief Clinton Rickard.* Syracuse, N.Y.: Syracuse University Press, 1973.

Greenstein, Fred I. *The Hidden-Hand Presidency: Eisenhower as Leader.* New York: Basic Books, 1982.

Hagan, William T. *American Indians.* 2nd ed. Chicago, Ill.: University of Chicago Press, 1979.

Hale, Horatio. *The Iroquois Book of Rites,* Edited by William N. Fenton. Toronto, Ont.: University of Toronto Press, 1963.

Hamby, Alonzo L. *Beyond the New Deal: Harry S. Truman and American Liberalism.* New York: Columbia University Press, 1973.

Hartman, Susan M. *Truman and the 80th Congress.* Columbia, Mo.: University of Missouri Press, 1971.

Hauptman, Laurence M. *The Iroquois and the New Deal.* Syracuse, N.Y.: Syracuse University Press, 1981.

Hechler, Ken. *Working with Truman: A Personal Memoir of the White House Years.* New York: Putnam, 1982.

Hertzberg, Hazel W. *The Search for an American Indian Identity: Modern Pan-Indian Movements.* Syracuse, N.Y.: Syracuse University Press, 1973.

Hess, Stephen. *Organizing the Presidency.* Washington, D.C.: Brookings Institution, 1976.

Hewitt, J. N. B. *Iroquoian Cosmology.* Part 1, 21st Annual Report of the Bureau of American Ethnology. Washington, D.C.: U.S.G.P.O., 1928.

Humphrey, George. *The Basic Papers of George E. Humphrey, Secretary of the Treasury, 1953–1957.* Cleveland, Oh.: Ohio State University Press, 1965.

Ismaelillo and Robin Wright, eds. *Native Peoples in Struggle: Cases from the Fourth Russell Tribunal and Other International Forums.* Bombay, N.Y.: Akwesasne Notes, 1982.

Javits, Jacob K. *Discrimination—U.S.A.* Rev. ed. New York: Washington Square Press, 1962.

———. *The Autobiography of a Public Man.* Boston, Mass.: Houghton Mifflin, 1981.

Johannsen, Christina B. and John P. Ferguson, eds. *Iroquois Arts: A Directory of a People and Their Work.* Warnerville, N.Y.: Association for the Advancement of Native North American Arts and Crafts, 1983.

Johnson, Lyndon B. *The Vantage Point: Perspectives of the Presidency, 1963–1969.* New York: Holt, Rinehart and Winston, 1971.

Johnson, Richard T. *Managing the White House.* New York: Harper and Row, 1974.

Josephy, Jr., Alvin M. *Now that the Buffalo's Gone: A Study of Today's American Indians.* New York: Alfred A. Knopf, 1982.

———, ed. *Red Power: The American Indians' Fight for Freedom.* New York: American Heritage Press, 1971.

Kelly, William H., ed. *Indian Affairs and the Indian Reorganization Act: The Twenty Year Record.* Tucson, Ariz.: University of Arizona Press, 1954.

Kearns, Doris. *Lyndon Johnson and the American Dream.* New York: Harper and Row, 1976.

Kellogg, Laura Cornelius. *Our Democracy and the American Indian.* Kansas City, Mo.: Burton, 1920.

Kickingbird, Kirke, et al. *Indian Sovereignty.* Washington, D.C.: Institute for the Development of Indian Law, 1977.

Kickingbird, Kirke and Karen Ducheneaux. *One Hundred Million Acres.* New York: Macmillan, 1973.

Kvasnicka, Robert and Herman Viola, eds. *The Commissioners of Indian Affairs, 1824–1977.* Lincoln, Neb.: University of Nebraska Press, 1979.

Lawson, Michael. *Dammed Indians.* Norman, Ok.: University of Oklahoma Press, 1982.

Leuchtenburg, William E. *The Shadow of FDR: From Harry Truman to Ronald Reagan.* Ithaca, N.Y.: Cornell University Press, 1983.

Liberty, Margot, ed. *American Indian Intellectuals.* St. Paul, Minn.: West, 1978.

Little Bear, Leroy, Menno Boldt, and J. Anthony Long, eds. *Pathways to Self-Determination: Canadian Indians and the Canadian State.* Toronto, Ont.: University of Toronto Press, 1984.

Lodge, Henry Cabot, Jr. *As It Was: An Inside View of Politics and Power in the 1950's and 1960's.* New York: Norton, 1976.

Lubove, Roy. *Twentieth Century Pittsburgh: Government Business and Environmental Change.* New York: John Wiley, 1969.

————, ed. *Pittsburgh: A Documentary History.* New York: New Viewpoints, 1976.

Lurie, Nancy and Stuart Levine, eds. *The American Indian Today.* Rev. ed. Baltimore, Md.: Penguin, 1968.

Mabee, Carleton. *The Seaway Story.* New York: Macmillan, 1961.

McCoy, Donald R. *The Presidency of Harry S. Truman.* Lawrence, Kan.: University Press of Kansas, 1984.

McCoy, Donald R. and Richard Ruetten. *Quest and Response: Minority Rights and the Truman Administration.* Lawrence, Kan.: University Press of Kansas, 1973.

McKelvey, Blake. *Rochester: An Emerging Metropolis, 1925–1961.* Rochester, N.Y.: Christopher Press, 1961.

McNickle, D'Arcy. *Indian Man: A Life of Oliver LaFarge.* Bloomington, Ind.: Indiana University Press, 1971.

————. *Native American Tribalism: Indian Survivals and Renewals.* Rev. ed. New York: Oxford University Press, 1973.

————. *They Came Here First.* Rev. ed. New York: Octagon, 1975.

Madigan, LaVerne. *The American Indian Relocation Program.* New York: Association on American Indian Affairs, 1956.

Matthiesson, Peter. *Indian Country.* New York: Viking Press, 1984.

————. *In the Spirit of Crazy Horse.* New York: Viking Press, 1983.

Morgan, Arthur E. *Dams and Other Disasters.* Boston, Mass.: P. Sargent, 1971.

————. *The Community of the Future and the Future of the Community.* Yellow Springs, Oh.: Community Service, 1957.

————. *The Making of the TVA.* Buffalo, N.Y.: Prometheus, 1974.

————. *The Philosophy of Edward Bellamy.* New York: King's Crown Press, 1945.

————. *The Small Community: Foundation of Democratic Life.* New York: Harper and Brothers, 1942.

Morgan, Lewis Henry. *The League of the Ho-de-no-sau-nee or Iroquois.* Rochester, N.Y.: 1851; Reprint, New York: Corinth Books, 1962.

Morrison, Joseph L. *Josephus Daniels: The Small-d Democrat.* Chapel Hill, N.C.: University of North Carolina Press, 1966.

Moscow, Warren. *Politics in the Empire State.* New York: Alfred A. Knopf, 1948.

Moses, Robert. *Tuscarora Fiction and Fact: A Reply to the Author of Memoirs of Hecate County and to His Reviewers.* New York: no publisher listed, 1960.

——. *Working for the People: Promise and Performance in Public Service.*
New York: Harper, 1956.

Murphy, Paul. *The Constitution in Crisis Times, 1918–1969.* New York: Harper
and Row, 1972.

Nevins, Allan. *Herbert H. Lehman and His Era.* New York: Scribner, 1963.

Nixon, Richard. *Memoirs of Richard Nixon.* New York: Grosset and Dunlap,
1978.

Noon, John A. *Law and Government of the Grand River Iroquois.* Viking
Fund Publications in Anthropology, 12. New York: Viking Fund, 1949.

Parker, Arthur C. *Parker on the Iroquois.* Edited by William N. Fenton. Syracuse, N.Y.: Syracuse University Press, 1968.

Parman, Donald. *The Navajos and the New Deal,* New Haven, Conn.: Yale
University Press, 1976.

Parmet, Herbert S. *Eisenhower and the American Crusades.* New York: Macmillan, 1972.

——. *JFK: The Presidency of John F. Kennedy.* New York: Dial Press, 1983.

Paul, Justin F. *Senator Hugh Butler and Nebraska Republicanism.* Lincoln,
Neb.: Nebraska State Historical Society, 1976.

Peroff, Nicholas. *Menominee Drums: Tribal Termination and Restoration,
1954–1974.* Norman, Ok.: University of Oklahoma Press, 1982.

Philadelphia Yearly Meeting of Friends Indian Committee. *The Kinzua Dam
Controversy: A Practical Solution Without Shame.* Philadelphia: Philadelphia Yearly Meeting of Friends, 1961.

——. *The 1965 Challenge to Seneca Indians and to All Americans.* Philadelphia: Philadelphia Yearly Meeting of Friends, 1965.

Philp, Kenneth R. *John Collier's Crusade for Indian Reform, 1920–1954.* Tucson, Ariz.: University of Arizona Press, 1977.

Porter, Kirk H. and Donald B. Johnson, comps. *National Party Platforms,
1840–1964.* Urbana, Ill.: University of Illinois Press, 1966.

Prucha, Francis Paul. *American Indian Policy in the Formative Years: The
Indian Trade and Intercourse Acts, 1790–1834.* Cambridge, Mass.: Harvard University Press, 1962.

——. *The Great Father: The United States Government and the American
Indians.* 2 vols. Lincoln, Neb.: University of Nebraska Press, 1984.

Reichard, Gary W. *The Reaffirmation of Republicanism: Eisenhower and
the 83rd Congress.* Knoxville, Tenn.: University of Tennessee Press,
1975.

Reichley, James. *Conservatives in an Age of Change: The Nixon and Ford
Administrations.* Washington, D.C.: Brookings Institution, 1981.

Richards, Cara E. *The Oneida People.* Phoenix, Ariz.: Indian Tribal Series, 1974.

Richardson, Elmo. *Dams, Parks and Politics: Resource Development and
Preservation in the Truman-Eisenhower Era.* Lexington, Ky.: University
Press of Kentucky, 1973.

——. *The Presidency of Dwight D. Eisenhower.* Lawrence, Kan.: University Press of Kansas, 1979.

Ritzenthaler, Robert. *The Oneida Indians of Wisconsin.* Bulletin of the Public Museum of the City of Milwaukee, 19. Milwaukee, Wis.: Milwaukee Public Museum, 1950.

Rockefeller, Nelson A. *The Future of Federalism.* Cambridge, Mass.: Harvard University Press, 1962.

Roemer, Angelika. *The St. Lawrence Seaway, Its Ports and Its Hinterland.* Tübingen, Germany: Im Selbstverlag des Geographischen Instituts der Universitat, 1971.

Rose, Mark H. *Interstate: Express Highway Politics, 1941–1956.* Lawrence, Kan.: University Press of Kansas, 1979.

Salinger, Pierre. *With Kennedy.* Garden City, N.Y.: Doubleday, 1966.

Sandstrom, Roy, ed. *Educating the Educators: The American Indian Student in Higher Education, St. Lawrence University, July 12–30, 1971.* Canton, N.Y.: St. Lawrence University, 1971.

Schlesinger, Arthur, M., Jr. *A Thousand Days.* Boston: Houghton Mifflin, 1965.

———. *Robert Kennedy and His Times.* Boston: Houghton Mifflin, 1978.

Shimony, Annemarie A. *Conservatism Among the Iroquois at the Six Nations Reserve.* Publications in Anthropology, 65. New Haven, Conn.: Yale University, 1961.

Smith, Jane F. and Robert M. Kvasnicka, eds. *Indian-White Relations: A Persistent Paradox.* Washington, D.C.: Howard University Press, 1976.

Smith, Reed M. *State Government in Transition: Reforms of the Leader Administration, 1955–1959.* Philadelphia: University of Pennsylvania Press, 1961.

Smith, Richard Norton. *Thomas E. Dewey and His Times.* New York: Norton, 1982.

Sorenson, Theodore C. *Kennedy.* New York: Harper and Row, 1965.

Sorkin, Alan L. *American Indians and Federal Aid.* Washington, D.C.: Brookings Institution, 1971.

Spicer, Edward H. *A Short History of the Indians of the United States.* New York: Van Nostrand, 1969.

Spieler, Cliff and Tom Hewitt. *Niagara Power.* Lewiston, N.Y.: Niagara Power Publishers, 1959.

Stave, Bruce M. *The New Deal and the Last Hurrah: Pittsburgh Machine Politics.* Pittsburgh: University of Pittsburgh Press, 1970.

Steiner, Stan. *The New Indians.* New York: Harper and Row, 1968.

Stern, Theodore. *The Klamath Tribe: A People and Their Reservation.* Seattle: University of Washington Press, 1965.

Sufrin, Sidney C. and Edward E. Palmer. *The New St. Lawrence Frontier: A Survey of the Economic Potential in the St. Lawrence Area of New York State.* Syracuse, N.Y.: Syracuse University Press, 1956.

Szasz, Margaret C. *Education and the American Indian: The Road to Self-Determination, 1928–1973.* Albuquerque, N.M.: University of New Mexico Press, 1974.

Talbot, Allan R. *Power Along the Hudson: The Storm King Controversy and the Birth of Environmentalism.* New York: Dutton, 1972.

Taylor, Graham D. *The New Deal and American Indian Tribalism: The Administration of the Indian Reorganization Act, 1934–1945*. Lincoln, Neb.: University of Nebraska Press, 1980.

Taylor, Theodore W. *American Indian Policy*. Mt. Airy, Md.: Lomond, 1984.

————. *The Bureau of Indian Affairs*. Boulder: Westview Press, 1984.

————. *The States and Their Indian Citizens*. Washington, D.C.: U.S. Bureau of Indian Affairs, 1972.

Tooker, Elisabeth. *The Iroquois Ceremonial of Midwinter*. Syracuse, N.Y.: Syracuse University Press, 1970.

————, ed. *Iroquois Culture, History and Prehistory: Proceedings of the 1965 Conference on Iroquois Research*, Albany, N.Y.: New York State Museum and Science Service, 1967.

Truman, Harry S. *The Autobiography of Harry S. Truman*. Edited by Robert H. Ferrell. Boulder, Co.: Colorado Assoc. University Press, 1980.

————. *Memoirs*. 2 vols. Garden City: Doubleday, 1955.

————. *Off the Record: the Private Papers of Harry S. Truman*. Edited by Robert H. Ferrell. New York: Harper and Row, 1980.

Tyler, Daniel, ed. *Red Men and Hat Wearers: Viewpoints in Indian History*. Boulder, Co.: Pruett Publishing, 1976.

Tyler, S. Lyman. *A History of Indian Policy*. Washington, D.C.: U.S. Dept. of the Interior, 1973.

Underhill, Robert. *The Truman Persuasions*. Ames, Ia.: Iowa State University Press, 1981.

Upton, Helen M. *The Everett Report in Historical Perspective: The Indians of New York State*. Albany, N.Y.: New York State American Revolution Bicentennial Commission, 1980.

Waddell, Jack O. and O. Michael Watson, eds. *The American Indian in Urban Society*. Boston: Little, Brown, 1971.

Wallace, Anthony F. C. *The Death and Rebirth of the Seneca*. New York: Random House, 1970.

Wallace, Paul A. W. *Indians in Pennsylvania*. Harrisburg, Pa.: Pennsylvania Historical and Museum Commission, 1961.

Washburn, Wilcomb E. *The Indian in America*. New York: Harper and Row, 1975.

————. *Red Man's Land/White Man's Law: A Study of the Past and Present Status of the American Indian*. New York: Scribner, 1971.

————, ed. *The American Indian and the United States: A Documentary History*. 4 vols. Westport, Conn.: Greenwood, 1973.

Weaver, Sally. *Making Canadian Indian Policy: The Hidden Agenda*. Toronto, Ont.: University of Toronto Press, 1981.

————. *Medicine and Politics Among the Grand River Iroquois: A Study of the Non-Conservatives*. Ottawa, Ont.: Mercury Series, National Museum of Man, 1972.

Williams, Ted C. *The Reservation*. Syracuse, N.Y.: Syracuse University Press, 1976.

Willoughby, William R. *The St. Lawrence Waterway: A Study in Politics and Diplomacy.* Madison, Wis.: University of Wisconsin Press, 1961.

Wilson, Charles Banks, ed. *The Quapaw Agency Indians.* Miami, Ok.: n.p., 1947.

Wilson, Edmund. *Apologies to the Iroquois.* New York: Alfred A. Knopf, 1959.

———. *Letters on Literature and Politics, 1912–1972.* Edited by Elena Wilson. New York: Farrar, Straus and Giroux, 1977.

Zimmerman, Bill. *Airlift to Wounded Knee.* Chicago: Swallow Press, 1976.

Articles

Abler, Thomas. "Friends, Factions, and the Seneca Nation Revolution of 1848." *Niagara Frontier* 21 (Winter 1974): 74–79.

Abrams, George H. "The Cornplanter Cemetery." *Pennsylvania Archaeologist* 35 (August 1965): 59–73.

Benge, William B. "Law and Order on Indian Reservations." *Federal Bar Journal* 20 (1960): 223–29.

Bennett, Robert L. "Indian-State Relations in Their Historical Perspective." *Journal of the Wisconsin Indians Research Institute* 3 (September 1967): i–v.

———. "New Era for the American Indian." *Natural History* 76 (February 1967): 6–11.

Barsh, Russel L. "BIA Reorganization Follies of 1978: A Lesson in Bureaucratic Self-Defense." *American Indian Law Review* 7 (1979): 1–50.

Berkhofer, Robert F., Jr. "The Political Context of a New Indian History." *Pacific Historical Review* 40 (August 1971): 363–82.

Blanchard, David S. "Entertainment, Dance and Northern Showmanship." *American Indian Quarterly* 7 (1983): 2–26.

———. "High Steel! The Kahnawake Mohawk and the High Construction Trade." *Journal of Ethnic Studies* 11 (Summer 1983): 32–60.

Blumenfeld, Ruth. "Mohawks: Round Trip to the High Steel." *Transactions* 3 (1965): 19–22.

Boender, Debra R. "Termination and the Administration of Glenn L. Emmons as Commissioner of Indian Affairs, 1953–1961." *New Mexico Historical Review* 54 (October 1979): 287–304.

Bonney, Rachel A. "The Role of AIM Leaders in Indian Nationalism." *American Indian Quarterly* 3 (Autumn 1977): 209–24.

Campisi, Jack. "New York-Oneida Treaty of 1795: A Finding of Fact." *American Indian Law Review* 4 (Summer 1976): 71–82.

Carter, Luther J. "Dams and Wild Rivers: Looking Beyond the Pork Barrel." *Science* 158 (October 13, 1967): 233–42.

Clute, James W. "The New York Indians' Rights to Self-Determination." *Buffalo Law Review* 22 (Spring 1973): 985–1019.

Cohn, Bernard S. "History and Anthropology: The State of Play." *Comparative Studies in Society and History* 22 (April 1980): 198–221.

Corwin, R. David. "Dilemma of the Iroquois." *Natural History* 76 (June–July 1967): 6–7, 60–66.

Costo, Rupert. "Alcatraz." *Indian Historian* 3 (Winter 1970): 4–12, 64.

Day, Gordon M. "Oral Tradition as Complement." *Ethnohistory* 19 (Spring 1972): 99–108.

Deardorff, Merle H. "The Cornplanter Grant in Warren County." *Western Pennsylvania Historical Magazine* 24 (1941): 1–22.

De Luca, Richard. "The Indian Attempt to Reclaim Alcatraz Island." *California History* 62 (1983): 2–23.

Doherty, Matthew F. "Indian Education: Toward a Better Tomorrow." *New York State Education* 58 (April 1971): 16–17.

Dollar, Clyde D. "The Second Tragedy at Wounded Knee: A 1970's Confrontation and Its Historical Roots." *American West* 10 (September 1973): 4–11, 58–61.

Dowling, John H. "A 'Rural' Indian Community in an Urban Setting." *Human Organization* 27 (1968): 236–39.

Fadden, John and Louis Mofsie. "Student Reactions to Indian Teachers of Non-Indian Children." *Social Education* 36 (May 1972): 507–11.

Fenton, William N. "A Day on the Allegheny Ox Bow." *Living Wilderness* 10 (1945): 1–8.

———. "Seth Newhouse's Traditional History and Constitution of the Iroquois Confederacy." *Proceedings of the American Philosophical Society* 93 (1949): 141–58.

———. "Toward the Gradual Civilization of the Indian Natives: The Missionary and Linguistic Work of Asher Wright (1803–1875) Among the Senecas of Western New York." *Proceedings of the American Philosophical Society* 100 (1956): 567–81.

———. "Iroquoian Culture History: A General Evaluation." Bureau of American Ethnology, *Bulletin* 180 (1961): 253–77.

———. "This Island, the World on the Turtle's Back." *Journal of American Folklore* 75 (October–December 1962): 283–300.

———. "The Iroquois Confederacy in the Twentieth Century: A Case Study of the Theory of Lewis Henry Morgan in 'Ancient Society.'" *Ethnology* 4 (July 1965): 251–65.

———. "The Funeral of Tadodaho: Onondaga of Today." *The Indian Historian* 3 (1970): 43–47, 66.

———. "The New York State Wampum Collection: The Case for the Integrity of Cultural Treasures." *Proceedings of the American Philosophical Society* 115 (1971): 437–61.

———. "The Lore of the Longhouse: Myth, Ritual and Red Power." *Anthropological Quarterly* 48 (1975): 131–47.

———. "The Iroquois in the Grand Tradition of American Letters: The Works of Walter D. Edmonds, Carl Carmer, and Edmund Wilson." *American Indian Culture and Research Journal* 5 (1981): 21–39.

Freeman, John L., Jr. "A Program for Indian Affairs: Summary of the Report of the Hoover Commission Task Force on Indian Affairs." *American Indian* 7 (Spring 1954): 48–62.

Freilich, Morris. "Cultural Persistence Among the Modern Iroquois." *Anthropos* 53 (1958): 473–83.

Gillette, Charles H. "Wampum Beads and Belts." *Indian Historian* 3 (Fall 1970): 33–38.

Griffith, Robert. "Dwight D. Eisenhower and the Corporate Commonwealth." *American Historical Review* 87 (February 1982): 87–122.

Gunther, Gerald. "Governmental Power and New York Indian Lands—A Reassessment of a Persistent Problem of Federal-State Relations." *Buffalo Law Review* 8 (Fall 1958): 1–14.

Hagan, William T. "Tribalism Rejuvenated: The Native American Since the Era of Termination." *Western Historical Quarterly* 12 (January 1981): 5–16.

Harris, LaDonna. "Indian Education in New York State Education: Hope for the Future." *New York State Education* 58 (April 1971): 18–21.

Hauptman, Laurence M. "The American Indian Federation and the Indian New Deal: A Reinterpretation." *Pacific Historical Review* 52 (November 1983): 378–402.

———. "Senecas and Subdividers: Resistance to Allotment of Indian Lands in New York, 1875–1906." *Prologue* 9 (Summer 1977): 105–16.

Henry, Jeannette. "A Rebuttal to the Five Anthropologists on the Issue of Wampum Return." *Indian Historian* 3 (Spring 1970): 15–18.

Hill, Rick and Jim Wake. "The Native American Center for the Living Arts." *American Indian Art* 5 (Summer 1980): 22–25.

Hogan, Thomas E. "City in a Quandary: Salamanca and the Allegany Leases." *New York History* 55 (January 1974): 79–101.

Holm, Tom. "Fighting a White Man's War: The Extent and Legacy of American Indian Participation in World War II." *Journal of Ethnic Studies* 9 (Summer 1981): 69–81.

Hood, Susan. "Termination of the Klamath Tribe in Oregon." *Ethnohistory* 19 (Fall 1972): 379–92.

Howard, James. "Cultural Persistence and Cultural Change as Reflected in Oklahoma Seneca-Cayuga Ceremonialism." *Plains Anthropologist* 6 (1961): 21–30.

Howard, James H. "Environment and Culture: The Case of the Oklahoma Seneca-Cayuga." *Oklahoma Anthropological Society Newsletter* 18 (September 1970): 5–13.

"The Iroquois Wampum Controversy." *Indian Historian* 3 (Spring 1970): 4–14. [Includes several articles and statements.]

Iverson, Peter. "Building Toward Self-Determination: Plains and Southwestern Indians in the 1940s and 1950s." *Western Historical Quarterly,* 16 (April, 1985): 163–74.

Jacobson, Peter Maxwell. "Who Rules the Valley of the Six Nations?" *McGill Law Journal* 22 (1976): 130–47.

Koppes, Clayton R. "From New Deal to Termination: Liberalism and Indian Policy, 1933–1953." *Pacific Historical Review* 46 (November 1977): 543–66.

Lake, Randall A. "Enacting Red Power: The Consummatory Function in Native American Protest Rhetoric." *Quarterly Journal of Speech* 69 (May 1983): 127–42.

Landy, David. "Tuscarora Tribalism and National Identity." *Ethnohistory* 5 (1958): 250–84.

Lurie, Nancy O. "Menominee Termination: From Reservation to Colony." *Human Organization* 31 (Fall 1972): 257–70.

———. "The Voice of the American Indian: Report on the American Indian Chicago Conference." *Current Anthropology* 2 (1961): 478–500.

———. "Wisconsin: A Natural Laboratory for North American Indian Studies." *Wisconsin Magazine of History* 53 (Autumn 1969): 3–20.

Manley, Henry S. "Indian Reservation Ownership in New York." *New York State Bar Bulletin* 32 (April 1960): 134–38.

Margon, Arthur. "Indians and Immigrants: A Comparison of Groups New to the City." *Journal of Ethnic Studies* 4 (1976): 17–28.

Mathur, Mary E. Fleming. "The Jay Treaty and the Boundary Line." *Indian Historian* 3 (Winter 1970): 37–40.

Merrill, Arch. "Salamanca Lease Settlement." *American Indian* 1 (Spring 1944): 3–8.

Meyer, Eugene I. "Bury My Heart on the Potomac: Indians at the BIA." *Ramparts* 11 (January 1973). 10–12.

Mitchell, Joseph. "Mohawks in High Steel." *New Yorker* (September 17, 1949): 38–52. [Reprinted in Edmund Wilson's *Apologies to the Iroquois*.] ·

Montgomery, Malcolm. "Legal Status of the Six Nations in Canada." *Ontario History* 55 (1965): 93–105.

Nickerson, Steve. "The Structure of the Bureau of Indian Affairs." *Law and Contemporary Problems* 40 (Winter 1976): 61–76.

Oakes, Richard. "Alcatraz Is Not an Island." *Ramparts* 11 (December 1972): 35–38.

Painter, Levinus K. "The Seneca Nation and the Kinzua Dam." *Niagara Frontier* 17 (Summer 1970): 30–35.

Parman, Donald. "American Indians and the Bicentennial." *New Mexico Historical Review* 51 (July 1976): 233–49.

Philp, Kenneth R. "Termination: A Legacy of the Indian New Deal." *Western Historical Quarterly* 14 (April 1983): 165–80.

———. "Stride Toward Freedom: The Relocation of Indians to Cities, 1952–1960." *Western Historical Quarterly* 16 (April, 1985): 175–90.

Postal, Susan. "Hoax Nativism at Caughnawaga: A Control Case for the Theory of Revitalization." *Ethnology* 4 (1965): 266–81.

Prucha, Francis P. "American Indian Policy in the Twentieth Century." *Western Historical Quarterly* 15 (January 1984): 5–18.

Ritzenthaler, Robert E. and Mary Sellers. "Indians in an Urban Situation." *Wisconsin Archeologist* 36 (1955): 147–61.

Russell, Charles. "Centralizing New York Indian Schools: Report of a Survey." *American Indian* 7 (1955): 45–54.

Simpson, George E. and J. Milton Yinger, eds. "American Indians and American Life." *The Annals of the American Academy of Political and Social Science* 311 (May 1957): 1–165.

———. "American Indians Today." *The Annals of the American Academy of Political and Social Science* 436 (March 1978): 1–152.

Stefon, Frederick J. "The Irony of Termination: 1943–1958." *Indian Historian* 9 (September 1978): 3–14.

Talbot, Steve. "Free Alcatraz: The Culture of Native American Liberation." *Journal of Ethnic Studies* 6 (Fall 1978): 83–96.

Vernon, Howard. "The Cayuga Claims: A Background Study." *American Indian Culture and Research Journal* 4 (Fall 1980): 21–35.

Wasser, Martin B. and Louis Grumet. "Indian Rights—The Reality of Symbolism." *New York State Bar Journal* 50 (October 1978): 482–518.

Wilkinson, Charles F. and Eric R. Boggs. "The Evolution of the Termination Policy." *American Indian Law Review* 5 (1980): 139–84.

Wilkinson, Charles F. and John M. Volkman. "As Long as Water Flows or Grass Grows Upon the Earth—How Long a Time Is That?" *California Law Review* 63 (1975): 601–66.

Dissertations

Basehart, Harry W. "Historical Changes in the Kinship System of the Oneida Indians." Ph.D. dissertation, Harvard University, Cambridge, Mass., 1952.

Bulkley, Peter B. "Daniel A. Reed: A Study in Conservatism." Ph.D. dissertation, Clark University, Worcester, Mass., 1972.

Boyce, Douglas W. "Tuscarora Political Organization, Ethnic Identity, and Sociohistorical Demography, 1711–1825." Ph.D. dissertation, University of North Carolina, Chapel Hill, N.C., 1973.

Campisi, Jack. "Ethnic Identity and Boundary Maintenance in Three Oneida Communities." Ph.D. dissertation, State University of New York, Albany, 1974.

Daum, Raymond W. "A Film Study of Some Aspects of Urban and Rural Communities of a Twentieth-Century American Indian Group: The Mohawks of Caughnawaga and New York City." Ed.D. dissertation, Columbia University Teachers College, New York, 1976.

Dowling, John H. "The Impact of Poverty on a Wisconsin Oneida Indian Community." Ph.D. dissertation, University of Michigan, Ann Arbor, Mich. 1973.

Fixico, Donald Lee. "Termination and Relocation: Federal Indian Policy in the 1950's." Ph.D. dissertation, University of Oklahoma, Norman, Ok., 1980.

Flad, Harvey. "The City and the Longhouse: A Social Geography of American Indians in Syracuse, N.Y." Ph.D. dissertation, Syracuse University, Syracuse, N.Y., 1973.

Frisch, Jack A. "Revitalization, Nativism and Tribalism Among the St. Regis Mohawks." Ph.D. dissertation, Indiana University, Bloomington, Ind., 1970.

Geier, Philip Otto. "A Peculiar Status: A History of Oneida Indian Treaties and Claims: Jurisdictional Conflict Within the American Government, 1775–1920." Ph.D. dissertation, Syracuse University, Syracuse, N.Y., 1980.

Hasse, Larry J. "Termination and Assimilation: Federal Indian Policy, 1943 to 1961." Ph.D. dissertation, Washington State University, Pullman, Wash., 1974.

Hevesi, Alan G. "Legislative Leadership in New York State." Ph.D. dissertation, Columbia University, New York, N.Y., 1971.

Johannsen, Christina B. "Efflorescence and Identity in Iroquois Arts." Ph.D. dissertation, Brown University, Providence, R.I., 1984.

Katzer, Bruce. "The Caughnawaga Mohawks: Occupations, Residence and the Maintenance of Community Membership." Ph.D. dissertation, Columbia University, New York, N.Y., 1965.

Koppes, Clayton R. "Oscar L. Chapman: A Liberal at the Interior Department, 1933–1953." Ph.D. dissertation, University of Kansas, Lawrence, Kansas, 1974.

Landsman, Gail Heidi. "Ganienkeh: Symbol and Politics in an Indian/White Land Dispute." Ph.D. dissertation, Catholic University of America, Washington, D.C., 1982.

Ricciardelli, Alex F. "Factionalism at Oneida, An Iroquois Indian Community." Unpublished Ph.D. dissertation, University of Pennsylvania, Philadelphia, Pa., 1961.

Rosenthal, Harvey D. "Their Day in Court: A History of the Indian Claims Commission." Ph.D. dissertation, Kent State University, Kent, Ohio, 1976.

Underdal, Stanley J. "On the Road Toward Termination: The Pyramid Lake Paiutes and the Indian Attorney Controversy of the 1950's." Ph.D. dissertation, Columbia University, New York, N.Y., 1977.

Index

315

Danforth, Eva, 115–16
Danforth, John, photograph, 72
Danforth, Julius, 71–73
Danielan, N. R., 131
Daniels, Charles Cleaves, 33, 93,
 251n49; and Seneca leases (Forness
 case), 23–30
Daniels, Josephus, 23
David, Louis, 8
Dawes General Allotment Act (1887),
 20, 65, 77
Dayton flood (1913), 92
Dearborn, Henry, 154–55
Dearborn Tract, 154–55
de Casson, Dollier, 125
Decker, George P., 4, 189, 206
Declaration of Indian Purpose, 213
Deep Waterways Association, 125–26
Deere case (1927) (*Deere et al. v.
 State of New York, et al.*), 185–86
Deere, James, 185
Delaware Indians, 74, 183
Deloria, Jr., Vine, ix, 177, 205, 220
Dennison Dam, 112
Deskaheh (Levi General), 206–207
D'Ewart, Wesley, 49, 90, 99–100
Dewey, Thomas, 55, 139; photograph,
 126, 127
Diabo, Louis, 138–39
Diebold, Ruby Charloe, 76, 82; photo-
 graph, 240
Diefenbaker, John, 138
Dieppe, Battle of, 3
Doane College, 48
Douglas, William O., 173
Dowd, Thomas H., 35–36, 60
Draft cases. *See Ex Parte Green;
 United States v. Claus; Albany v.
 United States*
Draft controversy, 2, 5–9, 207, 240,
 243

Eagle Bay. *See* Ganienkeh
Eastern Shawnee Indians, 74
Economic conditions, 2, 9–10, 73–75,
 135, 137, 143–45
Education, 11–14, 82, 220–21, 239–40
Eels, Elon, 52

Eisenhower, Dwight D., 45, 74, 85,
 90, 94, 160; administration's In-
 dian policy, 97–104; Office of Pub-
 lic Works Planning, 105–22; Saint
 Lawrence Seaway, 125, 132; photo-
 graph, 125
Eisenhower, John, 109
Elijah, Amos, 194
Elijah, George, 194
Ellender, Allen, 97
Ellis (Metoxen) Loretta, 217
Elm, Lloyd, 217, 220
Elm, Ray, 192–94
"Emancipation" bills. *See* Butler bills
Emarthla, Lillian Johnson, 76
Emmons, Glen, 68, 82, 98, 172
Engineers, Army Corps of, 2, 83, 133,
 141, 239; Kinzua Dam, 91–122.
 See also Bragdon, John S.; Seneca
 Nation of Indians
Erie Canal, 142
Erie Railroad, 17
Everett Commission, 24, 58, 184
Everett, Edward A., 24, 184
Ex Parte Green (1941), 6, 240

Factionalism, Iroquois, xii, 38–39, 52–
 56, 71–76, 78, 158–60, 181, 194,
 202, 231–32
Fadden, John, 224
Fadden, Ray, 206, 222, 224; photo-
 graph, 223
Farnham, William, 176
Federal Power Act, 170–74
Federal Power Commission (FPC),
 141, 145, 153, 160, 241; and Tusca-
 roras, 168–74
Fenton, William N., 115, 265n35
Ferguson, John P., 233
Ferrin, A. W., 20
Fickinger, Paul, 76, 80–82
Flathead Indians, 46
Fogden, Gloria Tarbell, 231
Ford, Henry, 23
Forness case (1942) (*U.S. v. Forness*),
 37, 57, 93, 240–41; origins and im-
 pact, 15–31. *See also* Daniels,
 Charles Cleaves; Salamanca, City

The Iroquois Struggle for Survival
World War II to Red Power

was composed in 10-point Digital Compugraphic Trump Medieval and leaded 2 points,
with display type also in Trump Medieval
by Metricomp;
printed sheet-fed offset on 50-pound, acid free Warren's Old Style,
Smyth sewn and bound over 88-point binder's boards in Holliston Roxite B,
also adhesive bound with paper covers
by Thomson-Shore, Inc.;
with dust jackets and paper covers printed in 2 colors and film laminated
by Thomson-Shore, Inc.;
and published by

SYRACUSE UNIVERSITY PRESS
SYRACUSE, NEW YORK 13244-5160